THE SOCIALIST RE

SOCIALIST REGISTER 1990

Edited by
RALPH MILIBAND
LEO PANITCH
JOHN SAVILLE

THE MERLIN PRESS
LONDON

First published in 1990
by The Merlin Press Ltd
10 Malden Road
London NW5 3HR

British Library Cataloguing in Publication Data

The Socialist Register.-1990
  1. Socialism - Serials
  I. Miliband, Ralph   II. Panitch, Leo
  355′.005

ISBN 0–85036–395–0
ISBN 0–85036–396–9 Pbk

Printed and bound in Great Britain by
Biddles Ltd, Guildford and King's Lynn

TABLE OF CONTENTS

Preface

This twenty-sixth volume of the *Socialist Register* is devoted to the move away, as we see it, from earlier socialist positions on the part of Left intellectuals in the last decade. This trend has been particularly pronounced in regard to Marxism; but it has also involved a more general retreat from socialism conceived as a radical alternative to capitalism. The very notion of capitalism has come to be exceedingly blurred in much Left discourse; and the notion of a radical alternative to capitalism has been correspondingly devalued in the eyes of many intellectuals who had previously been committed to it.

There are of course many Left intellectuals who would say that there has been no move away at all, but an essential reappraisal of socialist positions in the light of the extraordinary transformations which have occurred in recent times, and which have created an entirely new context, so it is claimed, in which to conceive socialist change. We too believe that constant reappraisal is essential for socialism to advance. But we also believe that much of the reappraisal undertaken by Left intellectuals in recent years *has* marked a retreat from socialist perspectives; *and* that such a retreat is unwarranted.

The essays in this volume provide an analysis and a critique of many of the forms which the retreat has assumed; and we hope that the volume as a whole may play a modest part in halting the trend, and in creating an intellectual and ideological climate in the nineties very different from the climate which has prevailed on the Left in the past decade.

We are very grateful to our contributors for their help; and we wish to say, as usual, that neither our contributors nor the editors are necessarily committed to everything that appears in the volume. We also acknowledge with many thanks the help of Martin Eve, of Merlin Press, in producing this issue.

Norman Geras and Paul Cammack teach in the Department of Government at Manchester University; and Stephen Gill is the Harmsworth Fellow in Political Economy also at Manchester University. Ellen Meiksins Wood is Professor of Political Science at Glendon College, York University, Toronto; and Fredric Jameson is Professor of English Literature at Duke University, North Carolina. Terry Eagleton is a Fellow of Linacre College, Oxford; and Linda Gordon is Professor of History at the University of Wisconsin in Madison. Bryan Palmer is in the Department of History at Queen's University, Kingston, Ontario; and George Ross is Professor of Sociology at Brandels University. Eleanor MacDonald is in the Department of Political Science at York University, Toronto; and John Foster is in the Department of Sociology at the University of Oregon. Amy Bartholomew is in the Department of Law at Carleton University, Ottawa; and Arthur MacEwan teaches Economics at the University of Massachusetts, Boston. Richard Levins is Professor of Population Science at the Harvard School of Public Health, Harvard University.

John Saville has decided that the time had come for him to cease being a co-editor of the *Socialist Register*. This is a real wrench, for he was one of the two founders of the *Register* in 1964, and has been closely associated with it ever since. His steadiness, lucidity and good sense, and his sharp political intelligence, have been of immense value through the years; and we are very grateful to him. We are glad to think that, as in the case of the present volume, we shall be able to rely on his good advice and on his contributions in the future.

February 1990   R.M.   L.P.

SEVEN TYPES OF OBLOQUY:
TRAVESTIES OF MARXISM

NORMAN GERAS

One comes across the strangest arguments these days. If you happen to be interested in Marxist thought, whether as history of ideas or as ideas of history, you find yourself quite regularly surprised. You may find yourself startled even, at the character of some of what you encounter. I offer here a modest compilation of examples, with accompanying critical commentary.

The principles governing the compilation are few. Examples are all from writers of the Left and from writings of the 1980s. Seven broad types of argument are reviewed, each type prominent within contemporary socialist discussion – though I make no claim to their being exhaustive of the genre of criticism they represent. Together, the assembled examples provide a kind of snapshot of something, that is all. The sequence of them is interrupted here and there by a digression.

I. Smiling Marxists

'Obloquy', as generally understood, means something very pronounced: speaking ill of a person or – as it may also be and is here – tradition of thought. I use the word in that sense. Instances of the first type of obloquy, which I shall be considering in this section, are unified by (loosely speaking) their style rather than their substance. They differ in that from the six types to follow, whose unity is thematic. The style defining the first type of obloquy is that of the quick, casual disparagement, untroubled by effort of serious proof or even advocacy: the small, avoidable falsehood or lightminded absurdity; the rendering of an opposing viewpoint in transparently prejudicial terms; the passing caricature or easy oversimplification; each of these generally in cahoots with others like it in the same text – for authors permitting themselves one usually permit themselves many – and cumulatively producing a not very good impression of their object. Here are some examples of such a 'style' of recent critical discussion.

Jon Elster gives his readers to understand that Marx may have thought 'each individual. . .has all the capacities that any other has', a view he finds 'extremely' utopian, 'by its denial of any genetically determined differences in ability.' Curious here is that in support of the suggestion he adduces but one line from the *Grundrisse* which speaks, in a general way, about the artistic and scientific 'development' of individuals in a prospective – better – future. This seems different from saying that everyone has identical inherent abilities. It is all Elster offers. Except, that is, for a broad gesture towards 'the corpus as a whole, which never to my knowledge refers to differences in natural talents.' Also curious is that there is a famous passage in the *Critique of the Gotha Programme*, concerning the distributive principles suitable to a post-capitalist order, and in which Marx says things like: 'But one man is superior to another physically or mentally. . .'; and 'it [a particular distributive principle] tacitly recognizes unequal individual endowment and thus productive capacity as natural privileges'; and individuals 'would not be different individuals if they were not unequal'; and 'From each according to his abilities, to each according to his needs!' Elster discusses the passage at some length elsewhere in his own text. Oversights are perfectly possible. How odd, though, unless on the basis of the clearest statement or entailment to this effect, to credit someone with the belief that we all have the same natural aptitude to be sprinters, or weightlifters, or mathematicians.[1]

There is a certain kind of socialist, according to John Keane, by whom it is supposed that 'under conditions of genuine socialism. . .all decisions in public affairs, no matter how small or insignificant, will be taken directly by the community as a whole'. Whoever else he may be thinking of here, he is anyway thinking of the Marxist kind of socialist, for this is what Marx supposed, so we are told, in 'a species of the collective harmony myth': 'All communist beings would make decisions on all public matters, no matter how insignificant, and without resorting to separate political institutions for securing agreements or reconciling conflicts.' Amongst the many and difficult problems Marx bequeathed to the Marxist tradition through what he did and did not say about the regulative institutions of a future communist society, this one had, I confess, hitherto escaped my notice: that everybody would have to be directly involved in the siting of each road sign. I had come across Marx's references to the continued existence of a 'public power' and the mechanism of elections; Engels's scepticism towards the notion of being able to dispense with the 'authority of the majority over the minority'; some reflections, even, of August Bebel, concerning 'democratic' elections to 'positions of trust' in a central administration, with the possibility of recall and re-election 'if this is demanded by circumstances or the electors deem it desirable' – and had come across a bit more yet (some of it to be detailed later) pointing to a picture of communist public affairs slightly more mediated and less harmonious than Keane suggests. Keane is perhaps exaggerating. But how odd to exaggerate so.[2]

How very odd, really, when you reflect upon it, a society of people endowed with exactly the same natural talents; or of people all directly deciding about everything, 'no matter how small'. It would be itself, doubtless, excessive were we to say of this form of discourse about Marxism that it turns your average Marxist into someone who thinks all humankind will be permanently smiling 'after the revolution'; or into someone whose beliefs are consonant only with the wearing of an inane grin.

Stuart Hall commends Antonio Gramsci: 'Where Gramsci departs from classical versions of Marxism is that he does not think that politics is an arena which simply reflects already unified collective political identities, already constituted forms of struggle.' This is good for Gramsci but bad for classical Marxism. To that category we may take it Marx belongs, and Luxemburg and Lenin also. Now, it seems hard to give a clear meaning to Lenin's thinking on the revolutionary party, or on the strategy of proletarian-peasant alliance in pre-1917 Russia, if it was a matter for him of *already* unified collective political identities. Equally, it is hard on such a basis to understand the mass strike's significance for Luxemburg: as formative, educative, unifying indeed; as constitutive of a new and active, self-governing political identity for the working class. These two were familiar with the distinction Marx made between a class-in-itself and a class-for itself, and with what it implied about long, difficult struggles, about learning from the experience of them, about interruptions and defeats. Stuart Hall is familiar with the same distinction. He calls it 'Marx's formidable distinction between a class "in itself" and one which has developed sufficient political, cultural and strategic unity to become an active force in history – "for itself". . .' This seems rather better for classical Marxism. It could be the difference between Gramsci and less saintly figures in the tradition is poorly formulated.[3]

'Marxism's more scientific adherents. . .implicitly assumed the God's eye view of a transcendental, monological meta-subject able to grasp the whole from a presumed point exterior to it.' So says Martin Jay. That is some subject, all right: with a God's eye, and transcendental, and monological, and meta – and when Marxism's more scientific adherents have not been so sympathetic to notions of deity or transcendental subjecthood. It is perhaps merely an emphatic expression of the well-known and properly lamented tendency towards dogmatism in certain Marxist circles. No, it is not that. The target is other; contained in the words 'to grasp the whole'. Jay's target is 'totalistic knowledge'. What exact pejorative weight falls, for him, respectively on 'totalistic' and on 'knowledge' (as in 'more *scientific* adherents') is hard to say. But such, in any case, are the features of the historical-materialist enterprise – its aspiration to understand different forms of society, to explain their general character – which convict Marxism of the arrogant God's eye view.[4]

Another who is worried about totality is Jean Cohen. The problem which troubles her is Marx's 'one single totalizing logic, the logic of a "mode of production". . .[S]uch a totalistic theory dangerously excludes the possibility (which we of the twentieth century ought to know well) that there might be other modes of domination than socioeconomic class relations, other principles of stratification in addition to class (nationality, race, status, sex, etc.). . .' Note that the said totalistic theory, according to Cohen, does not merely give primary emphasis to class, nor even just understate, perhaps, the importance of other modes of domination. It 'excludes the possibility' of them. Cohen excludes the possibility of things I definitely remember reading: Marx saying that 'the general position of women in modern society is inhuman', and that 'Labour cannot emancipate itself in the white skin where in the black it is branded'; Engels saying of Germany that a nation which has allowed itself to be used as 'a tool of oppression against. . .other nations' must entirely renounce that past; Lenin following the two of them in declaring 'no nation can be free if it oppresses other nations'; Luxemburg remarking on the special sorrows of children; Trotsky, likewise, writing of the 'darkness' and 'dependence' of so many childhoods, and that a 'revolution does not deserve its name if it does not take the greatest care possible of the children'; and writing of 'Woman. . .at last free[ing] herself from her semi-servile condition'; Adorno speaking of 'the husband's barbarous power over the property and work of his wife' and of 'the lying ideology which sets up the man as superior'; Deutscher (yes, even in an essay with the title 'On Socialist Man') looking forward to the end of 'the present family, with. . .its dependence of woman and child on father' – and so, if need be, on.[5]

Stuart Hall also has something to say about all this singularity: 'We cannot imagine socialism coming about any longer through the image of that single, singular subject we used to call Socialist Man. Socialist Man, with one mind, one set of interests, one project, is dead. And good riddance. Who needs 'him' now. . .with 'his' particular sense of masculinity, shoring 'his' identity up in a particular set of familial relations, a particular kind of sexual identity? Who needs 'him' as the singular identity through which the great diversity of human beings and ethnic cultures in our world must enter the twenty-first century?'[6] These writers, it may be observed in passing, are ever so contemporary. They invoke the twentieth, or the prospect of the twenty-first, century; say 'we ought to know' and 'we cannot any longer imagine'. And they draw all the while a picture of these grinning – and shrunken – predecessors. Beware when the writer writes, 'We know, today. . .' Does she know, or is that currently the thing to say? And what he knows, was it perhaps also known yesterday? Was it known by someone, known at least in part?

Gösta Esping Anderson interprets Lenin: 'if socialists take parliamentary democracy seriously, they will betray the proletarian cause by helping obscure the nature of class struggle. Even worse, their participation will serve only to perpetuate and strengthen class exploitation, thus delaying the inevitable revolutionary moment.' By contrast with Kautsky, for whom 'parliamentary participation can develop the proletariat's capacity for socialist politics,' Lenin is said to have held that 'participation in bourgeois institutions. . .would corrupt working class politics.' This is the same Lenin as he whose strategic perspective for the Russian workers' movement over more than a decade was summed up thus: 'there is not, nor can there be, any other path to real freedom for the proletariat and the peasantry, than the path of bourgeois freedom and bourgeois progress'; who railed against 'the hoary Narodnik theory that. . .we do not need bourgeois political liberty', and against 'anarchism which denies any participation of the proletariat in bourgeois politics. . .in bourgeois parliamentarism'; who, in *State and Revolution* (Esping Anderson's alleged source), spoke of the benefits to the proletariat of the 'wider, freer and more open *form* of the class struggle' vouchsafed by the democratic-republican type of bourgeois state; who upheld in fact 'the viewpoint that it was. . .*obligatory* to participate even in a most reactionary parliament'; that 'participation in parliamentary elections and in the struggle on the parliamentary rostrum is *obligatory* on the party of the revolutionary proletariat.' Esping Anderson feels 'It is impossible to cling to Leninism when one engages in empirical analysis.' You can see what he means.[7]

The list of such examples could be extended at will. But this first type of obloquy is now sufficiently exemplified. The above instances of it are all representative of the style: off-the-cuff, belittling – and, upon examination, feeble. They are not chosen, however, only for the style. They also signal, loosely, the substantive themes of the other six types of obloquy, to be pursued after the following short digression.

D1. Snapshot

There is any number of reasons, cogent, intellectually arguable, morally understandable or otherwise worthy of respect, why a person might not be, not want to be or not choose to call herself or himself a Marxist; and there is any number of reasons therefore – again, cogent, intellectually arguable, morally understandable or otherwise worthy of respect – why, Marxist or not, someone might be critical of this intellectual tradition, whether individual aspects or whole areas of it.

They might feel that Marxism to date has had too little to offer towards a theory of the political institutions necessary for any genuinely democratic community, deficiency enough when problems of political mediation will be with us for good. Or might think that, in historical and social explanation, although Marxism explains something or even quite a lot, there is too much which it cannot explain. Or might hold, on the basis of their judgement of whatever evidence they take to be relevant, that its central theoretical claims are wrong or at least not proven. They might not wish to appear to identify themselves with a primary emphasis on the effort to end economic exploitation and class division, in a world with more inequities than these. Even recognizing the desirability of socialism, they might doubt its probability, whether because of the discredit brought upon it by the regimes that have claimed its name, or for older and deeper reasons. Or they might wonder from where, or from what, credible agencies or strategies of socialism will emerge. They might feel, from within the 'inwardness' of their own personal sphere and their sense of its importance to them, that Marxism will not help them much towards understanding or fulfilment here. Or feel that its major thinkers have had too little time for problems of moral philosophy, germane though these are to any project of human emancipation. Or feel, in the light of a religious or other metaphysical belief, that Marxism has had nothing or not the right sort of thing to say to them about the most profound meanings of life and death. They might just think that contributions to our knowledge of the social world have been too many and varied for it to be sensible to identify oneself with a label deriving from the name of one man.[8]

There is, to put it otherwise, plenty of room for difference with, and for difference within, this tradition of thought; for serious substantive criticism of it; for argument over its shortcomings that is precise and worthwhile. Why, then, with no lack of matter for sober critical discussion, is there on the Left today such a volume of caricature, ill-informed oversimplification and generally facile disputation in the treatment of Marxist thought? Note the specifications of time and milieu in the question. For Marxism has always been subject to this sort of thing. The sources of it, moreover, were generally not hard to see: overt political hostility, prejudice and the like. But the same easy critical themes, the same kinds of misrepresentation and distortion as were fed by such sources, now come from writers of the Left overtly open to what is positive in Marxist thought, and sometimes professing, indeed, a form of Marxism themselves. And they come from them after two decades in which a flourishing of debate and scholarship in this area has nuanced and enriched Marxism itself, as well as confounding the more vulgar representations of it which prevailed at the beginning of the period, during the Cold War. The point can be accentuated still further. It is possible to identify the themes and inflections of this new obloquy even confining oneself, as I mostly do here, to work of some quality: to the writings of serious scholars, some of them of considerable intellectual standing.

Whatever the explanation for it, the phenomenon itself is unmistakable. Amongst writers and academics across a significant sector of the Left, an impulse has lately grown towards the taking of some 'extra' distance, so to say, from Marxism. That is the subject of this snapshot: for the record, a moment of intellectual history when good reasons did not suffice; the actual standard of some of the reasons put forth.

II. Amazing Reductions

There are three common variants of the discursive form to be treated next. Its theme was foreshadowed more than once in Section I. It is that Marxism is – inescapably – reductionist.

An example of this second type of obloquy, in the first of the three variants I distinguish, is provided by Jean Cohen. She writes: 'The base/superstructure model, according to which the state, law, and ideology are conceived as determined ("in the last instance") by the mode of production. . .implies that political power and domination represent something else: the social relations of domination of the only sphere with real weight in the historical materialist framework, the economy.' It obviously follows, if the economy is the only sphere with real weight in the model, that no other sphere has real weight in it; and it must seem reasonable, if that is so, to say that the 'reduction' thereby perpetrated 'precludes the investigation of the internal dynamics of the political sphere and the nature of the power of those who occupy its ranks.' Cohen says it. She is very quick on the subject of what Marxism precludes. Before, remember, it was other modes of domination than class; now, it is merely investigation of the dynamics of the political sphere.[9]

This first variant is the simple one. It simplifies. Marxism has here been rather pared down; reduced, in fact. For Cohen's is not the only version of the base/superstructure model. What student of Marxism can really be unaware of that today? She herself allows to peep out at us from between scare-quotes the phrase, 'in the last instance'. It has two immediate associations: a letter from Engels to Bloch, and the writings of Louis Althusser. Expressly argued in both is that the economy is *not* the only sphere with real weight, that it would be 'senseless' indeed (Engels) so to construe it.[10] On a conservative estimate, this must now have been argued by several dozen Marxist writers. Cohen just discounts the fact. And, with respect to 'the internal dynamics of the political sphere and the nature of the power of those who occupy its ranks', she discounts a few other things as well. Marx's analysis of Bonapartism, for example, is mentioned by her in this connection, but as exceptional only, 'an extraordinary deviation from the paradigm of class rule'. Also exceptional, one must suppose, would be Thalheimer or Trotsky on fascism, and Gramsci on hegemony, and Althusser on repressive and ideological state apparatuses, Miliband or Poulantzas on the capitalist state, virtually the whole classical Marxist tradition on the difference between parliamentary-democratic and autocratic forms of rule, and a certain amount of recent discussion of the notion of relative autonomy – to some of which material Cohen even refers.

It seems not to be enough to say that reductionist forms of explanation have been a problem within Marxist thought, a recurring tendency or temptation there; and one to which some Marxists may have succumbed more than others. This sort of critical observation, the import of which is undeniable, would obviously allow, for the problem, the possibility of solutions; for the tendency, the existence of other tendencies; for the temptation, a resistance to it also. It would allow that there might be Marxisms which were not reductionist. It is a criticism too weak for the tastes of some. There is more to the matter, however, than taste; arguments would also be to the point. An argument, in particular, as to why the base/superstructure model might not be rendered with a base which has real weight but is not the only sphere which has, would be most pertinent.

Moving on to a less blinkered variant of this theme, I benefit from the momentary support of Barry Hindess. Hindess rejects such simplification:

'No serious exponent of class analysis maintains that class analysis tells us all we need to know about the political forces at work in the modern world. The assertion that we must avoid reductionism is commonplace in the literature and everyone now presents some version of Marx and Engels' insistence that other elements must be given their due.' Further: 'Marxists have always insisted that economism is something to be avoided.' And: 'Much of post-war marxist theory. . .has been devoted to developing non-reductionist interpretations of that [base/superstructure] model.'[11] Marxism then, for Hindess, is more complex than for Cohen. It is not irredeemably reductionist. If we look again, though, we will find that he thinks, after all, it is irredeemably reductionist. He offers two criticisms. One, that Marxist theory has yet to specify clearly 'the precise mechanisms' of the relationship between base and superstructure, provides a perfectly good issue for critical discussion.[12] But it amounts to the claim that Marxist types of explanation of political structures and events in terms of class or economic causes have generally not been good enough; and this is a matter of judgement, in which Hindess's view will not necessarily prevail with everyone. Talk of 'precise mechanisms' in the domain of social and historical analysis does nothing to strengthen the claim. It looks like an attempt, rather, to impose on Marxist theory standards which no other social theory has yet been able to attain, to the best of my knowledge. Still, this at least is criticism of a kind that can be seriously debated.

Hindess's other criticism is of another kind. It gives us the second standard variant of the second type of obloquy. It comes down to this, that by their refusal of reductionism Marxists fall into inconsistency – because they remain committed to what they refuse. Marxism, Hindess says, 'has insisted on maintaining two incompatible accounts of the connections between economic relations and other elements of social life.' Its problem 'arises not so much from reductionism as from the attempt to combine apparently opposed positions: the economy is the ultimately determining element, but other elements must also be given their due; politics and the state are autonomous, but only relatively so.' Again: '[Marxism] is openly committed to reductionist principles of explanation (the primacy of class struggle and determination by the economy in the last instance) – and it insists that other elements must be given their due.' As he also puts this: 'Class analysis. . .promises to combine an insistence on the irreducibility of political life with the promise of reductionism. But how the trick is done remains obscure.'[13] Indeed. It would have to; until someone comes up with a way of fulfilling mutually incompatible promises.

It escapes Hindess's reckoning, evidently, that a Marxist for whom political life, the state, or whatever, is not reducible to a mere expression of economic structures or of class interests, is then not committed rather than still committed to reductionist principles of explanation. One who believes that 'other elements must be given their due' will not generally believe this together with the view that economic structures explain everything, but will believe it together with the view that they do not. The conviction of a relative autonomy, a specific effectivity, of superstructures – as in, say, the work of Althusser – is not simply *added on* to a notion of the base as sole effective historical determinant. It undoes it. 'Primacy' of class and 'last instance' determination in such a context no longer signify, therefore, the same (reductive) promise of an 'only sphere with real weight'. They signify something less weighty than that. The logical point here is elementary and its neglect a little puzzling. To use again an analogy I have drawn elsewhere, it is as though someone, thinking a certain family was composed entirely of vegetarians, were then to find that several members of it regularly ate beef, and say: 'These are not so much vegetarians as inconsistent eaters. Their meat-eating is incompatible with their open commitment to. . .well, vegetarianism; as manifested in their continuing to eat a lot of Brussels sprouts and spinach.' At the risk of labouring a point: vegetarianism is not the eating of many vegetables. And reductionism is not the hypothesis of an *explanans* thought to be weighty, even very weighty. And if one simply lays it down that 'primacy' of class or 'last instance' determination must stand for something *all*-explanatory, and hence incompatible with relative autonomy and the like, the question is: why must it?[14]

We have come back to the place we were before. We could still do with an argument, some reasons, why the base/superstructure model might not be rendered with a base which has real, even preponderant, but not total determining and explanatory weight.

The third variant of this disparaging theme consists precisely of the denial of such a 'middle' way. There can be no third way, it is claimed, between a reductionist conception giving total explanatory weight to class, the economy, etc., on the one hand, and a simple pluralism of factors or elements, on the other. The contention, thus nakedly exposed, is inane. It forbids the possibility that one thing might just be more important than others. Unpresentable in this form, it is nevertheless a contention that is remarkably common with contemporary critics of Marxism. It sidles unobtrusively out of their prose. Here it is, for instance, from Christopher Pierson:

> [T]he point is not to deny the interdependence of state and economy or, more broadly conceived, of state and society but rather to challenge the claim that the nature of this state can be derived from, for example, the 'irreconcilability of class contradictions' or 'the capital form'. For such a claim necessarily entails the subordination of political (and ideological) struggle to economic forms and a sublimation of struggles around differing political axes to struggles based upon class. The consequence of this Marxist position seems to be that (all) politics is, in some sense, class politics.[15]

The movement of thought here is: interdependence is fine; but to assign a Marxist-type priority within the interdependence 'necessarily entails' that class is all. Primacy then – as a matter not of what has sometimes been done, but of logic – *is* wholesale reductionism. As to why a Marxist might not think class generally more important than other 'axes' without going quite this far, no reason is offered. None could be. It is what plenty of Marxists have actually thought.

Now, here is the same sort of thing from Martin Jay:

> To avoid the reduction of the whole to a mere aggregate of disparate and autonomous elements, Marxist holism necessarily sought to locate an essential level of determination within the whole. . . Even when Louis Althusser attacked Hegelian Marxism for its expressivist notion of the totality, he held on doggedly to the belief in a dominant structure, an economic mode of production that was determinant in a last instance that paradoxically never came. With the collapse of the Althusserian project. . .the search for a privileged key to unlock the structural mechanism determining the whole has been all but abandoned.[16]

'Essential level' in the first sentence has to be taken in the sense of an original essence, to which all other levels are related as its epiphenomena – an inference, this, from the next proposition, about Althusser having attacked 'expressivist' notions of totality. It may be asked, therefore, why the quest for such an absolutist centre is said here to be a 'necessary' one for avoiding the 'mere aggregate of disparate and autonomous elements'. How about a less simplified social whole, constituted by levels, or sites, or structures, of differential causal weight, and in which one of them is by and large preponderant? Not possible, apparently. A vigorous and sustained argument for just this kind of conception is so characterized ('*Even*. . .Althusser. . .*held on doggedly* etc.') as to suggest that it is not a genuine option logically: eschewing the 'mere aggregate', did Althusser not fall back, with that 'dominant structure', on an expressivist essence? We learn at the finish that the search for what Jay calls, neutrally, 'a privileged key' to the social whole is now all but abandoned. He names a few people who have abandoned it. Once more, however, there is not the hint of a reasoned argument. Names alone cannot show why there is no logical space for thinking, for example, both that a fundamental feature of certain societies is that they are capitalist societies and that this is not the only significant feature of them.

As for a last instance, here is one. It comes in the shape of a question from Les Johnston. The question is formulated not as expecting an answer, but rhetorically, to encapsulate a problem which Marxism supposedly cannot resolve. '[I]f class struggle is given primacy over state institutions, how does one recognize the effects of those institutions?' That is the question. Amazing but true. If *p* is primary, how can *e* be recognized as having effects? Johnston is not brought up short by it. To him it makes the best possible sense. He is, you see, like Barry Hindess, a partisan of the radical contradiction in Marxist thought, the 'classical dilemma': of the state as reductionist 'expression' or the state as effective 'means of power'.[17] Well, if primacy just *is* economic reductionism, then Johnston's is a hard question, indeed. And if primacy is less? This is a hard question for several people today.

The issue, the danger, of reductionism has been a serious and a necessary theme in the history of Marxist thought. But it is now a very tired theme, wheeled out over and over again, without deliberation or discrimination as to when or where it might be apt. There is scarcely ever pause to reflect on what is the difference between explanation that is reductionist and explanation, period. It is not a sufficient basis for the complaint of reductionism that a given thinker explains certain features of one phenomenon by reference to certain features of another. He or she does not have to suppose that there are no other contributing or conditioning factors at work, or that there are no other dimensions of the phenomenon to be understood. It is actually banal, but necessary in this context to observe, that it is integral to the very act of explanation that some things are picked out, given prominence. A 'mere aggregate of disparate elements' will not take one very far.

Marxists pick out class and economic structures because they consider them to have powerful effects, both shaping and constraining, on institutions like the state, on political and other social practices. One aspect of this particular hypothesis, however, deserves to be emphasized. If the state matters, in Marxist theory, for the dominant economic class, this is by virtue of helping to stabilize or reinforce that class's economic wealth and power. The state matters, that is to say, because it is itself *not* nothing. It is not an empty space; not a mere appearance; not a facade; not just the same thing as the dominant class; and not a mere reflection of it. It is – and it matters because it is (but must I now say 'not only'?) – the site of something different, separate, substantial: namely, concentrated authoritative and coercive power. The nature of such power, various modalities of organizing and dividing it, different ways of wielding or limiting it, exactly whose hands it is in: these are then, obviously, critical issues. One can grasp this, and also believe that politics is not quite autonomous, since it is affected, massively, by the distribution of economic resources.

Some of these contemporary critics of Marxism could do worse than to ponder the words of Stuart Hall; not in that same mode we have seen him up to now, which could only be agreeable to their own inclinations; but speaking, rather, so: 'It is well-nigh impossible on the left to affirm the importance and specificity of a particular level of analysis or arena of struggle without immediately being misunderstood as saying that, because it is important, it is the only one.'[18] The level Hall here refers to is, as it happens, another level, but no matter. The point is good.

III. A Socialist Heaven
Obloquy of the third kind, encountered once already in a preliminary way, occurs when it is suggested that Marx and the tradition coming down from him look forward to an altogether harmonious and untroubled – sometimes also, uniform – future condition. In the Marxist vision of it, we are told, a society without classes will be not merely a radically better society, it will be out of this world.

The equality of talents imputed by Elster to Marx is criticism of this type. So is the same author's contention that Marx 'ignores the conflict between the self-actualization of man and of men that could arise because the frustration of unsuccessful individuals is an inevitable by-product of a system that allows a full development of human talents.' What Elster has in mind by this is given in an example: of the 'artist or scientist who throughout his life is desperately unhappy', unable to attain the standards he aspires to. '[P]recisely because of his great power and insight', he can see how far his work falls short. According to Elster, 'It is implicit in Marx's psychology that he did not believe such cases would arise in communism.' Then there is the 'mythology of abundance in an Eden of harmony', as formulated by Jean Cohen; 'the myth of collective harmony', where 'no serious conflicts of interest will arise among individuals or groups', as formulated by John Keane; and the notion, from Christopher Pierson, that 'all disputes over which it makes sense to appeal to democratic forms of conflict resolution would be eliminated with the transcendence of class society.'[19]

Taking stock provisionally: everyone with identical talents, no one miserable through failure to achieve their self-actualizing goals, abundance construed as Eden, no conflicts of either individual or group interest, the advent of universal agreement – it begins to look like a pretty tall order. Actually, no. The genuine goals of socialism, including of Marxian socialism, have always been a tall order. The picture here, I think one can reasonably say, is more hopeless than that. It is hopeless intellectually and hopeless practically. Such accents are, in any case, pervasive. They are found in writers much friendlier to Marxism, and more fair-minded, than are (now) those whose work I have drawn on heretofore. David Held, for example, in *Models of Democracy*, itself generally a model of balanced scholarship, propagates, when it comes to Marx, another of these standard depreciatory themes (to be taken up in due course as the sixth category in the present typology). Excerpted from it, we have this: that 'in communism all remnants of classes will have disappeared and with them the basis of all conflicts'; and that it will then be the case that 'everyone agrees on basic matters of public policy'. Kate Soper, too, referring to 'certain sources of tension in human relations. . .not traceable to economic causes. . .[and which] would persist even in societies that had corrected major iniquities and forms of exploitation', throws doubt on whether Marx was aware of such other sources of tension. It *'might* be mistaken', she says, to suppose he thought them eradicable; 'whether he did so or not', the expectation is 'problematic'.[20]

Others agree with this. Martin Jay looks favourably on the more moderate, less 'totalistic' sensibility he now detects in socialist thought vis-à-vis what came before. He speaks of the 'many. . .socialist theoreticians who have been disabused of the goal of complete normative totalization in the Hegelian Marxist mold'; of 'the yearning for totality. . .[now] all but abandoned'; of 'a corresponding acceptance of the inevitable imperfections of whatever social order humans might create'; of 'the utopian hope of perfect reconciliation. . .quietly laid to rest'; of 'the nostalgic *cum* utopian hope for total dedifferentiation expressed in the socialism of redemption'; and of 'the daunting model of a normatively totalized, fully redeemed social order.'[21] Daunting it certainly is; all 'complete' and 'perfect' and 'total' and 'fully redeemed'. For, by a twist, the vision is not really that perfect, after all. This is supposed to be for human beings: embodied, emotional, thinking, heterogeneous sort of folk. Stuart Hall: 'Who needs a socialist heaven where everybody agrees with everybody else, where everybody's exactly the same? God forbid.'[22] Quite. Who needs it?

Finally, for good measure, here is Jon Elster once more:

> Marx never to my knowledge discussed these [retardation, mental illness, senility] or other fatalities that may befall men, such as disease or accident, nor does he refer to the implications of man's mortality. Yet the limited and unknown span of human life has profound consequences for human nature, as has also the constant possibility of debilitations of various kinds.[23]

The judgement is offered in connection, not with Marx's thinking about a classless society, but with his view of human nature. It has a bearing, nevertheless, on our present preoccupations by the suggestion of a certain inattention on Marx's part to permanently troublesome features of the human predicament aside from class. One who could pass over the consequences for human nature of such matters as senility, disease, accident and the implications of human mortality, might very well have set in train a fully redeeming, rather smiling sort of tradition.

There are grounds, all the same, for thinking that these various claims and characterizations do not give an altogether rounded or accurate picture of the tradition in question. In his 'Preface' to the *Critique of Political Economy*, Marx talks of the 'bourgeois mode of production' as 'the last antagonistic form of the social process of production'. It is a well-known Marxian thesis. But he also, and immediately, specifies: 'antagonistic not in the sense of individual antagonism but of an antagonism that emanates from the individuals' social conditions of existence'. He is plainly alluding to class antagonism. Do not say now: but for Marx all antagonism is, at bottom, class antagonism. That is in question. One would need to explain why, if it were so, he should feel it appropriate to enter the qualification he does: antagonistic not in *this* sense but in that. The 'Preface' could scarcely be described as one of Marx's more obscure texts. It would seem to leave space (*pace* Keane) for serious conflicts of interest among individuals, unsettling the myth of harmony.[24]

In *The Holy Family*, Marx discusses punishment. He speaks, in a way unlikely to surprise anyone, of the need to destroy 'the anti-social sources of crime'. But he says also, with reference to Hegel's theory of punishment, that 'under *human* conditions punishment will *really* be nothing but the sentence passed by the culprit on himself. No one will want to convince him that *violence* from *without*. . .is violence which he had done to himself.'[25] This will doubtless strike many readers as a quite utopian idea of punishment and, for all I know, it is. Notice, however, that even a utopian idea of punishment entails the thought that under what Marx here calls human conditions there might still be something to 'punish': wrong-doing, hurt or harm by some to others, that sort of thing. Marx's earlier writings, it is generally acknowledged, tend rather more to utopianism than does his mature work. This one of them, at any event, is not so utopian as to envisage a world in which people never trespass against one another. With the 'Preface' passage aforementioned, it leaves space for doubting (*pace* Held) that Marx thought the basis of all conflicts would disappear with classes.

In the *Economic and Philosophical Manuscripts*, reflecting on the power of money, Marx invokes, once again, the prospect of more human conditions.

> Assume *man* to be *man* and his relationship to the world to be a human one: then you can exchange love only for love, trust for trust, etc. . . . if you want to exercise influence over other people, you must be a person with a stimulating and encouraging effect on other people. . .If you love without evoking love in return – that is, if your loving as loving does not produce reciprocal love; if through a *living expression* of yourself as a loving person you do not make yourself a *beloved one*, then your love is impotent – a misfortune.[26]

Marx shows himself aware of a source of personal unhappiness not (generally) attributable to class. That is not so remarkable. It is a widely experienced form of adversity, misfortune in love. Equally unremarkable, in virtually any other context than this, would be the implication in the above lines that, even in the 'good society', there might be occasions of mistrust; more and less trustworthy people; failures to influence others; even persons dissatisfied, perhaps, through not being possessed of 'a stimulating and encouraging effect' on those around them. Here, it is all relevant. With the 'Preface' and *Holy Family* passages aforementioned, it shows an awareness on Marx's part (Kate Soper's doubts on this score notwithstanding) of sources of tension in human relations not traceable to economic causes.

Turning now from the matter of interpersonal disharmony to other issues, I contest Jon Elster's suggestion that Marx did not believe there would be cases of frustration in communist society due to failed or incompletely realized creative projects; cases of people unhappy through having fallen short of their own ideal aims and standards. Marx's vision, to be sure, was one of all-round self-development or self-realization. But the evidence that this was not understood by him in any simple-minded spirit is right there in Elster's hands, in a familiar passage from the *Grundrisse* which informs his own discussion of the point. Marx argues 'that the individual, "in his normal state of health, strength, activity, skill, facility", also needs a normal portion of work, and of the suspension of tranquillity'; that the 'overcoming of obstacles is itself a liberating activity', a medium of 'self-realization'; and that to comprehend work thus 'in no way means that it becomes mere fun, mere amusement, as Fourier, with *grisette*-like naivete, conceives it. Really free working, e.g. ccomposing, is at the same time precisely the most damned seriousness, the most intense exertion.'[27]

It is not consistent with the sensibility here displayed that Marx could have overlooked the possibility – in any kind of society – of people sometimes failing or falling short in such enterprises, and of the potential meaning to them, emotional or psychological, of doing so. He knew something of what he spoke in this regard. In the nature of an obstacle, especially such as must call forth intense exertion to overcome it, is that it will not always be overcome; and in the nature of intense exertion is that, failing in its purpose, it often brings serious disappointment. It may well be that, in context of his overall expectations about communism, Marx would have thought disappointment so generated or, worse, unhappiness, to be of another and more bearable order, or just more acceptable morally, than the miseries and injustices he wrote of at length and lamented. But that is something different from what Elster so freely imputes to him.

I challenge, equally, the facile mockery by which Jean Cohen suggests (in plenty of company, it should be said) that the type of communist 'abundance' Marx must have had in mind is obviously ridiculous. I have argued elsewhere, in a way I merely summarize here, that where In *Critique of the Gotha Programme* he anticipates a time when 'the springs of co-operative wealth flow *more* abundantly' (my emphasis), Marx does not say enough to indicate precisely what sort or level of abundance he envisages. We know from other evidence that he does not mean only a sufficiency relative to some minimal standard of subsistence. But there is no textual basis for supposing, either, that he entertained the fantastic notion of a plenty without limits. We have a text that suggests otherwise: that, 'in all social formations and under all possible modes of production', there must be a 'realm of necessity'; a sphere, in other words, of labour that is 'determined by necessity and mundane considerations', by the imperative of maintaining and reproducing life. Given the high value Marx placed on *free time* – time beyond this sphere of necessity, time for autonomous individual development – any society, even a communist one, which must limit this kind of good in order to provide others, still lies within recognizable boundaries of a form of economic scarcity. The conclusion is unavoidable that what Marx looked forward to was a satisfaction of human needs, material and other, which, as ample or generous as it might be, would have to meet some standard of what was economically possible and socially 'reasonable'.[28]

One cannot help being struck by a certain lightmindedness in the dismissive, parodying way so many have with this Marxian theme, when large numbers of human beings still fall some way short of being able to enjoy any such standard; and a rather large number of these some way short even of a minimal sufficiency. Was *that* not the principal point of the man's life's work? Was it to entice an already flourishing humanity with dreams of boundless riches?

I beg, further, to differ with the opinion that Marx never discussed such features of the human condition as senility, disease, accident, or the implications of human mortality. Naturally, since these implications are many and varied and the said features, taken all in all, make up a large subject, one will be able to think of a lot which he did not say about it. Should he have said everything? There seems on occasion to be an unspoken, unconscious assumption, shared by some critics of Marx with the most dogmatic Marxist fundamentalism, that his ideas ought to have been completely comprehensive. Short of so extravagant an assumption, the only worthwhile question raised by Elster's opinion is whether Marx displayed a sensitivity to the permanent problems of human frailty and finitude. Well, he knew – this has actually to be written – that death is harsh, 'a harsh victory of the species over the *particular* individual'; and that as a living, material being the human being is a limited, sentient being: 'Man as an objective, sensuous being is therefore a *suffering* being – and because he feels that he suffers, a *passionate* being.'[29] And Marx not only knew but discoursed lengthily on at least some significant implications of this mortality and propensity for suffering. He observed, for example, that the duration of people's lives is of consequence to them and that it matters if their lives are shorter than necessary; or are afflicted by avoidable accident, injury and disease; or are so toilsome and oppressive that they become, these people, 'prematurely' old. I offer a handful of references to Chapter 10 of the first volume of *Capital*.[30] Marx knew also that in communist society the labour of those who could, must make provision for those who could not (any longer) work.[31] Did he have to spell out the various 'debilitations' in the human predicament in letters of fire?

So much for Marx himself. As to the tradition he began, I shall do no more, in concluding this section, than to sample some of the kinds of reflection to be found in its later thinkers. Isaac Deutscher wrote of death as a tragedy besetting humankind, and of aggressive drives still needing to find outlets for sublimation under socialism. 'We do not maintain,' he wrote, 'that socialism is going to solve all predicaments of the human race.' Herbert Marcuse, likewise, wrote of the 'ultimate necessity' of death; but of the exigency also of fighting for the difference between 'death after a fulfilled life' and dying before one must. Leon Trotsky reflected on the 'inexorable arch between birth and the grave', on the beauty of youth in the light of old age and death: on the 'pang of pity' experienced for the vanished youth of a loved one. Rosa Luxemburg spoke of the anguish and the conflicts born out of physical disability 'beyond all human interference'. And August Bebel (with how many others?) wrote of socialist society taking care of 'its aged, sick and incapacitated'.[32]

Theodor Adorno impugned the notion of some endless 'dynamism'; he could imagine a future 'tired of development' and willing to 'leave possibilities unused, instead of storming under a confused compulsion to the conquest of strange stars'. And he commented on the problem of exclusive personal relationship, 'erotic conflict' arising out of 'prior engagement': 'Even, and precisely, in a society cured of the anarchy of commodity production, there could scarcely be rules governing the order in which one met people.' And he thought, Adorno, that we should 'conceive the better state as one in which people could be different without fear.'[33] And then Trotsky, again, did indeed conceive the better state as a condition marked by certain differences. He saw it as one in which the planning of towns, and of the environment more generally, would be of interest not only to technical specialists. Around such questions would 'be formed true peoples' parties, the parties of the future for special technology and construction, which will agitate passionately, hold meetings and vote.' Further:

> The care for food and education, which lies like a millstone on the present-day family, will be removed, and will become the subject of social initiative and of an endless collective creativeness. Woman will at last free herself from her semi-servile condition. Side by side with technique, education. . .will take its place as the crown of social thinking. Powerful 'parties' will form themselves around pedagogic systems. Experiments in social education and an emulation of different methods will take place to a degree which has not been dreamed of before.[34]

There may be more 'dynamism' to this than Adorno, for his part, would have liked. There seems to have been space within the Marxist tradition, in any case, for thinking – and thinking differently – about some enduring human problems, about a degree of mundane complexity, imperfection and friction, beyond the end of class division. There was space for something else (*pace* Jay) than full redemption, total dedifferentiation, perfect reconciliation; something else (despite Held or Pierson) than agreement on all significant matters of public policy. One could perhaps say, borrowing from a remark of Terry Eagleton's on William Empson, that this intellectual tradition understood something – *not* everything or enough – of the 'complexity and ambiguity any programme of social transformation must encompass, without regarding that transformative end as in any sense unworthy.'[35]

D2. Edgar

Karl Marx knew a thing or two – and I do not mean about history or political economy. In 1855, he lost a beloved son, Edgar, who died at the age of eight. Marx was inconsolable, his family distraught with grief. He wrote, three months later, to Lassalle:

> Bacon says that really important people have so many relations to nature and the world, so many objects of interest, that they easily get over any loss. I am not one of those important people. The death of my child has shattered me to the very core and I feel the loss as keenly as on the first day. My poor wife is also completely broken down.[36]

Marx never to my knowledge discusses the experience of grief in his theoretical writings. He never discusses grief as a feature of a future communist society.

In 1972, Barrington Moore published a book called *Reflections on the Causes of Human Misery*, in the preface to which he observed:

> I am somewhat struck by how little I have had to say about what we loosely call personal

unhappiness and misery. . .while on the other hand I have always regarded [the various causes of it] as a major source of misery for the mass of humanity. There is nevertheless a reason for this apparent gap. Though some portion of personal unhappiness is probably an inevitable part of human fate, a very large portion is due to institutional causes.[37]

I am puzzled by the 'probably' here, in view of what precedes it, but that is a quibble.

A large, creative body of ideas, a tradition of thought, is a complex thing indeed. It will contain central theses and peripheral themes, original insights and unresolved problems, exaggerations and other insufficiencies, intellectual weaknesses as well as strengths. Amongst the weaknesses there will be false or one-sided hypotheses, actual obstacles to clear or fresh thinking about a given range of theoretical difficulties. And there will be also, always, unavoidably – within any such large body or tradition of ideas – gaps. The gaps may be partial or total. They may be too, in their way, a kind of obstacle to further thought. But a gap is also a space in which to think, in which someone *else* can think. She can think, so to put it, inside the tradition in which it is a gap; or outside it. Or he can think inside it but drawing from the outside; or outside it and drawing from the inside; or think just somewhere astride a line between these different intellectual regions. There will still be other gaps. It is a difficult business. It is made no easier by a style of intellectual exegesis which rushes to fill any gap, even a partial one, with costless frivolities.

One must, to a degree, separate the text from the thinker. All the same, there is the death of the child, Edgar.

IV. Absolute Knowledge

Obloquy of the fourth type occurs when Marxism is said to be a form of epistemological absolutism. The point of the charge is not that there have been Marxists given to absolutist certainty, uncritical, dogmatic modes of thought. It goes deeper: to the very heart of the Marxist (as well as many another) intellectual project. Since the fundamental reason for the charge – though not, be it noted, the content of it – is a commitment that Marxism genuinely owns to, it is not appropriate here, as in earlier sections it was, to assess this type of obloquy against sundry features of the tradition it purports to, but does not fairly, characterize. We may gauge it differently: by inspecting the quality of assertion and argument to be found in one altogether representative example of the genre. The word now, therefore, is to John Keane.

Marx, according to this writer, embraced the 'positivist assumption that absolute knowledge of modern civil society and the state' was attainable, an assumption Keane also describes as involving 'absolute truth claims' and – understandably in the circumstances – as 'arrogant'.[38] This 'traditional claim to absolute knowledge', this continuation of 'the intellectualist bid for power', this pretence of a 'totalizing meta-discourse', this 'search for foundations and totalizing truth' – that is the sorry picture that is Marxism.[39] The contrast is most stark between it and what Keane himself commends, namely, a theory offering 'accounts of social and political life. . .[which] understand themselves as *interpretations*. . .subject to self-contradiction, unforeseen social and political developments, drastic revision.' His is a commitment to 'cognitive relativism': a 'self-consistent relativism', and which he qualifies, for its part, as 'humble'.[40] It 'is opposed to the arrogant search for ultimate truth'; to 'the futile search. . .for definite truths of human existence'; devotes itself to 'disarticulating all essentialist or absolutist truth claims'.[41] The indictment is a very strong one; just so long as the reader asks no questions.

First question. What, theoretically, underlies this critique? What is the ground for ascribing to Marx and to Marxism an ambition to *absolute* knowledge? It is nothing but this: that Marxists have dared to entertain a concept of truth. Marx's theory, Keane informs us, 'falls victim to the assumption, common to all scientism, that it is true knowledge.' Or, as he also says, it presents 'its own language game as empirically true. . .hence unassailable'.[42] There you see it: the assumption of 'true knowledge'; and – 'empirically true. . .*hence* unassailable'. It is all the basis to the critique there is. In a couple of phrases, the equation is made: between knowledge and absolute knowledge. This, of course, squeezes out any idea intermediate between cognitive absolutism and cognitive relativism, such as the idea of a conditional, probabilistic kind of knowledge. It excludes a knowledge which, while indeed subject to critical questioning and the need for revision in the light of new theory or evidence, can be provisionally categorized nevertheless (when it can be) as knowledge. It can be so in virtue of the test of something outside itself, certain 'foundations' precisely, empirical, objective, realist, or what have you. These can also, and do all too frequently – as, in Keane's own words, through 'unforeseen social and political developments' – disabuse people of what they have wrongly taken for knowledge.

Scorning as hubris the very assumption of grounded knowledge, Keane's critique claims not to make any claims to a 'privileged' truth itself, enjoying its modest place within the discursive plurality it celebrates. We shall see about that in a moment. His theme, it may be noted first, is much current, part of a wider philosophical contestation, in which Marxism finds itself in some good company. A special object, perhaps, of this kind of 'absolutist' disparagement, still it does not stand alone. It stands, as the basis of Keane's critique reveals, alongside rather a lot of non-Marxist thinkers, past and present, also arrogant enough to believe it necessary, and who tried so far as they were able, to distinguish truth from falsehood.

Second (age-old) question. Are we to take it, then, that as Keane will not avail himself of the assumption that these, his own views are empirically true or knowledge, he will be willing to forego any claims for them to (let us just say) intellectual cogency? The answer to this, entirely predictably, is unclear. For the procedure he favours escapes, he says, the classical contradiction of relativism: the contradiction that, falling under its own generalization, it undermines its own truth; or not falling under it, it falsifies itself, by being itself a truth. It escapes this contradiction, according to Keane, by presenting itself as only a 'logic of particularity'; 'as neither a more universal logic nor a "truer truth".' And the kind of critical theory Keane aims at does not 'presume itself to be a privileged language game.'[43] May we indeed infer, then, rephrasing our second question, that between Keane's views, whether about knowledge and interpretation or about politics and society, and other contrary views, there is nothing to choose in the way of intellectual cogency? Must we choose in the way that we choose, say, between flavours of ice cream? Apparently not. '[R]elativism,' Keane says, 'certainly cannot cling naively to the complacent view (with which it is often stereotyped by its critics) that "every belief about every matter is as good as every other".' Some beliefs – possibly his – *can* be better than other beliefs.[44]

Third question, therefore. What are the criteria for assessing this sort of thing? We are surely, now, owed some. And they will need to be free of the taint of absolutist or 'essentialist' foundations, or else the entire relativizing construction would seem to be (in the theoretical, not the psychological sense) fraudulent. So, what are the criteria? None are offered, none whatsoever. Instead, there is a linguistic sideways hop. The direct sequel to Keane's statement that relativism does not entail every belief being as good as every other is this: 'Relativism *rather* [my emphasis] implies the need for democracy, for institutional arrangements and procedures which guarantee that protagonists of similar or different forms of language games can openly and continuously articulate their respective forms of life.' Well, democracy is excellent: for relativists, and for empiricists and realists also, to speak only of these. It is a superior way of negotiating matters of political and ethical disagreement. But, here, it is an evasion of the issue confronting this *cognitive* relativism: the issue as to how one belief might be adjudged better than, or not as good as, another. I cannot imagine Keane could mean that questions of knowledge or, as he would prefer, interpretation, should be settled by voting; or what he would say, if he does mean that, as to how one should make up one's mind which way to vote (unless it be by trying to anticipate the outcome of the procedure itself). If he does mean that and knows some non-arbitrary criteria for making up one's mind which way to vote; or if he does not mean it and this is, as it appears, only a sideways hop; one awaits, as one will endlessly from this kind of intellectual outlook, some foundation-free means for distinguishing cognitively better from cognitively worse.

Meanwhile, one can only observe what the relativist (always) does, as opposed to says. Here, for instance, is some criticism – you will see how humble – directed by Keane at Lucio Colletti. He refers to Colletti's distinction 'between parliament (which could be eliminated by a future socialist state) and political and civil liberties, which are inviolable, and

thus a necessary feature of socialism'; to his claim that 'public liberties –
the suffrage, freedom of expression, the right to strike – are not identical
with parliament.' And Keane then continues:

> This is undoubtedly true [sic]. The liberties of a democratic civil society encompass activities
> deeper and wider than parliament and its associated political freedoms. And yet Colletti's
> hint that civil and political liberties could be preserved and strengthened *without* parliament
> forgets their inner connection: the liberties of an active, self-organizing civil society cannot
> be defended without a central parliamentary assembly, which enables the particular interests
> of civil society to argue their case and to resolve their differences, openly, non-violently and
> without state repression. There has never been a political regime which simultaneously nurtured
> democratic civil liberties and abolished parliament. Nor has there ever existed a political regime
> which simultaneously maintained a democratic parliament and abolished civil liberties.[45]

There are reasons for thinking that Keane is substantially right here against
Colletti, with one or two qualifications (concerning, for example, the absence
of state repression; or whether the last proposition is defensible without
tautology). But neither the main substance nor the qualifications are the
point. Look at how Keane talks: 'undoubtedly true'; and 'forgets'; and
'the liberties. . .*cannot* be defended', with not so much as a whiff of a
qualification, whether 'as a rule' or 'generally' or 'probably'. And then,
finally: this simply is how it is and always has been, this is the *reality* of
the thing. If it be said that, oh, it is only a way of talking, I think one can
legitimately ask what entitles someone so to talk, invoking truth and what
gives every appearance of being foundations, empirical or realist, when it
is that sort of appeal precisely that motivates the charge against others of
seeking an absolute God. This is the (nearly?) universal practice of relativism,
a practice at odds with its own theory, because the theory is itself rather
unpersuasive. In itself, that is not such a terrible thing, after all. Who has
not fallen down, one way and another, trying to explore the treacherous
landscape of knowledge or interpretation? But a genuine intellectual humility
would be more hesitant before condemning as arrogant what it practises itself,
however it may preach.

Quite how unself-aware this sort of outlook can be, walking quietly away
from every difficulty, may be observed, to conclude here, from the following.
Reflecting on the mutual relation between democracy, on the one hand,
and 'indeterminacy', 'the destruction of the old reference points of ultimate
certainty', the refusal of any 'universal metalanguage', on the other, Keane
contends that to defend democracy is to 'reject every ideology which seeks
to stifle this indeterminacy by demanding the general adoption of particular
forms of life that are clothed in a broad repertoire of old and new metaphors'.
He gives some examples of such ideologies, going on to describe them as
inimical to democracy and containing 'a fanatical core'. 'Fortified by *their*
Truth', they seek to 'crash into the world, throttling everything which crosses
their path.' Here are the examples:

> [E]very woman needs a man, as the herd needs the shepherd, the ship's crew a captain, the
> proletariat the party, and the nation a Moral Majority or Saviour; mankind is the master and

possessor of nature; scientific evidence is the most rational criterion of knowledge; capitalism is the chief guarantor of liberty; the end justifies the means; doctors know best; whites are superior to blacks; and so on.

You see how easy a language game can be. Keane manifestly wants to assemble some (we must not say untruths, so let us call them) poor generalizations: discredited, questionable or odious. But the point cannot be made in that way. For it purports to be about rejecting *all* 'ideologies', such as 'contradict the particularity of their own language games' by calling for 'general adoption'. He needs consequently to write, if he would put the argument to a genuine test, something like this:

> Every person needs food and shelter, as the flower needs the sun, the ship's crew periodic sleep, citizens civil liberties, and the country a democratic parliament or free press; people do not like to be cruelly tortured or slaughtered; critical scepticism is a useful precaution against the claims of intellectual arrogance; capitalist exploitation or other grave social injustices tend to vitiate individual liberties; people have rights against personal violation for the ends of others; doctors know something; a society free of racism is superior to one not free of it; and so on.

One does not have to believe any or all of these to be absolute truths to see that they are somewhat different from Keane's innocent assembly. It would be interesting to know how many, and which, of them he would find fanatical or unworthy of general adoption.[46]

V. One Class of Actor

Obloquy of the fifth type occurs when an author discovers that a basic form of Marxian explanation, namely, of political events by reference to class, is no good at all, not really explanation. Just as in the last section there was no question of needing to deny that Marxism has been committed to the quest for knowledge, here too it will not be a matter, obviously, of seeking to show from the texts that Marxists do not proffer explanations of this form. They do – sometimes more and sometimes less successfully. It is a matter again of sampling, in one representative case, the character of argument by which such explanations are urged to be inherently invalid. Since the case I take is that of Barry Hindess, it may be recalled that he it was who proposed the thesis that Marxism is, even when it is not, reductionist. He might have saved himself the trouble of that. If you cannot explain anything in terms of class, it seems uneconomical to contort oneself over whether Marxists explain everything in terms of it, since they undoubtedly do so explain quite a lot.

Hindess challenges the assumption that 'classes [are] themselves collectivities engaged in struggle', that classes are 'collective actors'. According to him, 'classes are not social forces at all. Discussion of politics in terms of class struggle is at best a rather complex allegory and at worst thoroughly misleading.'[47] Here is the argument for this:

> An actor is a locus of decision and action, where the action is in some sense a consequence of the actor's decisions. Actors' decisions play a part in the explanation of their actions. . .Reference to an actor, then, always presupposes some definite means of reaching and formulating

decisions, definite means of acting on them, and some connections between the two. Human individuals are certainly actors in this sense, but they are clearly not the only things that reach decisions and act accordingly. Capitalist enterprises, state agencies, political parties and trade unions are all examples of actors other than human individuals.

Such collectivities as classes, on the other hand, 'have no identifiable means of formulating decisions, let alone of acting on them.' To treat as actors 'collectivities that have no means of formulating decisions' is to provide, says Hindess, 'a spurious explanation'.[48] The whole critical job has been done with a definition.

We might, of course, question the definition, but let us not. Let us accept it. Classes are not, then, actors. But why may they not be 'social forces' still, and there be social forces other than actors, of some explanatory importance? Or if 'forces' are definitionally equivalent with 'actors', why may classes not be social aggregates of another kind than actors and forces, and of explanatory importance? Consider, to come to the substance of the thing, this Collectivity. Large or very large numbers of its members become aware that some other collectivity or some institution is acting or about to act in a way prejudicial to what they cherish as their aims. There is within the Collectivity talk about it, this way and that: informal, spontaneous, in some places more organized. Sub-groups within the Collectivity, whether pre-existing or newly formed, structured or loose, confer. Some learn what others think directly by hearing from them; and some learn what others think indirectly through what they are told. Inferences are drawn from the known views of yet others. Partly because of this process, partly because even without it there is a widely-shared reaction amongst members of the Collectivity to the threat they perceive, actions now take place of a more or less consistent or even concerted kind. People take to the streets, say; or use money or positions of influence towards exerting other sorts of pressure upon a government.

Hindess leaves something unclear. Would the kind of process just described be a 'definite' or 'identifiable' means of formulating and acting upon decisions? His definition alone, perhaps, does not exclude that it would. In that case wider and looser types of collectivity than those he cites as examples could be actors after all and classes be amongst them. But if we interpret the definition in the light of his examples, he would appear to require, before we can talk of actors, that there be rule-governed, formally-constituted decision procedures. For, without exception, all of his examples are of formal organizations (capitalist enterprises, state agencies, political parties and trade unions).

Interpreting him in this light, our Collectivity is no social actor. But so what? On what basis will it now be said not to be a social force (or aggregate), and which can be used legitimately in explanation? It is not relevant, although it is true, that not all members of the Collectivity participate in deciding upon action and in acting. This is generally the case also with formal organizations. Nor is it relevant, although it is again true, that such concerted or convergent actions as are decided on and taken are the product of a series of individual and sub-group activities. Not only is that, too, the case with the formal decisions and actions of the organizations Hindess allows to be genuine social forces. Further, it does not follow from it that the concerted or convergent actions from within the Collectivity are reducible without residue, are fully explicable in terms of, these constituent activities. They will not be so if – as I suppose here, because the supposition is often enough realistic – these constituent activities are themselves motivated by objectives (material interests or ideal values) which members of the Collectivity have formed in virtue of being members of it.

It is worth noting that the conception of 'social forces' implicit in Hindess's examples would render formal organizations the rock bottom of valid explanation in terms of such forces. One could not explain the character or conduct of these organizations themselves by reference to any wider or looser social aggregates. If, for example, a particular organization is not merely random in its social composition, must we then say that more members of one social group than another just happen, by coincidence, to have joined it? Or if we say, so as to avoid this conclusion, that more members of one social group are attracted by the organization's policies and principles, is that differential attraction itself not explicable to some significant extent in terms of differential dispositions people acquire by being differently located within social aggregates of the wider sort?

The question takes us into a companion argument from Hindess; one impugning the notion of class interests, interests based upon social location within the structure of capitalist society. Interests, he says, 'should not be regarded as structurally determined'. With this second argument I shall be brief, since its logical deficiency is manifest (and extraordinary). The shape of it is as follows: people's reasons for action are *not* dependent on structurally defined class interests, because they are *also* dependent on other things. Hindess asserts that 'insofar as interests have an explanatory role, they are always dependent on definite discursive and other kinds of conditions, and their identification is always open to dispute.' This is so because interests are effective 'insofar as they provide reasons for actors' decisions'; hence only as 'conceptions', which are the 'products of assessment'. What reasons for action are recognized in a given situation will therefore depend on 'the forms of assessment' available to social actors. They can depend also on 'the work of individuals, political parties, unions and other agencies.' The point seems quite reasonable. But Hindess then concludes from it: 'the forms of assessment available to actors are not *uniquely* determined by their social location. It follows that the interests actors recognize and act upon cannot be *uniquely* determined by social location either.'[49]

If the burden of the argument is – as it is – to disqualify explanation in terms of social location and its effects through interests, Hindess needs to tell us and to have established that the forms of assessment available to actors and the reasons actors have for acting are not at all – or not significantly, at least – governed by social location. That would be a more exacting argument to make. It is also where his dissertation on this matter began. 'Not uniquely determined' backs away from it, allowing that actors' reasons for action are determined by social location to some extent; in which case Hindess's effort to disqualify class analysis and explanation as at best merely allegorical fails.

VI. The End of Politics

Obloquy of the sixth type occurs when a statement is made to the effect that Marxists foresee a society without politics. The thesis was lately ventured by Michael Walzer in *New Statesman and Society*, the Marxian view of politics as 'nothing more than the superstructural enactment of class conflict' being said by him to entail that with the end of social classes 'there will be no politics'. It is a popular thesis, found in a goodly proportion of the critics referred to in this essay. Pierson: 'under communism there would be no specifically political institutions over which it would be appropriate to seek to exercise constraint or control' but, rather, an 'end of politics'. Jay: 'socialist traditions, like Leninism, that promised the end of politics'. Cohen: a 'communist society without the aid of political institutions', 'the dissolution. . .of politics itself', and '[t]he *Communist Manifesto*. . .singing the praise of the destruction of politics'. Keane: everyone deciding about everything, no matter how small, without the need of 'separate political institutions'.[50]

There is a certain conceptual elision here, most visible, as it happens, in the writer from amongst all these whose treatment of Marxism is the most sympathetic one. I mean David Held. In introducing for his part the end-of-politics theme, Held writes – as is accurate – that the end of the state for Marx involved 'the dismantling of politics as an institutionally distinct sphere in society used in the perpetuation of class rule.' Citing, like Cohen, a well-known passage from the *Manifesto* in support of this contention, as well as another from *The Poverty of Philosophy*, Held then goes on to offer, however, the following gloss upon them: that 'since class relations determine the key dimensions of power and axes of conflict in state and in society. . .when classes are finally transcended, all political power will be deprived of its footing and the state – and politics as a distinct activity – will no longer have a role.'[51] Note the extension of meaning that has occurred: from politics in a determinate, particular sense, to 'all' politics. Note, equally, a debit in the reasoning for this extension: since 'key' aspects of the stuff of politics disappear, therefore politics *tout court* disappears. We shall need to ask if the passages Held cites do, in fact, license such an extension of meaning.

Let it be emphasized, first, that it is no part of the argument I shall make, to suggest that Marx or the tradition after him did offer an adequate theory or sketch of the political institutions of a classless society. They did not, not even remotely, and it has been a grievous lack. My point is a more limited one:

that the Marxist canon in this matter contains a space and some resources for making the deficiency good, and is not just the obstacle, which these critics one-sidedly depict, to the presently urgent task of elaborating models of a socialist polity. As the defence to be mounted is thus limited, it may be said that nothing much turns on it; the more especially since, in trying to make its deficiency good here, Marxist thought undoubtedly has a lot to learn from other intellectual traditions, in particular that of liberalism. What difference, then, whether Marxism is merely an obstacle or whether it leaves room and a few resources for thinking about the question, when there are in any case alternative points of departure? This difference. It matters whether Marxism is just disabled, by erroneous theses integral to it, from engaging seriously with the crucial issue of a feasible socialist polity; or whether there is space, *within* the framework of Marxism, a gap in the sense of our earlier digression (D2), large but not total, and in which Marxists, as well as anybody else who wants to, can today work to contribute to the discussion of that issue. The sixth type of obloquy would abolish such space. What follows displays it.

Let us consider what it is, precisely, that is invoked to support the projection of an end of politics, following upon the end of classes. Beyond the notion of communist uniformity – that everyone in a classless society will be the same and/or agree about everything including matters of public policy – it is the classical formula of the withering away or abolition of the state. I simply set aside the former notion, of uniformity, as not founded on anything substantial, and incapable consequently of furnishing a defensible basis for the theme. It is contradicted not only by texts cited in Section III above, but also by two central and perfectly familiar Marxian theses, when taken in conjunction. The first is that communism will achieve a conscious, collective control over social and economic processes which have hitherto escaped such control and indeed understanding, having taken place 'behind the backs' of individuals. The second – another side, this, of Marx's expectations concerning communist disalienation – is the thesis of an unprecedented flourishing of human individuality. Giving the lie as it does (just like that) to the talk about universal 'sameness', this second thesis also prompts one to ask how likely it is that Marx might have thought people, all of them, under such conditions of a flourishing individuality, would agree about all matters; and all matters to do with the public life of a large, modern society. It is unlikely. This is, to be sure, merely an inference. But it is an inference from something real and substantial in his work. One wants the material that will weigh against it, on the other side of the scale. Marx perhaps did speak also in a contrary sense. Did he?

I turn to the formula of the end of the state. Now, it falls out that Marx had a way of expressing this, over and again – in the passages Held and Cohen give and elsewhere – which seems positively to thrust upon the reader a point these two, and the other critics, nevertheless overlook. Here is the *Manifesto* passage:

When, in the course of development, class distinctions have disappeared . . . the public power will lose its political character. Political power, properly so called, is merely the organized power of one class for oppressing another.

And, here, the passage from *The Poverty of Philosophy*:

The working class, in the course of its development, will substitute for the old civil society an association which will exclude classes and their antagonism, and there will be no more political power properly so-called, since political power is precisely the official expression of antagonism in civil society.

Here, again, is a passage from a less familiar text, the review of a book by Emile de Girardin:

The abolition of the state has only one meaning to the Communists, as the necessary result of the abolition of classes, whereupon of itself the need for the organized power of one class for the suppression of another ceases to exist.[52]

These formulations reveal the nature of the conceptual elision I have spoken of. The end-of-politics construal of Marx begins from an independently given meaning of politics (roughly, interpersonal deliberation, negotiation and authoritative decision-making in matters of public scope or concern), and then reads him as saying in such passages as these that all politics, in *that* sense, is the product of classes and class antagonism, and so must disappear with them. But the passages, I submit, are of another import, and virtually cry out that they are so. Marx offers a different, rather narrow meaning of politics – 'properly so-called', by definition, it is class power and class antagonism – and says that politics, in *this* sense, will disappear 'of itself' with classes. The abolition of the state, he writes, 'has only one meaning to the Communists', and this is it. But beyond the state so defined, i.e. as an oppressive class institution, a 'public power' will continue to exist. Marx's repeated, forcible expression of the point renders the deduction compelling that 'politics' and a 'state', on meanings of these terms broader than the one he here stipulates, would be part of a classless society.

If, as I propose, the texts cited are so clear on this point, how is it that so many commentators do not see it, even if only as a sort of shadow falling upon their chosen theme and which they must try to remove? It is not easy to say. The point is not an eccentric insight of the present writer. It is well-covered within modern Marx scholarship.[53] It is confirmed, moreover, by other material in Marx's writings. In *Critique of the Gotha Programme*, for example, he writes that 'Freedom consists in converting the state from an organ superimposed upon society into one completely subordinate to it'; a formula suggesting not only the continued existence of a kind of (converted) 'state', but also its democratic foundation.[54] This democratic theme, again perfectly familiar, recalls and reaffirms the substance of some of Marx's earliest theoretical reflections: on Hegel, and on the Jewish question.

Then, too, in his marginal notes on Bakunin's *Statism and Anarchy* – which yet once more says of the end of the state: 'This merely means: when class rule has disappeared, there will no longer be any state in the present political sense of the word' – Marx makes it plain that the 'state' or 'public power' he envisages will have an elective basis. It is true that he also speaks of the subject of elections, in this context, as having become a 'business matter'. This is read by some as betokening an antithesis with politics. But the antithesis is with politics in Marx's restricted sense; for what he actually says is 'a business matter which does not afford any room for domination'.[55] The notion is of a democratic process which, freed from the contestation of classes, is no longer coercive in character, because Marx allowed himself to foresee a kind of community that would be willing to respect the outcomes of democratic deliberation. If even this is, as many will think, a highly utopian expectation, it is nonetheless a different expectation from that of an end of politics, in the broad sense. A non-coercive 'state', in which elections are democratically contested is one, we must presume, open to disputes over issues of public policy. Whether such a non-coercive 'state' is possible or not, it is anyway a terrain of politics, in the meaning that sundry commentators deny that it is.

A similar observation must be made concerning the notorious formula that, as Engels put it, 'public functions will lose their political character and be transformed into. . .simple administrative functions'. This was not, it has to be said, a happy usage, and it is not worth defending, much less perpetuating. Apart from its unlikely suggestion of a prospective simplicity of functions in a future society, the connotations of 'administration', as a (purely) technical sphere, are hard to put aside. Still, here again, it is not legitimate to abstract from the specifically Marxist – class-coercive – meaning of 'political', in interpreting the distinction between politics and administration. Engels, as was registered earlier, commented witheringly on the anarchist idea of getting rid of 'the authority of the majority over the minority'; dismissing the possibility of 'a society of even only two people' in which each does not 'give up some of his autonomy'. A society in which there is still the necessity of majorities and minorities, as there are still (and is implied by) contested elections, would seem to be a space of public dispute, a space for politics.[56]

Lenin, finally, to spare a word for him, believed not only in the end of the state but also – as we are told by Pierson – that democracy itself, being 'simply one form of the state', is 'destined to "wither away"' with the disappearance of classes.[57] This sounds bad. Is it true? Yes, it is; but only in a sense. In addition to the circumstance that Lenin, too, made clear his particular, Marxist understanding of the meaning of the 'state' ('The state withers away insofar as there are no longer any capitalists, any classes, and, consequently, no *class* can be *suppressed*'), there is also this: he went to some trouble to explain that he construed the withering away of democracy just *qua* state-form on this meaning. 'We do not,' he wrote, 'expect the advent of a system of society in which the principle of subordination of the minority to the majority will not be observed.'[58] Around what would minorities and majorities have been expected by him to form? And should it not be said, particularly by someone not attached to the narrow Marxist meaning of the 'state', that Lenin did not, then, actually anticipate the disappearance (without qualification) of *democracy*?

Looking out menacingly, you see, from behind this figure of the end-of-politics rendition of Marxism, is a close and a not very pretty friend. Its presence should not go unremarked. I mean a disposition to give out that Marxist ideas in this area were (not to put too fine a point on it) proto-Stalinist. Held puts the thing gently: that Marx's conception, by delegitimizing disagreement and dispute, implied 'a propensity to an authoritarian form of politics'. Keane thinks that Marx showed 'a lack of respect or enthusiasm' for, among other things, the right to vote. Cohen would have it that, in the communist society Marx envisioned, the 'private' or the 'particular' was to be abolished, 'would no longer exist'. And Jay is pleased to note in this fin-de-siècle a 'widespread reassessment of the value of bourgeois democracy as more than a *mere ideological smokescreen*' (my emphasis).[59] What is one to say? Such opinions are in themselves unastonishing, for having been so widely canvassed by now. But one has also come to expect, by now, with the quantity and quality of available scholarship on Marxism, rather better than this. You can still be surprised by it in some of the places it is found.

VII. Privilege

An example of the seventh type of obloquy, the last type of this series, will not be given. Readers are invited to find specific examples where they will, for there is today no shortage of them. They occur in discussion of the interrelationships between socialism, the working class, other types of social agent or political subject, and the various forms of exploitation and oppression: economic, gender, national, ethnic, and so on. It is, clearly, neither a small nor a simple set of issues, and I have no intention of trying to offer here anything like a thorough or sufficient treatment of them. I focus merely on one current anti-Marxist trope: that, in postulating a special connection between the prospect of achieving socialism and the movement and struggles of the working class, Marxism was and is guilty of a kind of arbitrary favouritism, privileging this particular agent at the expense of others, in a would-be universalizing discourse that is actually undemocratic.

A preliminary question about this is whether proponents of the criticism themselves regard socialism as a solution to all these aforesaid different oppressions. Typically they do not. It is, in fact, usually a companion argument to the one I focus upon that Marxism was wrong to conceive socialism in such an all-encompassing way, as the precondition for ending every human oppression; or – in extreme variants of this companion argument – as automatically bringing with it complete and universal liberation. The contention, in this extreme variant, is one more caricature, which I do not bother to contest at length, proffering merely two or three quite 'orthodox'

Marxist reference points to the contrary.[60] That Marxists have generally overstated, however, the interdependence between achieving socialism and the overcoming of the other social oppressions is fair criticism. Beyond continuing to register how different forms of domination can often feed off and mutually reinforce one another, socialists have to recognize that socialism, ambitious and difficult of attainment as it has proved to be, is one goal, relatively distinct from other emancipatory goals; which are of their own pressing urgency, the obstacles and resistances to them being the source of plenty human misery and stifled potentialities. There is still good enough reason for movements or agencies in support of these several goals to accept and to press the validity of each other's specific claims. Any battle against one grave systemic injustice diminishes itself by ignoring other such equally grave injustices, or by making light of them.

A contemporary universalism, therefore, may find its basis in the reciprocal recognition amongst different emancipatory struggles of what they share, as struggles against injustice or arbitrary power. It should not be founded on a claim that one such struggle is master or mistress of them all. If a feminist socialism and a socialist feminism, a socialist anti-racism or anti-racist socialism, are possible and necessary, still socialism, feminism and the struggle against racism train their sights on different objectives, none of which simply subsumes the others.

In this light, now, what is to be made of the argument that to see the working class as central, crucial, to any possible socialist future is arbitrarily to privilege it; that every kind of oppressed subject or social identity is a potential agency of socialism quite equally with this one? If the argument exploits a notion of socialism as, definitionally, only that kind of society from which all forms of social oppression have been removed, then socialism has been redefined again as universal, all-encompassing goal, and the whole point of insisting on its specificity and its distinction from other goals is lost. One might just as well say that the working class, or ethnic minorities, are equal potential agencies with women for overcoming gender oppression – understood, this, as the end of all oppressions. To establish, in other words, an equality amongst various putative agencies of socialism, the current critiques of Marxism on this point have quietly to take back what they forthrightly – and justly – put forward concerning the non-comprehensive, the particular, nature of the aim of a classless society.

If, on the other hand, this is not taken back, then the argument against 'privileging' the working class as agency of socialism, or that to do so is undemocratic, is unconvincing. Across the variety of conceptions of what is socialism, a core idea has always been the removal of that form of (economic) exploitation which is associated with class division. Cutting through the thorny issue of the boundaries of the working class, if we say it is composed roughly of all the victims – organized and not, male and female, black or white, ethnically diverse, and of whatever sexual orientation – of economic exploitation, then there are at least two good reasons to suppose that it is this constituency that is the primary constituency of socialism.

First, it has an interest (Hindess notwithstanding) in opposing capitalist exploitation, in a way that alternative constituencies, alternatively defined, do not. Women, just as women, for example, do not; unless it can be shown persuasively that the significantly wealthy among them, by birth, or by marriage, or by professional or commercial success, are in their generality just as likely to come to a consciousness of the injustices of capitalism as are women workers; or unless it can be shown persuasively why the struggle against gender inequality is, just as such, intrinsically anti-capitalist, and consequently socialist. Apart from restoring, once again, the sort of spurious universalism that is criticized in traditionally inflated socialist claims, this amounts to saying – as has been said rather too often, wrongly – that capitalism by its very nature could not accommodate or adapt to this or that particular democratic goal. Who will confidently say it about either gender or ethnic equality? What in the nature of capitalism definitively forbids the one or the other? Capitalism, as Marxists are all too frequently lectured, is not the cause of all ills. And it is not at all clear that to fight to remove these of them from existing capitalist societies must be to fight in vain.

Second, the idea – considered normatively now rather than predictively – that exactly those on the receiving end of a given form of oppression or injustice might be the primary agents of its liquidation is the opposite of undemocratic. It is a rather old idea and scarcely exclusive to Marxism: that genuine social liberations are not (as a rule at any rate) delivered to people by someone else. Within Marxism this theme has had the name of proletarian self-emancipation, and the problem with it has often been seen to be, not the theme itself, but that no Marxists have really taken it seriously (as, unhappily, *many* Marxists have not), going in for various, elitist substitutionisms. Of a sudden, it turns out that it is the sentiment itself that is at fault, underwriting a kind of privilege. Quite how far things have gone today in the development of facile criticisms of Marxism across a sector of the Left may be gauged by imagining what the reaction would be, were a parallel of this 'privileging' argument to be tried out in relation to some other type of oppression. If someone were to suggest, for instance, that one should not specially focus on women as the primary constituency of the battle against women's oppression; or that black people in South Africa had no privileged (!) place in the current struggle against apartheid – it is a safe bet there would be many who would not even cross the road to respond to the suggestion.

Conclusion
This critical commentary was composed, though all the material engaged and criticized by it predates the period, in the months spanning the turn into the 1990s, when momentous events, far from played out, were unfolding in Eastern Europe. Whatever other consequences may follow upon these

events, it seems not improbable that one consequence will be a further impetus to the propagation of material of a similar kind. Already it is possible to detect, within the spectrum of early reactions, one that might be called retrospective Stalinism or at least Brezhnevism: by which I mean a tendency, amongst people who have thought, insisted, for years that the Soviet and Eastern European regimes were not a genuine embodiment or product of Marxist belief, to wonder if the entire tradition is not now bankrupted by their wreckage – as though the ideas and values of Marxism were then, after all, wrapped up in these regimes, as before they were said not to be.

The sense in which it is likely to be true that a tradition is ended, is that the time of mass-based socialist movements which conceived themselves as specifically Marxist may well be up. There are good reasons, as well as bad ones, for drawing a line under it. Any socialist movement that seeks now to define itself by reference to one label or doctrine, that does not contain at its heart a vigorous, committed pluralism, intellectual and political, is doomed to be, not a movement, but a sect. At the same time, if socialism has any future, the movement for it needs to know where it has come from, not only the resources it lacks, but also the ones it has. It needs a proper form of self-accounting. Making a mess of its own past, of the different strands or currents within it, will not be a rewarding procedure. And this is to say nothing, all politics of the thing set aside, of the elementary care and sense of proportion which each generation of thinkers owes to the efforts of generations of thinkers before it.

NOTES

1. References for this paragraph: Jon Elster, *Making Sense of Marx*, Cambridge 1985, pp. 522, 88 – and cf. pp. 220–22, 526; Karl Marx, *Grundrisse*, Harmondsworth 1973, p. 706; and 'Critique of the Gotha Programme', in Karl Marx and Frederick Engels, *Selected Works*, Moscow 1970, Vol. 3, pp. 18–19. The starting point for Elster's discussion of this issue is actually a passage from *The German Ideology* in which it is said, 'it was not their [the utopian socialists'] view, as Sancho [Max Stirner] imagines, that each should do the work of Raphael, but that anyone in whom there is a potential Raphael should be able to develop without hindrance.' See Karl Marx and Frederick Engels, *Collected Works* (hereafter CW), London 1975 ff., Vol. 5, p. 393.
2. See John Keane, *Democracy and Civil Society*, London 1988, pp. 54, 63; for the Marx references, notes 52–55 below; Engels to Theodor Cuno 24/1/1872, in Karl Marx and Frederick Engels, *Selected Correspondence* (hereafter MESC), Moscow n. d., p. 336; and August Bebel, *Society of the Future*, Moscow 1971, p. 23.
3. Stuart Hall, *The Hard Road to Renewal*, London 1988, pp. 169, 242.
4. Martin Jay, *Fin-de-Siècle Socialism, and other essays*, London 1988, p. 5 – which has also 'those who arrogate to themselves knowledge of the whole'.
5. References for this paragraph: Jean L. Cohen, *Class and Civil Society*, Oxford 1983, p. 193; Marx, CW, Vol. 4, p. 195, and *Capital*, Vol. I, Moscow 1961, p. 301; Engels, CW, Vol. 7, p. 92; V. I. Lenin, *Collected Works*, Moscow

1960–1970, Vol. 22, p. 149; Rosa Luxemburg, 'The Spirit of Russian Literature: Life of Korolenko', in Mary-Alice Waters, *Rosa Luxemburg Speaks*, New York 1970, p. 349; Leon Trotsky, *My Life*, New York 1960, p. 1, and *Problems of Everyday Life*, New York 1973, p. 53, and *Literature and Revolution*, Ann Arbor 1960, p. 253; Theodor Adorno, *Minima Moralia*, London 1974, pp. 32, 173; and Isaac Deutscher, *Marxism in our Time*, London 1972, p. 236.

6. *The Hard Road to Renewal*, pp. 169–70.
7. See Gösta Esping Anderson, *Politics Against Markets*, Princeton 1985, pp. 12, 18, 24 – and xiii; and Lenin, *Collected Works*, Vol. 9, pp. 112, 49 (and cf. pp. 23, 29, 52, 56, 83, 98), Vol. 25, p. 454, and Vol. 31, pp. 36, 59 (and pp. 56–65 passim).
8. On the last point here, see Raymond Williams, *Resources of Hope*, London 1989, p. 66.
9. For this and the next paragraph, see *Class and Civil Society*, pp. 103–4 – and p. 244 notes 60 and 64.
10. Engels to Joseph Bloch 21–22/9/1890, in MESC, pp. 498–500 (and cf. Karl Marx, *Capital*, Vol. III, Moscow 1962, p. 772).
11. Barry Hindess, *Politics and Class Analysis*, Oxford 1987, pp. 8, 88 – and cf. pp. 94. 101.
12. Ibid., pp. 89, 102, 103–4.
13. Ibid., pp. 89–90, 94–5, 102.
14. See my *Discourses of Extremity*, London 1990, p. 143; and more generally, on this issue of reductionism, pp. 73–5, 84, 86–7, 93–4, 130–36, 166 n. 13.
15. Christopher Pierson, *Marxist Theory and Democratic Politics*, Cambridge 1986, p. 173.
16. *Fin-de-Siècle Socialism*, p. 4.
17. Les Johnston, *Marxism, Class Analysis and Socialist Pluralism*, London 1986, p. 78 – and pp. 50, 62, 67–8.
18. *The Hard Road to Renewal*, p. 156.
19. Elster, *Making Sense of Marx*, pp. 86, 91; Cohen, *Class and Civil Society*, p. 188; Keane, *Democracy and Civil Society*, pp. 54, 63–4; Pierson, *Marxist Theory and Democratic Politics*, p. 28.
20. David Held, *Models of Democracy*, Cambridge 1987, p. 131; and Kate Soper, 'Marxism and Morality', *New Left Review* 163, May/June 1987, pp. 105–6 (my emphasis).
21. *Fin-de-Siècle Socialism*, pp. 10, 12, 13.
22. *The Hard Road to Renewal*, p. 173.
23. *Making Sense of Marx*, p. 61 n. 3.
24. Karl Marx, *A Contribution to the Critique of Political Economy*, London 1971, p. 21.
25. CW, Vol. 4, pp. 131, 179.
26. CW, Vol. 3, p. 326.
27. *Grundrisse*, p. 611.
28. See 'Critique of the Gotha Programme', *Selected Works*, Vol. 3, p. 19; *Capital*, Vol. III, p. 799; and 'The Controversy About Marx and Justice', in my *Literature of Revolution*, London 1986, pp. 51–4 (or *New Left Review* 150, March/April 1985, pp. 81–4).
29. 'Economic and Philosophical Manuscripts', CW, Vol. 3, pp. 299, 336–7.
30. *Capital*, Vol. I, pp. 245, 246, 251, 252, 254–5, 263–4 n., 266, 269, 270.
31. *Capital*, Vol. III, pp. 826, 854.
32. Respectively: Deutscher, *Marxism in our Time*, pp. 237–8; Herbert Marcuse, *Eros and Civilization*, New York 1961, p. 215; Leon Trotsky, *Trotsky's Diary in Exile*, London 1958, pp. 56–7; *Rosa Luxemburg Speaks*, p. 354; Bebel *Society of the Future*, p. 107.

33. *Minima Moralia*, pp. 155–7, 78–80, 103.
34. *Literature and Revolution*, pp. 249, 253–4.
35. Terry Eagleton, *Against the Grain*, London 1986, p. 165.
36. Marx to Ferdinand Lassalle 28/7/1855, CW, Vol. 39, p. 544; and see David McLellan, *Karl Marx: His Life and Thought*, London 1973, pp. 274–5.
37. Barrington Moore Jr., *Reflections on the Causes of Human Misery*, London 1972, p. xvi.
38. *Democracy and Civil Society*, pp. 219, 228.
39. Ibid., pp. 229, 220, 232, 234.
40. Ibid., pp. 228, 229 (and pp. 230, 235), 236, 234–5.
41. Ibid., pp. x, 238, 236–7.
42. Ibid., pp. 220, 235.
43. Ibid., pp. 233, 235.
44. Ibid., p. 237.
45. Ibid., p. 182.
46. See Ibid., pp. 238–41. Those interested in the debate on 'essential contestability' may consult here also a small new contribution to it. The view of democracy which Keane defends 'acknowledges its essentially contested quality'. But then that view – 'a pluralist civil society guarded by an open and accountable state' – is at once said to comprehend that what is seen as democratic 'at any given time and place can be maintained. . .only through *these* democratic procedures' (Keane's emphasis). 'This means. . .that democracy cannot be interpreted as merely one language game among others'. So it goes.
47. *Politics and Class Analysis*, pp. 108–9.
48. Ibid., pp. 110–11.
49. Ibid., pp. 112–19 – emphases added.
50. See Michael Walzer, 'The Good Life', *New Statesman and Society*, 6 October 1989, pp. 28–9; Pierson, *Marxist Theory and Democratic Politics*, pp. 28, 30; Jay, *Fin-de-Siècle Socialism*, p. 9; Cohen, *Class and Civil Society*, p. 107 (and cf. pp. 108–9, 187, 190); Keane, *Democracy and Civil Society*, pp. 62–3 (and 54).
51. *Models of Democracy*, pp. 123–4 (and 131).
52. CW, Vol. 6, pp. 505, 212; and Vol. 10, p. 333 (translation modified).
53. See especially, for their care and clarity, Hal Draper, 'The Death of the State in Marx and Engels', in Ralph Miliband and John Saville (eds.), *The Socialist Register 1970*, London 1970, pp. 201–307; and Michael Evans, 'Karl Marx and the Concept of Political Participation', in Geraint Parry (ed.), *Participation in Politics*, Manchester 1972, pp. 127–50.
54. *Selected Works*, Vol. 3, p. 25.
55. See David McLellan, *Karl Marx: Selected Writings*, Oxford 1977, p. 563 (and cf. Held, *Models of Democracy*, p. 131).
56. *Selected Works*, Vol. 2, p. 378; and MESC, p. 336.
57. Pierson, *Marxist Theory and Democratic Politics*, p. 79.
58. *Collected Works*, Vol. 25, pp. 455–6, 467.
59. Held, *Models of Democracy*, pp. 137–8; Keane, *Democracy and Civil Society*, p. 59; Cohen, *Class and Civil Society*, p. 184; Jay, *Fin-de-Siècle Socialism*, p. 8.
60. Lenin: 'By transforming capitalism into socialism the proletariat creates the *possibility* of abolishing national oppression; the possibility becomes *reality* "only" – "only"! – with the establishment of full democracy in all spheres, including the delineation of state frontiers in accordance with the sympathies of the population.' *Collected Works*, Vol. 22, p. 325. Trotsky: the text to note 34 above; or this (reductionist?) observation, that 'culture was the main instrument of class oppression. But it also, and only it, can become the instrument of socialist emancipation.' *Problems of Everyday Life*, p. 236.

MARXISM TODAY: AN ANATOMY

JOHN SAVILLE

What do we expect from a monthly journal of the Left? Obviously it must be different, and distinguishable, from weekly journals such as *Tribune* and the *New Statesman and Society*. And with the explicit title of *Marxism Today*, which it must be assumed indicates a specific commitment to a marxist analysis in the elucidation of society, past, present and future, it would be reasonable to expect a serious review of the contemporary world. We would assume an historical perspective upon the world around us, one which included the kind of constant questioning of social reality to be found in the correspondence between Marx and Engels. It has always been the aim and purpose of Marxist analysis to help situate the individual within historical time; to relate the past to the present and to offer a variety of perspectives for the future; to make sense of individual purpose, a matter of self-enlightenment, within a wider social-political framework and setting. We have often been wrong, confused and blinded by a dogmatic reference to the past which has encouraged a false or one sided understanding of the present, and a mistaken prognosis of things to come. We are all, that is to say, human; but we have not always been mistaken, and readers of a journal that is titled *Marxism Today* expect a sharpness of intellectual approach which is serious, perceptive, and an encouragement to political action. Alongside all the criticisms we can make of ourselves, the last three decades have witnessed a significant revival of the critical spirit which moved the founding fathers. *Marxism Today*, after a decade or so of new editorial direction, has established itself as representative of a particular trend of thinking which it is the purpose of this present article to analyse; and to that end, the twelve issues of the year 1988 have been taken to illustrate the tendencies in editorial approach and thinking[1].

Let us begin with *Marxism Today*'s own survey of 1987 in the January 1988 issue as an index to their political and intellectual approach to the world as they see it. The survey covers twenty two pages, of which four are adverts, so there were eighteen pages of print and photographs. The Arts (music, films, theatre, TV) took eleven pages; fashion two; and one each to politics, political books, and one on Aids. And that was the year that was. The politics of 1987 were written up in a few limp words by Anthony Barnett. They made a passing reference to the general election of 1987 which was won for the third time by

Thatcher, but no analysis was offered nor was there any comment upon the state of the Labour Party other than a defence of the Chesterfield conference by Hilary Wainwright which was outside the review section proper. Nor was there any serious reference, or discussion, of the Stock Exchange crash of 1987. It is, indeed, interesting that the editorial direction thought it proper to devote two pages to fashion against one to politics. The fashion article was listed in the Table of Contents as 'Sarah Mower examines the economics of the rising hemline', and the heading over the article itself was 'The New Legshow', a double spread with three legfull pictures of models wearing expensive dresses with such cute captions as 'Sweetie Pie:Dressing for Lacroix born again dolly bird' and 'Gianni Versace's inflated idea of wit in fashion'. Ms Mower was not, however, wholly abstracted from the real world, and she did at least mention the great crash of '87 with a reference to 'the climate of fear' that was its immediate aftermath. She even predicted a 'utility look' for 1988 in keeping with what she thought might be the harsher climate of the year to come.

This was certainly not the view of the editorial collective of *Marxism Today*. In earlier years as well as 1988 which is being considered here, there was a more or less constant refrain about the changes in British society that have been brought about by the economic successes presided over by Mrs Thatcher; and 1988, when all the signs were beginning rapidly to accumulate concerning the fundamental weaknesses of large parts of the economy, was just the year when *Marxism Today*'s halleluyah chorus reached a high note. The editors have never been much taken with economic analysis; they have long cut any connection between base and superstructure, and it is ideology that is at the centre of their analysis of the New Times that we are now living in; but even they have on occasion to relate, however distantly, their description of the new society we now inherit to what it is that is providing all the wonderful new choices now opening before us.

There was no economic analysis in the January issue, and only a passing reference in February to our high economic growth in an article on foreign policy. But in March Frances Cairncross ('edits the Britain section of the *Economist*') wrote a page analysis of the background to the forthcoming budget of Nigel Lawson and what might be expected from it. Her approach was along the lines of editorial thinking. Britain, she wrote:

is now showing clear symptoms of post-election boom. Economists argue over whether the boom represents a once-for-all change in the economy's productivity. There are some signs that it does.

That argument begins from the Tory government's abolition of exchange controls and trade-union reforms. As a result, it postulates, British firms are now free to use capital and labour more efficiently. Their profits have therefore soared by 150% since 1980. That bonanza has allowed British firms to step up investment: imports of capital equipment have grown by 120% since the start of the 1980s. The modern machinery British companies have has been operated by fewer workers, working more effectively. Output per worker in manufacturing barely changed between 1974 and 1980; in the following six years, it rose by 40%.

As a result, British firms can now produce more, per worker and per pound of machinery, than ever before and can work closer to capacity than they ever used to. On this theory, the boom is sustainable at something not far from present levels for many months to come.

And then, as is the economist's wont, Ms Cairncross offered certain qualifications: there were early signs of overheating of the economy, for example; but the general tone of the rest of her article clearly suggested that she was confident Lawson had matters pretty well under control. In his budget, Lawson would be carefully considering tax reductions 'which will not add too much to demand', by giving more to the rich ('who save more than the poor'), to companies ('who invest') and generally to encourage savings.

Ms Cairncross would be well advised to forget this particular piece of journalism, since most of its information was proved to be wrong. I write in November 1989 when the disastrous consequences of the Lawson occupation of No 11 Downing St have become evident to the world; and as will be recorded below, not all specialist commentators were as superficial as Ms Cairncross. There were warnings in plenty of the serious weaknesses of the British economy throughout the Thatcher years. Before coming to what the facts of the economic situation reveal about the British condition in the 1980s, it may be helpful to provide the reader with examples of the ways in which the editorial team of *Marxism Today* interpreted the Cairncross analysis for the enlightenment of their constituency. Frank Mort toured the *Daily Mail* Ideal Home Exhibition and in the March 1988 issue he summarised what he believed to be the thinking of the salesmen and advertisers, with whom, it was clear, he was in full sympathy. He noted:

the new lifestyle politics of the 1980s; the move to intensely personal private consumption. This is not just a return to earlier, traditional values. Nor does it line up as straight cultural conservatism. . .Changing class relations, the cultural impact of recession and feminism, the youth markets, and the 'new man' – this is what is up for grabs in campaigns. The argument goes like this. . .Cultural as well as economic splintering of what were in the 60s and 70s solid market blocs (the working class, youth, the housewife etc) calls for a rethink. The market has filled up with segmented consumer profiles both up and down the scale: C 1 and C 2s, yuppies, sloanes, the working woman, gay men, the young elderly. A changed situation demands a different type of campaign. This is where the design input comes in. Lifestyle advertising, where the message is more 'emotional' than rational and informational, feeds off design and visual imagery. The idea is to create mood, where consumers experience their quintessential indivuality in the product. Levis jeans, Saga holidays, Dr. White's, all work with this brief. Life style advertising is about differentiating oneself from the Joneses', not, as in previous decades, keeping up with them. . .

And so on. Two months later, Mort co-authored an article with Nicholas Green which was listed in the Table of Contents as a look at the consumer boom, and the need to come to terms with the politics of prosperity. Its opening words:

Everywhere I go, up and down the country, I can't help noticing how prosperous people are looking. No, it's not Harold Macmillan's 'you've never had it so good' Britain, but we might be forgiven for thinking it is. Prosperity is in the air and the Tories are making the most of it. And it is not just about spending power. It goes hand in hand with a *cultural* vision of lifestyles and social identities. Suddenly, as Janet Street-Porter put it, everyone wants a degree in creative shopping. How the Left responds to this – whether it engages with the politics of prosperity or retreats into fundamentalism – is at the heart of the debate over socialist renewal.

Let the pundits and commentators argue it out whether there really has been that economic miracle. Looked at from the inside – from key sectors of the consumer economy – business has never been better. . .Part and parcel of the retail spiral is the boom in credit. The current flexibility and innovations of finance capital have set some of the conditions. Britons have taken to charge cards and plastic money like no other EC country. . .

Of course, the authors went on to comment, we know we have a growing current account deficit; we know that there has been an increasing casualisation of the labour market; and we know about the growing part-time youth and female work that is low paid, non-unionised and without basic employment rights. However:

But the point is we are talking about *cultural images* of prosperity here, not just economic theories and statistics. On that score – and at the level of popular experience – personal consumption has become a very potent emblem of national recovery indeed. The extra quid a week in the pay packet, the ability to muscle on in there and grab a piece of the action, to take out that loan – these things don't just provide a sense of personal power for 'you and yours', they have a way of saying symbolically that things must be all right in the country as a whole. If we are in work, Mrs Thatcher and the chancellor don't lecture us any more about backs to the wall, there is no alternative. Can't pay, won't pay. We get a pat on the back and cash in hand for enterprise and initiative rewarded

It was a long article that insisted on de-politicisation as a by-product of rising living standards and the increasing range of choice that more prosperous lifestyles brought with them. And for the future?:

As so often, Thatcherism's successes have forced the Left's hand. The current consumer boom has rudely pushed the issue on to Labour's agenda, demanding some sort of response. Where you stand on consumption seems to be becoming a litmus test over the whole issue of socialist renewal. In the redder than red corner stands Bennism and the fundmantalist Left. In a rhetoric resonant of its evangelical past, markets here are cast as the very apogee of capitalist immorality, denying real freedoms and social decision making.

It is the recognition of consumer aspirations that must form the starting point for the socialist politics of the decades to come: the cultural politics of prosperity, as the authors sum up. The editorial collective of *Marxism Today* had already offered practical help by launching their own credit card (CRED CARD) in the January 1988 issue; and their publicity blurb to encourage membership must be taken as reflecting their own understanding of how their readers were reacting to the New Times ahead:

You might be feeling a little out of pocket this Christmas. Next year need not be the same. We are not suggesting you give up all those little luxuries that make life worth living: the odd meal at a restaurant, outings to cinemas, theatres, nightclubs, and gyms, not to mention saturday's shopping spree. But, we can try to make them less expensive. You can save a small fortune with our plastic discount card. It's accepted all over the country at the most convenient and stylish places.

And there followed a list – a short list – of shops, theatres etc where *Marxism Today*'s Cred Card would be accepted; and this was followed by the rather surprising information that 'Our discounts include free meals for a third person, two tickets for the price of one, free bottles of wine and club membership, as well as press invites. You can't afford to miss out'.

It is not clear how many did miss out since after this first advertisement there was no further notice in *Marxism Today* for the next twelve months; either they were overwhelmed with subscriptions or so many people missed out that the scheme folded. But it was an enlightening episode, not least for its implications of the good life as understood by *Marxism Today*'s promoters.

The febrile statements that have been quoted above must not be thought to be out of line with the mainstream thinking of the editorial team of *Marxism Today*. In an article published in the *Guardian* on 31 March 1988, Martin Jacques, *MT*'s editor, summed up his political approach in three main points of which the Left must take full account in all policy developments in the future. The first was 'The economy and competitiveness'; the third was 'The culture of the Labour Party', the need to recognise the new heterogeneous world in which we now live; and the middle point was 'Choice and the Consumer':

> Thatcherism, over the past couple of years, has made these its own. Perhaps more than any other issue, they symbolise how Thatcherism feels of the moment, In the new world where leisure, consumption and the consumer have become more and more important, so choice has taken on a new significance. It is a way people express themselves, assert their identity and exercise their power.
>
> By way of contrast, the Left still speaks only of basic provision and access. That's not wrong, but it's only part of the problem, and as such seems to address only the past, an old declining world where choice was simply about having or not having.
>
> The Benn-Heffer position has nothing to say about choice and consumers. It moves in the traditional world of producers and production, forgetting that all those producers are consumers, and that consumption (be it video recorders, clothes, homes or holidays) occupies an increasingly important part in their lives.
>
> The Kinnock-Hattersley position again is more flexible, more adaptive, but lives, one feels, in the shadow of Thatcherism.
>
> Labour should be decisively in favour of a culture of consumerism, but one where access to it is not denied by the poverty of an underclass. If consumption now looms so large, then society has an obligation to ensure that everyone has access to certain social resources. Moreover, just as Labour wishes to see a shift in power from employer to worker so it should clearly stand for the consumer against the corporation. It might in rhetoric (when it remembers to say so): in practice it doesn't.

There is, naturally, a grand theory behind the emphasis upon the individual and the consumer society. It is most explicitly stated in the writings of Stuart Hall, a member of the editorial board or collective, but not of the editorial team. It is Stuart Hall's theoretical approach however that clearly infuses the editorial mind. In general, it is possible to identify a number of the central concepts that combine to form the *Marxism Today* analysis of contemporary society, and much of the illustration given below is taken from the published work of Stuart Hall, most of it in the journal itself.

1) Politics is overwhelmingly a matter of cultural discourse within ideology. Classical marxism, so Hall argued 'depended upon an assured correspondence between the 'economic' and the 'political': one could read off our political attitudes, interests and motivations from our economic class interests and position' (2) And this can today no longer be accepted. The 'correspondence' has disintegrated, both in theory and in practice, and the language of politics has therefore moved over to the cultural side. In his introduction to a volume of collected essays published in 1988, (3) Stuart Hall acknowledges that a main criticism of his writings had been the over-emphasis upon politics and ideology (Introduction, p.3) He accepted that Thatcherism was not only an ideological phenomenon and that he had given no 'substantial assessment' of the political economy of Thatcherism (pp.9 and 3); but – and it was a very large 'but' – matters of ideology and culture were not factors that were in any way secondary or dependent, and they must be understood to play a key role in the politics of the hegemonic perspective. 'Ideology' he argued, 'has its own modality; its own ways of working and its own forms of struggle'; and he reminds us of Gramsci's insistence that all economic and political processes have ideological 'conditions of existence', and that, in Gramsci's own words, 'popular beliefs. . .are themselves material forces'.[2]

Ideology, then, is of crucial importance, and it is the ideology of a new epoch: one that is distinct from the previous period of mass production, sometimes described as 'post-industrial', although Stuart Hall favours 'Post-Fordism'. The era of post-Fordism embraces a range of new or newly developing characteristics: the decline in the traditional manufacturing sector and the rise of computer based industries; the falling proportions of the skilled, male, working class and the increase in the numbers of white collar workers and above all the 'feminisation' of the workforce; the increasing domination of the world economy by multinational companies and the globalisation of financial markets. It is emphasised in Hall's analysis that the processes of change are always uneven, and that it is necessary to look for the 'leading' edges of change to appreciate what the world of the twenty first century will be like. These changes at the base, although Hall does not phrase it in this way, are associated with broader social and cultural changes, and it is at this point that we begin to move into the area of ideology. There is taking place a weakening of the traditional solidarities, and the newly developing work processes, which offer flexibilities not hitherto enjoyed are linked with 'the maximisation of individual choices through personal consumption'. A new individuality is being created, away from 'the lines of continuity which hitherto stabilised our social identities'. This re-forging of individuality leading to a transformation of social identities is a central concept in the New Times thinking of *Marxism Today*. A key passage from Stuart Hall's October 1988 article, from which the quotations given above have been taken, sets out the new analysis in striking words:

One boundary which 'new times' have displaced is that between the 'objective' and subjective dimensions of change. The individual subject has become more important, while our models of 'the subject' have altered. We can no longer conceive of 'the individual' in terms of a whole and completed Ego or autonomous 'self'. The 'self' is experienced as more fragmented and incomplete, composed of multiple 'selves' or identities in relation to the different social worlds we inhabit, something with a history, 'produced', in process. These vicissitudes of the 'subject' have their own histories which are key episodes in the passage to 'new times'. They include the cultural revolutions of the 1960s; '1968' itself, with its strong sense of politics as 'theatre'; feminism's slogan that 'the personal is political'; pyschoanalysis, with its rediscovery of the unconscious roots of subjectivity; the theoretical revolutions of the 60s and 70s – semiotics, structuralism, post-structuralism – with their concern for language and representation.

This 'return of the subjective' aspect suggests that we cannot settle for a language in which to describe 'new times' which respects the old distinctions between the objective and subjective dimensions of change. But such a conceptual shift presents problems for the Left. The conventional culture of the Left, with its stress on 'objective contradictions', 'impersonal structures' and processes that work 'behind men's (sic) backs', has disabled us from confronting the subjective in politics in any coherent way.

It was following this passage that Hall argued the assumed correspondence between the economic and the political no longer obtained, and that ideology is now an independent factor, hard, a material fact, as he says elsewhere.[3]

If we assume that the 1988 issues of *Marxism Today* represent reasonably well the thinking in the editorial office, and of the editorial board, then what must be emphasised is the continual re-iteration of the success of the Thatcher years. Thatcherism, as Judith Williamson phrased it in her critique of the New Times approach, has been 'perceived as an endlessly adaptable, almost indomitable force'.[4] Throughout 1988 there was constant reference to the successes of Thatcherite ideology; to the intellectual and moral hegemony which Thatcher had secured; and to the recognition by the Thatcherites that the ideological struggle was of crucial importance. The reader could be forgiven for thinking that Thatcherism was unassailable. The sub-editors of the journal regularly provided striking confirmation of the apparently dogmatic belief in the political astuteness of Mrs. Thatcher herself, and of those around her. As late as November 1988, an article by Andrew Gamble on the economy – one of only two main articles in the whole year on the subject – was given the heading: "ON, AND ON, AND ON. . .? The Thatcher revolution keeps on rolling. A dominant party system could be in the making. The only cloud on the horizon, argues Andrew Gamble, is the economy". In the Table of Contents, the subtitle read: "As the Tories look forward to 10 more years, Andrew Gamble looks for clouds on the economic horizon". A subtle difference, it will be perceived. In one heading Gamble is searching for clouds on the economic horizon, which presumably might not be there, and above the article itself the reference is to 'The only cloud on the horizon'.

The intellectual subservience to Thatcherism, and to Mrs. Thatcher herself, was sharply etched for the readers in an article on foreign policy, in the February issue, by Malcolm Rutherford, another of the *Financial Times'* writers who seem to spend much of their spare time working for *Marxism*

Today. This was a highly instructive piece in three columns, containing within its short compass most of the illusions that crowd the minds of the editorial team. 'A Power Abroad' was the heading, and it began:

> British foreign policy is not what it used to be. Since the general election last year it has become more self-confident, and although the policy itself may not have changed much, Britain has begun to carry more weight around the world'

One reason for Britain's changed stature, we were told, was that Thatcher has both experience, because of her many years in office, and, "abroad at least – respect as an elder statesperson". Another reason was "the halting and perhaps reversal of Britain's long relative economic decline". Britain also had, if not a special then a very close relationship with the United States; the old quarrels with Europe were over; Thatcher can now speak to the Americans with the backing and support of Paris and Bonn; and as a result east Europeans regard Britain "as in a pivotal position and Thatcher as a leader with some clout". After all, he went on, "she did not *invent* her relationship with Gorbachov, but it exists. It is as much his doing as hers". And he began to sum up:

> One may dispute whether British foreign policy in all these areas [referring to Africa and the Middle East] is right or wrong, or even how it should be defined beyond a general desire to maintain stability. But it has become harder than it used to be to argue that it is not of much consequence and is all based on posturing.

Set into the article was a small photograph of Thatcher and Gorbachov waving to the camera, and subtitle: "Making waves in the world".

It is difficult not to describe this analysis as rigmarole, almost every word of which was either not true at the time it was written or has been proved wildly inaccurate in the months which followed its publication. But it was all too symptomatic of the thinking of the editorial team of *MT*. No one would guess, from a reading of all the *MT* of 1988 that the world has been a bitter and bloody planet ever since the end of World War II; that there have been dozens of wars, large and small, and that millions and millions have died or been maimed; that it is not only when the United States has been involved that large scale destruction has occurred, although we should never forget the infamous destruction and obliteration of so much of Korea and Vietnam; that these innumerable conflicts between Third World regimes have been consistently and steadily supplied with arms from the industrialised powers of the world; that the international trade in arms has become a significant part of the balance of trade of the United Kingdom – as in other countries. Once upon a time – before World War II – the labour movement in Britain regarded the arms manufacturers as immoral beings and the international trade in arms as obscene.[5] No more, and certainly not a subject these days for *MT* to debate and discuss. There is a very small country in central America called Nicaragua. The struggle of its government against rebel forces has affinities with the civil war in Spain between 1936 and 1939, although the world wide sympathy of all decent people for the Spanish Republic has not been reproduced on the same scale for Nicaragua in spite of Solidarity committees in many countries. Why this is so will provide academic research with much interesting discussion in fifty years time when, as Tawney once remarked 'passion has cooled into curiosity, and the agonies of peoples have become the exercise of the schools'. The passion has already cooled for *MT*, for 1988 saw not one specialist article on Nicaragua. The only discussion came in Fred Halliday's serious and informative article in the June issue which surveyed the relations between the USA and the USSR and which – it really is so typical – was given the title by the sub-editors as 'The Ron and Mik' show. But Halliday considers the most important single matter of world politics: the fact that since World War II the United States has been at the centre of world reaction and has used its enormous resources to crush, curb and contain democratic and progressive movements in all continents. Halliday for the most part restricts his analysis to the last twenty years (as in his *The Making of the Second Cold War*) where his thesis is that in the 1970s, and especially towards the end of that decade, there were fourteen social revolutions which weakened the international position of the US, but that since 1980 there have been no further successful revolutions, and the balance in the 1980s shifted in favour of the United States. The 'Reagan Doctrine' involved active support, financial and military, for right-wing guerrillas in the Third World. In American jargon, this is known as Low Intensity Conflict, military intervention short of a direct role for US troops. While the US support for the contras in Nicaragua has not overthrown the Sandinista government, the physical damage to the country has been enormous. But then, this is standard practice. Since World War Two the United States, as a result of direct or indirect intervention, has left a wide trail of devastation round the world. The Americans are stained with the blood of the millions of Third World citizens who have been butchered to keep the world safe for the property owners of the world; and America has been actively supported by its allies among the advanced capitalist countries and not least by the United Kingdom, whose record of subservience to America in world affairs has not been equalled by any of the other major states in the world.

In the introduction, already quoted, to his collection of essays, Stuart Hall emphasised our need to 'Submit everything to the discipline of present reality, to our understanding of the forces which are really shaping and changing our world'.[6] We may begin the process of submission by looking at the background to the euphoria – that is the correct word – the editorial team of *MT* have constantly expressed about the consumer society and in particular the consumer boom of the past few years. The basic facts however are not in dispute, nor have they been hidden from public view. Throughout the 1980s there have been serious commentators – financial journalists and professional economists – who have never believed the populist hype spread around by much of the media, or the more academic pronouncements of Frances Cairncross et al.[7]

The British economy has for many decades been in relative economic decline compared with the most advanced industrial countries. Evidence of a lag in productivity in the manufacturing sector preceded World War I, and by 1939 the gap between the most advanced – the United States first and then Germany – was considerable. In the immediate aftermath of World War II the deficiencies in British manufacturing were becoming widely known. Wartime production had exposed grave deficiencies in the machine tool sector. The failure of the combined efforts of the War Office and British industry to produce a tank comparable in fighting power with those of Germany or the Soviet Union was in large measure an indictment of the engineering industry, although the stupidities of the planners in the War Office were not helpful. The Board of Trade files during wartime contain abundant documentation of the inefficiencies of much industrial production, and after the war there were a series of Working Parties as well as the Reports of the Anglo-American delegations concerned with productivity which offered a stream of evidence of what was wrong. There was also the beginning of academic enquiry, notably the work of the Hungarian-born economist Rostas, who worked at the National Institute of Economic and Social Research. Rostas calculated that in the years before the outbreak of war in 1939, physical output per head in American manufacturing was over twice as high as in the United Kingdom, although if all branches of the economy were included the American superiority was somewhat reduced to between 1.6 and 1.8. The years of the Labour Governments after the war saw certain improvements but nothing of a radical kind, largely because Britain was in a seller's market, and all one had to do was to attract sufficient labour, and produce as much as possible, mostly along the traditional lines of organisation and management. In 1950 productivity in manufacturing in Germany was nearly forty per cent lower than in the United Kingdom; but then the story began to change. By 1980 manufacturing productivity in Germany was about thirty per cent higher than in Britain; and the same comparisons for the later period can be made with all other manufacturing countries. Labour productivity, and therefore the standard of living in Britain, have increased at a slower rate than in all Western Europe and Scandinavia. In Britain, the highest level of employment in post-war manufacturing was in the year 1968, since when there has been an uneven but steady decline by around forty per cent; and of that decline by far the largest share has taken place since 1979. This decrease in employment in the manufacturing sector by 3.5 million has been partly offset, but only partly, by an expansion in the service sector, and in other occupations. The corollary was an increase in unemployment: quite marked after the oil crisis of 1973 but accelerating sharply after 1979.[8]

The world crisis of 1973, the immediate cause of which was the very sharp increase in oil prices, was followed by a decade of slower growth; and this was the situation inherited by the new Thatcher government in the summer of 1979. As a direct result of the policies of the new government – Geoffrey Howe was Chancellor of the Exchequer – Britain experienced the deepest recession of the twentieth century. Between 1979 and 1981 total output fell by over three per cent; manufacturing output declined by seventeen per cent; and unemployment rose from one million to 2.5 million. Inflation soared. The effective exchange rate, as a result of very tight fiscal and monetary policies, rose sharply; and about twenty per cent of Britain's manufacturing base was wiped out. By the end of 1981, the Thatcher government was deeply unpopular, and what saved the Tory Party was a combination of the gross ineptitude and bumbling incompetence of the Labour Opposition at Westminster, where Michael Foot was leader; the rapidly growing revenues from North Sea oil; and the Falklands War. Oil revenues reached a peak in 1984–5, and in all some £ 80 billion of tax will have been collected between 1979–80 and 1988–89. The total was diminishing fast in the closing years of the decade. There also flowed into the Exchequer the considerable profits from privatisation and from the steady and unrelenting squeeze on welfare benefits of all kinds: a matter which is further discussed below. The government has also benefitted from increased revenues following the upturn in the economy. After the devastating years of the early eighties, the economy began to pick itself up, and from about 1984 growth was considerable: not so markedly in the manufacturing sector, which only achieved the 1978–9 output levels nearly ten years later, but in the economy as a whole, as a result of the rise in consumer demand.

The Thatcher government came to power in 1979 with mostly unclear ideas about strategic economic policy except on two counts: breaking the trade unions and privatisation. They developed a stance which everyone, within the government and outside, believed was monetarist. In 1981 there was published the Financial Statement and Budget Report which emphasised that inflation could only be reduced by controlling the money supply, along with agreed fiscal policy; and in this Financial Statement target rates were set for the growth in money supply. These allowed fluctuations between a low range of sixteen per cent for the years 1981–4, with an upper limit of thirty per cent. As it turned out, the money supply rose by no less than fifty per cent in the three years 1981–4, and then, instead of slowing down as predicted in the Financial Statement, it accelerated sharply. Between 1984 and 1988 the money supply has increased at the rate of round about twenty per cent per annum, so that it has just about doubled in this period.[9]

The consequences have been crucial for the British economy. The first is consumer spending at levels not previously achieved. Since 1984 the growth in consumer spending has been at a rate of increase of five per cent a year: a record for any comparable period in the post-war years. The recovery in domestic output, for the most part, has been the result of this consumer boom, much fuelled, of course, by the very rapid enlargement of credit facilities of all kinds. It was the enormous increase in imports that represented the most important consequence of government policy. For the first time in the industrial history of Britain there developed a deficit on the manufacturing balance of trade. In 1982 exports and imports of manufactured goods were almost equal, but beginning with 1983, when the difference was small, the gap between imports and exports has steadily widened. The manufacturing basis of the British economy was now too narrow, and it has remained so. De-industrialisation was already taking place long before 1979 – in part it is a by-product of increasing technical sophistication – but as an historical process it has been much more noticeable in Britain than in other industrial countries, and it was savagely increased in the deep recession of 1979–81. When consumer spending increased so rapidly from 1983–4, imports were sucked in at an ever increasing rate. The overall deficit on the balance of payments grew rapidly from 1987–8, and the estimate for 1989 is around 20 billion.

It is often argued that the growth of the service sector will make up for the loss of manufacturing enterprises. This is true only in part, although the argument has been widely used by apologists of the Thatcher government. In October 1985 there was published the Report of a House of Lords Select Committee on Overseas Trade. Its chairman was Lord Aldington, a former M.P. and deputy chairman of the Conservative Party, and the House of Lords debated the Report on 3 December 1985. The Chancellor of the Exchequer, Nigel Lawson, had already dismissed the Report on 13 November as not 'a helpful contribution to the debate' and he later added that the government 'wholly rejects the mixture of special pleading dressed up as analysis, and assertion masquerading as evidence, that leads the Committee to its doom-laden conclusion'. What the Report said was that since it was only manufacturing that created wealth, the decline in British manufacturing must be halted, and then reversed. They noted that manufacturing output in the 1983–4 years was 12 per cent lower than in 1973, while in the rest of the EEC, in the USA and in Japan, it was substantially higher. The Committee went on to demolish the myth that the services sector can compensate for the decline in manufacturing. And for two reasons: first, that an important part of the services sector depends on the manufacturing sector; and second, that the value-added of manufacturing exports is three times higher than services exports, with the result that a one per cent fall in manufacturing exports requires a three per cent rise in the export of services to make up the difference. The Report further noted that the share of world trade taken by British invisible exports has been declining at a faster rate than the fall in the share of manufactured exports. The House of Lords Select Committee took an impressive body of evidence from written statements and individual witnesses, and its Report represents a major statement of Britain's economic problems.[10]

What is constantly quoted by government apologists is that in spite of all the problems confronting the British economy, it is in fitter shape, with greater productivity, than at any previous period in post war history. Certainly it is true that there have been substantial productivity increases in recent years, but they have not been as spectacular as often suggested, and they have, in fact, not been greater than in certain earlier periods of the post-war era, for which see below:

Growth Rates in Manufacturing Output: Per Cent per annum

Period	Output	Productivity
1950–55	3.21	1.75
1955–60	2.92	2.36
1960–64	3.16	3.67
1964–68	3.13	3.17
1968–73	2.78	3.77
1973–79	−0.70	0.68
1979–86	−0.67	3.64

Source: National Institute of Economic and Social Research: Economic Review, February 1989, p. 64.

The growth of Labour productivity rose in each successive cycle until 1973, to be followed by a marked slowdown in the 1970s, followed by a recovery in the 1980s (and if figures for 1987 and 1988 were available the rise in productivity would probably be greater and the output level also higher). But with these qualifications, it will be appreciated that the 1980s record in manufacturing output and productivity was of a different order from any previous period: higher productivity on levels of output low by comparison with earlier years. It is when these trends are translated into international competitiveness that the seriousness of the British position in the world economy becomes clear. Britain's share of the world market in manufacturing in the 1980s remained well below the levels of earlier decades, and all the indices relevant to the measurement of competitiveness on the world market are showing adverse trends. At the end of the 1980s exports were growing at half the rate of imports, and only in chemicals and specialist drugs was Britain holding its share of the international market.

The international position of Britain during the Thatcher years has, then, worsened steadily, and the effects will work their way through to domestic levels of investment and employment in the decade which follows. But almost none of these basic facts were made available to the readers of *Marxism Today* through 1988. There was one article, and only one article, in the whole of 1988 that stated clearly the core problems confronting the British economy. This was in the July issue: an analysis by a Cambridge economist named John Wells which set forth in straightforward terms the grim facts of the British situation. The other article on the economy, by Andrew Gamble, was nothing like as rigorous. But quite obviously the Wells' analysis made no impact at all upon the thinking of the editorial team; and they continued their irresponsible way, extolling the New Times of the consumer society and repeating the myths of Thatcherite success. So we find in November 1988 a review by Peter Riddell – another of the *Financial Times* helpers, this time a former political editor of the paper – which commented on Andrew Gamble's *The Free Economy and the Strong State* and Stuart Hall's *The Hard Road to Renewal*. Riddell makes one point of note, namely, that both authors assume a coherence to Thatcherism that is not to be found in practice; and that is a fair point, provided it is appreciated that Thatcherism is centrally concerned with making the rich richer and many of the poor poorer. Riddell ends on a typically *MT* assessment on the 'unassailability of Thatcher' thesis. There is nothing, he wrote 'in these books to cheer Labour supporters from their current depression about their prospects, or to disturb Tories in their current self-confidence' (p. 49). This was written, it must be recalled, in November 1988 when the problems which led to the resignation of Nigel Lawson in 1989 were already becoming very clear to most observers.

Marxism Today has misread the history of the 1980s in quite remarkable ways. They have mistaken a consumer boom, financed by politically motivated cuts in direct taxation together with the very high growth of the money supply in the public sector, and the rapid expansion of credit facilities in the private sector, for a turn-around in the continued decline of the British economy. The very large increases in oil revenues were used to pay for the redundancies and widespread unemployment which followed the twenty per cent reduction in the manufacturing sector between 1979 and 1981. The consumer boom had no basis at all in the real state of the British economy. The slide into a balance of trade deficit on manufactured goods was already beginning in 1983, and industrial investment and output remained below the levels of previous decades until the closing years of the decade. But it has been upon the consumer boom that the editorial collective have erected their own interpretation of social change, central to which is the belief in the successful development of what they commonly describe as the Thatcher project. They have, that is, examined only the surface phenomena of this past decade and assumed that this was the projection for the future. 1989 has confirmed their errors, and in particular has blown apart their singular acceptance of Tory propaganda about the unassailability of Thatcherism as a way of life. Recognition of their wrongheadedness, however, seems to be taking some time, as witness the keynote speech of *Marxism Today's* editor, Martin Jacques, to the British Communist Party Congress in late November 1989.

An analysis of the economy of a society is not, however, limited to the general factors making for fast or slow growth, or to a macro-economic discussion of the broad movements of the balance of payments or the relationship between economic growth and productivity in manufacturing industry. The internal evolution of income distribution and the ownership of wealth are equally important, and bear immediately upon standards of living, and their changes. Very high growth rates set against a steep inequality of income distribution do little or nothing to help the poor, and may indeed make the poor poorer. Changes in the structure of the tax system – except for movements in direct income tax – are for the most part not comprehended by the mass of people. It is easy enough to appreciate the basic rate of income tax has been cut from 33 per cent to 25 per cent, and that the rate applied to the highest income from 83 per cent to forty per cent; but it is much more difficult to grasp the impact of changes in National Insurance Contributions, Capital Gains Tax, V.A.T., local rates; and so on. The importance of these different forms of taxation is underlined by the fact that during the decade of the eighties the revenue raised by direct taxation (income tax) fell from 32 per cent of all government income to 24 per cent (1978–9 to 1988–9).

In the years immediately following its assumption of office, the Thatcher government ended the link between pensions and other long term benefits, and average earnings; and instead benefits were now related to prices, which increased on an annual basis at a lower rate than earnings. The list of such benefits continued to be extended and by 1984 the Budget surplus from the savings incurred amounted to about four billion pounds. Lawson then abolished earnings-related unemployment pay. Pensions, of course, come out of the National Insurance Fund which is fed by contributions from those in employment, and it was therefore to be expected that when the economy started moving out of recession the National Insurance Fund began showing ever larger surpluses. The latest infamy has been to freeze child benefit for the last three years.

What we have had since 1979 has been a very marked redistribution from those on low incomes to the better off. If all direct taxes are taken into account – that is, all taxes plus all benefits – over the population as a whole and for the ten years to 1988–9, the bottom sixty per cent of the income distribution have lost while the top thirty per cent, and especially the top ten per cent, have gained. Expressed in figures, the bottom half of the population have lost £6.6 billion and the top ten per cent have gained £5.6 billion. Within that top ten per cent the gain for the top five per cent has been £4.8 billion. If *Marxism Today* wanted to single out one component of the Thatcher project, this massive shift from the poor to the rich should be used to illustrate the real meaning of the project. Tax reductions for the rich go right across the board. Company tax rates, for example, are now among the lowest of all the advanced countries. At thirty five per cent (the tax is on undistributed profits) the British company tax rate compares with fifty six for Germany and fifty two for Sweden. With all the tax concessions that have been introduced in the past ten years it would be theoretically possible for someone with an income of a million pounds a year to avoid tax altogether.[11] With such generous concessions to the rich, the very sharp increases in salary which company directors have been awarding themselves in the past few years makes very good sense. For the year to June 1989 the Guardian Index of Top Executives pay showed an average increase of 28 per cent after annual reports from 91 of the top 100 companies. Stuart Hall in the introduction to his recent volume, indicated how difficult he found the identification of the class interests represented by Thatcherism. These were his words:

> . . .the effectivity of Thatcherism has rested precisely on its ability to articulate different social and economic interests within this political project. It is therefore a complicated matter to say in any precise sense which class interests are represented by Thatcherism (multinational capital 'lived' through the prism of petty bourgeois ideology?) since it is precisely class interests which, in the process of 're-presentation', are being politically and ideologically defined (pp. 4–5)

The first and obvious answer to Stuart Hall's difficulties is quite simply 'the rich'; and we could then take the class analysis from there. Whether these very wealthy beneficiaries of ten years of Thatcherism have difficulty in seeing themselves as they are, or whether it is through the prism of petty bourgeois ideology, darkly or clearly, may be left for another discussion; but whether at their watering holes in London's clubland or luxury hotels, they really have a problem of self identification may perhaps be doubted. There is no doubt, of course, that the Conservative Party did win considerable support from a wide spectrum of the electorate and that there are substantive economic and social changes constantly working upon attitudes, outlooks and perspectives, but we should not forget the absence of a political opposition for just about a decade; and we should not neglect the role of human agency in the formation of political ideas different from those of the dominant classes.

Reading these twelve issues of 1988 provides a strong sense of the incoherence in the politics of the editorial collective. They have seized upon certain characteristics of our contemporary scene and either mostly, or completely, ignored others. Eric Hobsbawm wrote a powerful analysis and criticism of three recently published pamphlets, the most important of which was the Kinnock-Hattersley *A Statement of Democratic Socialist Aims and Values*. His article appeared in the April 1988 issue of *MT* and also included comments on pamphlets by Tony Benn and a third by David Blunkett and Bernard Crick; but his main concentration was upon the Labour leaders. Their approach, he wrote, reflected two major weaknesses in Labour's thinking. The first was provincialism: 'the world beyond the seas is more remote and unimportant than in real life' (p. 15). And he went on to observe that not one other country was mentioned:

> even when one might think it directly relevant to Britain. Sweden, for instance, is just the sort of country which one might expect to inspire anti-Thatcherite democratic socialists. It represents everything that Thatcherites blame for the failures of Britain in the dark pre-Maggie era: it has been run by Labour, has one of the highest ratios of public expenditure to gross domestic product, high taxes, no fondness for the unrestricted free market, and plenty of controls. Yet Sweden, which must have one of the highest standards of living in the world, together with

low unemployment, has a much higher rate of growth than the USA and remains at the forefront of technological progress. Why should British Labour not get a little mileage out of the achievements of its opposite number elsewhere?

The second weakness, Hobsbawm went on to argue, was intellectual: a failure of vision divorced from an historical understanding of the ways in which Britain's past development has provided the framework for the present crisis. His essay was a highly pertinent commentary on the Kinnock-Hattersley approach and it happens also to be of direct application to the journal in which he was writing. It is extraordinary that during the whole year of 1988 there was not one major article on the place of Britain in the world. There were essays on the super-powers (by Fred Halliday), several articles on the USSR including interviews of intellectuals by Monty Johnstone, one extensive survey of Eastern Europe and for the rest short pieces on various countries round the world that were currently in the news: Zimbabwe, Angola and Namibia, Campuchea and so on. But no young socialist reading the pages of Marxism Today would gain that deep sense of the world family of women, men and children; of the universal presence of exploitation, in its many different forms; of the innumerable ways in the rich countries have always bled, and are still bleeding, the poor countries of the Third World; of a continuing support for the liberation movements round the globe. Does a regular reading of Marxism Today encourage a sense of solidarity with our brothers and sisters of the African National Congress?; or renew our support for the Intifada, or strengthen our commitment to Nicaragua?. We in the United Kingdom have had a civil war within our boundaries for the past two decades. It has led to many and serious breaches of the traditional civil liberties theoretically enjoyed under British constitutional practice; to over 2,000 deaths; to wholly illegal actions such as the shootings in Gibraltar; and to an almost total silence from the 1988 Marxism Today. In good Establishment company, let it noted. There have been seven general elections since British troops moved in to Northern Ireland and at not one election on the mainland did the Irish question move from the bottom of the agenda. Mostly it was never discussed.

It has always been one of the accepted characteristics of socialism, certainly in its marxist version, that internationalism – vigorous, supportive internationalism – is at the centre of its general ideas – and it is a tradition that finds regrettably little expression in the pages of MT. Of course, many of those in the past whom Marxists have honoured for their struggle against the evil forces of world capitalism would have been too dogmatic, too narrowly economistic, too ready to 'read off' ideas from class interests, to suit the modern-day ci-devant sophisticates of Marxism Today for whom the crudities of the past are best forgotten. This presumably is at least part of the complex of reasons for the absence of any sense of history in the pages of Marxism Today. There is almost certainly no doubt of the theoretical inadequacies of the dogmatism of those who led The Long March; or of these German

Communists whose record in the concentration camps was so astounding and heroic; or of the 70,000 French communists who were killed in the Resistance movement; or the guerillas in El Salvador today and their nearby comrades in Nicaragua. The latter, undoubtedly, would be in better theoretical shape if only they had access to *MT*'s elaboration of the 'New Times' we now live in.

To consider further Hobsbawm's criticism of the intellectual weakness of the Kinnock-Hattersley pamphlet: its lack of an historical vision. This absence of history from the pages of *Marxism Today* has been commented on above, but it is very striking. It is, no doubt, a sign of the New Times the journal is preaching, for there has never been a marxist journal previously which has failed to relate the present with the past. Not always judiciously, of course, but whatever the failings, it is not in the intellectual nature of marxism to ignore the past. *Marxism Today* does just that, and this accounts for what was described earlier as the incoherence of its politics. Over the year, there were a number of serious articles published: some have already been quoted and in addition there was a an excellent piece by Andy Green on education in the January issue; a long and interesting essay on feminism by Cynthia Cockburn (April); Pat Devine on market socialism (June a good month's issue in general); Richard Smith on Alcohol and alcoholism. Most issues have something that is interesting, but there is too much candy floss and occasionally straight dross. The fault can only be editorial and this must at least in part be due to political confusion. Why, for example, do we have to have long interviews with well-known Tories: a flashy vulgarian called Edwina Currie; a man out of power such as Edward Heath, and the frenziedly ambitious Heseltine: these last two in the 1988 issues? And why does the page of letters on International Women's day (March) have to include one from Teresa Gorman, a Tory MP, who informed *MT*'s readers that International Women's Day was'a lot of nonsense, nothing but hype'? It can be understood, given the general attitude towards Thatcherism, that readers had to see seven photographs or drawings of Thatcher herself in 1988 – in case any one forgot how successful the Thatcherite hegemony was, but this continuous effort to bring readers into touch with Tory ideas must be seen as the editorial belief that the business of learning from Thatcherism – one of *MT*'s slogans – is far from completed. And here we come upon a matter of fundamental theoretical importance. What Stuart Hall, Martin Jacques and presumably the rest of the editorial collective, have failed to appreciate from the writings of Antonio Gramsci is that when he elaborated the idea of intellectual and moral hegemony he was describing the complicated web of institutions, social relations and ideas as a result of which the dominant class or classes were helped to maintain their political control. But he never assumed that coercion was absent from state power, and he always assumed that the central aim and purpose of the intellectuals allied with the working class movement was to attack the dominant ideas of the hegemonic classes and create a counter-hegemony. And where do we find this counter-attack, this ruthless subjection of bourgeois ideas to dissection and critique, within the pages of *Marxism Today*? Almost nowhere; and what genuinely critical pieces there are, as with John Wells' analysis of the consumer boom, are neither followed through nor, it would seem, do they make any impact upon the thinking of the editorial collective who continue to misconceive the Thatcher project. In his commentary upon Bukharin in the *Prison Notebooks*, Gramsci underlined the crucial importance of leaving the minor figures to 'petty daily polemic':

> A new science [by which he meant Marxism] proves its efficacy and vitality when it demonstrates that it is capable of confronting the great champions of the tendencies opposed to it and when it either resolves by its own means the vital questions which they have posed or demonstrates, in peremptory fashion, that these are false problems.
>
> It is true that an historical epoch and a given society are characterised rather by the average run of intellectuals, and therefore by the more mediocre. But widespread, mass, ideology must be distinguished from the scientific works and the great philosophical syntheses which are its real cornerstones. It is the latter which must be overcome, either negatively by demonstrating that they are without foundation, or positively, by opposing to them philosophical syntheses of greater importance and significance. Reading the *Manuel* [of Bukharin] one has the impression of someone who cannot sleep for the moonlight and who struggles to massacre the fireflies in the belief that by doing so he will make the brightness lessen or disappear (p. 433)

Gramsci would have been surprised to discover any group of Marxists so bemused by what they felt to be the apparent unassailability of the hegemony exercised by the propertied classes that they had virtually abandoned any serious critique of its intellectual and moral basis. Gramsci would have expected a serious and sustained critique of its leading ideas, and certainly not what this particular group of British disciples have offered: criticisms of marginal matters together with a large black hole of intellectual nothingness at the centre. We have seen that their understanding of the political economy of Thatcherism was woefully misinformed, and they have largely refrained from serious political discussion, which must involve the Labour Party, its policies and its personalities because that would, or might, have put them out of joint with mainstream Labour whose ambience apparently is congenial. An example of both the rejection of a radical past and an unwillingness to tread anywhere but the safe centre was the article on the Monarchy by Rosalind Brunt (September 1988).

The sub-editor's heading to her article was: "The Right Royal Opposition. The Royal Family is riding high in the popularity stakes – except with the government. But shouldn't it worry us, asks Rosalind Brunt, that the Monarchy is the best on offer in the way of moral opposition". One cannot usually fault authors with the absurdities of the sub-editors of any journal or paper, but on this occasion the phrases were not out of line with the tenor of the article. Brunt writes 'as a convinced republican who remains "enchanted" with the Royal Family' (and she is using 'enchanted' in Tom Nairn's sense in his *The Enchanted Glass*). At the same time, as is made clear later, she has no wish to be identified with the 'cranky down-with-the monarchy stuff'. Her essay is a remarkably confused piece of writing and argument. Her sense of history, and certainly of radical history, is meagre. It may be assumed that Tom Paine has never lived for Rosalind Brunt, and the famous denunciation of the monarchy in *Common Sense* and *The Rights of Man* have remained unread by her.[12] Republicanism, of course, has not been a serious issue of English politics since the early 1870s; but socialists have always recognised that the monarchy is a central part of the conservative establishment, and not just because of the mummery involved. In a decently ordered society, that is to say, a democratic society, there would be no room for a centre of political conservatism such as the monarchy in Britain has always occupied. Ms Brunt makes much of the personal qualities of some members of the present monarchy, and offers the comparison with Mrs Thatcher, but the comparison is trivial and, in political terms, marginal. It is a somewhat elementary point to suggest that what matters in society is who has the power and who determines policy. As Disraeli told Hyndman in the spring of 1881, England 'is a very difficult country to move', and the conservatism to which Disraeli was referring has always been assisted and nourished by the existence of the monarchy.

The book pages are not at all helpful to many of the novitiates who service *MT*'s editorial needs. There was an advertisement in the January 1988 issue of *Marxism Today* from the Journeyman Press. They were advertising *The Murals of Diego Rivera* at £12.95, and they added the comment: 'Just one of Journeyman's many feminist and socialist books not reviewed or mentioned by *Marxism Today* in the last twelve years'. It was a fair criticism. The book pages of *Marxism Today* do not rank as among the journal's chief glories. Marxism, in its many forms – and deformations – has always accepted intellectual debate and discussion. In its political meetings the platform has always reminded the audience of the bookstall at the back of the room. But for *Marxism Today* books are obviously not important. The numbers of books noticed are few; the level of reviewing is indifferent; and, as would be expected, there is almost no coverage of historical subjects. Occasionally there are useful things: a page on Virago's celebration of 15 years of publishing (July); another on Kagarlitsky in the month following; and a page of short notices of books on South Africa and Apartheid (June). It is, however, not only the regrettably little space allocated to book reviews, but *MT*'s usual political promiscuity. In October they again showed their fascination with the Tories by asking Jeffrey Archer what his reading habits were. In three columns, and the slop per inch was as could have been predicted. JEFFREY ARCHER! . . . in the section of the journal headed CULTURE. Just as unfortunate was the full page review, in the same issue as the unspeakable Archer, of the Kray brothers. The reviewer was Jimmy Boyle, an interesting personality who however is quite incapable of writing anything but an anecdotal account. *Marxism Today* must have a special line to the Krays because in February 1989 they published a memoir written by Reg Kray of a young 18 year old murderer who was hanged. It took one and a half pages of the journal and was also included in the 'Culture' section.

The October 1988 issue of *MT* was largely devoted to a discussion of New Times, the centrepiece of all the editorial discussions and approaches. Much of it was similar to the Communist Party discussion document *Facing Up to the Future* which was published in the September issue. In the following month there was first a letter from Ernesto Laclau extolling the document as 'a major breakthrough in the political strategy of the British Left' and a second letter from three signatories to the document who explained that they had not seen the final draft with which they had 'substantial disagreements'. They went on to make the point that there was no link between the analysis and any strategy of advance towards socialism. And that was the last *MT* readers heard about these political differences since apparently it had already been agreed that the political debate around the document should be carried on in the CP weekly, *7 Days*. Reasonable, no doubt, given *MT*'s aversion to serious political discussion. The method so often used by *MT*, the round table discussion, tends to superficiality and cosiness.

The matter of New Times has not been absent from the British labour movement in the past, and indeed there are certain striking similarities to the period of the 1950s. But both the leadership of Labour and the intellectuals of the movement have often had difficulty in coming to terms with improving living standards. It was a constant theme of the lib-lab trade unionists at the end of the 19th century. They were always looking back at their early days, when the levels of exploitation were so brutally apparent and when living standards were so precarious, and contrasting those times with their present position. It all helped to encourage and extend the conservative character of the Labour leadership down to the first World War. There was little of that nostalgia during the interwar years, but with World War II and the election of a Labour government, against a background of full employment, it was now the turn of the Labour Party's intellectuals to proclaim the advent of New Times. They actually believed, and explained, the social revolution which had come about as a result of income redistribution, the introduction of a range of welfare benefits, and what they believed to be the state's responsibility for full employment. What Tony Crosland called 'The Transition from Capitalism' was the theme of a series of articles published in *New Fabian Essays* in 1952. Crosland repeated the arguments, although not quite in their earlier stark illiteracy, in his major work *The Future of Socialism* which first appeared in 1956; and even in the 1962 edition he was arguing that considerable income redistribution had taken place, and that he would still be prepared to argue that we were no longer living in a capitalist society. By this time, it should be added, Richard Titmuss, among others, had already demolished the Crosland arguments concerning income distribution and the ownership of wealth.[13]

We now have another group of intellectuals who are telling us about the

New Times we are currently living in, their importance to the Thatcherite hegemony, and the much needed changes in the Left's political strategies to match the rapidly changing situation. There is certainly no doubt about the rapidity of change, but the fact that we are supposed to be living, or moving into, the post-Fordist era, says nothing about the ownership of wealth, the distribution of income, or the relationship between economic power and political control. On these matters the New Times advocates are notably hazy. It has been emphasised above that the directors of *Marxism Today* have completely misread the political economy of the Thatcher years. Much less has been said about the absence of an effective political opposition during the whole decade of Thatcherism, but it has been a material fact of the greatest importance, since does it not have consequences for the supposedly successful hegemony of the Thatcher project? And it is not only the economic history of the Thatcher years which has been misunderstood, so have the social consequences. Poverty is not a subject often discussed in *Marxism Today*, and it is difficult to know why this has been so. New Timers are always sensitive to changes around them; they are always looking for the areas of growth in society, and are never backward in chiding the Left upon its tendency to remain rooted in a conservative past. Now today poverty is a growth area and as such ought surely to have engaged the attention of the editorial team of *Marxism Today* in their search for what is new and developing. Since 1975 the number of poor people in Britain has risen by more than three million. In the years 1973–77 Britain ranked second in the poverty table of 12 EC countries, with one nation only having a lower proportion of poor. By 1984–5 Britain had fallen to sixth place, with Belgium, Netherlands, Luxembourg, Germany and Italy all with lower proportions than Britain. The definition of 'poor' were those with less than half the average equivalent disposable income of their own country, and the figures are therefore a guide to growing income inequalities as much as a sign of absolute poverty; and on these figures poverty between the dates indicated has grown more sharply in Britain than anywhere else except Ireland (The figures quoted were prepared for the European Commission and leaked to Gordon Brown, of the Labour Shadow Cabinet).

The trouble with the New Times people is that they cannot get away from the consumer society, and their horizons are bounded by words like choice, individualism, increased individual responsibility, flexibility, and the like. As with the Crosland revisionists of the 1950s, it does not apparently seem credible that if individuals and families have improved living standards their ideas do not necessarily have to regress into petty bourgeois modes of thinking. On the contrary: the radical sections of advanced capitalist societies in the 20th century have often come from the better paid workers among the working class as a whole, and there is no reason whatsoever why the relatively modest economic improvements of the past decades should be accompanied by a slide into conservative attitudes. There must, of course, be a vigorous political and intellectual centre of opposition, and this has certainly been absent in recent years: to which, it may be added, *Marxism Today* has unfortunately made its own special contribution. For what has been missing is the projection of the kind of society that produces both choice and justice; that offers the vision of a country that puts the education of its young people at the centre of its purposes; that provides for the welfare of its disadvantaged and disabled as a major responsibility; that restores and maintains working practices and conditions of work independent of the ravages of the free market; that decentralises power and breaks down the pervasive authoritarianism that has developed so strongly these past ten years: not a socialist society, for that is not on the immediate agenda, but the first beginnings of something better.

In the meantime we have New Times: after ten years of Mrs Thatcher, the British economy is in serious and growing trouble, with the highest inflation in western Europe, the highest interest rates and a massive balance of payments deficit; with a manufacturing output increase over the years 1973 to 1988 of 3.2 per cent, compared with 33.53 per cent for Italy, 17.5 per cent for West Germany, and 13.26 for France; with our homeless total higher than ever before at well over 100,000; with more people in prison than in any other country of the EC, and with the worst overcrowding ever experienced; with 125 out of 338 beaches failing to meet EC standards, chiefly because of sewage pollution; with the UK's rate for full time education and training in the 16 to 18 age groups at 35 per cent in 1988, compared with 79 per cent in the US, and 77 per cent in Japan, Holland and Belgium.

This is only the beginning of a catalogue of economic and social ills that are pushing Britain downwards in the hierarchy of second class world powers. We already occupy around the seventeenth place in the world league of gross domestic product per head; and if present world trends continue, we shall continue to move down. If Galbraith's private affluence is limited to a minority of the British people, public squalor has been a rapidly growing feature of the British urban environment during the Thatcher years. Much more serious is the public corruption in high places that has been such a striking characteristic of this past decade. Westland, Gibraltar, the Stalker affair, the financial gerrymandering to encourage the processes of privatisation, the lies that government ministers are constantly telling each other, Parliament, and the European Commission: known about mostly because of the constant leaks from Whitehall by civil servants who cannot stomach the level of duplicity that is now common practice. And in the business and financial worlds fraud and deception are the staple of the daily lives of those who exist by making money breed more money. We are members of a society in which there are growing tumours of decadence. New Times indeed; and why, in this new found era, cannot a new title be discovered for a journal that is seriously misinforming its readers as to its contents?

A close reading of these twelve issues of 1988 has been an exceedingly dispiriting experience. We already know that when historians come to look back upon the 1980s the most striking political fact will have been the absence of a serious opposition at Westminster and in the country at large. A political opposition can only come about with an informed, relevant and sharply critical approach to the dominant ideas and policies of those in power, and to those who uphold them. An opposition must be constantly probing and denouncing. All political movements of the Left must be able to rely upon their writers and intellectuals to provide interpretations and judgements that will come together to form a coherent programme: one which not only provides the basis for continuous attack but which offers constant encouragement to its own supporters. *Marxism Today* is described on its front page as the theoretical and discussion journal of the Communist Party; and the intellectual feebleness and absence of a steadfastly critical approach must have some relationship with the continued decline of the Communist Party as a political force. No one who read *Marxism Today* in 1988 would have become enthused and excited about political activity. At its best, occasionally, *Marxism Today* was interesting; too often it was wordy, dull and not interesting. Above all the absence of political debate left a very large hole in what purports to be a theoretical discussion journal of the Left. If it continues in the grooves of 1988, this is not a journal for the politically committed: what is needed is more debate, more discussion, and a social exploration that is not bound by the shallow and superficial trivia known as New Times.

NOTES

1. I wish to make it clear that this article was planned in the closing months of 1988, and written during November/December 1989. As the text makes plain, it is essentially a study of the twelve issues of 1988, and it does not purport to register the changes over time which editorial policy may have initiated. In particular, there are some contributors over the years since Martin Jacques became editor whose theoretical approach has been important for the development of the journal, but whose approach has not been analysed in this present article since they wrote only occasionally during 1988. I refer especially to Eric Hobsbawm and Bea Campbell.
2. *MT*, October 1988, p. 25.
3. *The Hard Road to Renewal. Thatcherism and the Crisis of the Left* (Verso, 1988)
4. *New Statesman and Society*, 7 July 1989, pp. 32–5.
5. For a brief introduction, with bibliography of some of the leading items, see John Saville, 'May Day 1937', in *Essays in Labour History, 1918–1939* (ed. Briggs and Saville, 1977) p. 252. Public opinion forced the National government in 1935 to set up a Royal Commission on the Private Manufacture of Arms.
6. *The Hard Road to Renewal*, p. 14.
7. The commentators who were most consistent during the 1980s for their critical understanding of the political economy of the Thatcher government included Wynne Godley, professor of applied economics at Cambridge; Victor Keegam

of the *Guardian*; Christopher Huhne of the same paper; William Keegan of the *Observer*. I have been especially indebted to the writings of William Keegan for the analysis developed in this article.

8. The literature on Britain's economic decline relative to the rest of the industrialised world is now voluminous. For a succinct account, Sir Alec Cairncross, 'Britain's industrial decline', *Royal Bank of Scotland Review*, No 159 (September 1988) pp. 3–18.

9. Wynne Godley, 'A growth in the heart of the economy', *Observer*, 7 August 1989; Will Hutton and J. Story, 'The Slide to Skid Row', *New Statesman and Society*, 13 October 1989, pp. 12–13.

10. The report is discussed by its chairman, Lord Aldington, 'Britain's Manufacturing Industry', *Royal Bank of Scotland Review*, No 151 (September 1988) pp. 3–13.

11. All the data on tax and benefits are taken from the remarkable analysis by John Hills, *Changing Tax. How the Tax System Works and how to change it* – 64pp. The booklet, which is a very detailed account of the tax system in the past decade, is published by the Child Poverty Action Group (1988) and is an indispensable guide to the ways in which the burden of taxation has been steadily shifted from the well-off to the less well-off.

12. 'A French bastard landing with an armed banditti and establishing himself King of England, against the consent of the natives, is, in plain terms, a very paltry, rascally original. It certainly hath no divinity . . . The plain truth is that the antiquity of English monarchy will not bear looking into' *Common Sense* (1776).

13. There is a discussion of the post-war Labour Party New Times' thinkers of the 1950s in John Saville, 'Labour and Income Re-distribution', *Socialist Register* (1965) pp. 147–162.

THE USES AND ABUSES OF 'CIVIL SOCIETY'

ELLEN MEIKSINS WOOD

We live in curious times. Just when intellectuals of the Left in the West have a rare opportunity to do something useful, if not actually world-historic, they – or large sections of them – are in full retreat. Just when reformers in the Soviet Union and Eastern Europe are looking to Western capitalism for paradigms of economic and political success, many of us appear to be abdicating the traditional role of the Western left as critic of capitalism. Just when more than ever we need a Karl Marx to reveal the inner workings of the capitalist system, or a Friedrich Engels to expose its ugly realities 'on the ground', what we are getting is an army of 'post-Marxists' one of whose principal functions is apparently to conceptualize away the problem of capitalism.

The 'post-modern' world, we are told, is a pastiche of fragments and 'difference'. The systemic unity of capitalism, its 'objective structures' and totalizing imperatives, have given way (if they ever existed) to a bricolage of multiple social realities, a pluralistic structure so diverse and flexible that it can be rearranged by discursive construction. The traditional capitalist economy has been replaced by a 'post-Fordist' fragmentation, where every fragment opens up a space for emancipatory struggles. The constitutive class relations of capitalism represent only one personal 'identity' among many others, no longer 'privileged' by its historic centrality. And so on.

Despite the diversity of current theoretical trends on the left and their various means of conceptually dissolving capitalism, they often share one especially serviceable concept: 'civil society'. After a long and somewhat tortuous history, after a series of milestones in the works of Hegel, Marx and Gramsci, this versatile idea has become an all-purpose catchword for the left, embracing a wide range of emancipatory aspirations, as well – it must be said – as a whole set of excuses for political retreat. However constructive its uses in defending human liberties against state oppression, or in marking out a terrain of social practices, institutions and relations neglected by the 'old' Marxist left, 'civil society' is now in danger of becoming an alibi for capitalism.

The Idea of Civil Society: A Brief Historical Sketch

The current usage of 'civil society' or the conceptual opposition of 'state' and 'civil society', has been inextricably associated with the development of capitalism. There has certainly been a long intellectual tradition in the West, even reaching back to classical antiquity, which has in various ways delineated a terrain of human association, some notion of 'society', distinct from the body politic and with moral claims independent of, and sometimes opposed to, the state's authority. Whatever other factors have been at work in producing such concepts, their evolution has been from the beginning bound up with the development of private property as a distinct and autonomous locus of social power. For example, although the ancient Romans, like the Greeks, still tended to identify the state with the community of citizens, the 'Roman people', they did produce some major advances in the conceptual separation of state and 'society', especially in the Roman Law which distinguished between public and private spheres and gave private property a legal status and clarity it had never enjoyed before.[1] In that sense, the modern concept of 'civil society', its association with the specific property relations of capitalism, is a variation on an old theme. At the same time, any attempt to dilute the specificity of this 'civil society', to obscure its differentiation from earlier conceptions of 'society', risks disguising the particularity of capitalism itself as a distinct social form with its own characteristic social relations, its own modes of appropriation and exploitation, its own rules of reproduction, its own systemic imperatives.[2]

The very particular modern conception of 'civil society' – a conception which appeared systematically for the first time in the eighteenth century – is something quite distinct from earlier notions of 'society': civil society represents a separate sphere of human relations and activity, differentiated from the state but neither public nor private or perhaps both at once, embodying not only a whole range of social interactions apart from the private sphere of the household and the public sphere of the state, but more specifically a network of distinctively *economic* relations, the sphere of the market-place, the arena of production, distribution and exchange. A necessary but not sufficient precondition for this conception of civil society was the modern idea of the state as an abstract entity with its own corporate identity, which evolved with the rise of European absolutism; but the full conceptual differentiation of 'civil society' required the emergence of an autonomous 'economy', separated out from the unity of the 'political' and 'economic' which still characterized the absolutist state.

Paradoxically – or perhaps not so paradoxically – the early usages of the term 'civil society' in the birthplace of capitalism, in early modern England, far from establishing an opposition between civil society and the state, conflated the two. In 16th and 17th century English political thought, 'civil society' was typically synonymous with the 'commonwealth' or 'political society'. This conflation of state and 'society' represented the subordination of the state to the community of private-property holders (as against both monarch and 'multitude') which constituted the political nation. It reflected a unique political dispensation, in which the dominant class depended for its wealth and power increasingly on purely 'economic' modes of appropriation, instead of on directly coercive 'extra-economic' modes of accumulation by political and military means, like feudal rent-taking or absolutist taxation and office-holding as primary instruments of private appropriation.

But if English usage tended to blur the distinction between state and civil society, it was English conditions – the very same system of property relations and capitalist appropriation, but now more advanced and with a more highly developed market mechanism – which made possible the modern conceptual opposition between the two. When Hegel constructed his conceptual dichotomy, Napoleon was his inspiration for the 'modern' state; but it was primarily the capitalist economy of England – through the medium of classical political economists like Smith and Steuart – that provided the model of 'civil society' (with certain distinctively Hegelian corrections and improvements). Hegel's identification of 'civil' with 'bourgeois' society was more than just a fluke of the German language. The phenomenon which he designated by the term *bürgerliche Gesellschaft* was a historically specific social form. Although this 'civil society' did not refer exclusively to purely 'economic' institutions (it was, for example, supplemented by Hegel's modern adaptation of medieval corporate principles), the modern 'economy' was its essential condition. For Hegel, the possibility of preserving both individual freedom and the 'universality' of the state, instead of subordinating one to the other as earlier societies had done, rested on the emergence of a new class and a whole new sphere of social existence: a distinct and autonomous 'economy'. It was in this new sphere that private and public, particular and universal, could meet through the interaction of private interests, on a terrain which was neither household nor state but a mediation between the two.

Marx, of course, transformed Hegel's distinction between the state and civil society by denying the universality of the state and insisting that the state expressed the particularities of 'civil society' and its class relations, a discovery which compelled him to devote his life's work to exploring the anatomy of 'civil society' in the form of a critique of political economy. The conceptual differentiation of state and civil society was thus a precondition to Marx's analysis of capitalism, but the effect of that analysis was to deprive the Hegelian distinction of its rationale. The state-civil society dualism more or less disappeared from the mainstream of political discourse.

It required Gramsci's reformulation to revive the concept of civil society as a central organizing principle of socialist theory. The object of this new formulation was to acknowledge both the complexity of political power in the parliamentary or constitutional states of the West, in contrast to more openly coercive autocracies, and the difficulty of supplanting a system of class domination in which class power has no clearly visible point of concentration in the state but is diffused throughout society and its cultural practices. Gramsci thus appropriated the concept of civil society to mark out the terrain of a new kind of struggle which would take the battle against capitalism not only to its economic foundations but to its cultural and ideological roots in everyday life.

The New Cult of Civil Society

Gramsci's conception of 'civil society' was unambiguously intended as a weapon against capitalism, not an accommodation to it. Despite the appeal to his authority which has become a staple of the 'new revisionism', the concept in its current usage no longer has this unequivocally anti-capitalist intent. It has now acquired a whole new set of meanings and consequences, some very positive for the emancipatory projects of the left, others far less so. The two contrary impulses can be summed up in this way: the new concept of 'civil society' signals that the left has learned the lessons of liberalism about the dangers of state oppression, but we seem to be forgetting the lessons we once learned from the socialist tradition about the oppressions of civil society. On the one hand, the advocates of civil society are strengthening our defence of non-state institutions and relations against the power of the state; on the other hand, they are tending to weaken our resistance to the coercions of capitalism.

The concept of 'civil society' is being mobilized to serve so many varied purposes that it is impossible to isolate a single school of thought associated with it; but some common dominant themes have emerged. 'Civil society' is generally intended to identify an arena of (at least potential) freedom outside the state, a space for autonomy, voluntary association and plurality or even conflict, guaranteed by the kind of 'formal democracy' which has evolved in the West. The concept is also meant to reduce the capitalist system (or the 'economy') to one of many spheres in the plural and heterogeneous complexity of modern society. The concept of 'civil society' can achieve this effect in one of two principal ways. It can be made to designate that multiplicity itself as against the coercions of both state and capitalist economy; or, more commonly, it can encompass the 'economy' within a larger sphere of a multiple non-state institutions and relations.[3] In either case, the emphasis is on the plurality of social relations and practices among which the capitalist economy takes its place as one of many.

The principal current usages – which will be the main focus of this discussion – proceed from the distinction between civil society and state. 'Civil society' is defined by the advocates of this distinction in terms of a few simple oppositions: for example, 'the state (and its military, policing, legal, administrative, productive, and cultural organs) and the non-state (market-regulated, privately controlled or voluntarily organized) realm of civil society';[4] or 'political' vs. 'social' power, 'public' vs. 'private' law, 'state-sanctioned (dis)information and propaganda' vs. 'freely circulated public opinion.'[5] In this definition, 'civil society' encompasses a very wide range of institutions and relations, from households, trade unions, voluntary associations, hospitals, churches, to the market, capitalist enterprises, indeed the whole capitalist economy. The significant antitheses are simply state and non-state, or perhaps political and social.

This dichotomy apparently corresponds to the opposition between *coercion*, as embodied in the state, and *freedom* or voluntary action, which belongs – in principle if not necessarily in practice – to civil society. Civil society may be in various ways and degrees submerged or eclipsed by the state, and different political systems or whole 'historical regions' may vary according to the degree of 'autonomy' which they accord to the non-state sphere. It is a special characteristic of the West, for example, that it has given rise to a uniquely well-developed separation of state and civil society, and hence a particularly advanced form of political freedom.

The advocates of this state-civil society distinction generally ascribe to it two principal benefits. First, it focuses our attention on the dangers of state oppression and on the need to set proper limits on the actions of the state, by organizing and reinforcing the pressures against it within society. In other words, it revives the liberal concern with the limitation and legitimation of political power, and especially the control of such power by freedom of association and autonomous organization within society, too often neglected by the Left in theory and practice. Second, the concept of civil society recognizes and celebrates difference and diversity. Its advocates make *pluralism* a primary good, in contrast, it is claimed, to Marxism, which is, they say, essentially monistic, reductionist, economistic.[6] This new pluralism invites us to appreciate a whole range of institutions and relations neglected by traditional socialism in its preoccupation with the economy and class.

The impetus to the revival of this conceptual dichotomy has come from several directions. The strongest impulse is now undoubtedly coming from Eastern Europe, where 'civil society' has become a major weapon in the ideological arsenal of opposition forces against state oppression. Here, the issues are fairly clear: the state – including both its political and economic apparatuses of domination – can be more or less unambiguously set against a (potentially) free space outside the state. The civil society/state antithesis can, for example, be said to correspond neatly to the opposition of Solidarity to Party and State.[7]

The crisis of the Communist states has, needless to say, also left a deep impression on the Western left, converging with other influences: the limitations of social democracy, with its unbounded faith in the state as the agent of social improvement, as well as the emergence of emancipatory struggles by social movements, not based on class, with a sensitivity to dimensions of human experience all too often neglected by the traditional socialist left. These heightened sensitivities to the dangers posed by the state and to the complexities of human experience have been associated with a wide range of activisms, taking in everything from feminism, ecology and peace, to constitutional reform. Each of these projects has often drawn upon the concept of civil society.

No socialist can doubt the value of these new sensitivities, but there must be serious misgivings about this particular method of focusing our attention on them. We are being asked to pay a heavy price for the all-embracing concept of 'civil society'. This conceptual portmanteau, which indiscriminately lumps together everything from households and voluntary associations to the economic system of capitalism, confuses and disguises as much as it reveals. In Eastern Europe, it can be made to apprehend everything from the defence of political rights and cultural freedoms to the marketization of post-capitalist economies or even the restoration of capitalism. 'Civil society' can serve as a code-word or cover for capitalism, and the market can be lumped together with other less ambiguous goods like political and intellectual liberties as an unequivocally desirable goal.

But if the dangers of this conceptual strategy and of assigning the market to the free space of 'civil society' appear to pale before the enormity of Stalinist oppression in the East, problems of an altogether different order arise in the West, where capitalism does actually exist and where state-oppression is not an immediate and massive evil which overwhelms all other social ills. Since in this case 'civil society' is made to encompass a whole layer of social reality which does not exist in post-capitalist societies, the implications of its usage are in some important respects even more problematic.

Here, the danger lies in the fact that the totalizing logic and the coercive power of capitalism become invisible, when the whole social system of capitalism is reduced to one set of institutions and relations among many others, on a conceptual par with households or voluntary associations. Such a reduction is, indeed, the principal distinctive feature of 'civil society' in its new incarnation. Its effects is to conceptualize away the problem of capitalism, by disaggregating society into fragments, with no over-arching power structure, no totalizing unity, no systemic coercions – in other words, no capitalist system, with its expansionary drive and its capacity to penetrate every aspect of social life.

It is a typical strategy of the 'civil society' argument – indeed, its *raison d'être* – to attack Marxist 'reductionism' or 'economism'. Marxism, it is said, reduces civil society to the 'mode of production', the capitalist economy. 'The importance of *other* institutions of civil society – such as households, churches, scientific and literary associations, prisons and hospital – is devalued.'[8]

Whether or not Marxists have habitually paid too little attention to these 'other' institutions, the weakness of this juxtaposition (the capitalist economy and 'other institutions' like hospitals?) should be immediately apparent. It must surely be possible even for non-Marxists to acknowledge, for example, the very simple truth that in the West hospitals are situated *within* a capitalist economy which has profoundly affected the organization of health care and the nature of medical institutions. But is it possible to conceive of an analogous proposition about the effects of hospitals on capitalism? Does Keane's statement mean that Marx did not *value* households and hospitals, or is it rather that he did not attribute to them the same historically determinative force? Is there no basis for distinguishing among these various 'institutions' on all sorts of quantitative and qualitative grounds, from size and scope to social power and historical efficacy? In the usage adopted here by John Keane – which is far from atypical – the concept of civil society evades questions like this. It also has the effect of confusing the *moral* claims of 'other' institutions with their determinative power, or rather of dismissing altogether the essentially empirical question of historical and social determinations.

There is another version of the argument which, instead of simply evading the systemic totality of capitalism, explicitly denies it. The very existence of other modes of domination than class relations, other principles of stratification than class inequality, other social struggles than class struggle, is taken to demonstrate that capitalism, whose constitutive relation is class, is not a totalizing system. The Marxist preoccupation with 'economic' relations and class at the expense of other social relations and identities is understood to demonstrate that the attempt to 'totalize[d] all society from the standpoint of one sphere, the economy or the mode of production,' is misconceived for the simple reason that other 'spheres' self-evidently exist.[9]

This argument is circular and question-begging. To deny the totalizing logic of capitalism, it is not enough merely to indicate the plurality of social identities and relations. The class relation which constitutes capitalism is not, after all, just a personal identity, nor even just a principle of 'stratification' or inequality. It is not only a specific system of power relations but also the constitutive relation of a distinctive social process, the dynamic of accumulation and the self-expansion of capital. Of course it can be easily – self-evidently – shown that class is not the only principle of 'stratification', the only form of inequality and domination. But this tells us virtually nothing about the totalizing logic of capitalism. To substantiate the denial of that logic, it would have to be convincingly demonstrated that these other 'spheres' do not come – or not in any significant way – within the determinative force of capitalism, its system of social property relations, its expansionary imperatives, its drive for accumulation, its commodification of all social life, its creation of the market as a *necessity*, a compulsive mechanism of self-sustaining 'growth', and so on. But 'civil society' arguments (or, indeed, 'post-Marxist' arguments in general) do not typically take the form of historically and empirically refuting the determinative effects of capitalist relations. Instead, (when they do not take the simple circular form: capitalism is not a totalizing system because other spheres exist) they tend to proceed as abstract philosophical arguments, as internal critiques of Marxist theory, or, most commonly, as moral prescriptions about the dangers of devaluing 'other' spheres of human experience.

In one form or another, capitalism is cut down to the size and weight of 'other' singular and specific institutions and disappears into a conceptual night where all cats are grey. The strategy of dissolving capitalism into an unstructured and undifferentiated plurality of social institutions and relations cannot help but weaken both the analytic and the normative force of 'civil society', its capacity to deal with the limitation and legitimation of power, as well as its usefulness in guiding the 'new social movements'. The current theories occlude 'civil society' in its distinctive sense as a social form specific to capitalism, a systemic totality within which all 'other' institutions are situated and all social forces must find their way, a specific and unprecedented sphere of social power, which poses wholly new problems of legitimation and control, problems not addressed by traditional theories of the state nor by contemporary liberalism.

Capitalism, 'Formal Democracy', and the Specificity of the West

One of the principal charges levelled against Marxism by the advocates of 'civil society' is that it endangers democratic freedoms by identifying Western 'formal democracy' – the legal and political forms which guarantee a free space for 'civil society' – with capitalism: 'civil' = 'bourgeois' society. The danger, they claim, is that we might be tempted to throw out the baby with the bath water, to reject liberal democracy together with capitalism.[10] We should instead, they argue, acknowledge the benefits of formal democracy, while expanding its principles of individual freedom and equality by *dissociating* them from capitalism in order to deny that capitalism is the sole or best means of advancing these principles.

It must be said that criticism of contemporary Western Marxism on these grounds must disregard the bulk of Marxist political theory since the sixties, and especially since the theory of the state was revived by the 'Miliband-Poulantzas' debate. Certainly civil liberties were a major preoccupation of both the principals in that controversy, and of many others who have followed in their train. Even the contention that 'classical' Marxism – in the person of Marx or Engels – was too indifferent to civil liberties is open to question. But without reducing this discussion to a merely textual debate about the Marxist ('classical' or contemporary) attitude to 'bourgeois' liberties, let us accept that all socialists, Marxist or otherwise, must uphold civil liberties (now commonly, if somewhat vaguely, called 'human rights'), principles of legality, freedom of speech and association, and the protection of a 'non-state' sphere against incursions by the state. We must acknowledge that some institutional protections of this kind are necessary *conditions* of any democracy, even though we may not accept the *identification* of democracy with, or its confinement to, the formal safeguards of 'liberalism', and even if we may believe that 'liberal' protections will have to take a different institutional form in socialist democracy than under capitalism.[11]

Difficulties nevertheless remain in the 'civil society' argument. There are other ways (indeed the principal ways in Marxist theory) of associating 'formal democracy' with capitalism than by rejecting the one with the other. We can recognize the historical and structural connections without denying the value of civil liberties. An understanding of these connections neither compels us to devalue civil liberties, nor does it oblige us to accept capitalism as the sole or best means of maintaining individual autonomy; and it leaves us perfectly free also to acknowledge that capitalism, while in certain historical conditions conducive to 'formal democracy', can easily do without it – as it has done more than once in recent history.

There are, on the contrary, real dangers in *failing* to see the connections or mistaking their character. There are real dangers in giving an account of Western democracy as an autonomous development, independent of the historical processes which produced capitalism. And the dangers affect both sides of the equation, limiting our understanding of both democracy and capitalism.

The historical and structural connection between formal democracy and capitalism can be formulated in terms of the separation of the state from civil society.[12] Much depends, however, on how we interpret that separation and the historical process which brought it about. There is a view of history, and a concomitant interpretation of the state-civil society separation, which cannot see the evolution of capitalism as anything but progressive. It is a view of history commonly associated with liberalism or 'bourgeois' ideology, but one which seems increasingly to underlie conceptions of democracy on the Left.

Let us sketch the traditional liberal version first. A few essential characteristics stand out: 1) a tendency to view history as a process of progressive *individuation*, generally associated with the evolution of private property, as communal or 'gentile' institutions and property-forms increasingly give way to more individualized modes of appropriation and consciousness; 2) a conception of the state as a response to this evolution from communal principles to individuality and private property, which calls for new, *political* institutions to replace old communal forms inadequate to deal with this degree of individuation; 3) a view of history, progress and the evolution of freedom which locates the principle of historical motion in the contradiction between individual and state, or perhaps between state and civil society – as an aggregate of (often mutually antagonistic) individuals – in contrast, for example, to a focus on class contradictions or relations of exploitation; 4) a tendency to identify milestones in the ascent of the propertied classes as the principal landmarks of history: Magna Carta, 1688, the establishment of constitutional principles whose object was to strengthen the hand of the propertied classes against both monarchical power *and* the multitude.[13] At some critical point, these developments begin to be called 'democratic' – so that, for example, American and European school-children are taught to think of such advances in the power of the landed aristocracy as the pivotal moments in the evolution of democracy. Such a definition of democracy would never have occurred to the major participants in the relevant historical events, for whom consolidating the power of the landed classes was, by definition, for good or for evil, *anti*-democratic.

Marx himself did not subject the liberal view of history to the same thorough critique that he applied to classical political economy.[14] But from the beginning, there was a different view of history at the core of his own distinctive life's work: history as the development of exploitative relations and the progressive separation of producers from the conditions of labour, property as alienation, the specificity of capitalism and its laws of motion – in short, everything implied by the critique of political economy. What we seem to be witnessing now is a new left version of the old liberal history without this other side.

The historical presuppositions underlying the advocacy of 'civil society' are seldom explicitly spelled out. There is, however, a particularly useful and sophisticated account by a Hungarian scholar, recently published in English in a volume devoted to reviving 'civil society' (East and West), which may serve as a model of the relevant historical interpretation.

In an attempt to characterize three different 'historical regions of Europe' – Western and Eastern Europe and something in between – Jeno Szücs (following Istvan Bibo) offers the following account of the 'Western' model, in 'a search for the deepest roots of a "democratic way of organizing society"'.[15] The most distinctive 'characteristic of the West is the structural – and theoretical – separation of "society" from the "state"'[16], a unique development which lies at the heart of Western democracy, while its corresponding absence in the East accounts for an evolution from autocracy to totalitarianism. The roots of this development, according to Szücs, lie in Western feudalism.

The uniqueness of Western history lay, according to this argument, in 'an entirely unusual "take-off" in the rise of civilizations. This take-off took place amidst disintegration instead of integration, and amidst declining civilization, re-agrarianization and mounting political anarchy.'[17] This fragmentation and disintegration were the preconditions of the separation of 'society' and 'state'. In the high civilizations of the East, where no such separation took place, the political function continued to be exercised 'downwards from above'.

In the process of feudal 'fragmentation' in the West, the old political relations of states and subjects were replaced by new social ties, of a contractual nature, between lords and vassals. This substitution of social-contractual relations for political relations had among its major consequences a new principle of human dignity, freedom and the 'honour' of the individual. And the territorial disintegration into small units each with its own customary law produced a decentralization of law which could resist '"descending" mechanisms of exercising power'.[18] When sovereignty was later reconstructed by the Western monarchies, the new state was essentially constituted 'vertically from below'.[19] It was a 'unity in plurality' that made 'freedoms' the 'internal organizing principles' of Western social structure 'and led to something which drew the line so sharply between the medieval West and many other civilizations: the birth of "society" as an autonomous entity.'[20]

There is much in this argument that is truly illuminating, but equally instructive is the bias in its angle of vision. Here, in fact, are all the staples of liberal history: the progress of civilization (at least in the West) as an unambiguous ascent of individual 'freedom' and 'dignity' (if there is a critical difference between Szücs's account and the traditional liberal view, it is that the latter is more frank about the identification of individuality with private property); the prime focus on the tension between individual or 'society' and the state as the moving force of history; even – and perhaps especially – the tendency to associate the advance of civilization, and democracy itself, with milestones in the ascent of the propertied classes. Although there was nothing democratic about the medieval West, Szücs concedes, this is where the 'deepest roots' of democracy are to be found. It is as if the 'constitutive idea' of modern democracy were *lordship*.

The same 'fragmentation', the same replacement of political relations by social and contractual bonds, the same 'parcellization' of sovereignty, the same 'autonomy of society', even while their uniqueness and importance in the trajectory of Western development are acknowledged, can be seen in a different light, with rather different consequences for our appreciation of 'civil society' and the development of Western democracy.

Suppose we look at the same sequence of events from a different angle. The divergence of the 'West' from the 'Eastern' pattern of state-formation began, of course, much earlier than medieval feudalism. It could be traced as far back as early Greek antiquity, but for our purposes a critical benchmark can be identified in ancient Rome[21]. This divergence, it needs to be stressed, had to do not only with political forms but above all with modes of appropriation – and here developments in the Roman system of private property were decisive. (It is a curious but 'symptomatic' feature of Szücs's argument that modes of appropriation and exploitation do not figure centrally, if at all, in his differentiation of the three historical regions of Europe – which may also explain his insistence on a radical break between antiquity and feudalism. At the very least, the survival of Roman law, the quintessential symbol of the Roman property regime, should have signalled to Szücs some fundamental continuity between the Western 'autonomy' of civil society and the Roman system of appropriation.)

Rome represents a striking contrast to other 'high' civilizations – both in the ancient world and centuries later – where access to great wealth, to the surplus labour of others on a large scale, was typically achieved through the medium of the state (for example, late-imperial China, which had a highly developed system of private property but where great wealth and power resided not in land so much as in the state, in the bureaucratic hierarchy whose pinnacle was the court and imperial officialdom). Rome was distinctive in its emphasis on private property, on the acquisition of massive land-holdings, as a means of appropriation. The Roman aristocracy had an insatiable appetite for land which created unprecedented concentrations of wealth and a predatory imperial power unrivalled by any other ancient empire in its hunger not simply for tribute but for *territory*. And it was Rome which extended its regime of private property throughout a vast and diverse empire, governed without a massive bureaucracy but instead through a 'municipal' system which effectively constituted a federation of local aristocracies. The result was a very specific combination of a strong imperial state and a dominant propertied class autonomous from it, a strong state which at the same time encouraged, instead of impeding, the autonomous development of private property. It was Rome, in short, which firmly and self-consciously established private property as an autonomous locus of social power, detached from, while supported by, the state.

The 'fragmentation' of feudalism must be seen in this light, as rooted in the privatization of power already inherent in the Roman property system and in the Empire's fragmented 'municipal' administration. When the tensions between the Roman imperial state and the autonomous power of private property were finally resolved by the disintegration of the central state, the autonomous power of property remained. The old political relations of rulers and subjects were gradually dissolved into the 'social' relations between lords and vassals, and more particularly, lords and peasants. In the institution of *lordship*, political and economic powers were united as they had been where the state was a major source of private wealth; but this time, that unity existed in a fragmented and privatized form.

Seen from this perspective, the development of the West can hardly be viewed as simply the rise of individuality, the rule of law, the progress of freedom or power from 'below'; and the autonomy of 'civil society' acquires a different meaning. The very developments described by Szücs in these terms are also, and at the same time, the evolution of new forms of exploitation and domination (the constitutive 'power from below' is, after all, the power of *lordship*), new relations of personal dependence and bondage, the privatization of surplus extraction and the transfer of ancient oppressions from the state to 'society' – that is, a transfer of power relations and domination from the state to private property. This new division of labour between state and 'society' also laid a foundation for the increasing separation of private appropriation from public responsibilities which came to fruition in capitalism.

Capitalism then represents the culmination of a long development, but it also constitutes a qualitative break (which occurred 'spontaneously' only in the particular historical conditions of England). Not only is it characterized by a transformation of social power, a new division of labour between state and private property or class, but it also marks the creation of a completely new form of coercion, the market – the market not simply as a sphere of opportunity, freedom, and choice, but as a compulsion, a necessity, a social discipline, capable of subjecting all human activities and relationships to its requirements.

'Civil Society' and the Devaluation of Democracy
It is not, then, enough to say that democracy can be expanded by detaching
the principles of 'formal democracy' from any association with capitalism.
Nor is it enough to say that capitalist democracy is incomplete, one stage
in an unambiguously progressive development which must be perfected by
socialism and advanced beyond the limitations of 'formal democracy'. The
point is rather that the association of capitalism with 'formal democracy'
represents a contradictory unity of advance and retreat, both an enhancement
and a devaluation of democracy.[22] To put it briefly, capitalism has been able
to tolerate an unprecedented distribution of political goods, the rights and
liberties of citizenship, because it has also for the first time made possible
a form of citizenship, civil liberties and rights which can be abstracted
from the distribution of social power. In this respect, it contrasts sharply
with the profound transformation of class power expressed by the original
Greek conception of democracy as rule by the demos, which represented
a specific distribution of class power summed up in Aristotle's definition
of democracy as rule by the poor. Access to political rights in societies
where surplus extraction occurs by 'extra-economic' means and the power
of economic exploitation is inseparable from juridical and political status and
privilege has a very different meaning from what it does in capitalism, with
its expropriated direct producers and a form of appropriation not directly
dependent on juridical or political standing. In other words, in Athens, where
citizenship remained a critical determinant in relations of exploitation, there
could be no such thing as purely 'formal' political rights or purely 'formal'
equality. It was capitalism which for the first time made possible a purely
'formal' political sphere, with purely 'political' rights and liberties.

That historical transformation laid the foundation for a redefinition of
the word 'democracy'. If capitalism made this reconceptualization possible,
political developments in a sense made it necessary. As it became more
difficult for dominant classes simply to denounce democracy, with the
intrusion of the 'masses' into the political sphere, the concept of democracy
began to lose its social connotations, in favour of essentially procedural or
'formal' criteria. The concept was, in other words, domesticated, made
acceptable to dominant classes who could now claim commitment to 'democratic' principles without fundamentally endangering their own dominance.
Now, the purely 'formal' principles of liberalism have come to be *identified*
with democracy. In other words, these formal principles are treated not simply
as good in themselves, nor even as necessary conditions for democracy in the
literal sense of popular rule, but as synonymous with it or as its outer limit.
More than that, it has now become possible even to describe undemocratic
practices – like the restriction of trade union rights by Thatcher or Reagan
– as democratic, while denouncing 'extra-parliamentary' popular politics
as 'undemocratic'. 'Formal democracy', in short, certainly represents an

improvement on political forms lacking civil liberties, the rule of law and the principle of representation. But it is also, equally and at the same time, a *subtraction* from the substance of the democratic idea, and one which is historically and structurally associated with capitalism.[23]

The 'civil society' argument insists that we should not allow our conception of human emancipation to be constrained by the identification of 'formal democracy' with capitalism. Yet the irony is that this very argument, by obscuring the connections, may have the effect of allowing capitalism to limit our conception of democracy. And if we think of human emancipation as little more than an extension of liberal democracy, then we may in the end be persuaded to believe that capitalism is after all its surest guarantee.

The separation of the state and civil society in the West has certainly given rise to new forms of freedom and equality, but it has also created new modes of domination and coercion. One way of characterizing the specificity of 'civil society' as a particular social form unique to the modern world – the particular historical conditions which made possible the modern distinction between state and civil society – is to say that it constituted a new form of social power, in which many coercive functions that once belonged to the state were relocated in the 'private' sphere, in private property, class exploitation, and market imperatives. It is, in a sense, this 'privatization' of public power which has created the historically novel realm of 'civil society'. 'Civil society' constitutes not only a wholly new relation between 'public' and 'private' but more precisely a wholly new 'private' realm, with a distinctive 'public' presence and oppressions of its own, a unique structure of power and domination, and a ruthless systemic logic. It represents a particular network of social relations which does not simply stand in opposition to the coercive, 'policing' and 'administrative' functions of the state but represents the *relocation* of these functions, a new division of labour between the 'public' sphere of the state and the 'private' sphere of capitalist property and the imperatives of the market, in which appropriation, exploitation and domination are detached from public authority and social responsibility.

'Civil society' has given private property and its possessors a command over people and their daily lives, a power accountable to no one, which many an old tyrannical state would have envied.[24] Those activities and experiences which fall outside the immediate command structure of the capitalist enterprise, or outside the political power of capital, are regulated by the dictates of the market, the necessities of competition and profitability. Even when the market is not, as it commonly is in advanced capitalist societies, merely an instrument of power for giant conglomerates and multinational corporations, it is still a coercive force, capable of subjecting all human values, activities and relationships to its imperatives. No ancient despot could have hoped to penetrate the personal lives of his subjects – their choices, preferences, and relationships – in the same comprehensive and minute detail, not only in the workplace but in every corner of their lives. Coercion, in other words, has been not just a *disorder* of 'civil society' but one of its constitutive principles.

This historical reality tends to undermine the neat distinctions required by current theories which ask us to treat civil society as, at least in principle, the sphere of freedom and voluntary action, the antithesis of the irreducibly coercive principle which intrinsically belongs to the state. These theories do, of course, acknowledge that civil society is not a realm of perfect freedom or democracy. It is, for example, marred by oppression in the family, in gender relations, in the workplace, by racist attitudes, homophobia, and so on. But these oppressions are treated as *dysfunctions* in civil society. In principle, coercion belongs to the state while civil society is where freedom is rooted, and human emancipation, according to these arguments, consists in the autonomy of civil society, its expansion and enrichment, its liberation from the state, and its protection by formal democracy. What tends to disappear from view, again, is the relations of exploitation and domination which irreducibly *constitute* civil society, not just as some alien and correctible disorder but as its very essence, the particular structure of domination and coercion that is specific to capitalism as a systemic totality.

The New Pluralism and the Politics of 'Identity'

The rediscovery of liberalism in the revival of civil society thus has two sides. It is admirable in its intention of making socialists more sensitive to civil liberties and the dangers of state oppression. But the cult of civil society also tends to reproduce the mystifications of liberalism, disguising the coercions of civil society and obscuring the ways in which state oppression itself is rooted in the exploitative and coercive relations of civil society. What, then, of its dedication to *pluralism*? How does the concept of civil society fare in dealing with the diversity of social relations and 'identities'?

It is here that the cult of civil society, its representation of civil society as the sphere of difference and diversity, speaks most directly to the dominant preoccupations of the new new left. If anything unites the various 'new revisionisms' – from the most abstruse 'post-Marxist' and 'post-modernist' theories to the activisms of the 'new social movements' – it is an emphasis on diversity, 'difference', pluralism. The new pluralism goes beyond the traditional liberal recognition of diverse interests and the toleration (in principle) of diverse opinions in three major ways: 1) its conception of diversity probes beneath the externalities of 'interest' to the psychic depths of 'subjectivity' or 'identity' and extends beyond political 'behaviour' or 'opinion' to the totality of 'life-styles'; 2) it no longer assumes that some universal and undifferentiated principles of right can accommodate all diverse identities and life-styles (women, for example, require different rights from men in order to be free and equal); 3) the new pluralism rests on a view that the essential characteristic, the historical *differentia specifica*, of the contemporary world – or, more specifically, the contemporary capitalist world – is not the totalizing, homogenizing drive of capitalism but the unique heterogeneity of 'post-modern' society, its unprecedented degree of diversity, even fragmentation, requiring new, more complex pluralistic principles.

The arguments run something like this: contemporary society is characterized by an increasing fragmentation, a diversification of social relations and experiences, a plurality of life-styles, a multiplication of personal identities. In other words, we are living in a 'post-modern' world, a world in which diversity and difference have dissolved all the old certainties and all the old universalities. (Here, some post-Marxist theories offer an alternative to the concept of civil society by insisting that it is no longer possible to speak of *society* at all, because that concept suggests a closed and unified totality.[25]) Old solidarities – and this, of course, means especially class solidarities – have broken down, and social movements based on other identities and against other oppressions have proliferated – having to do with gender, race, ethnicity, sexuality, and so on. At the same time, these developments have vastly extended the scope of individual choice, in consumption patterns and life-styles. This is what some people have called a tremendous expansion of 'civil society'.[26] The Left, the argument goes, needs to acknowledge these developments and build on them. It needs to construct a politics based on this diversity and difference. It needs both to celebrate difference and to recognize the plurality of oppressions or forms of domination, the multiplicity of emancipatory struggles. The Left needs to respond to this multiplicity of social relations with complex concepts of equality, which acknowledge people's different needs and experiences.[27]

There are variations on these themes, but in broad outline, this is a fair summary of what has become a substantial current on the left. And the general direction in which it is pushing us is to give up the idea of *socialism* and replace it with – or at least subsume it under – what is supposed to be a more inclusive category, *democracy*, a concept which does not 'privilege' class, as traditional socialism does, but treats all oppressions equally.

Now as a very general statement of principle, there are some admirable things here. No socialist can doubt the importance of diversity, or the multiplicity of oppressions that need to be abolished. And democracy is – or ought to be – what socialism is about. But an emancipatory theory is more than just a statement of general principles and good intentions. It also involves a critical view of the world as it is, a map of the existing terrain which informs our understanding of the obstacles to be overcome, an insight into the conditions of struggle. And an emancipatory theory takes us beyond the limiting and mystifying ideological categories which support existing dominations and oppressions.

What, then, does the cult of civil society tell us about the world as it is? How far does it take us beyond the ideological limits of current oppressions? We can test the limits of the new pluralism by exploring the implications of its constitutive principle. What we are looking for is a general concept which can encompass – equally and without prejudice or privilege – everything from gender to class, from ethnicity or race to sexual preference. For lack of a better word, let us call it by its currently most fashionable name, 'identity'.

For the sake of brevity, we can assess the value of this all-embracing concept (or any analogous one) by conducting a thought experiment. Imagine a democratic community which acknowledges all kinds of difference, of gender, culture, sexuality, which encourages and celebrates these differences, but without allowing them to become relations of domination and oppression. Imagine these diverse human beings united in a democratic community, all free and equal, without suppressing their differences or denying their special needs. Now try to think in the same terms about *class* differences. Is it possible to imagine class differences without exploitation and domination? Does our imaginary democratic society celebrate class differences as it does diversities of life styles, culture, or sexual preference? Can we construct a conception of freedom or equality which accommodates class as it does gender differences? Would a conception of freedom or equality which *can* accommodate class differences satisfy our conditions for a democratic society?

There are serious problems in the concept of identity as applied to any of these social relations, but there is a particular problem in the case of class. When I perform this thought experiment, the results I get for class are very different from those I get for other 'identities'. I can conceive of a democratic society with gender or ethnic diversity, but a democracy with class difference seems to me a contradiction in terms. This already suggests that some important differences are being concealed in a catch-all category like 'identity' which is meant to cover very diverse social relations like class, gender or ethnicity.

But let us go on to the connection between the concept of identity and the idea of *equality*, and consider the notion of a 'complex' or pluralist equality which purports to accommodate diversity and difference. What happens when we try to apply the concept of equality to various different forms of domination? Clearly, class equality means something different and requires different conditions from gender or racial equality. In particular, the abolition of class inequality would by definition mean the end of capitalism. But is the same necessarily true about the abolition of gender or racial inequality? Gender and racial equality are not in principle incompatible with capitalism. The disappearance of class inequalities, on the other hand, by definition *is* incompatible with capitalism. At the same time, although class exploitation is *constitutive* of capitalism as gender or racial inequality are not, capitalism subjects *all* social relations to its requirements. It can co-opt and reinforce inequalities and oppressions which it did not create and use them in the interests of class exploitation.[28]

How should we deal theoretically with these complex realities? One possibility is to retain a concept of equality that does not raise the problem of capitalism – perhaps the old liberal concept of *formal* legal and political equality, or some notion of so-called 'equality of opportunity', which presents no fundamental challenge to capitalism and its system of class relations. This concept of equality gives no privileged status to class. It may even have radical implications for gender or race, because in respect to these differences, no capitalist society has yet reached the limits even of the restricted kind of equality which capitalism allows. But formal equality cannot have the same radical implications for class differences in a capitalist society. In fact, it is a specific feature of capitalism that it has created a particular kind of universal equality *without* such radical implications – that is, precisely, a formal equality, having to do with political and legal principles and procedures rather than with the disposition of social or class power. Formal equality in this sense would have been impossible in pre-capitalist societies where appropriation and exploitation were inextricably bound up with juridical, political and military power.

If the liberal-democratic conception of formal equality seems unsatisfactory, what about 'complex' or 'pluralist' conceptions as a way of dealing with diverse inequalities in a capitalist society without 'privileging' class? These differ from the liberal-democratic idea in that they are directed at a whole range of social inequalities (including class) but also in that they acknowledge the complexities of social reality by applying different criteria of equality to different circumstances and relations. In this respect, pluralist notions of this kind may have certain advantages over more universalistic principles, even if they may lose some of the benefits of such universal standards.[29] The trouble is that these 'complex' or 'pluralistic' conceptions beg the question of capitalism because they fail to deal with its overarching totality as a social system, which is *constituted* by class exploitation but which shapes *all* our social relations.

There is another possibility: to differentiate not less but much more radically among various kinds of inequality and oppression than even the new pluralism allows. We can acknowledge that, while all oppressions may have equal *moral* claims, class exploitation has a different *historical* status, a more strategic location at the heart of capitalism; and class struggle may have a more universal reach, a greater potential for advancing not only class emancipation but other emancipatory struggles too. But this is just the kind of differentiation the new pluralism will not permit, because it suggests that class is somehow privileged. If we want, then, to avoid giving class any kind of privileged historical status, if we want to avoid differentiating in this way among different inequalities, we shall have to accommodate ourselves to capitalism; and we shall also be obliged very drastically to limit our emancipatory project. Is that really what we want?

It is possible that the new pluralism, like other 'new revisionisms', is leaning toward the acceptance of capitalism, at least as the best social order we are likely to get. The crisis of the post-capitalist states has undoubtedly done more than anything else to encourage the spread of this view. At least, it has become increasingly common to argue that, however pervasive capitalism may be, its old rigid structures have more or less disintegrated, or become so permeable, opened up so many large spaces, that people are free to construct their own social realities in uprecedented ways. That is precisely what some people mean when they talk about the vast expansion of civil society in modern ('post-Fordist'?) capitalism.[30]

But even if we stop short of openly embracing capitalism, we can simply evade the issue. That is the effect of all-purpose concepts like 'identity' or 'civil society' as they are currently used. The capitalist system, its totalizing unity, can be conceptualized away by adopting loose conceptions of civil society or by submerging class in catch-all categories like 'identity' and by disaggregating the social world into particular and separate realities. The social relations of capitalism can be dissolved into an unstructured and fragmented plurality of identities and differences. Questions about historical causality or political efficacy can be side-stepped, and there is no need to ask how various identities are situated in the prevailing social structure because the existence of the social structure can be denied altogether.

In a sense, the concept of 'identity' has simply replaced the 'interest groups' of pluralist theories in conventional political science, whose object was to deny the importance of class in capitalist democracies. According to both the old and the new pluralisms 'interest groups' or 'identities' are separate but equal, or at least equivalent, *plural* rather than *different*. And our democracy is a kind of market-place where these interests or identities meet and compete, though they may come together in loose alliances or political parties. Both pluralisms, of course, have the effect of denying the systemic unity of capitalism, or its very existence as a social system; and both insist on the heterogeneity of capitalist society, while losing sight of its increasingly global power of homogenization.

The irony is that the new pluralism, with its demand for complex ideas of freedom and equality which acknowledge the multiplicity of oppressions, ends up by *homogenizing* these differences. What we get is *plurality* instead of difference. And here is an even more curious paradox. One of the distinctive features of the new social movements is supposed to be their focus on *power*, an antagonism to all power relations in all their diverse forms. Yet here, in these theories one of whose principal claims is their capacity to speak for the new social movements, we find a conceptual framework which, just like the old pluralism, has the effect of making invisible the power relations which constitute capitalism, the dominant structure of coercion which reaches into every corner of our lives, public and private.

The final irony is that this latest denial of capitalism's systemic and totalizing logic is in some respects a reflection of the very thing which it seeks to deny. The current preoccupation with 'post-modern' diversity and fragmentation undoubtedly expresses a reality in contemporary capitalism, but it is a reality seen through the distorting lens of ideology. It represents the ultimate 'commodity fetishism', the triumph of 'consumer society', in which the diversity of 'life-styles', measured in the sheer quantity of commodities and varied patterns of consumption, disguises the underlying systemic unity, the imperatives which create that diversity itself while at the same time imposing a deeper and more global homogeneity.

What is alarming about these theoretical developments is not that they violate some doctrinaire Marxist prejudice concerning the privileged status of class. Of course, the whole object of the exercise is to side-line class, to dissolve it in all-embracing categories which deny it any privileged status, or even any political relevance at all. But that is not the real problem. The problem is that theories which do not differentiate – and, yes, 'privilege', if that means ascribing causal or explanatory priorities – among various social institutions and 'identities' cannot deal critically with capitalism at all. The consequence of these procedures is to sweep the whole question under the rug. And whither capitalism, so goes the socialist idea. Socialism is the specific alternative to capitalism. Without capitalism, we have no need of socialism; we can make do with very diffuse and indeterminate concepts of democracy which are not specifically opposed to any identifiable system of social relations, in fact do not even recognize any such system. What we are left with then is a fragmented plurality of oppressions and a fragmented plurality of emancipatory struggles. Here is another irony: what claims to be a more universalistic project than traditional socialism is actually less so. Instead of the universalist project of socialism and the integrative politics of the struggle against class exploitation, we have a plurality of essentially disconnected particular struggles.

This is a serious business. Capitalism is constituted by class exploitation, but capitalism is more than just a system of class oppression. It is a ruthless totalizing process which shapes our lives in every conceivable aspect, and everywhere, not just in the relative opulence of the capitalist North. Among other things, and even leaving aside the sheer power of capital, it subjects all social life to the abstract requirements of the market, through the commodification of life in all its aspects. This makes a mockery of all our aspirations to autonomy, freedom of choice, and democratic self-government. For socialists, it is morally and politically unacceptable to advance a conceptual framework which makes this system invisible, or reduces it to one of many fragmented realities, just at a time when the system is more pervasive, more global than ever.

The replacement of socialism by an indeterminate concept of democracy, or the dilution of diverse and different social relations into catch-all categories like 'identity' or 'difference', or loose conceptions of 'civil society', represent a *surrender* to capitalism and its ideological mystifications. By all means let us have diversity, difference, and pluralism; but not this kind of *undifferentiated* and unstructured pluralism. What we need is a pluralism which does indeed acknowledge diversity and difference – and that means not just *plurality* or *multiplicity*. It means a pluralism which also recognizes historical realities, which does not deny the systemic unity of capitalism, which can tell the difference between the constitutive relations of capitalism and *other* inequalities and oppressions with *different* relations to capitalism, a *different* place in the systemic logic of capitalism, and therefore a different role in our struggles against it. The socialist project should be *enriched* by the resources and insights of the new social movements, not impoverished by resorting to them as an excuse for disintegrating the struggle against capitalism. We should not confuse respect for the plurality of human experience and social struggles with a complete dissolution of historical causality, where there is nothing *but* diversity, difference, and contingency, no unifying structures, no logic of process, no capitalism and therefore no negation of it, no universal project of human emancipation.

Postscript

In the face of the current crisis in the post-capitalist world, it is easy for the Western left to lose its nerve. We certainly have a lot of rethinking to do. But while we are about it, the apologists of capitalism are having a field day. There could hardly have been a more welcome and timely diversion from various troubles at home. There is nothing like the trumpet of triumphalism to drown out the worrisome noises from our own backyard. The very wildness of these triumphalist pronouncements should make us suspicious. Not just the triumph of capitalism or liberal democracy over socialism, long before the game is over, but even the end of history??[31]

Of course Stalinism was a disaster for the Soviet Union, Eastern Europe, and the whole socialist movement. But let us put things into perspective. In the 'richest country in the world', the capital city is riddled with poverty and crime, as sleek civil servants cohabit with beggars. In the first half of 1989, the infant mortality rate in Washington D.C. apparently rose by 40% over the previous year, in large part because of the spread of crack-cocaine addiction. At 32.3 deaths per 1000 births, this mortality rate exceeds, among others, those of China, Chile, Jamaica, Mauritius, Panama, and Uruguay, according to World Bank statistics. One end of the country is dominated by a city, New York, the heartland of the nation's wealth, where unparalleled luxury coexists with the most abject squalor, poverty, crime, drug addiction and homelessness. At the other end, in Los Angeles, the city's core is being eaten away by drugs and gang-warfare, while privileged whites increasingly retreat into fortified enclaves where every manicured lawn sports a notice that its owner is protected by one of many and multiplying security services, with the menacing announcement: 'Armed Response'. In many places, the school system is a shambles, producing illiterate graduates; and millions of Americans cannot afford health care. It is estimated that 20 million workers in the US take illegal drugs (not to mention many more with alcohol problems), and that drug and alcohol abuse is costing US companies more than $100 billion a year (*Guardian*, November 17, 1989). In Britain, the birthplace of capitalism, under a government more implacably committed than any other to the values of 'free enterprise', the infrastructure crumbles, mass unemployment persists, public services decline, education even at the primary level becomes less accessible, and squalor deepens, while the poor and homeless multiply. The much vaunted 'economic miracle' in Italy has spawned a large and growing population of near-slaves in the form of Third World immigrants, many of them illegal, who have become the objects of yet another lucrative trade for the Mafia. In Japan, the well-spring of consumerism, ordinary citizens typically work longer hours than in any other developed country, live in postage-stamp-size flats, and take no holidays. As I write, here in prosperous Toronto, the richest city in Canada, one of the city's two major newspapers is conducting a food drive to feed the hungry – not in Ethiopia, but in Metropolitan Toronto, where property developers are making a killing while people go hungry because 70% of their income goes to pay impossibly high rents. The Daily Bread Food Bank, representing 175 emergency food programmes, today helpfully supplied paper bags with every newspaper, inscribed with the following information: '217,000 people a year [84,000 a month, according to the Toronto *Star*] in Metro need food help [out of a population of about 3.4 million]. Half of them have gone without food for a day or more. One Metro [Metropolitan Toronto] child in seven belongs to a family who needed food help last year. Daily Bread now distributes as much food in a week as it did in all 1984.'

And that is just in the prosperous corners of capitalism. If these are the successes of capitalism, what standards should we use in comparing its failures to those of the communist world? Would it be an exaggeration to say that more people live in abject poverty and degradation within the ambit of capitalism than in the Soviet Union or Eastern Europe? How should we weigh the well-fed and highly educated East Germans streaming into the West against, say, the shanty-town dwellers of São Paolo or the rubber-tappers of the Amazon – or, for that matter, against the millions in advanced capitalist countries who 'escape' from intolerable conditions by means of drug addiction and violent crime? (In fact, maybe we need to consider how to balance such apolitical reactions to the oppressions of 'civil society' against political resistance to a repressive state.) And if anyone objects that East Germany vs. Brazil is not comparing like with like, perhaps they should consider the 'third-world' areas of the Soviet Union itself. How about Tashkent as against Calcutta? Or what about this: if destruction of the environment in the post-capitalist world has resulted from gross neglect, massive inefficiency, and a reckless urge to catch up with Western industrial development in the shortest possible time, how are we to judge this against the capitalist West, where a far more wide-ranging ecological vandalism is not an index of failure but a token of success, the inevitable by-product of a system whose constitutive principle is the subordination of all human values to the drive for accumulation and the requirements of profitability?

Solidarity's new minister of finance, seeking a model for the regeneration of Poland, looks to South Korea, a repressive regime whose 'human rights' record hardly represents an improvement over that of the regime which Solidarity was so keen to replace, and whose economic 'miracle' was achieved by means of a low-wage economy, with a working class even more overexploited and overworked than the Japanese (never mind that Poland, if the project of 'restoring capitalism' works at all, may turn out to be not a 'successful' South Korea but a squalid peripheral capitalism on a Latin American model). It is perhaps time for us in the West to tell a few home truths about capitalism, instead of hiding them discreetly behind the screen of 'civil society'.

NOTES

1. For an argument that the Romans, specifically in the person of Cicero, had a concept of 'society', see Neal Wood, *Cicero's Social and Political Thought*, Berkeley and Los Angeles 1988, esp. pp. 136–42.
2. Much of John Keane's argument in *Democracy and Civil Society*, London 1988, is, for example, predicated on a criticism of Marxism for its identification of 'civil society' with capitalism, which he opposes by invoking the long tradition of conceptions of 'society' in the West.
3. Something like the first conception can, for example, be extracted from Jean L. Cohen, *Class and Civil Society: The Limits of Marxian Critical Theory*, Amherst 1982. The second view is elaborated by John Keane in *Democracy and Civil Society*. (For his criticism of Cohen's conception, see p. 86n.)
4. John Keane ed., *Civil Society and the State*, London 1988, p. 1.
5. Keane, *Civil Society and the State*, p. 2.
6. Norman Geras debunks such myths about Marxism in this volume.
7. For the application of 'civil society' to events in Poland, see Andrew Arato, 'Civil Society Against the State: Poland 1980–81', *Telos* 47, 1981, and 'Empire versus Civil Society: Poland 1981–82', *Telos* 50, 1982.
8. Keane, *Democracy and Civil Society*, p. 32.
9. Cohen, p. 192.
10. See, for example, Cohen, p. 49; Keane, *Democracy and Civil Society*, p. 59; Agnes Heller, 'On Formal Democracy', in Keane, *Civil Society and the State*, p. 132.
11. I have discussed these points at greater length in my *The Retreat from Class: A New 'True' Socialism*, London 1986, chap. 10.
12. The rest of this section is drawn largely from a paper delivered at the Roundtable 'Socialism in the World', Cavtat, Yugoslavia, October 1988.
13. The tendency to conflate aristocratic 'constitutionalist' principles with democracy is very widespread and not confined to the English language. Another notable example is the canonization of the Huguenot resistance tracts, in particular the *Vindiciae Contra Tyrannos*, as classics of democratic political thought, when they more precisely represent the reassertion of feudal rights especially by lesser provincial nobles – those who benefitted least from the favours of the

Court and from access to high state office – against an encroaching monarchy. 'Constitutionalism' has, in fact, historically often been aristocratic, even feudal, in its motivations; and while this does not disqualify it as an important contribution to the development of 'limited' and 'responsible' government, a certain caution should attend any effort to identify it with 'democracy'.

14. For a powerful discussion of this point, see George Comninel, *Rethinking the French Revolution: Marxism and the Revisionist Challenge*, London, 1987, chapters 3, 5 and 6.

15. Jeno Szücs, 'Three Historical Regions of Europe', in Keane, *Civil Society and the State*, p. 294.

16. Szücs, p. 295.

17. Szücs, p. 296.

18. Szücs, p. 302.

19. Szücs, p. 304.

20. Szücs, p. 306.

21. I have discussed the specificity of Greece in *Peasant-Citizen and Slave*, London 1988, where the relation between this unique formation and the growth of chattel slavery is also explored.

22. I develop this point at greater length in 'Capitalism and Human Emancipation', *New Left Review* 167, January/February 1988, especially pp. 8–14.

23. The defence of formal democracy is sometimes explicitly accompanied by an attack on 'substantive' democracy. Agnes Heller, in 'On Formal Democracy', writes: 'The statement of Aristotle, a highly realistic analyst, that all democracies are immediately transformed into anarchy, the latter into tyranny, was a statement of fact, not an aristocratic slandering by an anti-democrat. The Roman republic was not for a moment democratic. And I should like to add to all that that even if the degradation of modern democracies into tyrannies is far from being excluded (we were witness to it in the cases of German and Italian Fascism), the endurance of modern democracies is due precisely to their formal character.' (p. 130) Let us take each sentence in turn. The denunciation of ancient democracy as the inevitable forerunner of anarchy and tyranny (which is, incidentally, more typical of Plato or Polybius than Aristotle) is, precisely, an anti-democratic slander. For one thing, it bears no relation to real historical sequences, causal or even chronological. Athenian democracy brought an end to the institution of tyranny, and went on to survive nearly two centuries, only to be defeated not by anarchy but by a superior military power. During those centuries, of course, Athens produced an astonishingly fruitful and influential culture which survived its defeat and also laid the foundation for Western conceptions of citizenship and the rule of law. The Roman republic was indeed 'not for a moment democratic', and the most notable result of its aristocratic regime was the demise of the republic and its replacement by autocratic imperial rule. (That undemocratic Republic was, incidentally, a major inspiration for what Heller calls a 'constitutive' document of modern democracy, the US Constitution.) To say that the 'degradation of modern democracies into tyrannies is far from being excluded' seems a bit coy in conjunction with a (parenthetical) reference to Fascism – not to mention the history of war and imperialism which has been inextricably associated with the regime of 'formal democracy'. As for endurance, it is surely worth mentioning that there does not yet exist a 'formal democracy' whose life-span equals, let alone exceeds, the duration of the Athenian democracy. No European 'democracy', by Heller's criteria, is even a century old (in Britain, for example, plural voting survived until 1948); and the American republic, which she credits with the 'constitutive idea' of formal democracy, took a long time to improve on the Athenian exclusion of women and slaves, while free working men – full citizens

in the Athenian democracy – cannot be said to have gained full admission even to 'formal' citizenship until the last state property qualifications were removed in the nineteenth century (not to mention the variety of stratagems to discourage voting by the poor in general and blacks in particular, which have not been exhausted to this day). Thus, at best (and for white men only), an endurance record of perhaps one century and a half for modern 'formal democracies'.

24. This paragraph is drawn largely from my article on civil society in *New Statesman and Society*, 6 October, 1989.

25. This is, for example, the view of Ernesto Laclau and Chantal Mouffe in *Hegemony and Socialist Strategy*, London 1985.

26. See, for example, Stuart Hall in *Marxism Today*, October 1988.

27. The notion of complex equality is primarily the work of Michael Walzer, *Spheres of Justice: A Defence of Pluralism and Equality*, London 1983. See also Keane, *Democracy and Civil Society*, p. 12.

28. These points are developed in my 'Capitalism and Human Emancipation', *New Left Review* 167, January/February 1988.

29. For a discussion of both the advantages and disadvantages in Walzer's conception of complex equality, see Michael Rustin, *For a Pluralist Socialism*, London 1985, pp. 76–95.

30. Such an analysis of capitalism, for example, constitutes the core of *Marxism Today*'s conception of 'New Times', which purports to provide a platform for a modern Communist Party in Britain. See the special issue, *New Times*, October 1988, and *A Manifesto for New Times*, June 1989.

31. The argument that we have reached a kind of Hegelian end of history, with the triumph of liberal democracy over all other ideologies, is the latest conceit of the American right, as elaborated by Francis Fukuyama in *National Interest*, Summer 1989.

DEFENDING THE FREE WORLD

TERRY EAGLETON

Towards the end of his essay entitled 'Solidarity', Richard Rorty, having just argued that those who helped Jews in the last world war probably did so less because they were fellow human beings than because they belonged to the same city, profession or other social grouping as themselves, asks us to consider why contemporary American liberals should help miserable young American blacks. 'Do we say that these people must be helped because they are our fellow human beings? We may, but it is much more persuasive, morally as well as politically, to describe them as our fellow *Americans* – to insist that it is outrageous that an *American* should live without hope'.[1]

Rorty's case here seems to me unworkably global. There are, after all, rather a lot of Americans, of various shapes and sizes, and there is surely something rebarbatively abstract about basing one's compassion on such grandiosely general grounds. It is almost as though 'Americanness' operates here as some sort of meta-discourse or metaphysical essence, conflating into some unitary phenomenon the vast variety of creeds, life-styles, skin-colours and so on which go to compose the United States. Better, surely, to found one's ethics on a *genuine* localism, such as, for example, the city block. This is still perhaps a little on the homogenising side, since your average city block does of course contain a fair sprinkling of different sorts of people; but it is surely a more manageable basis for justice and compassion than an abstraction like 'America'. One could demonstrate compassion towards those in the next apartment, for example, while withholding it from those a mile down the street. Personally, I only ever manifest compassion to fellow graduates of the University of Cambridge. It's true that such credentials aren't always easy to establish; indeed I have occasionally tossed a coin towards some tramp whom I thought I dimly recognised as a member of the class of '64, only to retrieve it again furtively when I recognised my mistake. But it suffices, whatever the practical difficulties, as a rule of thumb, and the implications of any alternative moral strategy are fairly dire. Once one begins extending one's compassionate reach to graduates of Oxford too, there seems no reason not to go on to London, Warwick and even Wolverhampton Polytechnic, and before one knows it one is on the slippery slope to Habermas, universalism, foundationalism and the rest.

Incidentally, I haven't as yet withdrawn from the Campaign for Nuclear Disarmament, merely adjusted my reasons for membership. I now object to nuclear war not because it would blow up some metaphysical abstraction called the human race but because it would introduce a certain unpleasantness into the lives of my Oxford neighbours. The benefit of this adjustment is that my commitment as an anti-nuclear campaigner is no longer the anaemic, aridly intellectualist affair it was when I used to think in terms of theoretically disreputable universals like 'humanity', but lived sensuously on the pulses, brought home to me as richly concrete experience. If Oxford survives a nuclear catastrophe, I really couldn't give a damn about the University of Virginia. I have, however, resigned my membership of the Christian church, as there is clearly something theoretically dubious about the Good Samaritan.

Rorty is quite correct to believe that what is at stake in these issues is something called America, though not at all in the sense he thinks. We professional America-watchers, perched in our European fastness, are accustomed to witnessing the inhabitants of the Land of the Free engaging from time to time in spasms of smug self-congratulation. It is just that we were a little slow to appreciate, being at something of a distance, that the name of such narcissism had shifted so rapidly from Reaganism to neo-pragmatism. Another version of the case can be found in Barbara Hernstein Smith's *Contingencies of Value*, which argues at one point that 'it is perhaps just as well for "our society" that its norms are a "melange", that they constantly multiply, collide, and transform each other, that conflicts of judgement are negotiated ad hoc, and that normative authority itself is multiple and recurrently changes hands, variously strengthening and becoming diffuse'.[2] I don't quite know what those scare-quotes are doing nervously shielding the phrase 'our society', but Hernstein Smith's formulation inspires the dreadful suspicion, surely unworthy, that she actually takes herself here to be giving a thumbnail sketch of a country known as the United States. I can't believe that this is true, but the suspicion, for all one's charitable disposition, stubbornly lingers. It would be intriguing to know what Allende would have made of that multiple, recurrently changing authority, or whether the Nicaraguans have got round to savouring the pluralist, humbly ad hoc nature of US political judgements. That probably doesn't matter, since if Rorty is anything to go by they can be more or less written off anyway. One doesn't get too strong a sense that Rorty's 'American' stretches to Peruvian peasants or El Salvador guerilla fighters. In any case, it is relieving to know that, let's say, the CIA manifests a rich melange of ceaselessly variable norms, even if it's a little hard to appreciate when they have just been busy suborning your democratically elected government.

Rorty and Hernstein Smith, along with most other liberal or radical American critics, would appear united in their faith that difference, conflict, plurality, open-endedness and heterogeneity are 'absolute', unquestionable goods in themselves. (I place the term 'absolute' in charitable scare-quotes, since these critics seem to have one or two problems with it). It is a position I have long shared myself. It has always struck me as unduly impoverishing of British social life, for example, that we can only muster a mere two or three fascist parties. Instead of a ceaselessly varied, robustly proliferating, infinitely differentiated fascistic scene, with energising conflicts and ad hoc negotiations between its various currents, we are stuck with the dreary monism of the National Front and the British Movement. The postmodernist imperative to multiply small narratives at all costs has certainly not caught on among our local Nazis, who seem not to have read their Lyotard. If they really took literally what many American pragmatists, postmodernists and deconstructionists have been insisting on so 'absolutely' – that difference and plurality are good in themselves regardless of their political substance – then they would surely begin to spawn into eighty-three or so different movements rather than a mere boring two or three. The political left would then be kept energetically engaged in chasing them around the country, identifying their latest shifting positions in order to combat them, spreading its forces thin as fascists popped up in the most unpredictable places.

A similar lack of internal conflictiveness and multiplicity characterises such organisations as the African National Congress. Instead of learning from American postmodernists that unity is *ipso facto* a negative phenomenon – 'closure', 'essentialism', 'terroristic totalisation' and so on – they obtusely continue to strive to achieve the maximum degree of agreement and solidarity among the people of the townships in order to bring the apartheid regime to its knees. Bishop Tutu can't possibly have read his Smith, Rorty, Hartman, Hillis Miller, Felmann, Weber, or indeed hardly any left-leaning American critic at all. He certainly cannot have been reading most American feminist critics. There is now, among all such critics, an impressive degree of consensus that consensus is inherently oppressive.

Much the same goes for the current political struggles in Northern Ireland. The trouble with Sinn Fein is its disastrous abandonment of indeterminacy, even if it has the cheek to dub itself 'Provisional'. It actually seems to believe that it is an unquestionably bad thing that British soldiers kill indiscriminately on the streets of West Belfast; that it is 'true' (things go from bad to worse) that no lasting solution to the Irish question can be achieved without the withdrawal of these troops; and that in this process the 'closure' of unified, determinate political goals on its own part may prove productive. Whether or not Sinn Fein ever achieves those goals, it can certainly kiss goodbye to contributing to *Diacritics*. Far better, surely, to breed a republican movement with stimulating internal divisions, so that they could wrangle all day among themselves while men of the second paratroop regiment smashed up their furniture while pretending to hunt for arms. Such a transformed republicanism would find itself exhilaratedly unsure of exactly what it was doing when it found itself up against British guns; and though this exhilaration would have only a brief time-span, it would surely provide a more theoretically sophisticated way to die for a number of Irishmen and women currently trapped in the metaphysical delusion that the foreign occupation of their soil is unequivocally to be denounced.

An American feminist critic wrote recently about the need to multiply different idioms – idioms of gender, of race, and – so she added – of class. It is indeed another impoverishment of British society, whatever may be true of the United States, that we have *far too few social classes*, even if there are a few monistic metaphysicians around the place who suspect that we might have one or two too many. What we should strive to do is to generate as many social classes as possible, perhaps two or three new bourgeoisies and a fresh clutch of aristocracies. It all adds to the rich variety of social life. 'The more classes, the merrier' might then act as an appropriate slogan for radical pluralism. There is surely still room towards the bottom end of the social scale for a range of new sub-classes: there is already a kind of lumpen intelligentsia in Britain, given the shortage of academic jobs, and any pluralist sufficiently committed to the absolute value of heterogeneity would no doubt be able to dream up a few more ways of skilfully variegating our current somewhat restricted categories of oppression.

Social class tends nowadays to crop up as one item in the celebrated triptych of 'class, race and gender', a formula which has rapidly assumed for the left the kind of authority which the Holy Trinity exerts for the right. The logic of this triple linkage is surely obvious. Racism is a bad thing, and so is sexism, and so therefore is something called 'classism'. (I haven't encountered this feeble concept anywhere outside North America; its European meaning – roughly, 'class-reductionism' – is quite different). Marxists, however, churlishly refuse to subscribe to the fashionable orthodoxy that social class is a Bad Thing. Indeed they find it difficult to imagine how anyone regarding themselves as even vaguely politically radical could bring themselves to credit such an absurdity. For Marxism, the working class is an excellent thing, since without it we would never be able to expropriate the bourgeoisie. The bourgeoisie may be by and large a bad thing today, but it was an exceedingly good thing in its heyday, not least when it courageously resisted the brutalities of feudalist absolutism and bequeathed to us a precious liberal tradition. We might even go the whole hog and hand one or two accolades to that fine class of feudalist exploiters who did so much to end the slave mode of production. The pluralists and postmodernists who speak up for heterogeneous styles of thought are on the whole unaccustomed to such nuanced historical distinctions, which once upon a time went under the name of the dialectic. It is not that one is requesting such theorists to *agree* with these propositions; one is merely asking them to recognise that such, in effect, is what Marxism has traditionally held, and that this is a rather different theory from the abstract moralism which holds that class, like salt and smoking, is not very nice. Marxists have never been quite arrogant enough to believe that the whole of the Enlightenment was up a gum tree, and that suddenly, perhaps around 1972, we all began to read Saussure and get our act together. The crass triumphalism of this case, which like any other caricature has more than its kernel of truth, makes Georg Lukács look like Arthur Schopenhauer. It has been Marxism, not liberal pluralism, which has regularly accorded admiration and respect to its historical antagonists.

Viewed in this light, then, the 'class, race and gender' formula comes near to involving what the philosophers might call a category mistake. But this is true in other senses too. On the surface, the triplet appears convincing enough: some people are oppressed because of their race, some on account of their gender, and some in accordance with their class. But this is of course grossly misleading. For it is not that some individuals manifest certain characteristics known as 'class', which then result in their oppression; on the contrary, to be a member of a social class just *is* to be oppressed, or to be an oppressor. Class is in this sense a wholly social category, as being black or female is not. To be black or female is a matter of Nature as well as culture. This, of course, is hardly the most acceptable pronouncement to the ears of that rampant left culturalism which has held sway over recent years – a culturalism which lays rhetorical claim to the title of 'materialist' and then proceeds to suppress the most obviously materialist bits of human beings, their biological make-up. Somewhere around the early 1970s, it was as though all attention to biology became 'biologistic' overnight, just as all concern with history became 'historicist' and all preoccupation with the empirical 'empiricist'. The social oppression of women is a matter of gender, which is entirely a social construct; but women are oppressed *as women*, which involves the kind of body one biologically has. Being a proletarian, by contrast, is not a question of biology, though it is true that we working-class North-of-Englanders tend to be small, dark and stunted. There will be no proletarians in an emancipated society, though there will certainly be women and Chinese. There can be liberated women, in the sense of people who are at once women and liberated, but there cannot be liberated serfs or workers in the sense of individuals who are at once both. Moreover, the *fact* that one is black or female is not because there are males or whites around, as the fact that one is proletarian is entirely because there is a bourgeoisie. The *social* constitution of categories like black and female is, like social class, a wholly relational affair; but nobody is black because someone else is white, in the sense that some people are only landless labourers because there are gentlemen farmers around the place. This distinction may not be of great political importance, but sloppy thinking about such crucial issues is always perilous.

In any case, Marxism is not definitively to do with social class at all. As Marx himself once commented, the distinctiveness of his and Engels's discovery was not the existence of a phenomenon known as social class, which had been as salient as Mont Blanc for quite a long time. It was, Marx claimed, the much more challenging and specific thesis that the genesis, evolution and demise of social classes is closely bound up with the development of historical modes of production. It is this which demarcates Marxism from those forms of so-called 'classism' which simply attend to the more visible effects of class oppression in the present. Once again, pragmatists and postmodernists may not *agree* with this hypothesis, but they have a responsibility to attend a little more closely to what exactly it is that Marxists have been arguing for the last century or so. Marxism is not just some high-sounding theoretical way of finding it somewhat distasteful or 'privileged' that some people belong to one social class and some to another, as it might be thought objectionable that some people get to attend cocktail parties while others have to make do with a can of beer from the ice-box. Marxism is a theory of the role played by the struggle between social classes in a much wider process of historical change, or it is nothing. And on this theory, social class cannot be said to be unequivocally a bad thing, as opposed to racism and sexism, about which there was never a good word to say.

There is another possible political error encouraged by the class, race and gender triplet. What these social groupings have in common is of course the fact that they are variously oppressed, denied their full humanity; but Marxism's interest in the working class is not at all in the first place to do with the fact that they are denied their full humanity. The proletariat is not a potential agent of revolutionary change because it suffers a good deal. As far as suffering goes, there are many better candidates for revolutionary agency than the working class: vagrants, perhaps, or impoverished students or prisoners or senior citizens. Many of these individuals suffer more than your average worker who drives a Renault and holidays annually in Greece. I do not wish to be misunderstood here: some of my best friends are vagrants, impoverished students, prisoners and senior citizens, and I have no personal grudge whatsoever against any of these groupings. But none of them is even potentially an agent of socialist transformation, as the working class is. Unlike the latter, these groups are not so objectively located within the capitalist mode of production, trained, organised and unified by that very system, as to be able to take it over. It is not Marxism which selects the proletariat as a potential revolutionary instrument, but capitalism, which as Marx wryly commented gives birth to its own gravedigger. Radical politics is not just a matter of looking around the place, determining who is most needy or desperate, and backing them against the system. Historical materialists can leave such a strategy to guilt-stricken middle-class liberals.

Marxists have always held to a belief in the unity of theory and practice, sometimes rather piously so. Some years ago I used to sell political newspapers with a comrade who once told me, in solemnly self-righteous terms, that he 'derived his theory from his practice'. No doubt this meant that he had arrived at his judgement that Luxemburg's theory of imperialism had the edge over Hilferding's by selling newspapers outside the Oxford branch of Woolworth. Piety apart, however, it is a traditional tenet of Marxism that radical theory, bereft of any practical political context, will tend to fray at the edges and sag in the middle. This seems to me exactly what is now happening in some areas of radical American thought, given the apparently intractable practical problems which the political opposition in that society faces. When one stumbles across a formulation as fatuous as Rorty's comments on Americanism, one can be reasonably sure that there is more at stake here than a simple lapse of individual sensitivity. 'Dig here', such comments signal, and you are likely to find a deeper historical deadlock and disorientation. The reverence lavished on the work of Michel Foucault by the new historicism is a similar case in point. Viewed from eight thousand miles off, that enthusiasm for Foucault has a good deal to do with a peculiarly American left defeatism, guilt-stricken relativism and ignorance of socialism – a syndrome which is understandable in Berkeley but, as I write, unintelligible in Beijing. The unconscious ethnocentrism of much of the US appropriation of such theory is very striking, at least to an outsider. What seems on the surface like a glamorous theory of the Renaissance keeps turning out to be about the dilemmas of ageing 1960s radicals in the epoch of Danforth Quayle. I write this article while the Chinese students and workers are still massing outside the Great Hall of the People; and I find it rather hard to understand why the neo-Stalinist bureaucrats have not, so far anyway, moved among the people distributing copies of Derrida, Foucault and Ernesto Laclau. For the Chinese students and workers to learn that their actions are aimed at a 'social totality' which is, theoretically speaking, non-existent would surely disperse them more rapidly than water cannons or bullets.

Given the fact that there is at present little thriving socialist culture in the United States, it seems at times to pass there as quite unexceptionable that some (if by no means all) theorists engaged with particular emancipatory struggles – ethnic or gender-based, let us say – appear as ignorant of or insouciant about socialism as Mr Quayle himself. Another disabling effect of this relative paucity of socialist theory and practice is that a good many American theorists who don't much like Marxism do not need, or are perhaps unable, to confront it head-on. It only takes a faint whiff of leftist paranoia to see much current American postmodernist and post-structuralist theory as a splendid strategy for trying to undermine Marxism without actually suffering the embarrassment of politically engaging with it. We hear very little about why exactly Stanley Fish has not rushed to espouse the theory of surplus value, or what Richard Rorty thinks of neo-colonialism, or the precise nature of Jonathan Culler's views of feudal absolutism. We do not hear this, because there is in fact no need. You can save yourself the trouble of a detailed involvement with these issues, which does after all require rather a developed knowledge of Marxist traditions and quite technical bodies of thought, simply by trying to pull the ontological and epistemological carpet out from under radical thinking as such. Why bother to debate whether this or that Marxist concept does its job when you can argue instead, much more grandiosely, that all social analysis is blinded and indeterminate, that the 'real' is undecidable, that all action beyond a timorous reformism will proliferate perilously beyond one's control, that there are no subjects sufficiently coherent to undertake such actions in the first place, that there is no 'total' system to be changed anyway, or that there is such totality but it is always terroristic, that any apparently oppositional stance has always already been included within what it resists, and that the way the world is is no particular way at all, if indeed we can know enough about it in the first place even to assert that?

One of the benefits of trying to scupper a radical politics in this way is that it doesn't make you appear quite such a red-neck reactionary as you might otherwise look. You can seem to be talking about the ineluctability of belief systems or the fact that institutionality goes all the way down whereas in fact you are talking about preserving the possibility of turning a fast buck. Richard Rorty is at least honest enough to admit that he is strenuously defending the Free World, which is more than can be said for most of his apparently avant-garde colleagues. Most of the positions I have just enumerated above suffer from the embarrassment of differing hardly at all from good old-fashioned liberal humanism; most of them, in fact, can be found lurking around as far back as A Passage to India. But they have now been dressed up in rather flashier theoretical guise. It would appear, in fact, that not all that much has changed since the good old post-war days of the End of Ideologies, when American sociologists were prone to argue that the Soviet Union was in the grip of a fanatical metaphysical ideology whereas the United States saw things more or less as they actually were. Sending your tanks into Czechoslovakia is an effect of logocentric delusion; bringing down the elected government of Chile is a piece of modest, pragmatic social engineering. It is true that not many American theorists these days are much enamoured of the concept of seeing things as they actually are; but the current distinction between the ideologico-metaphysical and the micropolitical (which sometimes seems to mean a politics so tiny as to be invisible) is among other things a variant on the end-of-ideologies epoch. To call your micropolitical pragmatism Foucaulteanism separates you less than you might think from the post-war intellectual wing of the CIA.

One of the problems, however, with this ontological and epistemological undercutting is that it leaves political radicals with far too much elbow room, and so fails to achieve its purpose. We are extremely happy to admit that there is no transcendental vantage-point outside particular belief systems from which to launch a critique of Western society; in fact some of us hold that Marxism had been tediously insisting upon this fact long before the pragmatists got round to mentioning it. We do not mind in the least being informed that what we are doing is merely carrying on the conversation that is Western civilisation, a set of moves within an existing language game, as long as we can be allowed to get on and do it. If we in Britain are permitted to pull out of NATO, scrap our so-called independent nuclear deterrent, socialise industrial production under workers' self-management, dismantle the structures of patriarchy, return the Malvinas to the Argentinians and recall the troops from Northern Ireland, then it is really neither here nor there in our view whether what we are doing remains dismally imprisoned within a metaphysical problematic. Our theoretical opponents must either tell us that this means that we cannot really do it, a case which has a somewhat implausible ring to it, or that we *should* not really do it, in which case they are going to have to engage in a little more detailed political argument than they customarily do. They will have to come out from behind the cover of general theories of belief or anti-foundationalism or anti-logocentrism or the ontological ineluctability of micropolitics and let us know a little more clearly why they would like us to remain in NATO.

Somewhere in the later nineteenth century, the capitalist system found itself confronted by an awkward choice. Either it could continue to try to justify its activities by an appeal to metaphysical foundations, or it could simply abandon this whole project as a bad job. Neither alternative was very appealing. The problem with the former strategy, then as now, is that if such a society appeals to metaphysical values as part of its ideological self-legitimation, it will only succeed in exposing the farcical gap between such high-toned ethical or religious imperatives and the squalid nature of its actual marketplace practices. This is so because those practices belong to a rationalising, secularising current which tends continually to erode and discredit the very metaphysical discourses which are still necessary to it as a form of self-validation. Caught in this rather painful cleft stick, nineteenth-century bourgeois society was offered by Friedrich Nietzsche an alluring way out: don't bother trying to justify your practices at all. Forget about God, truth, morality, History, the state: let your activities become their own splendid, self-grounding justification, as marvellously self-born and self-generative as the work of art. It was, in fact, an aestheticising solution, and present-day American spokespersons for the death of meta-narrative and the collapse of ultimate legitimations are its aestheticising inheritors. Bourgeois society, however, was prudent enough to reject Nietzsche's audacious suggestion, and continues to do so today: it is canny enough to appreciate that without some perfunctory talk of God, Freedom and this Great Country of Ours, the marketplace is going to look rather a shaky, discreditable answer to the Meaning of Life. The seductive dream of throwing up the business of justification altogether, however, never quite receded, and in the midst of a sharp rightward-turn of the capitalist system is now once more back on the theoretical agenda. What Richard Rorty and his kind are saying to us is that there is no ultimate justification for the Western way of life. And this is exactly what we Marxists have been saying for a rather longer time.

NOTES

1. Richard Rorty, *Contingency, Irony, and Solidarity* (Cambridge, England, 1989), p. 191.
2. Barbara Hernstein Smith, *Contingencies of Value* (Cambridge, Massachusetts and London, England, 1988), p. 94.

POSTMODERNISM AND THE MARKET

FREDRIC JAMESON

Linguistics has a useful scheme that is unfortunately lacking in ideological analysis: it can mark a given word as either 'word' or 'idea' by alternating slash marks or brackets. Thus the word 'market', with its various dialect pronunciations and its etymological origins in the Latin for trade and merchandise, is printed as /market/; on the other hand, the concept «market», as it has been theorized by philosophers and ideologues down through the ages, from Aristotle to Milton Friedman, would be printed market'. One thinks for a moment that this would solve so many of our problems in dealing with a subject of this kind, which is at one and the same time an ideology and a set of practical institutional problems, until one remembers the great flanking and pincer-movements of the opening section of the *Grundrisse*, where Marx undoes the hopes and longings for simplification of the Proudhonists, who thought they would get rid of all the problems of money by abolishing money, without seeing that it is the very contradiction of the exchange system that is objectified and expressed in money proper and would continue to objectify and express itself in any of its simpler substitutes, like work-time coupons. These last, Marx observes dryly, would then simply turn back into money itself, and all the previous contradictions would return in force.

So also with the attempt to separate ideology and reality: the ideology of the market is unfortunately not some supplementary ideational or representational luxury or embellishment, which can be removed from the economic problem, and then sent over to some cultural or superstructural morgue, to be dissected by specialists over there. It is somehow generated by the thing itself, as its objectively necessary afterimage; somehow both dimensions must be registered together, in their identity as well as in their difference. They are, to use a contemporary but already outmoded language semi-autonomous: which means, if it is to mean anything, that they are not really autonomous or independent from each other, but not really at one with each other either. The Marxian concept of *ideology* was always meant to respect and to rehearse and flex the paradox of the mere semi-autonomy of the ideological concept – for example, the ideologies of the market – with respect to the thing itself – or in this case the problems of market and planning in late capitalism as well as in the socialist countries today. But the classical Marxian concept (including the very word 'ideology', itself something like the ideology of the thing, as opposed to its reality) often broke down in precisely this respect, becoming purely autonomous, and then drifting off as sheer 'epiphenomenon' into the world of the superstructures, while reality remained below, the professional responsibility of the professional economists.

There are of course many provisional models of ideology in Marx himself. The following one, from the *Grundrisse*, and turning on the delusions of the Proudhonists, has been less often remarked and studied, but is very rich and suggestive indeed. Marx is here discussing a very central feature of our current topic, namely the relationship of the ideas and values of freedom and equality to the exchange system; and he argues, just like Milton Friedman, that these concepts and values are real and objective and are organically generated by the market system itself, and dialectically, indissolubly linked to it. He goes on to add – I was going to say now *unlike* Milton Friedman, but a pause for reflection allows me to remember that even these unpleasant consequences are also acknowledged, and sometimes even celebrated, by the neo-liberals – Marx goes on to add, then, that in practice this freedom and equality turn out to be unfreedom and inequality. Meanwhile, however, it is a question of the attitude of the Proudhonists to this reversal, and of their miscomprehension of the ideological dimension of the exchange system and how that functions – both true and false, both objective and delusional, what we used to try to render with the Hegelian expression 'objective appearance':

> Exchange value, or, more precisely, the money system, is indeed the system of freedom and equality, and what disturbs [the Proudhonists] in the more recent development of the system are disturbances immanent to the system, i.e. the very realization of *equality and freedom*, which turn out to be inequality and unfreedom. It is an aspiration as pious as it is stupid to wish that exchange value would not develop into capital, or that labor which produces exchange value would not develop into wage labor. What distinguishes these gentlemen [in other words, the Proudhonists, or as we might say today, the social democrats] from the bourgeois apologists is, on the one hand, their awareness of the contradictions inherent in the system and, on the other, their utopianism, manifest in their failure to grasp the inevitable difference between the real and the ideal shape of bourgeois society, and the consequent desire to undertake the superfluous task of changing the ideal expression itself back into reality, whereas it is in fact merely the photographic image [*Lichtbild*] of this reality.[1] (vol. 28, p. 180)

So it is very much a cultural question (in the contemporary sense of the word), turning very much on the problem of representation itself: the Proudhonists are realists, we might say, of the correspondence model variety. They think (along with the Habermassians today, perhaps) that the revolutionary ideals of the bourgeois system – freedom and equality – are properties of real societies, and they note that on the Utopian ideal image or portrait of bourgeois market society these features are present, which are, however, absent and woefully lacking when we turn to the reality which sat as the model for that ideal portrait. It will then be enough to change and improve the model, and make freedom and equality finally appear, for real, in flesh and blood, in the market system.

But Marx is, so to speak, a modernist; and this very remarkable theory of ideology – drawing, only twenty years after the invention of photography itself, on very contemporary photographic figures (where previously Marx and Engels had favoured the pictorial tradition, with its various camera obscuras and so forth) – suggests that the ideological dimension is intrinsically embedded within the reality, which secretes it as a necessary feature of its own structure. That dimension is thus profoundly *imaginary* in a real and positive sense, that is to say, it exists and is real insofar as it is an image, marked and destined to remain as such, its very unreality and unrealizability being what is real about it. I think of episodes in Sartre's plays which might serve as useful textbook allegories of this peculiar process: the passionate desire of Electra to murder her mother, for example, which, however, turns out not to have been intended for realization. Electra, after the fact, discovers that she did not really want her mother dead ('dead', i.e. dead in reality) what she wanted was to go on longing in rage and resentment to have her «dead». And so it is, as we shall see with those two rather contradictory features of the market system which are freedom and equality: everybody wants to want them; but they cannot be realized – the only thing that can happen to them is for the system that generates them to disappear, thereby removing the 'ideals' and ideological afterimages in the process.

But to restore to 'ideology' this complex way of dealing with its roots in its own social reality would mean reinventing the dialectic itself, something every generation fails in its own way to do. Ours has, indeed, not even tried to do so; and yet the last attempt, the Althusserian moment, long since passed under the horizon along with the hurricanes of yesteryear. To want to try, of course, presumes something no longer taken for granted today, namely that Marxism is itself still alive (and that is another way of characterizing the topic of the present paper). If it is, then it makes sense to see whether we have ever really got the dialectic right, and how we might today do so. If not, then we might as well buckle down and bone up on analytic philosophy just like everybody else.

Meanwhile, I have the impression that only so-called discourse theory has tried to fill the void left by the yanking of the concept of ideology along with the rest of classical Marxism into the abyss (or should we say, the ashcan of History). I very much endorse Stuart Hall's programme, which is based, as I understand it, on the notion that the fundamental level on which political struggle is waged is that of the struggle over the legitimacy of concepts and ideologies; that political legitimation comes from that: and that for example Thatcherism and its cultural counterrevolution was founded fully as much on the delegitimation of welfare-state or social-democratic (we used to call it, liberal) ideology as on the inherent structural problems of the welfare state itself.

This now allows me to express the thesis of the present paper in its strongest form, which is that the rhetoric of the market has been a fundamental and central component of this ideological struggle, this struggle for the legitimation or delegitimation of left discourse. The surrender to the various forms of market ideology – on the *left*, I mean, not to speak of everybody else – has been imperceptible but alarmingly universal; everyone is now willing to mumble, as though it were an inconsequential concession in passing to public opinion and current received wisdom (or shared communicational presuppositions) – that no society can function efficiently without the market and that planning is obviously impossible. This is the second shoe of the destiny of that older piece of discourse, 'nationalization' – which it follows some twenty years later, just as in general full postmodernism (particularly in the political field) has turned out to be sequel, continuation and fulfillment of the old 50s 'end of ideology' episode. At any rate, we were then willing to murmur agreement to the increasingly widespread proposition that of course socialism had nothing to do with nationalization; the consequence is that today we find ourselves having to agree to the proposition that socialism really has nothing to do with socialism itself any longer. 'The market is in human nature': this is the proposition that cannot be allowed to stand unchallenged, and that is, in my opinion, the most crucial terrain of ideological struggle in our time. If you let it pass, because it seems an inconsequential admission, or, worse yet, because you've really come to believe in it yourself, in your heart of hearts, then socialism and Marxism alike will have effectively become delegitimated, at least for a time. Sweezy reminds us that capitalism failed to catch on in a number of places before it finally arrived in England; and that if the actually existing socialisms go down the drain, there will be other, better ones later on. I believe this also, but we don't have to make it a self-fulfilling prophecy. In the same spirit, I would want to add, to the formulations and tactics of Stuart Hall's 'discourse analysis', the same kind of historical qualifier: the fundamental level on which political struggle is waged is that of the legitimacy of concepts like planning or the market – at least *right now*, and in our current situation. At other times, politics may well take very different forms from that, just as it has done in the past.

And I would also want to add, finally, on this methodological point, that the conceptual framework of discourse analysis – although allowing us conveniently, in a postmodern age, to practise ideological analysis without calling it that – is no more satisfactory than the reveries of the Proudhonists: by autonomizing the dimension of the 'concept' and calling it 'discourse', it suggests that this dimension is potentially unrelated to reality and can be left to float off on its own, to found its own sub-discipline and develop its own specialists. I still prefer to call 'market' what it is, namely an ideologeme, and to premise about it what one must premise about all ideologies, that, unfortunately, we have to talk about the realities fully as much as about the concepts. Is the market discourse merely a rhetoric? It is and it isn't (to rehearse the great formal logic of the identity of identity and non-identity); and to get it right, you have to talk about real markets just as much as about metaphysics, psychology, advertising, culture, representations, and libidinal apparatuses. I don't know whether I'll be able to do that here, but it will be enough if you can glimpse what should have been done (over and above what I actually end up doing).

But this means somehow skirting the vast continent of political philosophy as such, itself a kind of ideological 'market' in its own right, in which as in some gigantic combinational system, all possible variants and combinations of political 'values', options, and 'solutions' are available, on condition you think you are free to choose among them. In this great emporium, for example, we may combine the ratio of freedom to equality according to our individual temperament, as when state intervention is opposed, because of its damage to this or that fantasy of individual or personal freedom; or equality is deplored because its values lead to demands for the correction of market mechanisms and the intervention of other kinds of 'values' and priorities. The theory of ideology excludes this optionality of political theories, not merely because 'values' as such have deeper class and unconscious sources than those of the conscious mind; but also because theory is itself a kind of form determined by social content, and reflects social reality in more complicated ways than a solution 'reflects' its problem. What can be observed at work here is the fundamental dialectical law of the determination of a form by its content – something not active in theories or disciplines in which there is no differentiation between a level of 'appearance' and a level of 'essence', and in which phenomena, like ethics or sheer political *opinion* as such, are modifiable by conscious decision or rational persuasion. Indeed, an extraordinary remark of Mallarmé – 'il n'existe d'ouvert à la recherche mentale que deux voies, en tout, où bifurque notre besoin, à savoir, l'esthétique d'une part et aussi l'économie politique'[2] – suggests that the deeper affinities between a Marxian conception of political economy in general and the realm of the aesthetic (as for instance in Adorno's or Benjamin's work) are to be located precisely here, in the perception shared by both disciplines of this immense dual movement of a plane of form and a plane of substance (to use an alternative language of the linguist Hjelmslev).

This would seem to confirm the traditional complaint about Marxism that it lacks any autonomous political reflection as such, something which however tends to strike one as a strength rather than a weakness. Marxism is indeed not a political philosophy of the *Weltanschauung* variety, and in no way 'on all fours' with conservatism, liberalism, radicalism, populism or whatever. There is certainly a Marxist practice of politics, but political thinking in Marxism, when it is not practical in that way, has exclusively to do with the economic organization of society, and how people cooperate to organize production. This means that 'socialism' is not exactly a political idea, or if you like that it presupposes the end of a certain political thinking. It also means that we do have our homologues among the bourgeois thinkers, but they are not the fascists (who have very little in the way of thought in that sense, and have in any case become historically extinct), but rather the neo-liberals and the market people: for them also, political philosophy is worthless (at least once you get rid of the arguments of the Marxist, collectivist enemy), and 'politics' now means simply the care and feeding of the economic apparatus (in this case the market rather than the collectively owned and organized means of production). Indeed, I will argue on the proposition that we have much in common with the neo-liberals, indeed virtually everything – save the essentials!

But the obvious must first be said, namely that the slogan of the market not merely covers a great variety of different referents or concerns, but also that it is virtually always a misnomer. For one thing, no free market exists today in the realm of oligopolies and multinationals: indeed, Galbraith suggested long ago that oligopolies were our imperfect substitute for planning and planification of the socialist type. Meanwhile, on its general use, market as a concept rarely has anything to do with choice or freedom, since those are all determined for us in advance, whether we are talking about new model cars, toys, or television programmes: we choose among those, no doubt, but we can scarcely be said to have a say in actually choosing any of them. Thus the homology with freedom is at best a homology with parliamentary democracy of our representative type. Then too, the market in the socialist countries would seem to have more to do with production than consumption, since it is above all a question of supplying spare parts, components and raw materials to other production units which is foregrounded as the most urgent problem (and to which the Western-type market is then fantasized as a solution). But presumably, the slogan of the market and all its accompanying rhetoric was devised to secure a decisive shift and displacement from the conceptuality of production to that of distribution and consumption: something it rarely seems in fact to do. It also, incidentally, seems to screen out the rather crucial matter of property as well, with which conservatives have had notorious intellectual difficulty: here, the exclusion of 'the justification of original property titles'[3] will be viewed as a synchronic framing that excludes the dimension of history and systemic historical change. Finally, it should be noted that for many neo-liberals, not only do we not yet have a free market, but what we have in its place (and what is sometimes otherwise defended as a 'free market' against the Soviet Union)[4] – namely a mutual compromise and buying off of pressure groups, special interests, and the like – is in itself, according to them, a structure absolutely inimical to the real free market and its establishment. This kind of analysis (sometimes called public choice theory) is the right-wing equivalent of the left analysis of the media and consumerism (in other words of what in the public area and the public sphere generally *prevents* people from adopting a better system and impedes their very understanding and reception of such a system).

The reasons for the success of market ideology can therefore not be sought in the market itself (even when you have sorted out exactly which of these many phenomena is being designated by the word). But it is best to begin with the strongest and most comprehensive metaphysical version, which associates the market with human nature. This view comes in many, often imperceptible, forms, but has been conveniently formalized into a whole method by Gary Becker in his admirably totalizing approach: 'I am saying that the economic approach provides a valuable unified framework for understanding *all* human behavior'.[5] Thus, for example, marriage is susceptible to a kind of market analysis: 'My analysis implies that likes or unlikes mate when that maximizes total household commodity output over all marriages, regardless of whether the trait is financial (like wage rates and property income), or genetical (like height and intelligence), or psychological (like aggressiveness and passiveness).'[6] But here the clarifying footnote is crucial and marks a beginning towards grasping what is really at stake in Becker's interesting proposal: 'Let me emphasize again that commodity output is not the same as national product as usually measured, but includes children, companionship, health, and a variety of other commodities.' What immediately leaps to the eye, therefore, is the paradox, of the greatest symptomatic significance for the Marxian theoretical tourist, that this most scandalous of all market models is in reality a production model! In it consumption is explicitly described as the production of a commodity or a specific utility, in other words a use value! (which can be anything from sexual gratification to a convenient place to take it out on your children if the outside world proves inclement). Here is Becker's core description:

> The household production function framework emphasizes the parallel services performed by firms and households as organizational units. Similar to the typical firm analyzed in standard production theory, the household invests in capital assets (savings), capital equipment (durable goods) and capital embodied in its 'labor force' (human capital of family members). As an organizational entity, the household, like the firm, engages in production using this labor and capital. Each is viewed as maximizing its objective function subject to resource and technological constraints. The production model not only emphasizes that the household is the appropriate basic unit of analysis in consumption theory, it also brings out the interdependence of several household decisions: decisions about family labor supply and time and goods expenditures in a single time-period analysis, and decisions about marriage, family size, labor force attachment and expenditures on goods and human capital investments in a life cycle analysis.
>
> The recognition of the importance of time as a scarce resource in the household has played an integral role in the development of empirical applications of the household production function approach.[7]

I have to admit that I think one can accept this, and that it provides a perfectly realistic and sensible view, not only of *this* human world, but of *all* of them, going back to the hominids. Let me underscore a few features of the Becker model which are crucial: the first is the stress on time itself as resource (another fundamental essay is entitled 'a theory of the allocation of time'): but this is of course very much Marx's own view of temporality, as that supremely disengages itself from the *Grundrisse*, where finally all value is a matter of time. My sense is that, particularly after the diffusion of psychoanalysis, but also with the gradual evaporation of 'otherness' on a shrinking globe and in a media-suffused society, very little remains that can be considered 'irrational' in the older sense of incomprehensible: the vilest forms of human decision-making and behaviour – torture by sadists and overt or covert foreign intervention by government leaders – are now for all of us comprehensible (in terms of a Diltheyan *Verstehen*, say), whatever we think of them. Whether such an enormously expanded concept of Reason then has any further normative value (as Habermas still thinks) in a situation in which its opposite, the irrational, has shrunken to virtual non-existence, is another, and an interesting, question. But Becker's calculations (and the word does not at all in him imply homo economicus, but rather very much unreflective, everyday, 'preconscious' behaviour of all kinds) belong in that mainstream; indeed the system makes me think more than anything else of Sartrean freedom, insofar as it implies a responsibility for everything we do – Sartrean choice (which of course in the same way takes place on a non-self-conscious everyday behavioural level) means the individual or collective production at every moment of Becker's 'commodities' (which need not of course be hedonistic in any narrow sense; altruism can very much be just such a commodity or pleasure). I'm actually more interested in the representational consequences of a view like this, an interest which leads me belatedly to pronounce the word postmodernism for the first time. Only Sartre's novels indeed (and they are samples, enormous unfinished fragments) give one any kind of sense of what a representation of life would look like that interpreted and narrated every human act and gesture, desire and decision, in terms of Becker's maximization models. This would be a world peculiarly without transcendence and without perspective (death is here for example just another matter of utility maximization), and indeed without plot in any traditional sense, since all my choices would be equidistant and on the same level. The analogy with Sartre, however, suggests that this kind of reading – which ought to be very much a demystifying eyeball-to-eyeball encounter with daily life, with no distance and no embellishments – might not be altogether postmodern, in the more fantastic senses of that aesthetic. I'm afraid Becker has missed the wilder forms of consumption available in the postmodern, which in other places is capable of staging a virtual delirium of the consumption of the very idea of consumption: in the postmodern, indeed, it is the very idea of the market that is consumed with the most prodigious gratification, as it were a bonus or surplus of the commodification process. Becker's sober calculations fall far short of that – not necessarily because postmodernism is inconsistent or incompatible with political conservatism – but rather primarily because his is finally a production and not a consumption model at all, as has been suggested above. Shades of the great 'introduction' to the *Grundrisse*, in which production turns into consumption and distribution and then ceaselessly returns to its basic productive form (in the enlarged systemic category of production Marx wishes to substitute for the thematic or analytic one)! Indeed, it seems to me possible to complain that the current celebrants of the market (of a theoretical conservative type) fail to show much enjoyment or *jouissance* (as we will see below, their market mainly serves as a policeman meant to keep Stalin from the gates, where in addition one suspects that Stalin in turn is merely a code word for Roosevelt).

As description, then, Becker's model seems to me impeccable, and very faithful indeed to the facts of life as we know it; when it becomes prescriptive, of course, we face the most insidious forms of reaction 'my two favourite practical consequences are 1) that oppressed minorities only make it worse for themselves by fighting back; and 2) that 'household production' [see above] is seriously lowered in productivity when the wife has a job). But it is easy to see how this should be so. The Becker model is postmodern in its structure as a transcoding: two separate explanatory systems are here combined, by way of the assertion of a fundamental identity (about which it is always protested that it is *not metaphorical*, the surest sign of an intent to metaphorize): human behaviour (preeminently, the family or the *oikos*) on the one hand, the firm or enterprise on the other. Much force and clarity is then generated by the rethinking of phenomena like spare time and personality traits in terms of potential raw materials. It does not follow, however, that the figural bracket can then be removed, as a veil is triumphantly snatched from a statue, allowing one then to reason about domestic matters in terms of money or the economic as such. But that is very precisely how Becker goes about 'deducing' his practical-political conclusions. Here too then he fails of absolute postmodernity, where the transcoding process has as a consequence the suspension of everything that used to be 'literal': Becker wants to marshall the equipment of metaphor and figural identification, only to return in a final moment, to the literal level (which has however in the meantime in late capitalism evaporated out from under him).

Why do I find none of this particularly scandalous and what could possibly be its 'proper use'? As with Sartre, in Becker choice takes place within an already pre-given environment, which Sartre theorizes as such – he calls it the 'situation' – but which Becker neglects. In both we have a welcome reduction of the old-fashioned subject, or individual, or ego, who is now little more than a point of consciousness directed onto the stock-pile of materials available in the outside world, and making decisions about that which are 'rational' in the new enlarged sense of what any other human being could understand (in Dilthey's sense, or in Rousseau's, what every other human being could 'sympathize' with). That means that we are freed from all kinds of more properly 'irrational' myths about subjectivity, and can turn our attention to that situation itself, that available inventory of resources, which is the outside world itself and which must now indeed be called History. The Sartrean concept of the situation is a new way of thinking history as such; Becker avoids any comparable move, for good reasons. I have implied that

even under socialism (as in earlier modes of production) people can very well
be imagined operating under the Becker model. What will be different is then
the *situation* itself, the nature of the 'household', the stock of raw materials,
indeed, the very form and shape of the 'commodities' therein to be produced.
Becker's market thus by no means ends up as just another celebration of the
market system, but rather as an involuntary redirection of our attention
towards history itself and the variety of alternative situations it offers.

We must suspect, therefore, that essentialist defences of the market
in reality involve other themes and issues altogether: the pleasures of
consumption are little more than the ideological fantasy consequences
available for ideological consumers who buy into the market theory, of
which they are not themselves a part. Indeed, one of the great crises in
the new conservative cultural revolution – and by the same token, one of its
great internal contradictions – was displayed when some nervousness began
to be shown by these same ideologues about the success with which consumer
America had overcome the protestant ethic, and was able to throw its savings
(and future income) to the winds in exercizing its new nature as the full-time
professional shopper. But obviously, you can't have it both ways, and enjoy a
booming functioning market whose customer personnel is staffed by Calvinists
and hard-working traditionalists who know the value of the dollar.

The passion for the market was indeed always political, as Albert
Hirschman's great book, *The Passions and the Interests*, taught us. The
market finally, for 'market ideology', has less to do with consumption than
it has with government intervention, and indeed with the evils of freedom
and human nature itself. Here is a representative description of the famous
market 'mechanism':

> By a natural process Smith meant what would occur, or which pattern of events would emerge,
> from individual interaction in the absence of some specific human intervention, either of a
> political kind or from violence.
>   The behaviour of a market is an obvious example of such natural phenomena. The self-
> regulating properties of the market system are not the product of a designing mind but are a
> spontaneous outcome of the price mechanism. Now from certain uniformities in human nature,
> including of course the natural desire to 'better ourselves', it can be deduced what will happen
> when government disturbs this self-regulating process. Thus Smith shows how apprenticeship
> laws, restraints on international trade, the privileges of corporations and so on, disrupt, but
> cannot entirely suppress, natural economic tendencies. The spontaneous order of the market
> is brought about by the *interdependency* of its constituent parts and any intervention with this
> order is simply self-defeating: 'No regulation of commerce can increase the quantity of industry
> in any part of society beyond what its capital can maintain. It can only divert a part of it into a
> direction which it otherwise would not have gone.' By the phrase 'natural liberty' Smith meant
> that system in which every man, provided that he does not violate the (negative) laws of justice,
> is left perfectly free to pursue his own interest in his own way and bring both his industry and
> capital into competition with those of any other man.[8]

The force, then, of the concept of the market lies in its 'totalizing' structure
as they say nowadays, that is, in its capacity to afford a model of a social
totality. It offers then another way of displacing the Marxian model: distinct

from the now familiar Weberian and post-Weberian shift from economics to politics, from production to power and domination. But the displacement from production to circulation is no less a profound and ideological one, and has the advantage of replacing the rather antediluvian fantasy representations that accompanied the 'domination' model – from *1984* to *Oriental Despotism*, narratives rather comical for the new postmodern age – with representations of a wholly different order (I will argue in a moment that these are not primarily consumptive ones either, even though they may have the shopping mall for a kind of imaginary backdrop).

What we first need to grasp is however the conditions of possibility of this alternate concept of the social totality. Marx suggests (again, in the *Grundrisse*) that the circulation or market model will for all kinds of reasons historically and epistemologically precede other forms of mapping and offer the first representation by which the social totality is grasped:

> Circulation is the movement in which general alienation appears as general appropriation and general appropriation as general alienation. Though the whole of this movement may well appear as a social process, and though the individual elements of this movement originate from the conscious will and particular purposes of individuals, nevertheless the totality of the process appears as an objective relationship arising spontaneously; a relationship which results from the interaction of conscious individuals, but which is neither part of their consciousness nor as a whole subsumed under them. Their collisions give rise to an *alien* social power standing above them. Their own interaction [appears] as a process and force independent of them. Because circulation is a totality of the social process, it is also the first form in which not only the social relation appears as something independent of individuals as, say, in a coin or an exchange value, but the whole of the social movement itself.[9]

What is remarkable about the movement of these reflections of Marx is that they seem to identify two things which have most often been thought to be very different from each other as concepts: Hobbes' *bellum omnium contra omnes* and Adam Smith's *invisible hand* (here appearing disguised as Hegel's *ruse of reason*). I would indeed argue that Marx's concept of 'civil society' is something like what happens when these two concepts (like matter and anti-matter) are unexpectedly combined. Here, however, what is significant is that what Hobbes fears is somehow the same as what gives Adam Smith confidence (the deeper nature of Hobbesian terror is in any case peculiarly illuminated by the complacency of Milton Friedman's definition, 'A liberal is fundamentally fearful of concentrated power'[10]). The conception of some ferocious violence inherent in human nature, and acted out in the English revolution, whence it is theorized ('fearfully') by Hobbes, is not modified and ameliorated by Hirschman's 'douceur du commerce'[11], it is rigorously identical (in Marx) with market competition as such. The difference is not political-ideological but historical: Hobbes needs state power to tame and control the violence of human nature and competition; in Adam Smith (and Hegel on some other metaphysical plane) the competitive system, the market, does the taming and controlling all by itself, without needing the absolute state any longer. But what is clear throughout the conservative tradition is its motivation by fear, and by anxieties in which civil war or urban crime are themselves mere figures for class struggle. The market is thus Leviathan in sheep's clothing: its function is not to encourage and perpetuate freedom (let alone freedom of a political variety), but rather to repress it; and about such visions, indeed, one may revive the slogans of the existential years – the fear of freedom, the flight from freedom. Market ideology assures us that human beings make a mess of it when they try to control their destinies ('socialism is impossible'), and that we are fortu,ate in possessing an interpersonal mechanism – the market – which can substitute for human hybris and planning and replace human decisions altogether. We only need to keep it clean and well-oiled; it now – like the monarch so many centuries ago – will see to us and keep us in line.

Why this consoling replacement for the divinity should be so universally attractive at the present time, however, is a different kind of historical question. The attribution of the new-found embrace of market freedom to the fear of Stalinism and of Stalin is touching but just slightly misplaced in time, although certainly the current Gulag Industry has been a crucial component in the 'legitimation' of these ideological representations (along with the Holocaust Industry, whose peculiar relations to the rhetoric of the Gulag demand closer cultural and ideological study).

The most intelligent criticism ever offered me on a long analysis of the Sixties I once published[12] I owe to Wlad Godzich who expressed Socratic amazement at the absence, from my global model, of the Second World, and in particular the Soviet Union. Our experience of perestroika has revealed dimensions of Soviet history that powerfully reinforce Godzich's point and make my own lapse all the more deplorable; so I will here make amends by exaggerating in the other direction. My feeling has in fact come to be that the failure of the Khrushchev experiment was not merely disastrous for the Soviet Union, but somehow fundamentally crucial for the rest of global history and not least the future of socialism itself. In the Soviet Union, indeed, we are given to understand that the Khrushchev generation was the last one to believe in the possibility of a renewal of Marxism, let alone socialism: or rather, the other way around, that it was their failure which now determines the utter indifference to Marxism and socialism of several generations of younger intellectuals. But I think this failure was also determinant of the most basic developments in other countries as well, and while one does not want the Russian comrades to bear all the responsibility for global history, there does seem to me to be some similarity between what the Soviet revolution meant for the rest of the world positively and the negative effects of this last, missed, opportunity to restore that revolution (and to transform the party, in the process) and to 'get it moving again' (to use the American slogan from those years). Both the anarchism of the 60s in the West and the cultural revolution are to be attributed to that failure, whose prolongation, long after the end of both, explains the universal triumph of what Sloterdijk calls 'cynical reason' in the omnipresent consumerism of the postmodern today. It is therefore no wonder that such profound disillusionment with political praxis should result in the popularity of the rhetoric of market abnegation and the surrender of human freedom to a now lavish invisible hand.

None of these things, however, which still involve thinking and reasoning, go very far towards explaining the most astonishing feature of this discursive development, namely, how the dreariness of business and private property, the dustiness of entrepreneurship and the wellnigh Dickensian flavour of title and appropriation, coupon-clipping, mergers, investment banking and other such transactions (after the close of the heroic or robber-baron stage of business) should in our time have proved to be so *sexy*. In my opinion, the excitement of the once tiresome old fifties representation of the free market derives from its illicit metaphorical association with a very different kind of representation, namely the media itself in its largest contemporary and global sense (including an infrastructure of all the latest media gadgets and high tech). The operation is the postmodern one alluded to above, in which two systems of codes are identified in such a way as to allow the libidinal energies of the one to suffuse the other, without however (as in older moments of our cultural and intellectual history) producing a synthesis, a new combination, a new combined language, or whatever.

Horkheimer and Adorno observed long ago, in the age of radio, the peculiarity of the structure of a commercial 'culture industry' in which the products were free.[13] The analogy between media and market is in fact cemented by this mechanism: it is not because the media is *like* a market that the two things are comparable; rather it is because the 'market' is as *unlike* its 'concept' (or Platonic idea) as the media is unlike its, that the two things are comparable. The media offer free programmes in whose content and assortment the consumer has no choice whatsoever, but whose selection is then rebaptized free choice.

In the gradual disappearance of the physical marketplace, of course, and the tendential identification of the commodity with its image (or brandname or logo), another, more intimate symbiosis between the market and the media is effectuated, in which boundaries are washed over (in ways profoundly characteristic of the postmodern) and an indifferentiation of levels gradually takes the place of an older separation between thing and concept (or indeed economics and culture, base and superstructure). For one thing, the products sold on the market become the very content of the media image, so that, as it were, the same referent seems to maintain in both domains. This is very different from a more primitive situation in which to a series of informational signals (news reports, feuilletons, articles) a rider is appended touting an unrelated commercial product. Today the products are as it were diffused throughout the space and time of the entertainment (or even news) segments, as part of that content, so that in a few well-publicized cases (most notably

the series Dynasty[14]) it is sometimes not clear when the narrative segment
has ended and the commercial has begun (since the same actors appear in
the commercial segment as well).

This interpenetration by way of the content is then augmented in a
somewhat different way by the nature of the products themselves: one's
sense, particularly when dealing with foreigners who have been inflamed by
American consumerism, is that the products form a kind of hierarchy whose
climax lies very precisely in the technology of reproduction itself, which now of
course fans out well beyond the classical television set and has come in general
to epitomize the new informational or computer technology of the third stage
of capitalism. We must therefore also posit another type of consumption,
which is consumption of the very process of consumption itself, over and
beyond its content and the immediate commercial products. It is necessary
to speak of a kind of technological bonus of pleasure afforded by the new
machinery and as it were symbolically reenacted and ritually devoured at each
session of official media consumption itself. It is indeed no accident that the
conservative rhetoric that often used to accompany the market one in question
here (but that in my opinion represented a somewhat different strategy of
deligitimation) had to do with the end of social classes – a conclusion always
demonstrated and 'proved' in the canonical argument by the presence of the
television set in workers' housing. Much of the high and the euphoria of
postmodernism indeed derives from this celebration of the very process of
high technological informatization (and the prevalence of current theories of
communication, language or signs is an ideological spinoff and aftereffect of
this more general 'world view'). This is then, as Marx might have put it, a
second moment in which (like 'capital in general' as opposed to the 'many
capitals') the media 'in general' as a unified process is somehow foregrounded
and experienced (as opposed to the content of individual media projections);
and it would seem to be this 'totalization' that allows a bridge to be made to
fantasy images of 'the market in general' or 'the market as a unified process'.

The third feature of the complex set of analogies between media and market
that underlies the force of the latter's current rhetoric may then be located
in the form itself. This is then the place at which we need to return to
the theory of the image, recalling Guy Debord's remarkable theoretical
derivation (the image as the final form of commodity reification)[15]. At
this point, the process is reversed, and it is not the commercial products
of the market which in advertising become images; but rather the very
entertainment and narrative processes of commercial television which are
in their turn reified and turned into so many commodities: from the serial
narrative itself, with its wellnigh formulaic and rigid temporal segments
and breaks, to what the camera shots do to space, story, characters, and
fashion, and very much including a new process of the production of stars
and celebrities that seems distinct from the older and more familiar historical
experience of these matters and that now converges with the hitherto 'secular'

phenomena of the former public sphere itself (real people and events in your nightly news broadcast, the transformation of names into something like news-logos, etc., etc.). Many analyses have shown how the news broadcasts are structured exactly like narrative serials. Some of us in that other area of official or 'high' culture have tried to show the waning and obsolescence of categories like 'fiction' (in the sense of something opposed to either the 'literal' or the 'factual'). But here I think a profound modification of the public sphere needs to be theorized, the emergence of a new realm of image reality which is both fictional (narrative) and factual (even the characters in the serials are grasped as real 'named' stars with external histories to read about), and which now – like the former classical 'sphere of culture' – becomes semi-autonomous and floats above reality, with this fundamental historical difference that in the classical period reality persisted independently of that sentimental and romantic 'cultural sphere', whereas today it seems to have lost that separate mode of existence, culture impacting back on it in ways that make any independent and as it were non- or extra-cultural form of reality problematical (in a kind of Heisenberg principle of mass culture which intervenes between your eye and the thing itself), so that finally the theorists unite their voices in the new doxa that the 'referent' no longer exists.

At any rate in this third moment the contents of the media itself have now become commodities, which are then flung out on some wider version of the market with which they become affiliated until the two things are indistinguishable. Here then, the media, as which the market was itself fantasized, now returns into the market and by becoming a part of it seals and certifies the formerly metaphorical or analogical identification as a 'literal' reality.

What must finally be added to these abstract discussions of the market is a pragmatic qualifier, a secret functionality such as sometimes sheds a whole new light – striking at a lurid mid-level height – upon the ostensible discourse itself. This is what Barry, at the conclusion of his useful book, blurts out as it were either in desperation or exasperation, namely that the philosophical test of the various neo-liberal theories can only be applied in a single fundamental situation, which we may call (not without irony) 'the transition from socialism to capitalism'.[16] Market theories, in other words, remain Utopian insofar as they are not applicable to this fundamental process of systemic 'deregulation': and he himself has already illustrated the significance of the judgement in an earlier chapter when, discussing the rational choice people make, he points out that the ideal market situation is for them as Utopian and unrealizable under present-day conditions as, for the left, socialist revolution or transformation in the advanced capitalist countries today. One wants to add that the referent here is two-fold: not merely the processes in the various Eastern countries which have been understood as an attempt to reestablish the market in one way or another, but also those efforts in the West, particularly under Reagan and Thatcher, to do away with the 'regulations' of the welfare state and return to some purer form of market conditions. We need to take into account the possibility that both of these efforts may fail for structural reasons; but we also need to point out tirelessly this interesting development that the 'market' turns out finally to be as Utopian as socialism has recently been held to be.

Under these circumstances, nothing is served by substituting for one inert institutional structure (bureaucratic planning) another inert institutional structure, namely the market itself. What is wanted is a great collective project, in which an active majority of the population participates, as something belonging to it and constructed by its own energies. The setting of social priorities – also known in the socialist literature as planning – would have to be a part of such a collective project: it should be clear, however, that virtually by definition the market cannot be a project at all.

NOTES

1. Marx and Engels. *Collected Works*, Volume 28 (New York: International; 1987). p. 180.
2. 'Only two paths stand open to mental research: aesthetics, and also political economy.' Stéphane Mallarmé, 'Magie', in *Variations sur un sujet*, in *Oeuvres complètes* (Paris: Editions de la Pléiade, 1945), p. 399. The phrase, which I used as an epigraph to *Marxism and Form*, emerges from a complex meditation on poetry, politics, economics and class at the very dawn of high modernism itself, written in 1895.
3. Norman P. Barry, *On Classical Liberalism and Libertarianism* (New York: St. Martin's, 1987), p. 13.
4. Ibid., p. 194.
5. Gary Becker, *An Economic Approach to Human Behavior* (Chicago: U. Chicago Press, 1976) p. 14.
6. Ibid., p. 217.
7. Ibid., p. 141.
8. Barry, op. cit., p. 30.
9. Marx and Engels, op. cit., vol. 28, pp. 131–132.
10. Milton Friedman, *Capitalism and Democracy* (Chicago: U. Chicago Press, 1962), p. 39.
11. See Albert O. Hirschman, *The Passions and the Interests* (Princeton: Princeton University Press, 1977), Part One.
12. 'Periodizing the Sixties', in *The Ideologies of Theory* (Minneapolis: U. Minnesota Press, 1988), Volume 2, pp. 178–208.
13. T.W. Adorno and Max Horkheimer, *Dialectic of Enlightenment*, trans. John Cumming (New York: Herder and Herder, 1972), pp. 161–167.
14. See Jane Feuer, 'Reading *Dynasty*: Television and Reception Theory', SAQ, Sept. 1989, Vol. 88, No. 2., pp. 443–466.
15. Guy Debord, *The Society of the Spectacle* (Detroit: Red and Black Press, 1977), chapter one.
16. See Barry, op. cit., pp. 193–196.

THE ECLIPSE OF MATERIALISM: MARXISM AND THE WRITING OF SOCIAL HISTORY IN THE 1980s

BRYAN D. PALMER

This is not a good time to be a historical materialist. It is not even a good time to be a historian.[1]

Explaining this negative conjuncture and detailing its dimensions would be a large project involving a many-sided appreciation of current economic, political and intellectual trends. Each strand in this rope strangling the possibilities of historical materialism and its project of understanding and appreciating the past so as to be able to change the present and transform the future would require exploration and critique.[2] Here I will only allude to the extent to which one decisive and determining force in this conjuncture has been Stalinism's final instance. For surely no specific process has more single-handedly opened the floodgates of attack on Marxism and its analytic categories and political project than the collapse of the degenerate and deformed workers states in which socialism/communism had supposedly been constructed. This world historic event, in the making since the mid-1920s, but associated most strongly with ruptures such as 1956 and 1968, reached a new culmination in the 1980s. It necessarily conditioned much of the climate in which the scholarship of that decade matured.[3]

Academics and intellectuals are not ones to stay with a sinking ship for long, however sound its original structure and guiding principles may have been. Many historians who once considered themselves historical materialists have been distancing themselves from Marxism for a number of years. With the current crisis of Stalinism, this process has accelerated. What is peculiar about the late 1980s is the extent to which a backing away from historical materialism has, within the peculiarities of the political economy of the moment, coincided with declarative statements about the end of history itself.

At its most blatantly ideological, this trend is nicely and neatly articulated in the statements of the Right. Thus Francis Fukuyama proclaimed in the summer of 1989: 'What we may be witnessing is not just the end of the Cold War, or the passing of a particular period of postwar history, but the end of history as such: that is, the end point of mankind's ideological evolution and the universalization of Western liberal democracy as the final form of human government.'[4] Such complacent and self-congratulatory politics are to be expected from some quarters, which have been far from slow in consolidating whatever ideological gain can be quickly and cheaply amassed from Stalinism's sordid denouement.

More interesting is the seemingly unrelated, but definitely parallel, development in the intellectual arena, where for some time historical materialism and history itself have been interrogated and jettisoned by those championing the discursive, centreless nature of a pervasive power which is bounded not so much by class relations and struggles, or the structures of historically determined political economy, but by discourse, representation, and a social construction weighted heavily toward the ideological. This is, simply put, the poststructuralism premise, the ideological/intellectual freight accompanying the postmodernist 'condition'.

Sande Cohen introduces a recent dissection of historical narration with words that link Marxism and history in a chain that it is his purpose to break in its entirety: 'Historical thought is a manifestation of reactive thinking-about, which blocks the act of thinking-to. The "perplexity of History" (Arendt's term), a Liberal projection which also includes, unhappily, most of Western Marxism, arises, I argue, from the ill-conceived act of trying to make "history" relevant to critical thinking. What actually occurs by means of "historical thought" is the destruction of a fully semanticized present.'[5] Less abrasive, but fundamentally compatible, is the position of the preeminent Derridean feminist, Gayatri Chakravorty Spivak, who, in alliance with Michael Ryan, has attempted to congeal Marxism and deconstruction. Spivak reduces 'the production of historical accounts' to 'the discursive narrativization of events.' 'Since the incursion of "theory" into the discipline of history, and the uncomfortable advent of Michel Foucault,' she declares in what is an amazingly reductionist and chronologically current collapse of theory into a singular body of thought, 'it is no longer too avant-garde to suspect or admit that "events" are never not discursively constituted and that the language of historiography is also language.'[6] The Althusserian and neo-Althusserian idealism that Edward Thompson pilloried so mercilessly in the late 1970s precisely because, among other things, it declared the study of history 'not only scientifically but also politically valueless,' has returned in different dress.[7]

History – as lived and written – is indeed at a specific crossroads. But it is not the self-indulgent unintelligibility of a postmodernist late twentieth-century swirl of excess, waste, and disaccumulation depicted in some ostensibly theoretical texts. Nor is it at its own end, as proclaimed from the pulpits of the ideological Right. Rather, capitalism is impaled on its own contradictions, while Stalinism is coming unglued in its final failures to construct anything resembling socialism out of its bureaucratic mismanagement, suppression of workers democracy, and corruption and deformation of the planned economy. The way out of this impasse is not, theoretically or practically, to buy into it and its logic of disintegration,[8] as both the ideologues of the Right and many on the fashionable post-structuralist Left would advocate. Historical materialism and Marxist analysis remain interpretive tools that aid in providing explanations of why the world – capitalist and socialist – is unfolding, if not as it should, at least as it is. Whatever small part the writing of a social history erected on these conceptual foundations can play in resisting the pressures of the moment will happen only if some refusals and denials begin to be made. This essay attempts to explore how that might be done.

It commences with an irony, and one that reinforces an appreciation of the extent to which Stalinism's costs are being exacted in ways that are as complex as they are often unanticipated. For if some of historical materialism's finest recent texts grew directly out of overt repudiation of Stalinism, their engagement with this Stalinism may well have unintentionally opened cracks in doors that would widen to explict assault on historical materialism in later years. What follows thus begins with the two-sidedness of the historical materialism of E.P. Thompson and Raymond Williams, arguably the most influential writers to register an impact on an entire generation of social historians. It then moves into a discussion of how social history is currently being written, with special reference to the repudiation of historical materialism via the appropriation of critical/discourse theory or post-structuralist thought. Finally, it suggests that much feminist writing, undoubtedly the single most influential – if highly differentiated – current within the contemporary writing of social history, feeds into this general context of post-structuralism to denigrate historical materialism and push history in specific and problematic directions.

A Paradoxical Legacy: Thompson, Williams, and the Break from Stalinism

Thompson's histories, which have spawned an industry of historiographic criticism in the 1980s, were forged in his break from Stalinism.[9] Theoretically, his exit from the Communist Party of Great Britain was posed in terms of his political and conceptual reading of the deficiencies of the orthodox Marxist metaphor of a determining economic base and a derivative superstructural realm. 'In fact,' he concluded, 'no such basis and superstructure ever existed; it is a metaphor to help us to understand what does exist – men, who act, experience, think, and act again.' On the political plane, all of this took on even more sinister trappings: 'It turns out that it is a bad and dangerous model, since Stalin used it not as an image of men changing in society but as a mechanical model, operating semi-automatically and independently of conscious human agency.' In Thompson's view, it was necessary to relearn what Marx and Engels understood well, 'that man is human by virtue of his culture, the transmission of experience from generation to generation; that his history is the record of his struggle truly to apprehend his own social existence,' a contest of liberation from 'false, partial, class consciousness,' thereby freeing humanity 'from victimhood to blind economic causation, and extending immeasurably the region of choice and conscious agency.'

Thompson worked this theoretical resistance to the metaphorical notion of a base and its reflective superstructures into writings of unrivalled historical richness, wrestling with determination in ways that could step outside of the rigidities of the base/superstructure metaphor. Yet none of this argument was ever meant to imply that critical processes of historical formation, such as class, exercised an independence of 'objective determinations' or could be 'defined simply as cultural formation.' The attempt to pigeon-hole Thompson's writings in some slot labelled 'culturalist,' associated with Richard Johnson and others affiliated with the Birmingham Centre for Contemporary Cultural Studies was, as Thompson quite rightly insisted, an 'invention' constructed 'from some sloppy and impressionistic' understandings of historical texts and contexts.[10]

As Thompson's critical engagement with the inadequacies of the base-superstructure metaphor unfolded within histories and polemics, Raymond Williams was staking out different, but complementary, ground in his theoretical elaborations on 'cultural materialism.' Less prone to reject the language of orthodox Marxism, Williams nevertheless paralleled Thompson in his relentless pursuit of the limitations of orthodoxy and, in particular, in his insistence that the base be conceived in such a way as to allow entry to the materiality of areas presumably once relegated irrevocably to the superstructure. In describing his theoretical purpose, Williams stated:

> I was trying to say something very much against the grain of two traditions, one which has totally spiritualized cultural production, the other which has relegated it to secondary status. My aim was to emphasize that cultural practices are forms of material production, and that until this is understood it is impossible to think about them in their real social relations – there can only ever be a second order of correlation. But, of course, it is true that there are forms of material production which always and everywhere precede all other forms. . . . The enormous theoretical shift introduced by classical Marxism – in saying these are the primary productive activities – was of the most fundamental importance.[11]

This Thompson-Williams influence has informed so much positive and exciting work within social history and Marxist theory that it will seem ungenerous to suggest that it has also forced a certain price to be paid. But that is what I will maintain. For as much as was gained in the necessary confrontation with the mechanical consequences of an undialectical and rigidly structuralist implementation of the one-sided notion of base and superstructure, so too was something lost in the assimilation of agency and structure, culture and materiality. Through no fault of their own, for they had charted much-needed and creative advances in the development of historical materialism, the theoretical claims of Thompson and Williams were all too easily incorporated into an emerging orthodoxy that closed its nostrils to the foul smell of economism without reflecting on the extent to which it was also, simultaneously, shutting its eyes to materialism and the process of historical determination. The cultural became the material; the ideological became *the* real. What Thompson and Williams argued with a strong sense of the need to grasp determination, what in Thompson was always subordinate to a tough-minded insistence on an exacting confrontation with the historical sources and what in Williams was always developed with a sense of theoretical complexity, others took up far more indiscriminatingly. In the case of Thompson the relatively understated role of the economic in his histories was always a product of his understanding of the collective project of a group of (overwhelmingly Marxist) historians, many of whom addressed the material transformation of British society and the transition from feudalism to capitalism.[12] The Thompson-Williams rethinking of base and superstructure thus unintentionally paved the way for the denigration of the material and the reification of the ideal. 'Culturalism' arrived, not with Thompson and Williams, but through a process of appropriation that disfigured their actual projects, that listened to only part of their statement.

This trend highlights the need, not to return to an unthinking mechanical Marxism, but to address the two-sidedness of the Thompson and Williams project, to begin to reconsider the now somewhat neglected importance of determination. This relationship of being and consciousness was always central to the materialist texts of social history and cultural studies associated with the writings of these authors, but that dialogue between structure and agency has recently been silenced in a one-sided act of borrowing and suppression, in which the economically material realm's capacity to erect boundaries and set limits has receded from analytic view. Nowhere is this more apparent than within current trends in the writing of social history, most especially in terms of the now fashionable attraction to poststructuralism.

Social History in the 1980s: The Eclipse of Materialism

It is not possible to survey adequately the entire field of social history in an article such as this. But it is apparent that historical materialism, once embraced by many practising social historians who looked to a wide array of writing associated with the British Marxist historians,[13] is no longer held to be of great importance in understanding the past.

William M. Reddy centres his recent discussion of money and liberty in modern Europe around the need to question the very concept of class, encasing his argument in rhetoric that exposes both an idealist understanding of what history entails and a willingness to employ a 'Thompsonian' misreading of Thompson's own arguments: 'A class in the making is not a class; a class that is fully made, in this world of becoming, this vale of tears that is history, is dead.'[14] More blunt are the words of Michael Kazin. 'It is time for the US left to shed a grand and fond illusion,' Kazin pronounces with confidence, adding that the working class in American history has 'seldom been more than a structural and rhetorical abstraction, employed primarily by socialist activists and intellectuals who hoped wage-earners would someday share their socialist analysis and vision of society.' Kazin 'reads' the political language of labour single-mindedly through the words of a handful of trade union leaders, dismissing in sweeping blows the history of the Knights of Labor, the American Federation of Labor, the Industrial Workers of the World, the Congress of Industrial Organization, and the League of Revolutionary Black Workers as one blurred failure that proves decisively the absence of class in American history. Within the labour movement, then, Kazin argues that it was understandable that 'an essentially home-grown political language developed,' taken up by discontented worker activists who thought of themselves more as virtuous representatives of the American "people" than as members of a class.' This is a perverse distortion of a century of unfolding class relations, resting on a methodological reductionism and simple-minded conflation of class experience and the rhetoric of a handful of trade union tops. But an old story has been given a new twist: out of the language of a classless people comes pluralistic America.[15]

Reddy and Kazin are new additions to the ongoing left populist parades marching not so much toward anything of political and intellectual worth as they are running scared from class. It has become something not to be associated with, not only on the Right, but also among many on the ostensible Left.[16]

The particular strain of retreat associated with the current dismissal of class first surfaced early in the decade, and was most dramatically discerned in the historical and political writings of Gareth Stedman Jones and in the essays of Michael Ignatieff. Both authors broke from class, as have Reddy and Kazin, in good measure on the basis of an elevation of language, which takes on a singular importance as a determining materiality.

For Stedman Jones, the discovery of language and recognition of its historical capacity to construct being was a decisive historiographic rupture that necessitated a rethinking of how historians operate and how they employ (heavily Thompsonian) terms such as experience, consciousness, and class:

What both 'experience' and 'consciousness' conceal – at least as their usage has evolved among historians – is the problematic character of language itself. Both concepts imply that language is a simple medium through which 'experience' finds expression – a romantic conception of language in which what is at the beginning inner and particular struggles to outward expression and, having done so, finds itself recognized in the answering experience of others, and hence sees itself to be part of a shared experience. It is in some such way that 'experience' can be conceived cumulatively to result in class consciousness. What this approach cannot acknowledge is all the criticism which has been levelled at it since the broader significance of Saussure's work was understood – the materiality of language itself, the impossiblity of simply referring it back to some primal anterior reality, 'social being', the impossibility of abstracting experience from the language which structures its articulation. In areas other than history, such criticisms are by now well known and do not need elaboration. But historians – and social historians in particular – have either been unaware or, when aware, extremely resistant to the implications of this approach for their own practice, and this has been so most of all perhaps when it touches such a central topic as class.

Stedman Jones went on, from these conceptual beginnings, to rewrite the history of Chartism, to claim against the weight of past Marxist interpretation that the mobilizations of the 1830s and 1840s were not the product of class antagonisms and struggles but, rather, were constructed out of the cross-class language of eighteenth-century radicalism. The Chartists were 'made', not in the structured relations of exploitation and accumulation and their human hostilities, but within a linguistic paradigm governed by attachment to 'natural rights,' and the fears that such rights were being usurped by parasitism, fraud, and force. As the supposed site of both these 'rights' and their debasement, the state, and not the process of class formation and degradation, was thus 'the principal enemy upon whose actions radicals had always found that their credibility depended.' He also offered a congruent argument about the contemporary condition of the Labour Party, suggesting that its revival in post-Thatcherite Britain could only be sustained by junking its long-standing reliance on a 'homogeneous proletarian estate whose sectional political interest is encompassed by trade unions.' The answer to the Labour Party's woes and the reinterpretation of Chartism came together in an embrace of a particular kind of popular frontism, in which class was held to be of marginal importance in the building of mass movements of resistance or the reversal of the skidding fortunes of electoralist socialism.[17]

The critical response to this reassessment of Chartism has established beyond doubt two significant flaws. First, the conceptual foundations of the argument are flimsy at best, irresponsible at worst. Constructed out of cavalier assertions, Stedman Jones's attachment to the new-found analytic potential of language has been justly attacked. It appears as little more than a demonstration of the unsubstantiated enthusiasms of an advocate who has yet to master the intricacies of a theoretical system. Second, as a reconstruction of historical happenings, Stedman Jones's Chartism is aridly one-dimensional: its language is that of the published vocabulary of the movement's national leadership to the exclusion of many other class-accented discourses and symbolic statements.[18]

Yet it would be wrong to imply that Stedman Jones's piece has been uninfluential. Many are the footnotes of nodding approval. Within writing on the American working class, for instance, most social historians who champion uncritically the positive contribution of a language of labour republicanism almost universally find themselves in agreement with Stedman Jones and in opposition to an interpretive stress on class consciousness. Thus Leon Fink, the most authoritative voice endorsing the labour republicanism of the Knights of Labor and the Great Upheaval of the 1880s, quotes favourably Robert Gray's rejection of 'the straw person model of a class conscious and revolutionary working class, equipped with a rigorous class ideology and theoretical understanding of the capitalist economy.' Gray's argument that such cases are rare echoes views put forward by the late Herbert G. Gutman and his collaborator Ira Berlin. Similarly, Sean Wilentz, who champions the labour republicanism of the 1830s, rails against the attempt to measure American workers against some essentialist notion of class consciousness by which they will supposedly be found wanting and 'exceptional'. The consequence is that discussion of class consciousness is either exorcised or diluted to the point that any and all opposition by workers constitutes its realization. Yet curiously enough, Gray's original opposition to an essentialized class consciousness was posed against the very same Stedman Jones to whom social historians of American labour such as Fink and Wilentz acknowledge a debt. What is involved in this contradictory confusion?[19]

On one level, it is a function of the internal inconsistencies of 'Rethinking Chartism,' which is pulled in one direction by Stedman Jones's recent attraction to popular frontist cross-class alliances, most evident in his essay, 'Why is the Labour Party in a Mess?', a trajectory preceeded by many others: Gorz's 'farewell to the working class'; Laclau's and Mouffe's rejection of proletarian politics in favour of a 'socialism' paced by popular social movements; Gavin Kitching's notion of socialist transformation as the outcome of capitalist prosperity and the 'intellectual sophistication' of mental workers.[20] The Stedman Jones of this fast 1980s track is a reconstructed, 'true' socialist, disillusioned with class and its long-standing political failures at home and abroad, willing to rest his argument on the determinations of discourse and to interpret historical experience on the ground of reified language. But there lies between the lines of 'Rethinking Chartism,' not unlike a Derridean 'trace', the high structuralism of the Stedman Jones of the 1960s and 1970s. And this pulls the rereading of Chartism in another direction. That Stedman Jones knew the poverty of empiricism and how to measure class consciousness with the refined idealism of an Althusserian gage block.[21] Critics of Stedman Jones are quite right to see an idealized understanding of class and class consciousness at work in his 'Rethinking Chartism,' an essay that undoubtedly rests on an assumption about a model of mature class consciousness against which Chartism is found wanting. But oddly enough such critics sidestep the questions that should then follow: why does Stedman Jones so resolutely avoid evidence of transitional consciousness? why does he pay so little attention to the bedrock of class consciousness, the level of development of production itself? and why, finally, does he conclude his reinterpretation with an attempt actually to deny any place to class consciousness's role in the rise and fall of Chartism?

The answer lies in the changed politics of Stedman Jones and in the unwillingness of critics drawn intuitively to this politics to question too deeply a problem that would demand that they themselves address the relationship of class, class consciousness, and the project of social transformation. In short, the answer lies within the realm of historical materialism. Stedman Jones has moved on its margins, drawing away from an earlier Marxist scholasticism fixated on an idealized class consciousness toward a reformist popular frontism in which class consciousness is immaterial. If Stedman Jones fails to shake off entirely his intellectual past, he nevertheless ends up sufficiently unambiguous in his espousal of a politics of broad classless opposition to the state – which is what Chartism's success was about, he argues, and what the Labour Party needs to cultivate now – that he finds support in many quarters which share this ultimate politics. Politics, then, makes particular bedfellows: it matters not that those social historians who find the very term 'class consciousness' unnecessary, if not offensive, end up snuggling up to an argument about Chartism that places it, in an idealized way, at the centre of an analytic revision. What is lost in this bedding down of disparate conceptual trends is any attachment to an orthodox Marxist appreciation of attention to some elementary categories of historical materialism: class, consciousness, struggle.

The point is not that these categories, as categories, must be preserved on faith, but rather, that they provide just the kind of explanatory power needed to understand the complexities of mass working-class mobilizations such as the Chartism of the 1830s and 1840s or the North American Great Upheaval of the 1880s. These were class movements; they were most emphatically about class struggle; and their rise and their fall can be interpreted only by attention to conjunctures of economic structure and class activism.[22] Their discourses were not uniformly cut from the same cloth (either in comparison with one another, or internally), however, and although they were undoubtedly languages of class and struggle, they were not always – understandably so – unadulterated voices of class consciousness. Stedman Jones makes too much of this, the American social historians who uncritically embrace labour republicanism too little. Against this reading of the past, so obviously structured out of the political retreat from class evident in 1980s intellectual life, there remains no better antidote than adherence to the tenets of historical materialism, where class, consciousness and struggle remain vital points of entry.[23]

Michael Ignatieff also gravitated to language, but he had less distance to travel in his opposition to Marxism. Ignatieff revealed how attraction to language could strike a concrete blow against class struggle and ingratiate its advocates with the structures of 'progressive' authority. In the words of Ellen Wood, Ignatieff became 'the darling of the British literary press, their favourite repentant socialist.'[24] His 'Strangers and Comrades' proved a timely, refined, caring blow against class and its politics:

> There are those on the Left who maintain that the miners' strike is a vindication of class-based politics after decades in which the agenda of the Left was defined by cross-class campaigns like feminism and CND. Yet the strike demonstrates the reverse: a labour movement which is incapable of presenting a class claim as a national claim, which can only pose its demands

in the language of total victory, which takes on the State and ends up on the wrong side of the law, cannot hope to conserve its support and legitimacy among the working class public. The miners' strike is not the vindication of class politics but its death throes. . . .The trouble with Arthur Scargill's politics is not that it doesn't have justice on its side, but that it utterly lacks a conception of how competing classes, regions, races, and religions can be reconciled with each other in a national community.

'What the Left needs,' concluded Ignatieff, 'is a language of national unity expressed as commitment to fellowship among strangers. We need a language of trust built upon a practice of social comradeship.'[25]

A year later, the logic of Ignatieff's linguistic turn had led him so far from class that his *Needs of Strangers* did not need to touch on issues like the miners' strike. Instead, in the manner of the 'true' socialists of the 1840s, it agonized over the conceptualization of liberty, finding a predictable resolution of the dilemmas of the modern market world in words:

We need words to keep us human. Being human is an accomplishment like playing an instrument. It takes practice. . . . Our needs are made of words: they come to us in speech, and can die for lack of expression. Without a public language to help us find our own words, our needs will dry up in silence. It is words only, the common meanings they bear, which give me the right to speak in the name of the strangers at my door. Without a language adequate to this moment we risk losing ourselves in resignation towards the portion of life which has been allotted to us.[26]

As Marx and Engels concluded in their attack on the German 'true socialism' of the 1840s: 'After these samples of. . .Holy Scripture one cannot wonder at the applause it has met with among certain drowsy and easy-going readers.'[27]

Ignatieff was never much of a historical materialist, but he was, at one time, something of a historian. He began his journey toward this scriptural end with a Foucauldian history of the prison.[28] As such, he provides a tentative link and implicit connection to the poststructuralism of French thought. More than any other body of theory, poststructuralism has influenced the writing of social history in the 1980s. In its emphasis on the discursiveness of power it has challenged historical materialism directly. Much of the Anglo-American writing alluded to above draws on the implosion of theory associated with poststructuralism. Nowhere is the impact of this poststructuralist thought more pronounced, however, than in writing on the French Revolution, once associated strongly with the materialist conception of history. In the late 1980s that materialism has been eclipsed.

The French Revolution stands as one of the most significant events of modern times. Like other revolutions, it was, in Marx's conception of history, 'a driving force.' One would expect debate and disagreement about this revolution, but the surprising intellectual reality is that interpretive hegemony has historically consolidated quickly, vanquishing analytic opponents with sharp, decisive polemical strokes that, like the guillotine, hold forth little possibility of reconsiderations and reassessments. Like the Revolution itself, these consolidating orthodoxies have passed through phases. What concerns us here is the movement from Jacobinism to Thermidorian Reaction.

From World War II to the mid-1960s, a period of important developments in which professional historians adopted new methods and took on a new stature, there could be no question of the dominance of what many have called a Marxist, and others more precisely, a Jacobin, conception of the French Revolution.[29] The broad, bold lines of interpretive direction had been drawn by Marx and Engels in the 1840s, although by no means in ways that were devoid of contradiction and ambiguity:

> The revolutions of 1648 and 1789 were not English and French revolutions, they were revolutions of a European type. They did not represent the victory of a particular class of society over the old political order, they proclaimed the political order of the new European society. The bourgeoisie was victorious in these revolutions, but the victory of the bourgeoisie was at that time the victory of a new social order, the victory of bourgeois ownership over feudal ownership, of nationality over provincialism, of competition over the guild, of the division of land over primogeniture, of the rule of the landowner over the domination of the owner of the land, of enlightenment over superstition, of the family over the family name, of industry over heroic idleness, of bourgeois law over medieval privileges.[30]

This interpretive skeleton was fleshed out by Georges Lefebvre and, later, by Albert Soboul, two modern historians who did more than any others to establish the orthodoxy of the leftist analysis of the Revolution. That orthodoxy insisted on the bourgeois nature of the Revolution and, especially with Soboul, laid stress upon the importance of class struggle in the making of 1789 and its aftermath, positing a confrontation in which the bourgeoisie, drawing on the popular classes of town and country, ousted the aristocracy.[31]

Alfred Cobban crystallized the early discontent with the Lefebvre-Soboul interpretation in a series of writings. This highly sceptical new revisionism argued that feudalism had ceased to be an operative social formation long before the outbreaks of 1789, that the term bourgeoisie was meaningless, and that the Revolution was an upheaval culminating in continuity rather than a class rupture with the past. Cobban has been followed by many others. According to the new orthodoxy, since there was no revolutionary bourgeoisie, the Marxist histories of Lefebvre and Soboul are fatally flawed. This revisionism has carried the day and among historians of the French Revolution the old left-leaning historiography is regarded as rather old hat, another casualty of the demise of historical materialism in the 1980s.[32]

Against this idealized caricature of a revolutionary bourgeoisie judged not to have existed, Marxist theory and history has long grappled with the class paradoxes of revolutionary transformation. As his preface to *Contribution to a Critique of Political Economy* made clear, Marx drew no necessary relationship between structural class position and consciousness of that position, which was always a far more confused and ambivalent process than the objective conditions of production. In the concrete case of the French Revolution, Marx recognized that much of the riddle of the class contradictions of transformation lay in Jacobinism, its language and its attempt to revolutionize society politically rather than socially and economically.[33]

Trotsky would later embrace a similar position, but the historiography of the Revolution, especially after Soboul began to make an impact, treated Jacobinism much more heroically, drawing on Lenin's sympathetic reading of the Jacobins and, perhaps, Gramsci's comparable comments in his *Prison Notebooks*. An analytic difference does exist, with Marx-Trotsky suspicious of the socioeconomic presence or 'reality' of Jacobin class 'interests,' and Lenin, Gramsci, and Soboul more likely to accept class force as a historical agent. But on the fundamental political level, this divergence recedes. Since proletarian revolution was not on the agenda in the 1790s, Jacobinism represented, in Trotsky's words, 'the maximum radicalism which could be produced by bourgeois society.' It is therefore not surprising that subsequent Marxists have leaned sympathetically toward the likes of Robespierre and St Just. Marx himself saw these Jacobins as tragic victims of confusions and abstractions overdetermined by the material limitations of their times.[34]

The revisionist assault on the Jacobin interpretation of the French Revolution seldom pauses to consider such matters. It knows class interest expresses itself unambiguously; it knows, consequently, that the failure of class interest to proclaim itself articulately and to personalize its presence in identifiable, countable human beings proves that class interest does not really exist. Marx's basic insight that the French Revolution 'did not represent the victory of a particular class. . .[but] proclaimed the political order of the new European society,' is thus beyond its conceptual grasp. Inasmuch as Soboul and others often seemed to telescope analysis of the Revolution into the confines of class struggle, gesturing all too weakly to the limitations of the structural features of productive life, they bear some responsibility for the new revisionism's discontents.[35] But the tendency to divorce the Revolution from material forces, including class alignments, is a retrogressive step. Fuelled by the fetishization of quantitative methodology and the rampant anti-Marxism of social science history in the 1970s and 1980s, this analytic action looks persistently to the personnel of the Revolution, but not its political outcomes. Indeed, it takes a principled stand against the very consideration of origins and outcomes, unconsciously pulling a leaf from the pages of hedonistic critical theory.[36] A faction of the new revisionist camp has not surprisingly followed the drift of the 1980s, opting for a privileging of discourse, seeing the Revolution itself as a language or text in which imagery, rhetoric, and poetics abound, but where classes, material processes of accumulation and struggle, and the consciousness that develops around them are surprisingly silent.

The imprint of the anti-Marxism of this trend is captured nicely in François Furet's *Interpreting the French Revolution*. Composed of three essays addressing approaches to the history of the Revolution and an opening rambling, declarative statement, entitled, appropriately and defiantly, 'The French Revolution is Over,' the book is a manifesto for those dissatisfied with the Jacobin interpretation of 1789. Two of the four essays are of particular concern here, Furet's assault on Soboul and other Marxists, originally published in *Annales* as 'The Revolutionary Catechism,' and his introductory musings. The first establishes the anti-Marxism of the Furet wing of the new revisionism, the latter its formal adherence to discourse.

Furet's 'Revolutionary Catechism' is a remarkably splenetic piece of scholarship. Commencing as a diatribe against a text written in opposition to Furet and Richet's popularly-aimed history of the Revolution, it quickly proceeds to argue that three pernicious influences haunt the Marxist-dominated historiography of 1789: the positing of a kinship between the French and Russian Revolutions, in which the former serves as mother to the latter; the substitution of a linear, simplistic Marxism for the more subtle, contradictory positions of Marx and Engels on the historical making of the French Revolution; and the consequent entrenchment of a 'neo-Jacobinist', 'Leninist-populist vulgate' as the sectarian motivation of a 'conservative spirit of a historiography that substitutes value judgements for concepts, final ends for causality, argument from authorities for open discussion' and, in the process, ensures a ritualistic denunciation of all other interpretation as counter-revolutionary and antinational. Furet is especially damning of a Marxist historiography – attributable to Soboul – that takes 'its bearings from the prevailing ideological consciousness of the period it sets out to explain.'[37]

Impassioned references to the Gulag and persistent Soviet bashing indicate how much this essay is skidding out of control. What is interesting is Furet's inability to pause and consider the unusual critical inversion he finds himself within, and its own contradictory pulse. On the one hand, he chastizes Soboul for writing history that conveys a sense of the past as it was actually lived. 'From Soboul's language and ideas,' complains Furet, 'the reader almost feels as if he were participating in the meeting held on the famous night of 4 August 1789.' What Furet fails to appreciate is the extent to which Marxist historians are admonished to create just this kind of history, attentive to the past as it was experienced. Marxist historians are uniformly and roundly taken to task for imposing their false and unfittable conceptual agendas on a past that resists stubbornly such so-called 'presentist' ideological premises. If this charge of reproducing the past on its own terms is not sufficient, Furet then reaches into a more familiar anti-Marxist bag of charges to call Soboul to order for his theoretical reliance on the metaphysical categories of class analysis. That this dual charge of reproducing the past as it was lived and of imposing on it a theoretical construction of class that floats above the actualities of the Revolution contains a contradiction does not seem to bother Furet, who seems intent on forcing Soboul into whatever polemical corners best suit the dismissals of the moment. His reduction of Soboul's depiction of the contradictory composition, consciousness, and historic role of the sans-culottes to a mechanical cul-de-sac of simplistic class conflict flies directly in the face of what Soboul actually wrote about the struggles of the 1790s.[38]

Against this caricature of Soboul, Furet posits the determinations of discourse. Oppression and discontent played little role in the unfolding events of 1789–1794. Rather, it was language that paced all, leading the people where structures of power and authority could not. Indeed, power for Furet 'had no objective existence at the social level, it was but a *mental representation of the social sphere* that permeated and dominated the field of politics.' After decades of scholarship on the French Revolution in which one of the major events in the history of the modern world has been routinely scrutinized in ways at least somewhat congruent with the premises of historical materialism, the 1980s culminates in historical writing lost in a swirl of circular idealism:

> The 'people' were defined by their aspirations, and as an indistinct aggregate of individual 'right' wills. By that expedient, which precluded representation, the revolutionary consciousness was able to reconstruct an imaginary social cohesion in the name and on the basis of individual wills. . . .The idea of plot was cut from the same cloth as revolutionary consciousness because it was an essential aspect of the basic nature of that consciousness: an imaginary discourse on power. That discourse came into being, as we have seen, when the field of power, having become vacant, was taken over by the ideology of pure democracy, that is, by the idea that the people are power, or that power is the people.[39]

Lest it be misunderstood that Furet's interpretive resurrection of idealism is a peculiarly idiosyncratic text, another recent, and highly acclaimed study, can be drawn upon to suggest the nature of the current trend within study of the French Revolution. Lynn Hunt's *Politics, Culture, and Class in the French Revolution* is less irritatingly opaque than Furet's collection of essays; neither is it as overtly polemical. Produced within an American idiom, it is not so concerned to distance itself from Marxism, a consequence, no doubt, of historical materialism's weaker presence in the United States. It is more explicit, however, in its debt to post-structuralism. For all of its straightforwardness and its immersion in archival sources, which mark it out from the grand posturing of Furet's *Interpreting the French Revolution*, it bears the same stamps of anti-Marxism and the reification of language.

Like Furet, Hunt privileges the political, especially its symbolic and linguistic components, which she sees as far more than a mere expression of 'underlying' economic and social interests. 'Revolutionary political culture,' she insists, 'cannot be deduced from social structures, social conflicts, or the social identity of revolutionaries.' Political culture in the revolution was made up of 'symbolic practices, such as language, imagery, and gestures.' Echoing Furet, whom she quotes as establishing that speech substituted itself for power during the Revolution, and that 'the semiotic circuit [was] the absolute master of politics,' Hunt is adamant that language was itself an expression of power, shaping perceptions of interests and reconstituting the social and political world. She proposes to treat this 'foremost instrument' of the Revolution 'as a text in the manner of literary criticism.' This method allows her to avoid any interpretive slide into the abyss of 'class' politics: as a literary theorist she knows that authorial intention is always uncertain, as was that of the revolutionary text, and she grasps that 'the French rhetoric of revolution had to provide its own hermeneutics.'

This results, as in Furet, in a conceptualization of the Revolution that rather wilfully ignores socioeconomic divisions and that reconstitutes the process of revolution through adherence to linguistic metaphors of the revolutionaries themselves. To explain the abrupt shifts in the Revolution, Hunt turns to Northrop Frye's *Anatomy of Criticism,* arguing that the course of the Revolution can be explained by 'the transformation of narrative structures that informed revolutionary rhetoric.' The 'generic plot' of revolution moved from comedy to romance, and in the process the conflictual but reconcilable characters are reconstructed in a set of mythical oppositions, with larger-than-life heroes pitted against cowardly villains. Hence the rise of the Radicals in 1792. Tragedy was around the corner, however, speaking its most dramatic lines in the person of Robespierre, and propelled forward by the revolutionary obsession with the conspiratorial plot. Capital, labour, exploitation, class struggle and accumulation were not the orchestrating principles here, but given the discourse of hostility to the aristocracy, Hunt suggests that this may have been a 'language of class struggle without class.' If you like your revolution neat, this is a drink for you.

Hunt then moves into a fascinating discussion of political symbolism and ritualism during the Revolution. She extends our knowledge of the importance of this realm but oversteps interpretive acceptability with the blunt extremism of her denial of the structural and material substance of power, which is never interrogated, and the force of political ideas and strata, which are dwarfed by the larger-than-life universe of determining images and representations. The result is a book in which the politics of revolution tend to be divorced from ideas, and revolutionaries galvanized solely by the cockade and the symbol. So, too, is politics considered outside of any material referents, such as work, wages, or social mobility.

Oddly enough, Hunt does acknowledge that the revolutionary political class that operated within the symbolic formation of revolutionary rhetoric and image was indeed 'bourgeois.' But so hegemonic is the new revisionism and its hostility to any notion of 'bourgeois' revolution that Hunt backtracks, arguing that the term bourgeois is too general to discriminate between revolutionary militants and their moderate opponents. It is as if any sense of class fractions within a moment of revolutionary turmoil must be exorcised if class is to have any meaning.

In the end, Hunt demonstrates the presence of class in the revolution but retreats to the higher ground of language, the argument wrapped in circularity: 'the left won elections where the Jacobins of the towns and villages were able to develop relationships and organizations favorable to the defence of liberty, equality, and fraternity, and the right won elections where royalists and/or partisans of a republic of order were able to galvanize their clients into movements against the innovating Republic.' Convinced that any search for structural origins or outcomes is suspect, Hunt reifies political representation, treating the principles and personnel of revolution as abstracted, unmediated essences anchored only in their own cultural moment and imagination. The linguistic turn proves a dead end.[40]

What has been killed along the way is any appreciation of the complex interaction of economic structure and historical agency, of imposed necessity and cultivated desire. In the case of the French Revolution what has been lost is an appreciation of politics as the outcome of such conjunctures and dialogues, just as much recent writing on the history of workers submerges class, class consciousness, and class struggle in the determinations of discourse. Ultimately this analytic trend, congruent with – if not bred of – cavalier or conscious identification with the tenets of poststructuralist thought, has gone a considerable distance toward eclipsing historical materialism as a presence within the writing of social history.

Feminism(s) and the Eclipse of Materialism

What a difference a decade makes. There can be no mistaking that an admittedly highly differentiated feminism is now a presence of considerable importance within intellectual life in general and academic circles in particular. If the shifting natures of various feminisms are extremely difficult to chart with precision, it is nevertheless apparent that over the course of the 1980s a striking generalized trend has occurred. The extent to which feminism, broadly defined, has established itself and its concerns and vocabularies is perhaps not unrelated to the virtual collapse of the attempt to connect Marxism and feminism and the emergence of a community of feminists increasingly antagonistic to, and flippantly dismissive of, Marxist scholarship and politics. If there remain some few feminists who insist that analysis of the experience of gender be related to *other* experiences of oppression (race/ethnicity/region), however gingerly, or suggest that class, as the site of exploitation, mediates gender and its commonalities in ways that produce divergent histories, they grew less in numbers by the year, their voices more subdued, if not drowned out in the clamour of hostile accusation questioning their commitment to feminism. This development has had a profound impact within the writing of social history and it has extended and deepened the attack on historical materialism. It is also not unrelated to the reception of post-structuralism within an admittedly variegated set of feminisms.

Nothing is more instructive in this regard than a comparison of the original 1980 publication of Michèle Barrett's *Women's Oppression Today* and the new introduction to the 1988 edition. Barrett proves something of a barometer of changes in feminism over the course of this decade, being so astute as actually to change the subtitle of her volume so as to line herself up with the mainstream of feminist thought. What she once authored under the banner 'Problems in Marxist Feminist Analysis,' she now chooses to promote as a text in 'The Marxist/Feminist Encounter.'

Barrett begins and closes her new introduction with gestures towards poststructuralism, commencing with praise for Spivak and others and ending with a startling conception of how much the world has supposedly changed in less than a decade:

> Here lies, perhaps, the greatest challenge to the assumptions within which *Women's Oppression Today* was written: the discourse of post-modernism is premised on an explicit and argued denial of the kind of grand political projects that both 'socialism' and 'feminism' by definition are. But post-modernism is not something that you can be for or against: the reiteration of old knowledges will not make it vanish. For it is a cultural climate as well as an intellectual position, a political reality as well as an academic fashion. The arguments of post-modernism already represent, I think, a key position around which feminist theoretical work in the future is likely to revolve. Undoubtedly, this is where the book would begin, were I writing it today.

This positioning with respect to 'postmodernism' is surely as blunt a statement of closure as any ever offered by the most mechanical of Marxisms.[41]

Sandwiched between this opening gesture of goodwill toward post- structuralist feminism and this closing of the analytic book on all of those who might have the temerity to question the post-modern condition, are a series of retreats from the materialist arguments of her earlier, 1980, text. Barrett now repudiates her critique of the indiscriminate and ahistorical, descriptive use of the term 'patriarchy' among feminists, stating, 'I have come to regret the aggressive tone of my criticisms of this concept – and my own very limited definition of its appropriate use – in the first chapter of the original text.' One part of Barrett's earlier discontent with the use of patriarchy was its shading into a kind of biological essentialism, associated with the writings of Kate Millett and Shulamith Firestone. But with the increasing influence of the radical feminism of Mary Daly, Andrea Dworkin, Dale Spender, and Adrienne Rich, the biological essentialism of the early 1970s has come back into vogue in the late 1980s: Barrett thus slides into acceptance of the recent feminist view of biological difference as 'an unadorned fact of existence.' She is also, not surprisingly, less captivated by the validity of class analysis, toying with a Foucauldian reading of power and its analytic possibilities.

The meaning of this, in terms of an author who used to situate herself sympathetically in relation to some variant of Marxism, is unambiguous. A hyphenated socialist-feminism has been split apart and the project of reconciling Marxism and feminism shelved. Poststructuralism, the ascent of radical feminism, and the writings of French feminists have, for Barrett, displaced the task of negotiating 'socialist-feminism with the issues of men and class.' Any alliance with Marxism is now 'very problematic.' Barrett's insistence that feminism is located within 'a liberal, humanist tradition' impale her on some awkward contradictions, for she appears to want to have the best of both the anti-humanist and humanist world views, but her ultimate reassessment of her earlier writing leaves no doubt about where she locates herself and her feminism in the late 1980s:

Finally, I want to add a word about the general philosophical climate of today in comparison with the one that informed the book's premises. Just as it would be impossible to write such a book without integrating a consideration of racism and ethnicity, so it would, I think, be impossible to write in such a confidently materialist vein. At the very least one would have to defend the assumptions made about epistemology, the concept of ideology, the purchase of Marxist materialism, and the definition of the subject. Thus there would have to be a consideration of whether, for example, Foucault's suspension of epistemology and substitution of 'discourse' and 'regimes of truth' for a theory of ideology was to be accepted or not. There would have to be a consideration of the arguments, put forward by Ernesto Laclau and Chantal Mouffe, that the substantive arguments of a Marxist analysis of capitalism must be superseded. There would have to be an engagement with the arguments that the theory of the subject embodied in the text was, whilst not the universal male identification of bourgeois ideology, nevertheless still a conception unacceptably tainted by a humanist perspective.[42]

Within the writing of social history the process exemplified by Barrett is unmistakable. Feminist histories are now more strongly hostile to Marxism and historical materialism than at any point in the post-1960 development of attention to gender. The extent to which poststructuralism has captivated the 'theoretical' side of feminist social histories is undoubtedly a significant factor in this newly-consolidating hostility to historical materialism and its insistence on material determination and the importance of class. To read the new French feminists – Kristeva, Irigaray, and Cixous – is to appreciate how distanced these writers are from Marxism.[43] Even within an Anglo-American feminist milieu, where poststructuralism is not part of the bedrock of engagement, the dominant analytic paradigm has shifted decidedly, the terms of feminist analysis now tilted unmistakably toward a one-sided emphasis on the ideological that runs its course in a fixation on the making of *identities* and the social constructedness of absolutely everything.[44] Not surprisingly, class and its material referents figure only peripherally, if at all, in this project. When two recent theorists write that, 'The very achievements of Western humanism have been built on the backs of women and people of color,' the lack of inclusion of the working class is more than accidental omission: it is a statement of political programme.[45] Indeed, if there is a prime mover that can be located within feminist histories of the 1980s, both in terms of historiography and history itself, it is sexuality, a socially-constructed centre of power bounded by a rather timeless masculinist, patriarchal authority.

To address this literature in all of its complexity, attentive to the accomplishments and richness of various important studies, is beyond the capabilities of an article such as this. At the risk of slighting the important contributions made by various feminist histories in this realm,[46] let me single out a particular writer who exposes the analytical and political tendencies of feminist writing in the 1980s, especially as this relates to historical materialism.

The choice of Jeffrey Weeks may seem an odd one. But it is not. Weeks represents the 'progressive' side of a debate among feminisms over sexuality and its discontents, standing, alongside of many women activists and authors, for the potential of sexual desire as opposed to a one-sided assertion of its dangers.[47] Attentive to the diversity of sexuality because of his status as a gay activist, Weeks steps outside of the tendency to collapse the history of gender into the narrative of women's experience. Weeks is also theoretically attracted to post-structuralism, especially those Foucauldian strains that are currently quite important to feminist analyses. And as a male who has opted consciously for feminism, Weeks epitomizes a certain course increasingly common within both academia and the left.

Of those writers who have thus tackled the difficult area of gender in ways that draw most explicitly on poststructuralism, Weeks stands out as among the most self-consciously theoretical and the most relentless in his insistence that the sexual is the site of much of significance. Weeks draws on Foucault to argue that discourses of sexuality are central in any understanding of power in Western society. 'Sexuality is as much about words, images, ritual and fantasy as it is about the body,' notes Weeks in the first sentence of his *Sexuality and its Discontents*, and he goes on to claim that 'politics operate through metaphors.' Another text, *Sexuality*, opens with a chapter on 'The Languages of Sex.' His exploration of the history of sexuality follows Foucault in its insistence that sexualities are constructed and invented, a changing set of articulations that have nothing to do with nature and everything to do with power, its consolidation, and the ways in which it makes meanings and regulations pivotal in its project. Weeks takes as his starting point Foucault's blunt statement that sex is 'the truth of our being' and then turns it on its head, propelling us into what he calls a 'whirlwind of deconstruction.' What is this truth, he asks? On what basis is something natural or unnatural? Who 'laws' what is sexually acceptable?[48]

Weeks has received little in the way of critical commentary. Precisely because he has pioneered the development of a new area of historical and sociological inquiry, an accomplishment enhanced by his sensible refusals of some of the outlandish positions espoused by radical (separatist/lesbian) feminists on matters such as heterosexuality as the enemy or a politics of antipornography that unites 'Moral Majority' and segments of the women's movement, Weeks is rightly championed among many leftists. His commitment to and engagement with the movement for gay rights, which extends in his writing into an unwillingness to sidestep difficult questions such as intergenerational sex (paedophilia) and the meaning of 'consent,' insures that Weeks is warmly received in certain circles. There are signs, however, that his advocacy of a radical sexual pluralism sidesteps matters of importance, some in the gay milieu arguing that it submerges the specificities of homosexuality in a reformist sea of any and all sexualities. There is also no doubt that Weeks's focus on contemporary gay identity, a 'homosexual' community, and the political movements associated with these developments, collapses into the very essentialism he has long been at pains to challenge, an irony that does not escape the attention of Weeks himself.[49]

These emerging areas of interpretive contestation are not unrelated to Weeks's fixation on sexuality as discourse. Among gay rights activists,

Weeks's embrace of radical pluralism (also Barrett's ultimate advocacy) and his Foucauldian insistence on the constructedness – and hence historically transitory/mobile meaning – of the 'homosexual' appears as a liberal evasion of both the particularities of oppression and the positive features of sexual-cultural life that both stigmatize homosexuality and allow for some small spaces of celebration and creativity, carved out of the dominant culture with much pain and effort. When Weeks, following basic post-structuralist premises, argues that because 'homosexuality' is a fragmented, volatile, constantly moving discourse and thus the category does not 'exist,' some gay writers react with hostility: their scepticism is rooted in a knowledge of how homophobic power is *lived* and *used* against them as something more than discourse/representation.

Weeks himself is caught on the horns of this dilemma, for in spite of his theoretical dependency on this kind of Foucauldian scaffolding he is sufficiently embedded in the politics of gay activism to privilege gay identity. He does this by greatly understating the class-ridden character of this 'community.' When it was apparent at the beginnings of the AIDS crisis that a horrible disease was in fact ravaging gays and that its spread was somehow related to the commercialized commodification of sex concentrated in specific North American urban centres, it was the powerful, literally monopolistic, bathhouse and bar owners who blocked attempts on the part of gay activists to stop the drift to epidemic. Too much money was being made off of the back of gay sexuality for this capitalistic component of 'the community' to act againt its class, as opposed to cultural/sexual, interests. In effect, the 'gay community,' long enclosed within the boundaries of capitalist America, succumbed to its own vision of itself as 'one,' as the 'Other,' and a tragic internalized popular frontism ran its course in the spread of a disease that ended up exacerbating homophobia, killing off whole realms of gay culture and sexuality, and decimating 'communities' of sexual identity in San Francisco, Toronto, New York, and elsewhere. To use this kind of language is not to lapse into the sensationalized moral panic of the media, but to state a specific kind of reality and to reach for a particular sort of analysis. This is not to blame the main North American victims of AIDS in the 1980s, gay males, but to point to the necessity of political responses to threats that are simultaneously material (health and death) and social (heightened homophobia and repression). It is also to reassert the basic connectedness of the economic and the cultural, and to point to the futility of a politics that ignores this link.[50]

Weeks's writing thus oscillates uneasily between its theoretical fixation and fixedness on sexuality as discourse, and all of the ramifications that this positioning entails, and its political acknowledgement that 'sex does not unproblematically speak its own truth,' and that those subjected to the categories and definitions of discourses of sexuality 'have taken and used the definitions for their own purposes.'[51] Where this ambivalence manifests itself most pointedly is in Weeks's failure actually to probe this history of human agency and his willingness to lapse analytically all too easily into the more accessible 'texts' of sexology, psychoanalysis, and other writings concerned with sex. Like Foucault, Weeks has his surrogates, which become the history of sexuality.

Within this substitutionism, recognition of the importance of class sometimes appears, but partially and often with vital qualifications.[52] Weeks is quick to pillory 'class reductionism,' but he is slow to address the material embeddedness of sexuality, save for the extent to which it relates to the proliferation of commodified sexuality in the post-World War II epoch. Class does not even enter into Weeks's list of 'the really fundamental issues around sexuality today: the social nature of identity, the criteria for sexual choice, the meaning of pleasure and consent, and the relations between sexuality and power.' Attentive to the unconscious to the extent that it is the site of desire and repression, Weeks cannot bring himself to see this realm as constructed, in part, out of the material world of actual, economically determined social relations. The hidden injuries of class are somehow all too peripheral in the making of sexualities and their many meanings.[53]

To say all of this is not to suggest that the sexual can be reduced to the economic. It is to claim that the two cannot be divorced and their relationship tossed off with a slap in the face of crude determinism. Yet this is what Weeks's Foucauldian framework allows him to do. Power can never be located, and resides always in the determinations of discourse, which spins itself in a never-ending and analytically and politically impenetrable Lacanian circularity: 'Society does not influence an autonomous individual; on the contrary the individual is constituted in the world of language and symbols, which come to dwell in, and constitute, the individual.' With this kind of theoretical focus, it is not surprising that Weeks can gravitate politically to what he calls a radical sexual pluralism; nor is it inconsistent for him to embrace what can only be regarded as a naive voluntarism. 'We have the chance to regain control of our bodies,' he ends a recent book, 'to recognise their potentialities to the full, to take ourselves beyond the boundaries of sexuality as we know it. All we need is the political commitment, imagination and vision. The future now, as ever, is in our hands.'[54] Yet if sex does indeed not speak its own truth, the potentialities and control Weeks and others seek will never be attained by a focus on it, and its discourses, alone. Bodies are never just the property of their occupants: they must labour and live through exploitation, alienation, and oppression. Sex is never just a process in the hands of those who are living it, doing it: sex is always unfolding within sets of determinations. Weeks avoids such relationships – among sex/not sex, discourse/not discourse – that are central to the possibilities of a human condition that reaches beyond many boundaries, those of sexuality among them. Historical materialism would tell you this much; Weeks, among many others, is not listening to its message.

What does this particularistic focus have to do with feminist social history writ large? In a word everything, for Weeks, like Barrett, is nothing less than a sign of the times. What he emphasizes has become the emphasis of feminist social history. What he loses sight of is, within this writing, not worth seeing. We can appreciate the generality of the problematic eclipse of materialism by considering, first, an analytic tendency, and, second, by closing this discussion with a look at two recent post-structurally-inclined feminist 'histories'.

Let us begin with a current analytic trend, spawned and perpetuated by feminist sensitivies. This trend is but a subset of the penchant to grant ideology increasing weightiness and determinative capacities and to understate the severe limitations imposed by mundane, material reality. It involves the virtually unquestioned 'social' or subjective construction of virtually everything, from gender itself to documentary reality. Feminist scholarship in general and feminist historical writing in particular, for all the differentiations of varied 'feminisms,' has occupied a central place in this influential process. 'Second wave' feminism was in part mobilized around the premise that the personal is political, and many feminists have pointed out how this perspective in fact anticipated many of the positions about the discursiveness of power associated with a Foucauldian reading of institutions, knowledges, and historical discourses. Under feminist scrutiny the explanatory authority of orthodox historical materialism, with its concerns located in economic and class structures, often appeared inadequate, as did the strategic emphasis placed on a vanguard party that was increasingly dismissed as a male form. The pervasive power of masculinist perspectives and constructions took on new and enhanced meaning, simultaneously destabilizing and decentring the conception of power and adding new interpretive weight to the ubiquitous realm of the ideological.[55]

It is possible to oppose this often one-sided stress on the ideological without falling prey to Barrett's rather sectarian caricature of Marxism's historical handling of the ideological realm. For Barrett the deficiencies of historical materialism are easily identified. 'In practice,' she declares, 'there is no way in which orthodox Marxists will accept any serious consideration of ideology.'[56] Consideration of the recent focus on the social construction of skill, especially as it pertains to gender relations, allows entry into precisely this question that Barrett answers so decisively, and, so simple mindedly.

Where class and gender habitually now meet, for instance, is along the ideological axis of skill as the constructed site of difference and male dominance, in which skill is depicted as little more than the capacity of powerful male workers to define their jobs as the preserve of men against women. In the words of two often-cited feminist theorists: 'Skill definitions are saturated with sexual bias. The work of women is often deemed inferior simply because it is women who do it.'[57]

The point is not to approach the relation of skill, gender, and class with one's resolutely historical materialist eyes closed to the ideological forces at work, as Barrett concludes all orthodox Marxists will. It would be foolhardy to rebut the role of ideology in the making of the undeniable reality of labour market segmentation in which gender figures forcefully, nor would it be productive to deny the ways in which skill is defined and defended in the context of gender relations. As far as this recent feminist sensibility to skill's construction has taken us in new and critically important directions, however, it has also skewed the treatment of skill, pressuring its conceptualization ideologically to the detriment of a more nuanced materialist reading cognizant of the two-sidedness of skill's making within the processes of production/reproduction and its consequences – often ambiguous – for class and gender relations. It has also tended toward an ahistorical assessment, the much-studied cauldron of sexual antagonism pitting skilled male labour against an 'intruding' lot of unskilled women in the tailoring/seamstress trade of the pre-1850 years. Yet to generalize from this experience across time, as is often done, understates the highly differentiated histories of context-bound skills, drawing too selectively on relations in a particular trade that was closely associated with the domestic arena – thus perhaps forced into a defensiveness around questions of intraclass, gender-defined relations of subordination – and acutely aware of the perilous incursions of petty technologies and debasing reorganizations of work.[58]

This historically contextualized two-sidedness of skill was grasped much more forcefully by Marx than is currently readily acknowledged by those advocating understanding skill as social construction. Marx anticipated the argument of some contemporary feminists when he noted in Volume I of *Capital*:

> The distinction between skilled and unskilled labour rests in part on pure illusion, or, to say the least, on distinctions that have long since ceased to be real, and that survive only by virtue of a traditional convention; in part on the helpless condition of some groups of the working class, a condition that prevents them from exacting equally with the rest the value of their labour-power.[59]

Yet Marx was also capable of understanding that skill is only in part illusory, that its reality is constructed, not only ideologically, but also in the material realm of historically changing production, representing, again, in part, a substantive side of the never-ceasing process of accumulation with important ramifications for workers as a class counterposed to the bourgeoisie:

> The accumulation of the skill and knowledge (scientific power) of the workers themselves is the chief form of accumulation, and infinitely more important than the accumulation – which goes hand in hand with it and merely represents it – of the *existing objective* conditions of this accumulated activity. These objective conditions are only nominally accumulated and must be constantly produced and consumed anew.

And in this ongoing production, consumption, and renewal of skill lay much of the history of class struggle and class/gender fragmentation. To slide past this history of skill on a skidding discourse-like theory of a timeless social construction of absolutely everything is to ensure that you find yourself at a particular end.[60] We glimpse that end in the recent writings of two post-structuralist feminist historians: Denise Riley and Joan Wallach Scott.

Riley explores feminism and the category of 'woman,' shattering historical time, ranging across centuries to echo Lacanian notions of 'women's' fictive status and a Derridean grasp of the 'undecidability' of 'woman.' She replaces Sojourner Truth's 1851 refrain 'Ain't I a woman?' with the rather more cumbersome 'Ain't I a fluctuating identity?' In Riley's view, there is no historically continuous 'woman' or 'women'; rather 'woman' is 'discursively constructed, and always relatively to other categories which themselves change.' 'History' itself is not an unproblematic category – this stands as nothing less than a foundation of most poststructuralist thought – and Riley's positioning vis-à-vis history is appropriately ambivalent, marked by the ubiquitous quotation marks: 'It is the misleading familiarity of "history" which can break open the daily naturalism of what surrounds us.'[61]

My complaint here is not with Riley's basic questioning of the meaning of 'woman,' or her interrogation of historical practice. Rather, my discontent is with her reification of the category as history itself, a conceptual point of departure that allows her to simplify and distort a history she wants to claim needs to be made more complex. The result is a history with a feminist political message, but a history that is unfortunately one-dimensional and unconvincing.

Riley's *Am I That Name* is dedicated to Joan Scott. This should come as no surprise, for no feminist historian has argued the case for post-structuralism more strenuously than Scott, who has attained an unrivalled stature within certain circles. Scott, like Barrett, is an indication of which ways the winds of interpretation are blowing within academic feminist circles. When it was fashionable to espouse 'Thompsonianism' in the 1970s, Scott was one of its most unquestioning advocates, framing her own work within it and pillorying those who did not, according to her, deliver its promise. In her early writing, feminism's impact is simply non-existent, and as late as 1980 Scott could co-author, with the British Marxist historian E.J. Hobsbawm, an essay on political shoemakers that studiously avoided gender. Indeed, in a recent interview in the *Radical History Review*, we get a clue as to what in part lies behind the making of Joan Scott. Discussing her background in the left teachers' community of New York City, where her father was victimized during the McCarthyite repression, Scott concludes: 'The formative lesson of those years for me was less an abiding Marxism than it was an abiding political mentality.' It was in the 1980s and under the influence of feminist literary theorists, that Scott began to distance herself overtly from anything smacking of Marxism, including so-called Thompsonianism.[62]

Scott's essays of the 1980s have recently been gathered together in *Gender and the Politics of History*. They contain much of interest and value, but in their promotion of a post-structural feminism that consciously dismisses Marxism and historical materialism some undeniable problems intrude. First, in spite of Scott's newly-articulated antagonism to Marxism and the extent to which her essays are marketed as a rich and invigorating source challenging historical materialism, it is apparent that Scott's engagement with Marxism is cavalier and caricatured: like much of North American mainstream historiography, what Scott does not know about Marxism, or what she mistakenly assumes concerning it, is far more telling than any supposed critique that emerges from her work.[63] Scott is more concerned with what she considers to be the controversies and problems flowing out of attempts to merge Marxism and feminism than she is with a sustained discussion of Marxist-feminism itself. She notes that 'the English have had greater difficulty in challenging the constraints of strictly deterministic explanations,' citing an extensive literature that developed in response to Barrett's 1980 edition of *Women's Oppression Today*, but she neglects substantive contact with the Barrett text itself. Indeed, Scott is incapable of discussing Marxism without pillorying crude determinism. She seems to misread Juliet Mitchell's recent reflections on feminism and the need to address the material realm as an overt attempt to dichotomize psychoanalytic and materialistic analyses of gender when Mitchell undoubtedly means to posit no such opposition. The point of Mitchell's essay is simply that the material must be addressed more rigorously than it often is in feminist circles, a recognition of just how much it determines. It is not a rejection of psychoanalysis, which Mitchell always conceived as a way into the materiality of the unconscious. As an indication of just how skewed is Scott's understanding of what is at stake in the relationship of Marxism and the writing of social history, consider this recent statement. 'Social history is more deterministic,' she argues, 'when it posits economic or material causes for human actions; some Marxists, for example, see class consciousness immanent in relations of production. Although their histories may focus on the heroism of workers, the determinants of worker action are placed elsewhere.' This rather strained depiction of Marxist social histories, which typically carries no concrete citation of any actual writing, is then followed by a corrective. Scott poses the novel argument that human agency is in fact action taken in specific contexts but not without constraint, as if this insight was not precisely what Marx's *Eighteenth Brumaire*, Thompson's histories, and Williams' theorizing were all about.[64]

Second, if Scott's theoretical engagement with Marxism is partial and inadequate, her own project of theorizing feminism through adoption of post-structuralism is no better. Her gravitation toward the implosion of theory, in both its acceleration over the last few years and in its rather quick grasp of what is at stake in the – for her – mainly French fragments of critical theory, is instructive in exposing the promise and problem of reinterpreting gender through the lens of poststructuralism.[65] Even highly sympathetic feminist colleagues have pointed out that Scott's brisk partisanship 'mysteriously exempts [poststructuralism] from critical dissection, employing it instead as a toolbox from which theories can be picked up and applied to historical problems.' When Scott reduces deconstruction to a project summed up by its understanding of 'the production of meaning. . .as a political process,' she is surely simplifying what deconstructionists have been about for the last three decades and, if she is right, how far does this take us beyond Marx's insistence that, 'The ideas of the ruling class are in every epoch the ruling ideas. . .the ideas of dominance?'[66] In her recent work Scott is at pains to deal with meaning, reality, authorial intention, and textual discourse, but in doing so she usually lapses into the very binary oppositions questioned by the poststructuralism she champions, an analytic positioning that allows her to embrace a universalistic feminist accomplishment. It also conditions a history that, as Claudia Koonz suggests, bypasses the complexity of women's experience in its articulation of the representation of women. Theoretically, this problem is addressed frontally in the writings of Jane Flax and Deborah Cameron, both of whom stand for a feminism attentive to discourse but conscious of the material boundaries within which language and signification develop. Empirically it virtually leaps off the pages of Scott's current historical writing and historiographic reevaluations, leading us toward the third problematic feature of her poststructuralist crusade.[67]

For in the stress on representation, Scott is led to some rather dubious conclusions, especially from the vantage point of historical materialism. Consider, for instance, her comments on discourse, Chartism, and the working-class family. 'The version of class that Chartists espoused,' she writes with confidence, 'affirmed a working-class family structure resembling middle-class ideals and susceptible to middle-class pressures: a family organization that no later radical theories of economics managed entirely to displace. From this perspective the working-class family was created within working-class political discourse, by the particular gendered conception of class evident in (though not invented by) the Chartist program.'[68] This argument is so thoroughly idealist and ahistorical in its premises of causality that it leaves one gasping for intellectual breath. So, too, does Scott's critique of Thompson's *Making of the English Working Class*. In 'Women in *The Making of the English Working Class*,' the only previously unpublished essay to appear in *Gender and the Politics of History*, Scott subjects Thompson's book to a deconstructionist feminist challenge in which the legitimate project of questioning the text's gendered discussion of class formation is submerged in strained misreadings of specific passages, explicit distortion of Thompson's meanings, and a questionable dichotomization of women's expressivity and men's rationality.[69]

Out of this theoretical and empirical set of difficulties emerges the final, problematic area of Scott's recent 'linguistic turn.' What are the politics of this poststructuralist feminist history? One comes away from Scott's assessment of women in *The Making of the English Working Class* quite shaken about the political meanings of a deconstructive feminism. Real women, the repositories of sexual difference, are expressive, domestic, spiritual, religious, undisciplined, and irrational, coded as feminine. Radical women, secular, combative, and rational, are depicted as the intellectual/political equivalents of men in public drag, coded, for all of their superficial disguise, as masculine. The awkward complexities of actual women, often situated within sets of paradoxes and battling against the numerous 'constructions' of their lives, remain all too little appreciated in Scott's rereading of Thompson's text and in her gestures toward politics.

Within Scott's new collection of essays, where politics are constantly alluded to, no space is actually more vacant and vacuously underdeveloped than the *political*. Scott appears a particular case of a general problem located by the literary critic Barbara Foley: 'there is an urgent necessity for literary critics to examine more closely the concept of the "political" as it applies to our investigations. We are quite willing these days to admit that all discursive activity is in some sense political, but we are ordinarily imprecise, even naive, when actual political questions arise.' What Foley is suggesting is that discourse theory, whatever its analytic potential, will not resolve a host of political matters, which are linked to larger and more potent structures of oppression, exploitation, and organization. But this context of discourse and not-discourse is actually obscured by Scott's view of politics as 'the process by which plays of power and knowledge constitute identity and experience,' a rather circular conception given her insistence on knowledge's all-encompassing and determining capacities.[70]

Barrett and Scott, Riley and Weeks. The list could be extended indefinitely. These are representative texts because, even granting feminism's many and diverse faces, they capture a specific drift that has accelerated and grown more influential over the course of the 1980s. That drift is against the long-standing currents of historical materialism and these authors, in their emphases, realignments, and theoretical focus have both constructed feminism in opposition to Marxism and reflect mainstream feminism's increasingly hostile attitude toward historical materialism. It is of course not the case that these trends and writers are unopposed, and there are those within the highly differentiated body of thought associated with feminism that cultivate positions more compatible with materialism. But these are minority voices within feminism's variegated project. For much of feminism, Marxism is a burden that it no longer wants even to try to carry. It welcomes the eclipse of materialism as a liberation at the same time as it founders in the analytic and political darkness of current fashion.

To Be A Historian, To Be A Historical Materialist. . .
These are not good times to be a historian, not good times to be a historical materialist. Politically, there can be no denying the hegemony of the Right and its ideas, both in the capitalist West and the East of actually existing, but disintegrating, Stalinist socialism. Intellectually, there has not been a time in

the post-World War II epoch when an irrationalist hostility to and denigration of history has so tenaciously gripped the very neck of bourgeois thought. Poststructuralism, in Ellen Wood's words, constructs a politics 'detached from the anchor of history. . .where rhetoric and discourse are the agencies of social change.' These political and intellectual trends have overwhelmed the populist left and infiltrated whole realms of ostensibly Marxist writing, converging in 'a cynical defeatism, where every radical programme of change is doomed to failure.' Their conjuncture is not accidental. As Perry Anderson noted more than a decade ago, 'Marxist theory. . .acquires its proper contours only in direct relation to a mass revolutionary movement. When the latter is effectively absent or defeated, the former is inevitably deformed or eclipsed.'[71] The 1980s has been a decade in which much has been eclipsed, and in the developing darkness much necessarily lost sight of. Receding from view, essential processes, especially those of determinative causalities and the relationship of the past, present, and future, have been not just forgotten, but delegitimized. The result is a time in which, to quote the *Communist Manifesto*, 'All that is solid melts into air, all that is holy is profaned,' but it is not a time in which men and women, most emphatically not those men and women writing social history, have seemed compelled to 'face with sober senses [the] real conditions of life.'[72] The political defeats of the international workers movement are preeminent in this plunge into chaos and obscurantism, especially as it is registered in Marxist theory, but the conscious adoption of ideas and analysis antagonistic to historical materialism cannot be discounted as unimportant. To be a historian, to be a historical materialist, is necessarily to register certain refusals in the face of those many and influential forces that have gathered in the darkness of the 1980s, clamouring for new lights of interpretive insight and political practice that illuminate, in the end, nothing so much as their own accommodations to the pressures of the moment. To stake out this elementary ground of opposition is, of course, to court curt dismissals and nasty excommunications. But it is time for historians, for historical materialists, to begin fighting back. The 1990s will be many things. Let them not, at least, be further years of eclipse in which we ourselves remain open-mouthed, wide-eyed, and silent.

NOTES

1. This kind of thing has been said before, but the extent to which the situation has actually worsened rather than improved is striking. Note, for earlier statements, Tony Judt, 'A Clown in Regal Purple: Social History and the Historians,' *History Workshop Journal*, 7 (Spring 1979), pp. 66–94; Elizabeth Fox–Genovese and Eugene D. Genovese, 'The Political Crisis of Social History: A Marxian Perspective,' *Journal of Social History*, 10 (Winter 1976), pp. 205–220.
2. I have attempted to criticize one part of this process in a discussion of 'critical theory' and its current influence in the writing of social history. See Bryan D. Palmer, *Descent into Discourse: The Reification of Language and the Writing of*

Social History (Philadelphia: Temple University Press 1990), a text that I draw upon liberally in what follows.

3. See Ralph Miliband, 'Reflections on the Crisis of Communist Regimes,' *New Left Review*, 177 (September–October 1989), pp. 27–36.

4. Quoted in 'How the West is Winning,' and elaborated on in Richard Bernstein, 'Judging "Post-History," The Theory to End All Theories,' *New York Times*, 'Ideas & Trends,' 27 August 1989.

5. Sande Cohen, *Historical Culture: On the Recoding of an Academic Discipline* (Berkeley: University of California Press 1988), p. 1.

6. See Gayatri Chakravorty Spivak, 'A Literary Representation of the Subaltern: A Woman's Text from the Third World,' in *In Other Worlds: Essays in Cultural Politics* (New York: Routledgc 1988), pp. 241–42; Michael Ryan, *Marxism and Deconstruction: A Critical Articulation* (Baltimore: Johns Hopkins University Press 1982). For forceful criticism of the Ryan–Spivak position see Barbara Foley, 'The Politics of Deconstruction,' in Robert Con Davis and Ronald Schlcifcr, eds., *Rhetoric and Form: Deconstruction at Yale* (Norman, Oklahoma: University of Oklahoma Press 1985), pp. 113–114. Note, as well, Nancy Fraser, 'The French Derrideans: Politicizing Deconstruction or Deconstructing Politics,' *New German Critique*, 33 (Fall 1984), esp. 129; Terry Eagleton, 'Frère Jacques: The Politics of Deconstruction,' in Eagleton, *Against the Grain: Selected Essays, 1975–1985* (London: Verso 1986), pp. 79–88.

7. The quote is from Hindess and Hirst, cited in Thompson, 'The Poverty of Theory: or, an Orrery of Errors,' in *The Poverty of Theory & Other Essays* (London: Merlin 1978), p. 194.

8. I borrow this phrase from Peter Dews' impressive *The Logics of Disintegration: Post-structuralist Thought and the Claims of Critical Theory* (London: Verso 1987).

9. On the Thompson industry see, as a beginning only: Perry Anderson, *Arguments within English Marxism* (London: Verso 1980); Bryan D. Palmer, *The Making of E. P. Thompson: Marxism, Humanism, and History* (Toronto: New Hogtown Press 1981); Paul Q. Hirst, *Marxism and Historical Writing* (London: Routledge & Kegan Paul 1985); Gregor McLennan, 'E. P. Thompson and the Discipline of Historical Context,' in Richard Johnson, et al., eds., *Making Histories: Studies in History-Writing and Politics* (London: Hutchinson 1982); Allan Dawley, 'E. P. Thompson and the Peculiarities of the Americans,' *Radical History Review*, 19 (Winter 1978–79), pp. 33–60; F. K. Donnelly, 'Ideology and Early English Working-Class History: Edward Thompson and His Critics,' *Social History*, 2 (May 1976), pp. 219–238; Richard Johnson, 'Thompson, Genovese, and Socialist-Humanist History,' *History Workshop Journal*, 6 (Autumn 1978), pp. 79–100; Harvey J. Kaye, *The British Marxist Historians* (Cambridge: Polity Press 1984), ← pp. 167–220; Craig Calhoun, *The Question of Class Struggle: Social Foundations of Popular Radicalism during the Industrial Revolution* (Chicago: University of Chicago Press 1982); and Harvey J. Kaye and Keith McClelland, ed., *E. P. Thompson: Critical Debates* (Cambridge: Polity Press, forthcoming 1990).

10. Quotes in the above paragraphs from E. P. Thompson, 'Socialist Humanism: An Epistle to the Philistines,' *The New Reasoner: A Quarterly Journal of Socialist Humanism*, 1 (Summer 1957), esp. pp. 113–114; 'Revolution Again! Or Shut Your Ears and Run,' *New Left Review*, 6 (November–December 1960), pp. 18–31; Thompson, *Whigs and Hunters: The Origin of the Black Act* (New York: Pantheon 1975), p. 260; Thompson, 'Eighteenth-Century English Society: Class Struggle Without Class?' *Social History*, 3 (May 1978), p. 149; Thompson, 'The Politics of Theory,' in Raphael Samuel, *People's History and Socialist Theory* (London: Routledge & Kegan Paul 1981), pp. 396–397. The most explicit Johnsonian

statement on the so-called 'moment of culture' is: 'Culture and the historians,' in John Clarke, Chas Critcher and Richard Johnson, ed., *Working Class Culture*, pp. 41–71.

11. For Thompson's early critical engagement with Williams see 'The Long Revolution I,' and 'The Long Revolution II,' *New Left Review*, 9 (May–June 1961), pp. 24–33; 10 (July–August 1961), pp. 34–39. Williams recollects his reaction to this critique in Raymond Williams, *Politics and Letters: Interviews with New Left Review* (London: Verso 1979), pp. 134–136. The quote is from *ibid.*, p. 353.

12. See Interview with 'E. P. Thompson,' in Henry Abelove et al., ed., *Visions of History* (New York: Pantheon 1983), p. 22.

13. For an introductory overview see Harvey J. Kaye, *The British Marxist Historians* (Cambridge: Polity Press 1984).

14. William M. Reddy, *Money & Liberty in Modern Europe: a Critique of Historical Understanding* (Cambridge: Cambridge University Press 1987), p. 203.

15. Michael Kazin, 'A People Not a Class: Rethinking the Political Language of the Modern U.S. Labor Movement,' in Mike Davis and Michael Sprinker, eds., *Reshaping the U.S. Left: Popular Struggles in the 1980s* (London: Verso 1988), pp. 257–286, esp. pp. 257–259. For other Kazin pronouncements, all variations on a common theme, see 'The Limits of the Workplace,' in 'A Symposium on *The Fall of the House of Labor*,' *Labor History*, 30 (1989), pp. 110–113; and 'The New Historians Recapture the Flag,' *New York Times Book Review*, 2 July 1989.

16. Among right-wing historians who have provided particularly crude dismissals of class see Norman McCord, 'A Touch of Class,' *History*, 70 (1985), esp. pp. 412–419; and Gertrude Himmelfarb, *The New History and the Old: Critical Essays and Reappraisals* (Cambridge: Belknap Press of Harvard University Press 1987). Ellen Meiksins Wood, *The Retreat From Class: A New 'True' Socialism* (London: Verso 1986) dissected deftly the left-leaning rejection of class a few years ago, but her sharp polemic did little to stop the fashionable escape from materialism.

17. Gareth Stedman Jones, *Languages of Class: Studies in English Working Class History, 1832–1982* (New York: Cambridge University Press 1983), esp. pp. 20–21, 256.

18. The literature posed against Stedman Jones's Chartism essay is now considerable. See, for a beginning: Palmer, *Descent into Discourse*, esp. pp. 128–133; Wood, *The Retreat from Class*, pp. 102–115; John Foster, 'The Declassing of Language,' *New Left Review*, 150 (March–April 1985), pp. 29–46; Paul A. Pickering, 'Class without Words: Symbolic Communication in the Chartist Movement,' *Past & Present*, 112 (August 1986), pp. 144–162; Joan Scott, 'On Language, Gender, and Working-Class History,' *International Labor and Working Class History*, 31 (Spring 1987), and the responses to Scott by Palmer, Stansell, and Rabinbach, pp. 1–36; Dorothy Thompson, 'The Languages of Class,' *Bulletin of the Society for the Study of Labour History*, 52 (No. 1 1987), pp. 54–57; Neville Kirk, 'In Defence of Class: A Critique of Recent Revisionist Writing on the Nineteenth-Century Working Class,' *International Review of Social History*, 32 (1987), pp. 2–47; Robert Gray, 'The Deconstructing of the English Working Class,' *Social History*, 11 (October 1986), pp. 363–373; James Epstein, 'Rethinking the Categories of Working Class History,' *Labour/Le Travail*, 18 (Fall 1986), pp. 195–208; Epstein, 'Understanding the Cap of Liberty: Symbolic Practice and Social Conflict in Early Nineteenth-Century England,' *Past & Present*, 122 (February 1989), pp. 75–118; Nicholas Rogers, 'Chartism and Class Struggle,' *Labour/Le Travail*, 19 (Spring 1987), pp. 143–152; Christopher Clark, 'Politics, Language, and Class,' *Radical History Review*, 34 (1986), pp. 78–86.

19. See, for instance, Leon Fink, 'The New Labor History and the Powers of Historical Pessimism: Consensus, Hegemony, and the Case of the Knights of Labor,' *Journal of American History*, 75 (June 1988), pp. 121, 123–124; Gray, 'Deconstructing the English Working Class,' p. 373; Ira Berlin and Herbert G. Gutman, 'Class Composition and the Development of the American Working Class, 1840–1890,' in Gutman, *Power and Culture: Essays on the American Working Class* (New York: Pantheon 1987), pp. 381–382; Sean Wilentz, 'Against Exceptionalism: Class Consciousness and the American Labor Movement, 1790–1920,' *International Labor and Working Class History*, 26 (1984), pp. 1–24; Wilentz, *Chants Democratic: New York City and the Rise of the American Working Class, 1788–1850* (New York: Oxford University Press 1984), p. 16. It is of course hardly surprising that Michael Kazin embraces the Stedman Jones approach in 'A People Not a Class,' p. 282, n. 2.

20. See, among others: André Gorz, *Farewell to the Working Class: An Essay on Post-Industrial Socialism* (London: Pluto 1982); Ernesto Laclau and Chantal Mouffe, *Hegemony and Socialist Strategy: Towards a Radical Democratic Politics* (London: Verso 1985); Gavin Kitching, *Rethinking Socialism: A Theory for a Better Practice* (London: Methuen 1983); Kitching, *Karl Marx and the Philosophy of Practice* (London: Routledge 1988).

21. See, for instance, Gareth Stedman Jones, 'The Pathology of English History,' *New Left Review*, 44 (July–August 1967), pp. 29–44; 'The Marxism of the Early Lukacs,' in New Left Review, ed., *Western Marxism: A Critical Reader* (London: Verso 1978), pp. 11–60.

22. See, for example, Dorothy Thompson, *The Chartists: Popular Politics in the Industrial Revolution* (New York: Pantheon 1984); Gregory S. Kealey and Bryan D. Palmer, *Dreaming of What Might Be: The Knights of Labor in Ontario, 1880–1900* (Toronto: New Hogtown Press 1987).

23. This is central to Palmer, *Descent into Discourse*. But note as well Peter Novick, *That Noble Dream: The 'Objectivity Question' and the American Historical Profession* (New York: Cambridge University Press 1988), pp. 522–572.

24. Wood, *Retreat from Class*, pp. 180–181.

25. Michael Ignatieff, 'Strangers and Comrades,' *New Statesman*, 14 December 1984. For other views see Raphael Samuel's reply in *New Statesman*, 11 January 1985; Huw Benyon, ed., *Digging Deeper: Issues in the Miners' Strike* (London: Verso 1985).

26. Michael Ignatieff, *The Needs of Strangers: An Essay on Privacy, Solidarity, and the Politics of Being Human* (New York: Viking 1984), pp. 141–142.

27. Marx and Engels, *The German Ideology* (New York: International 1969), p. 193.

28. Michael Ignatieff, *A Just Measure of Pain: The Penitentiary in the Industrial Revolution* (New York: Pantheon 1978).

29. See, among many other studies: William Doyle, *Origins of the French Revolution* (Oxford: Oxford University Press 1980), pp. 7–40; G. Ellis, '"The Marxist Interpretation" of the French Revolution,' *English Historical Review*, 90 (1978), pp. 353–376; François Furet, *Interpreting the French Revolution* (Cambridge: Cambridge University Press 1981); George C. Comninel, *Rethinking the French Revolution: Marxism and the Revisionist Challenge* (London: Verso 1987). Note the recent discussion in Michael Löwy, '"The Poetry of the Past": Marx and the French Revolution,' *New Left Review*, 177 (September–October 1989), pp. 111–124, a source that came to my attention too late to influence the following discussion.

30. Marx and Engels, *Collected Works*, 'Bourgeoisie and Counter-Revolution,' cited in Gerard Bekerman, *Marx and Engels: A Conceptual Concordance* (Oxford: Basil Blackwell 1983), p. 153. The importance of this passage is noted in Michael Löwy,

The Politics of Combined and Uneven Development: The Theory of Permanent Revolution (London: Verso 1981), p. 3.

31. Lefebvre's most influential book is undoubedly *The Coming of the French Revolution* (Princeton, N. J.: Princeton University Press 1947), although it could be argued that his most impressive writing focused on the peasantry and rural panic on the eve of 1789. See Lefebvre, *The Great Fear of 1789: Rural Panic in Revolutionary France* (London: New Left Books 1973). Note as well Lefebvre, *The Directory* (New York: Vintage, 1967); Lefebvre, *Napoleon: From Eighteen Brumaire to Tilsit, 1799–1807* (New York: Columbia University Press 1969). Soboul is justifiably known as the historian of the Parisian sans-culottes on the basis of *The Parisian Sans Culottes and the French Revolution, 1793–1794* (Oxford: Clarendon Press 1964), but see as well his two-volume history, *The French Revolution, 1789–1799* (London: New Left Books 1974). For portaits of Lefebvre and Soboul from their closest non-Marxist collaborator, Richard Cobb, see 'Georges Lefebvre,' in Cobb, *A Second Identity: Essays on France and French History* (London: Oxford University Press 1969), pp. 84–100; 'Albert–Marius Soboul: A Tribute,' in Cobb, *People and Places* (New York: Oxford University Press 1986), pp. 46–92.

32. The most precise statements are found in Alfred Cobban, *Aspects of the French Revolution* (London: Paladin 1971), especially the essay entitled, 'The Myth of the French Revolution.' Even as astute a Marxist commentator as Comninel, *Rethinking the French Revolution* is unduly deferential to this Cobban-inspired revisionism.

33. Karl Marx, 'Preface to the Critique of Political Economy,' in Marx and Engels, *Selected Works* (Moscow: Progress 1968), p. 183; Karl Marx, *The Holy Family* (London: Lawrence and Wishart 1956), pp. 160–167; and *Deutsche Brusseler Zeitung*, 11 November 1847, quoted in Shlomo Avineri, *The Social and Political Thought of Karl Marx* (Cambridge: Cambridge University Press 1968), p. 191. On Jacobinism see, as well, Ferenc Feher, *The Frozen Revolution: An Essay on Jacobinism* (New York: Cambridge University Press 1987).

34. Trotsky's discussion of 'Jacobinism and Social Democracy' forms the final chapter of *Our Political Tasks* (1904), written as a Menshevik polemic against Lenin. See Baruch Knei-Paz, *The Social and Political Thought of Leon Trotsky* (Oxford: Clarendon Press 1978), pp. 199–206; Tony Cliff, *Trotsky: I. Towards October, 1879–1917* (London: Bookmarks 1989), pp. 60–63; Antonio Gramsci, *Selections from the Prison Notebooks* (New York: International 1971), pp. 77–79; Walter L. Adamson, *Hegemony and Revolution: Antonio Gramsci's Political and Cultural Theory* (Berkeley: University of California Press 1980), pp. 184–188; Marx, *Holy Family*, pp. 164–165.

35. For a sensitive critique of Soboul see Michael Sonenscher, 'The Sans-Culottes in the Year II: Rethinking the Language of Labour in Revolutionary France,' *Social History*, 9 (October 1984), pp. 301–328.

36. Note the forceful discussion in Elizabeth Fox–Genovese and Eugene D. Genovese, 'On the Social History of the French Revolution,' in *Fruits of Merchant Capital: Slavery and Bourgeois Property in the Rise and Expansion of Capitalism* (Oxford: Oxford University Press 1983), pp. 213–248.

37. Furet, *Interpreting the French Revolution*, esp. 85–89, 91.

38. Furet, *Interpreting the French Revolution*, pp. 90–91, contrasted with Soboul, *The Sans Culottes: The Popular Movement and Revolutionary Government, 1793–1794* (Garden City, N. Y.: Doubleday 1972), pp. 251–264.

39. Furet, *Interpreting the French Revolution*, pp. 63, 27, 54.

40. Lynn Hunt, *Politics, Culture, and Class in the French Revolution* (London: Methuen 1986), pp. 12–13, 23–26, 35–51, 177, 147.

41. Michèle Barrett, *Women's Oppression Today: The Marxist/Feminist Encounter* (London: Verso 1988), pp. v–vi (Spivak) and xxxiv (quote).

42. Barrett, *Women's Oppression Today* (1988), pp. xxii, xviii–xix, xxii–xxiii, xxiv, xxxiii.

43. Different discussion of this trio and introduction to the literature on French feminism can be found in Rosemarie Tong, *Feminist Thought: A Comprehensive Introduction* (Boulder and San Francisco: Westview Press 1989), pp. 217–233.

44. See, for instance, Dorothy E. Smith, *The Everyday World as Problematic: A Feminist Sociology* (Toronto: University of Toronto Press 1987); Rowena Chapman and Jonathan Rutherford, *Masculinity: Unwrapping Masculinity* (London: Lawrence and Wishart 1988); Celia Kitzinger, *The Social Construction of Lesbianism* (London: Sage 1989).

45. Irene Diamond and Lee Quinby, ed., *Feminism and Foucault: Reflections on Resistance* (Boston: Northeastern University Press 1988), p. xv.

46. Among some impressive recent works see Ann Snitow et al., ed., *Powers of Desire: The Politics of Sexuality* (New York: Monthly Review 1983); Christine Stansell, *City of Women: Sex and Class in New York, 1789–1860* (New York: Knopf 1986); Kathy Peiss and Christina Simmons, ed., *Passion and Power: Sexuality in History* (Philadelphia: Temple University Press 1989).

47. This sex debate has an extensive literature. For an introduction to its content see Varda Burstyn, ed., *Women Against Censorship* (Vancouver: Douglas & McIntyre 1985); and Catharine A. MacKinnon, 'Desire and Power: A Feminist Perspective,' as well as the discussion of this essay in Cary Nelson and Lawrence Grossberg, ed., *Marxism and the Interpretation of Culture* (Urbana and Chicago: University of Chicago Press 1988), pp. 105–121.

48. Jeffrey Weeks, *Sexuality and its Discontents: Meanings, Myths, and Modern Sexualities* (London: Routledge and Kegan Paul, 1985), pp. 3, 6, 17; Weeks, *Sexuality* (London: Tavistock 1986), p. 13.

49. For an indication of a critique of Weeks's radical pluralism see Bryan Bruce, 'Modern Diseases: Gay Self-Representation in the Age of AIDS,' *cineACTION*, 15 (Winter 1988–89), esp. pp. 30, 37, drawing upon Leo Bersani 'Is the Rectum a Grave,' in *October #43* (Cambridge: MIT Press 1987), esp. pp. 205, 219. My thanks to Steven Maynard, who does not agree with all of my arguments, for bringing this source to my attention. On essentialism see especially Weeks, *Sexuality and its Discontents.*, pp. 185–195.

50. Randy Shilts, *And the Band Played On: Politics, People, and the AIDS Epidemic* (New York: St. Martin's Press 1987). I am aware that this text is not an unproblematic source, weighted down as it is with a kind of journalistic moralism and sensationalism. Nevertheless, it shows clearly the class-ridden character of the gay community and relates these class divisions to the beginnings of the spread of AIDS. For accounts of AIDS more amenable to gay activists see Cindy Patton, *Sex and Germs: The Politics of AIDS* (Montreal: Black Rose Books 1986); Simon Watney, *Policing Desire: Pornography, AIDS and the Media* (London: Methuen 1987).

51. Weeks, *Sexuality and its Discontents*, pp. 56, 170.

52. Note Weeks, *Sexuality*, pp. 37–38.

53. Note Weeks, *Sexuality and its Discontents*, pp. 56, 170. Another reading appears in Reimut Reiche, *Sexuality and Class Struggle* (London: New Left Books 1970).

54. Weeks, *Sexuality and its Discontents*, pp. 170–171, 260; Weeks, *Sexuality*, p. 37. Both Weeks's endorsement of radical sexual pluralism and his unduly voluntarist and overly subjective assessment of what is politically possible relate to positions espoused by Foucault. First, Foucault's political trajectory was toward classical liberalism. See 'Polemics, Politics, and Problemizations: An Interview with Michel

144 THE SOCIALIST REGISTER 1990

Foucault,' in Paul Rabinow, ed., *The Foucault Reader* (New York: Hill and Wang 1984). Second, note Foucault's statement that 'It is possible that the rough outline of a future society is supplied by the recent experiences with drugs, sex, communes, other forms of consciousness and other forms of individuality. If scientific socialism emerged from the Utopias of the nineteenth century, it is possible that a real socialization will emerge, in the twentieth century, from experiences.' Michel Foucault, *Language, Counter-Memory, Practice: Selected Essays and Interviews*, ed., by Donald F. Bouchard (Ithaca, N. Y.: Cornell University Press 1977), p. 231, quoted in J. G. Merquoir, *Foucault* (Berkeley: University of California Press 1985), pp. 154–155.

55. Perhaps one of the most influential early statements was Sheila Rowbotham, Lynne Segal, and Hilary Wainwright, *Beyond the Fragments: Feminism and the Making of Socialism* (London: Merlin 1979).

56. Barrett, *Women's Oppression Today* (1988), p. xviii.

57. Anne Phillips and Barbara Taylor, 'Sex and Skill: Notes Towards a Feminist Economics,' *Feminist Review*, 6 (1980), pp. 79–83. For a more nuanced, but decidedly feminist, approach to the same issue, see Sylvia Walby, *Patriarchy at Work: Patriarchal and Capitalist Relations in Employment* (Minneapolis: University of Minnesota Press 1986).

58. See the important studies: Barbara Taylor, '"The Men Are as Bad as Their Masters. . .": Socialism, Feminism, and Sexual Antagonism in the London Tailoring Trades in the 1830s,' in Judith Newton, Mary Ryan, and Judith Walkowitz, ed., *Sex and Class in Women's History* (London: Routledge & Kegan Paul 1983), pp. 187–220; Joan Wallach Scott, 'Men and Women in the Parisian Garment Trades: Discussions of Family and Work in the 1830s and 1840s,' in Pat Thane, Geoffrey Crossick, and Roderick Floud, ed., *The Power of the Past: Essays for Eric Hobsbawm* (Cambridge: Cambridge University Press 1983), pp. 67–94. Christine Stansell, *City of Women*, pp. 130–154 offers some commentary that is both fascinating and problematic for my argument.

59. Quoted in Gerard Bekerman, *Marx and Engels: A Conceptual Concordance* (Oxford: Basil Reference 1983), pp. 87–88.

60. Karl Marx, *Theories of Surplus Value* (translated by Emile Burns, 3 volumes) (Moscow: Progress 1963–1971), 3, pp. 266–267, quoted in David Montgomery, *The Fall of the House of Labor: The Workplace, the State, and American Labor Activism, 1865–1925* (Cambridge: Cambridge University Press 1987), p. 45, a text that successfully addresses the two-sidedness of skill. Note the discussions in Mike Holbrook–Jones, *Supremacy and Subordination of Labour: The Hierarchy of Work in the Early Labour Movement* (London: Heinemann 1982); Craig Heron, *Working in Steel: The Early Years in Canada, 1883–1935* (Toronto: McClelland and Stewart 1988); and Jane Gaskell, 'Conceptions of Skill and Work: Some Historical and Political Issues,' in Roberta Hamilton and Michèlle Barrett, *The Politics of Diversity: Marxism, Feminism, and Nationalism* (London: Verso 1986), pp. 361–380.

61. It is typical of histories of this sort to substitute terms of supposed complexity for terms of supposed simplicity. Thus Riley's woman/fluctuating identity duality is paralleled by William Reddy's insistence that in the place of class we need to appreciate a language and terminology whose meaning 'draws the mind up short. . . .begins to fade. . . .no one can use. . .without repeatedly rethinking what it refers to.' Thus for class Reddy substitutes 'monetary exchange symmetry.' See Reddy, *Money and Liberty in Modern Europe*, pp. 202–203; Denise Riley, *'Am I That Name': Feminism and the Category of 'Women' in History* (London: Macmillan, 1988), pp. 1–5.

62. See Joan Wallach Scott, *The Glassworkers of Carmaux: French Craftsmen and*

Political Action in a Nineteenth-Century City (Cambridge, Massachusetts: Harvard University Press, 1974), esp. p. ix. For a particularly dogmatic polemic see Scott's review of Peter N. Stearns, *Lives of Labor* (1975) in *American Historical Review*, 81 (June 1976), p. 565, where Scott refers to 'E. P. Thompson's compelling and sensitive exploration of working-class experience.' Note, as well, 'Interview with Joan Scott,' *Radical History Review*, 45 (Fall 1989), pp. 40–59; Eric Hobsbawm and Joan W. Scott, 'Political Shoemakers,' (original *Past & Present*), in Hobsbawm, *Workers: Worlds of Labour* (New York: Pantheon, 1984), pp. 103–130.

63. Joan Wallach Scott, *Gender and the Politics of History* (New York: Columbia University Press, 1988). A full-scale critique of this collection of essays appears in my *Descent into Discourse*, pp. 78–86, and 172–186. Readers interested in more detail are directed there. Other assessments include Lisa Duggan, 'Viva la difference: Joan Scott's Historical Imperatives,' *Voice Literary Supplement* (January–February 1989), p. 37; Claudia Koontz, 'Post Scripts,' *The Women's Review of Books*, 6 (January 1989), pp. 19–20. Lynn Hunt provides the dust-jacket promotional blurb adorning Scott's *Gender and the Politics of History*. Her concluding sentence reads: 'Our reading of Marx and our understanding of class differentiation will never again be the same.'

64. This paragraph draws on *Gender and the Politics of History*, pp. 36–37, 207; 'Interview with Scott,' p. 51. Regarding Juliet Mitchell, Scott did not have access to Mitchell's 'Reflections on Twenty Years of Feminism,' in Juliet Mitchell and Ann Oakley, ed., *What is Feminism?* (Oxford: Basil Blackwell, 1986), pp. 34–49, but took Mitchell's position from a set of seminars at Princeton. Note Angela McRobbie, 'An Interview with Juliet Mitchell,' *New Left Review*, 170 (July–August 1988), pp. 80–92.

65. Scott appears to be a particular case of a general phenomenon identified by Peter Dews, *Logics of Disintegration*, p. xv: 'For the reception of Derrida's work, perhaps more than that of any other recent French thinker has been marked by an astonishingly casual and unquestioning acceptance of certain extremely condensed – not to say sloganistic – characterizations of the history of Western thought, as if this history could be dismissed through its reduction to a set of perfunctory dualisms.'

66. Lisa Duggan, 'Scott's Historical Imperatives,' p. 37; Interview with Scott,' p. 50; Karl Marx and Frederick Engels, *The German Ideology* (New York: International, 1947), p. 39.

67. Note Scott, *Gender and the Politics of History*, p. 176; Koonz, 'Post Scripts,' p. 19. See also Jane Flax, 'Postmodernism and Gender Relations in Feminist Theory,' *Signs: Journal of Women in Culture and Society*, 12 (1987), pp. 621–643; Deborah Cameron, *Feminism and Linguistic Theory* (London: Macmillan, 1985).

68. Scott, *Gender and the Politics of History*, p. 65. This wording represents a slight change from the original article 'On Language, Gender, and Working Class History,' *International Labor and Working Class History*, 31 (Spring 1987), p. 11, where Scott says more bluntly that the working class family was established by the Chartist programme and its conception of class and that no radical economic theories were later able to entirely displace this construction. I take these changes to be improvements, but of a cosmetic sort.

69. Note, as well, Angela Weir and Elizabeth Wilson, 'The British Women's Movement,' *New Left Review*, 148 (November–December 1984), pp. 82–85.

70. Barbara Foley, 'The Politics of Deconstruction,' in Robert Con and Ronald Schleifer, ed., *Rhetoric and Form: Deconstruction at Yale* (Norman Oklahoma: University of Oklahoma Press, 1985), p. 115; Scott, *Gender and the Politics of History*, pp. 5, 2. Circular conceptions of power and causality permeate Scott's new approach. See, as well, 'Interview with Joan Scott,' pp. 47–48, where Scott

argues that gender is a meaning system that constructs difference and that political economy constructs, rather than reflects, sexual difference.

71. Perry Anderson, *Considerations on Western Marxism* (London: New Left Books, 1976), p. 109.

72. Karl Marx and Frederick Engels, 'Manifesto of the Communist Party,' in *Selected Works* (Moscow: Progress, 1968), p. 38.

STATISM, NEW INSTITUTIONALISM, AND MARXISM

PAUL CAMMACK

From the late 1970s on, a literature stressing the autonomy of the state developed rapidly in comparative sociology and political science, in direct confrontation with Marxism. In the middle 1980s it gave rise to the 'new institutionalism'. This essay addresses the relationship of each to Marxism. I argue that both approaches caricature Marxist arguments, and that the case they make for themselves as superior alternatives depends upon their so doing. Secondly, I suggest that classical and contemporary Marxism makes better sense of the material presented by statists and new institutionalists than they do themselves. The attempt to create a 'statist' alternative to Marxism largely failed, and the 'new institutionalism' is evidence of its failure.

STATISM

The four major early contributions to the 'new statism' were Stepan, *The State and Society: Peru in Comparative Perspective* (1978), Krasner, *Defending the National Interest: Raw Materials Investments and US Foreign Policy* (1978), Skocpol, *States and Social Revolutions: A Comparative Analysis of France, Russia and China* (1979), and Nordlinger, *On The Autonomy of the Democratic State* (1981). Each presented the statist approach as a superior alternative to Marxism. However, a close examination of each of the texts suggests that if Marxism was rejected in these accounts, it was as much for what it could explain, as for what it could not.

Prefacing his study of Peru under the Velasco regime, Stepan declares himself to have been dismayed to find, in the course of work on the Brazilian military, 'that many of the most important theoretical approaches to politics – pluralist and Marxist alike – assigned very little independent weight to the state'.[1] Yet when he turns later to classical Marxist theory, he proves to be well aware of strands within it that 'offer rich, nondeterministic theoretical insights about such crucial questions as the relative autonomy of the state', asserting only that 'a main line of argumentation. . .treats the state largely as a dependent variable'.[2] He then notes that Engels often formulates the relationship of the political superstructure to the economic structure in 'much more mechanistic terms' than Marx, yet justifies his *primary* reliance on Engels' work in the development of his critique with the assertion that 'it would be sociologically unacceptable to *exclude* his works when we are evaluating the legacy of classical Marxism in regard to the analysis of the state' (emphasis mine). It is sociologically *acceptable*, it appears, to reduce the classical Marxist legacy to one strand of Engels' thought. Even so, Stepan cannot yet find Marxism guilty as charged: after having claimed that the state 'at least in Engels's formulation, is exclusively the coercive instrument of the dominant class', he cites evidence which makes it perfectly clear that even Engels did not rule out substantial state autonomy. Finally, he announces that 'there are neglected subthemes in Marx and Engels that, if read properly and applied to the special conditions of late developing, dependent-capitalist societies such as those in Latin America, in fact provide much less theoretical foundation for the neglect of the state than do many conventional Marxist interpretations'.[3] All this is a prelude, it should be noted, to the assertion of the superiority of an organic-statist approach, and represents the last sustained consideration of Marxist theory in the text.

Despite his eager advocacy of an organic-statist approach over pluralism and Marxism, Stepan clearly demonstrates the ample basis in classical Marxism (carried further, as he notes, by Gramsci, Miliband, and Poulantzas) for consideration of the state as an autonomous force. He resolves the dilemma this creates by dwelling on elements out of which a one-sided case can be constructed, then *choosing* to discard Marxism for his preferred alternative.

Krasner shares with Stepan an explicit commitment to the establishment of a 'state-centric or realist paradigm', which he presents as superior to those offered by interest-group liberalism or Marxism.[4] However, in contrast to Stepan, he does systematically test *instrumental* and *structural* variants of Marxism against his case material. He finds that some of the cases studied, including every one in which investments were actively promoted by the state, were more or less compatible with liberal, Marxist and statist theories, while a second major group of cases, which showed 'a clear divergence between corporate and state preferences', 'support statist and structural Marxist positions over interest-group and instrumental Marxist ones'. He concludes from this that 'the two approaches whose relative merits are most difficult to assess are structural Marxism and statism. Both see the state as an autonomous actor concerned with long-term objectives'.[5] So far, then, he has no evidence for the superior analytical power of the statist approach. In order to find some, he has to turn from the issue of conflict between state goals and the goals of private capitalists over raw materials supply to cases of the use of overt or covert force by the United States abroad. It is precisely at this point that his argument is weakest. He notes that 'after 1945 all of these [cases] were clearly associated with the goal of preventing communist regimes from assuming or holding power. This aim can be comprehended from a structural Marxist perspective: communism does not enhance capitalism's long-term prospects'. But rather than concede the validity of a structural Marxist approach, he pins his hopes on the case of the Vietnam war, arguing that

The nonlogical manner in which American leaders pursued their anticommunism is not compatible with a structural Marxist position. The absence of means-ends calculations, coupled with misperception, led to policies that undermined the coherence of American domestic society, particularly in Vietnam. This is the very opposite result from the one predicted by a structural Marxist argument, but it is compatible with a view that sees the state as capable of defining its own autonomous goals.[6]

He is reduced to arguing that the unintended outcome of the Vietnam War provides evidence against a structural Marxist position, but not against his own preferred statist alternative. This entails two absurdities: first that structural Marxism insists that capitalist states will be successful in every policy they pursue, and second that the 'autonomous' US state *desired* defeat abroad and disorder at home. Such are the lengths to which he is driven in order to differentiate his arguments from their Marxist alternative.

Skocpol's *States and Social Revolutions* presents a slightly different case, in that it avowedly draws much of its inspiration from Marxism, although in the end Marxism is found wanting. Rejecting two approaches to understanding revolutions (aggregate-psychological and systems/value consensus) out of hand, she opts to 'rely extensively upon certain ideas adapted from the Marxist and political-conflict perspectives'.[7] She faults Marxism, however, along with its competitors, as voluntaristic, neglectful of international structures and world-historical developments, and guilty of either analytically collapsing state and society or reducing political and state actions to representations of economic forces and interests. The structure of the argument is eccentric. She describes Marx as seeing revolutions as 'class-based movements growing out of objective structural contradictions within historically developing and inherently conflict-ridden societies', and argues the need to supplement this *structural* analysis with Tilly's political-conflict approach on the grounds that 'it is one thing to identify underlying, potential tensions rooted in objective class relations understood in a manner. It is another thing to understand how and when class members find themselves *able* to struggle effectively for their interests'.[8] She *then* introduces Marx's contrast between class in itself and class for itself, which might throw light on that very issue, *only* as evidence of voluntarism, in defiance of the structural perspective she has drawn from Marx only pages earlier. Finally, she cites one Marxist, Hobsbawm, in support of her critique of voluntarism, and another, Brenner, in support of her critique of the neo-Marxist Wallerstein, on whom she has drawn at length for her sketch of international and world-historical contexts. The break with classical and contemporary Marxism is more apparent than real.

When she turns to the potential autonomy of the state, Skocpol accuses Marxists, among others, of a 'general way of thinking' which views the state as 'nothing but *an arena* in which conflicts over basic social and economic interests are fought out', claiming that they 'regard the state as a system of organized coercion that invariably functions to support the superordinant

position of dominant classes or groups over subordinate classes or groups.'
In making this claim she dismisses classical Marxism in two paragraphs on
the grounds that within its terms 'it is. . .virtually impossible even to raise
the possibility that fundamental conflicts of interest might arise between
the existing dominant class. . .on the one hand, and the state rulers on the
other.'9 No reference is made to transitional periods, or to Bonapartism, or
to any other qualification of this view in classical Marxism. Mysteriously,
though, she also notes that classical Marxists 'do not analytically collapse
state and society', and characterizes the classical Marxist view as being that
'states are not simply created and manipulated by dominant classes'.10 When
she turns to contemporary Marxism, she notes its concern with the structural
constraints upon states, and its suggestion that 'state rulers may have to be
free of control by specific dominant-class groups and personnel if they are to
be able to implement policies that serve the fundamental interest of an entire
dominant class'. Finding two neo-Marxists (Trimberger and Block) who *do*
treat the state as potentially autonomous, she declares herself to have been
greatly influenced by them, only to charge other (un-named) individuals
with having 'carefully avoided' this line of argument, and to conclude by
obliterating the distinction between instrumental and structural approaches
in the claim that virtually all Marxists assume that 'state rulers cannot possibly
act against the *basic interests* of a dominant class' (emphasis mine), and
making the charge, denied two pages earlier, that Marxism does reflect 'the
enduring sociological proclivity to absorb the state into society'.11 She goes on
to argue, as if in opposition to Marxism, that the administrative, policing and
military organizations of the state are 'at least potentially autonomous from
direct dominant-class control': states compete with the dominant classes for
resources, and may pursue objectives at variance with theirs; in pursuit of
the maintenance of order and competition with other states they 'usually
do function to preserve existing economic and class structures', but may
develop distinct interests of their own. On the maintenance of order, she
argues as follows:

> Although both the state and the dominant class(es) share a broad interest in keeping the
> subordinate classes in place in society and at work in the existing economy, the state's own
> fundamental interest in maintaining sheer physical order and political peace may lead it –
> especially in periods of crisis – to enforce concessions to subordinate-class demands. These
> concessions may be at the expense of the interests of the dominant class, but not contrary to the
> state's own interests in controlling the population and collecting taxes and military recruits.12

On competition with other states, she argues that 'international military
pressures and opportunities can prompt state rulers to attempt policies that
conflict with, and even in extreme instances contradict, the fundamental
interests of a dominant class', undertaking military adventures that divert
resources from domestic development or undermine the position of dominant
socioeconomic interests, or responding to threats from abroad by launching
fundamental socioeconomic reforms or intervening to alter the course of

national economic development. These are the grounds on which Skocpol asserts the need for a new statism. However, the first offers a straightforward structural Marxist position, while the second stands in an indeterminate relationship to Marxist arguments. The dominant classes have an interest in the survival and competitiveness of the state, and the relationship between military action by the state abroad and dominant class interests demands exploration, as it is initially an open question whether the former furthers or is intended to further some of the latter; it cannot be presented by definitional fiat as independent action on the part of the state. Skocpol pursues none of these issues, and therefore cannot differentiate her position from Marxism. Her accounts of classical and contemporary Marxism are partial and contradictory, and where she breaks with Marxism, she persistently draws upon Marxists and neo-Marxists to do so. At times, as we shall see below, she draws on Marx himself. Finally, she does not pursue the issues she raises far enough to establish a novel position. In particular, she fails to consider whether a coherent account of the potential autonomy of the state could be derived from sources in classical and contemporary Marxism.

For such a consideration, finally spurned in a demonstration of consumer sovereignty similar to that offered by Stepan, we must turn to Nordlinger. He spells out precisely the basis in classical and contemporary Marxism for a consistent account of the recurrent and frequent autonomy of the state in a capitalist society, then dismisses it as a prelude to his presentation of his own 'state-centred' approach.[13] He identifies a primary view of the state in Marxism in which the state is an instrument of capital and an agent of the bourgeoisie, but accepts that a supplementary structural view explicitly sees the state as acting against the immediate interests of each.[14] Marxism is the only variant of empirical democratic theory 'that allows for, indeed clearly insists, that the state is able to act on its preferences when these diverge from those of the politically weightiest actors'.[15]

Nordlinger then announces that in order to differentiate his own approach from Marxism, he will show 'that the liberal capitalist state acts contrary to the demands of the bourgeoisie far more *often* than acknowledged in Marxist writings' (emphasis in the original). Taking each of Marxism's generalizations as given, 'without amending, subtracting from, or adding to them', he will demonstrate that 'on a straightforward reading, without any tortuous textual interpretations, Marxist theory itself points to the frequent occurrence of Type I state autonomy' (in which public officials translate their preferences into authoritative actions when state-society preferences are divergent). In addition he will do 'what Marxist scholars have not done, identifying and pulling together those aspects of the theory that indicate when and why the capitalist state acts contrary to bourgeois demands'.[16] Having made these claims, he cites Miliband to the effect that the view in the *Communist Manifesto* of the state as a committee for managing the common affairs of the whole bourgeoisie implies a need for autonomy, and lists a number

of other arguments drawn from recent Marxist writing: political divisions in
the dominant class create a need for mediation by the state; if it is to retain
legitimacy the state must respond to some extent to the demands of other
classes; and it needs autonomy both to carry out necessary reforms and to
reconcile the rationalities of individual capitalists to the imperatives of the
overall process of accumulation.[17]

Nordlinger provides no new arguments of his own, nor does he derive
any new arguments from Marxism. He offers no arguments that conflict
with basic premises of Marxism, nor does he combine the arguments he
assembles into a new synthesis. He simply provides, from Miliband, Offe,
Poulantzas, Block, Habermas, O'Connor and Wolfe – staple fare, one might
think, in debates over Marxism in the middle to late 1970s – ample evidence
that some Marxists do acknowledge, and that fundamental propositions in
Marxism do imply, a need for frequent and recurrent state autonomy. He
then turns to other matters, taking up Marxist theory again later only to
differentiate his state-centred model from it. He can do this only by forgetting
what he has clearly demonstrated 'on a straightforward reading, without any
tortuous textual interpretations', and claiming *both* that Marxism holds that
the autonomy of the state must be consistent, almost invariable, virtually
unswerving, and unaffected by the degree of societal opposition (a far cry
from frequent and recurrent, and not supported by any textual evidence),
and that it claims, in its primary society-centred thrust, that the need for state
intervention against bourgeois preferences is rare. In other words, having
demonstrated clearly the robust basis for a coherent synthesis, he arbitrarily
separates out and distorts its elements in order to be rid of it again. As with the
other statists, it seems that he has a theory of the autonomy of the democratic
state in Marxism, if he wants it, but that he does not want it.

As noted above, Krasner finds that a structural Marxist approach makes
sense of most of his material. Nordlinger, in contrast, barely considers
empirical material in what is an extended theoretical essay. In order to assess
further the competing claims of Marxism and statism we must therefore turn
to the empirical analysis pursued by Stepan and Skocpol respectively. We
shall find strong confirmation of Sartre's observation, recently recalled by
Michael Löwy, 'that Marxism is the ultimate possible horizon of our age and
that attempts to go beyond Marx frequently end up *falling short* of him'.[18]

Stepan concludes his discussion of Marxist approaches to the state with a
question he declines to answer: what are the *limits* of the relative autonomy
of the state? His subsequent analysis of relations between the Peruvian state
under Velasco and foreign capital makes no reference to Marxist debates, but
provides an answer which bears them out entirely. He outlines the attempt by
the Peruvian military to build a new economic foundation that was 'neither
capitalist nor communist', describing it as 'not a theoretically impossible
position to maintain'.[19] This comment perpetuates a persistent confusion
between an organic-statist *ideology*, and a pattern of economic development

which was still based on capitalist accumulation, but in which the state sought to impose its own priorities on domestic and foreign capital. It came up against structural limits identified by Marxism, and faithfully reflected in Stepan's descriptive account. In the sugar sector, of low priority to foreign capital, most production was in domestic hands, and the state was able to expropriate unwanted foreign investors, in part, as a brief footnote tells us, because the American Chamber of Commerce in Lima rejected their appeals for support on the grounds that more significant US investors might be hurt. However, the Peruvian state remained just as vulnerable to the sharp fluctuations of the global sugar market as they had been before. In the high priority oil sector, where initial investment needs and technological demands were very high, the state had to enter into a series of agreements which increasingly favoured foreign capital. And in the manufacturing sector, it was able to exclude some unwanted inward investment, but unable to implement plans that would have given national investors and workers eventual control over existing foreign enterprises, or to attract new foreign investment in priority areas. Overall, its reformist policies prompted an investment strike on the part of foreign and domestic capital which could not be offset by increased saving on the part of the state. This in turn prompted increasing reliance on foreign borrowing and led to the first debt crisis in the region. As a result 'by the middle of 1975 Peru was increasingly dependent on the international financial community for credit to fund its development program',[20] and in 1976 it signed an IMF agreement which froze wages, cut public spending, cancelled the right to strike, re-opened oil exploration to foreign firms, and began a programme of privatisation of state companies. A better illustration of the structural constraints which limit state autonomy vis-à-vis capital in the absence of a decisive break with reliance on capitalist accumulation would be hard to find. By restricting himself to a descriptive account of the potential for state autonomy *within* these limits, and failing to offer any theoretical analysis of the limits themselves, Stepan falls far short of a Marxist analysis in one major respect, and fails to challenge it in any other.

Skocpol's analysis of the French, Russian and Chinese revolutions suffers from similar problems. She argues at length that one of the primary factors which motivated state rulers was the need to force the pace of modernization in order to resist the military and commercial power of emerging capitalist rivals, concluding that 'revolutionary political crisis emerged in all three Old Regimes because agrarian structures impinged upon autocratic and protobureaucratic state organizations in ways that blocked or fettered monarchical initiatives in coping with escalating international military competition in a world undergoing uneven transformation by capitalism'.[21] She is able to differentiate herself from Marxism only by *choosing* to present 'monarchical initiatives' as divorced from class interests. As she is at pains to point out, these were absolutist regimes in pre-capitalist societies facing challenges from emerging capitalist rivals, not the modern representative states which Marx and Engels describe as committees for managing the affairs of the whole bourgeoisie. As they argue in the very same text, the constant revolutionizing of production characteristic of capitalism creates a world market, destroys established industries, makes the introduction of new ones a matter of life and death, and 'compels all nations, on pain of extinction, to adopt the bourgeois mode of production'.[22] In these circumstances, while bourgeoisies are not yet in control of the state in the absolutist monarchies, the dominant landed upper classes are 'unable to live in the old way', and Skocpol quotes Lenin to this effect at the head of the chapter. It is not inconsistent with a classical Marxist perspective to identify in such cases independent state projects aimed at modernization which go against existing dominant class interests. It is exactly what Marx describes and expects. If the projects which Skocpol describes seem to offer evidence against a Marxist perspective, it is because she fails to discriminate theoretically between precapitalist and capitalist societies, and ignores the structural context from which foreign pressures and threats from abroad emerge. Her version of the state is independent of class forces by definition, as she *presents* it as concerned purely with external defence and the maintenance of order at home, refusing to address the question of its possible class content.

Given these weaknesses, it is not surprising that Skocpol fails to notice the relevance of a Marxist perspective to her material. In the case of France, she describes an 'absolutist' state never entirely able to impose its will on the dominant landed class, and brought down in the end because its leading officers had largely entered the nobility and merged with the ruling classes; hence the inability of Louis XVI, on which she cites Bosher at some length, to restore his financial circumstances through a Chamber of Justice. This lends support to a central tenet of Marxist theory: by the time of the revolution the French state no longer had the relative autonomy Marxist theory recognizes as necessary; the nobility successfully resisted taxation and brought down the absolutist state and themselves with it. Equally, having denied herself the theoretical apparatus necessary to do so, Skocpol cannot decipher the bearing of state action on differing dominant class interests. She does not ask who among the dominant classes had a direct interest in 'military aggrandizement' and who did not, nor does she venture to distinguish between anachronistic imperial adventures on the one hand, and military action aimed at defending or broadening the scope for French entrepreneurs abroad on the other. Hence she talks indifferently of 'the vindication of French honor' and 'the protection of seaborne commerce' as raisons d'être of the French monarchy.[23] It is impossible to challenge a Marxist analysis of state-society relations in the revolutionary period without systematically addressing the class content of the French state, and the question of whether the French monarchy was or could become a vehicle for furthering bourgeois interests.

Finally, Skocpol's account of state-building in post-revolutionary France reveals her absolute failure to go beyond Marxism. She questions 'the until recently dominant "social interpretation" – a view of largely Marxist inspiration, which holds that the Revolution was led by the bourgeoisie to displace feudalism and the aristocracy and to establish capitalism instead', and opposes to it an account of 'changes wrought by the French revolution in the structure and functioning of the French state'.[24] Interestingly enough, she does so by prefacing her chapter with a passage from Marx which locates the origins of the 'modern state edifice' in France in the revolution, incorporating the phrase in the title of the chapter itself, describing the passage from Marx as the best available expression of what the revolution did accomplish, and concluding the chapter with a restatement and endorsement of his words:

> Indeed, the Revolution is best understood as a 'gigantic broom' that swept away the 'medieval rubbish' of seigneurialism and particularistic privilege – freeing the peasantry, private wealth-holders, and the state alike from the encumbrances of the Old Regime.[25]

If she does not go beyond Marx here, though, she certainly falls short of him. For there is no further consideration of Marx's analysis of the French state after the revolution. There is no other reference to *The Civil War in France*, and no reference at all to *The Class Struggles in France* or to *The Eighteenth Brumaire of Louis Bonaparte*. The former, it might be recalled, dwelt in its opening pages upon the obstacles to state autonomy arising from the indebtedness of the state to the financial aristocracy and upon the significance of the international context of the events of 1848, while the latter not only raised the issue of state autonomy, but also expressed fully the central theme of Skocpol's 'statist' alternative to a Marxist perspective:

> The task of the first French revolution was to destroy all separate local, territorial, urban and provincial powers in order to create the civil unity of the nation. It had to carry further the centralization that the absolute monarchy had begun, but at the same time it had to develop the extent, the attributes and the number of underlings of the governmental power. Napoleon perfected this state machinery.[26]

However, Marx went on to point out the contradictions and degeneration of the French state under the second Bonaparte, noting that he had been 'forced to create, alongside the real classes of society, an artificial caste for which the maintenance of his regime is a question of self-preservation', and concluding that 'the political centralization that modern society requires can arise only on the debris of the military and bureaucratic government machinery originally forged in opposition to feudalism.'[27] In comparison to Marx's richly suggestive dialectical account, Skocpol's is one-sided in the extreme.

A detailed examination of the early work of the new statists shows that although they concede more to Marxism than to any other rival approach, they seem to be at great pains to distance themselves from it. This emerges not so much in the perfectly legitimate advocacy of an alternative approach, as in the contortions in which they engage in order to justify it. Stepan describes a powerful analytical framework provided by Marxism, then opts to ignore it; Nordlinger claims the credit for discovering the potential for state autonomy present in classical and contemporary Marxism, then also ignores it; Krasner involves himself in convoluted efforts to get the better of a Marxist reading of events which he finds convincing; and Skocpol eventually relies directly upon Marx himself to take her where Marxism fears to tread. There is never an attempt to grapple with Marxist theory as a whole; selective readings and consequential distortions and misunderstandings abound; where substantive issues are pursued, a fairly straightforward Marxist analysis still proves more fruitful than the statist alternative; and overall, on the evidence of these accounts, the attempt to establish a robust statist alternative to Marxism fails. Against this inauspicious background, the new statism was to assume programmatic form.

Bringing the State Back In

With the setting up in 1983 of the SSRC Research Planning Committee on States and Social Structures and the publication in 1985 of *Bringing the State Back In*, the new statism received the official blessing of the social science establishment in the United States, and delivered its public manifesto.[28] In some contributions, notably Skocpol's introduction and Stepan's analysis of military withdrawal from power in Latin America, the emphases of the early statists are carried forward and accentuated. Skocpol presents an even cruder caricature of the Marxist tradition, omitting the structural position entirely from her account, and immediately claiming as superior to Marxism an analysis which is entirely consistent with it. Stepan progresses from his earlier strategy of avoidance (stating the Marxist case but refusing to consider it) to Krasner's alternative strategy (showing how well a Marxist analysis works, then wriggling out of it on a pretext). At the same time, two new and rather contradictory dimensions are introduced. The first is the ambitious call for a paradigmatic reorientation of social science, involving the incorporation of elements of Weberian and Marxist traditions among others into a new synthesis; the second is a rejection of 'grand theory' which leads to a point-blank refusal to attempt any new synthesis or to spell out in any way the theoretical basis of the new stand taken. As a consequence key contributions to the collection confirm the emptiness of 'statism', and point the way back to Marxism.

In her introduction to the collection, Skocpol defends a view of states 'as social actors and as society-shaping structures'. She characterizes Marx as a 'society-centered' theorist who ignores the state (in defiance of her earlier qualification of this view, and her use of his work on the French state), and makes the mistaken assumption that 'nineteenth century British socioeconomic developments presaged the future for all countries and for the world as a whole'.[29] Having thus disposed of Marx, she presents contemporary neo-Marxism as addressing the lack of attention to the state in post-war US structure-functionalism, thus divorcing it from the theoretical tradition inaugurated by Marx. She can then present it as above all concerned with *the state*, rather than with *class*, and hence assimilable into a new synthesis if it will abandon its dogmatic assumption that 'at base, states are inherently shaped by classes or class struggles and function to preserve and expand modes of production'.[30]

Skocpol chides Marxists, then, with failing to grant 'true autonomy' to states. This formulation conceals an essential strategic ambiguity, between entire and permanent independence from class and social constraints on the one hand, and a temporary and partial autonomy on the other. In combination with her failure to address structural Marxist debates, it allows her to reject Marxism for failing to recognize the former, then to pass her own work off as superior because it demonstrates the latter. This is best observed in her use of her work with Finegold on New Deal agricultural policy, which she sees as providing evidence of autonomous state contributions to domestic policy making. In fact, a structural Marxist interpretation fits the case exactly, as, in Skocpol's own words, intervention involved 'policies that responded to a long-standing "agrarian crisis" but *not* simply in ways directly demanded by powerful farm interest groups'.[31] What is more, the institutions created for the purpose were geared primarily to price support, which hardly threatened dominant class interests, and the fragility of the interventionist effort was swiftly revealed, when commercial farmers' organizations took over within a couple of years and directly pursued their class interests through the new institutions. Finegold's own summary elsewhere confirms that the case offers no challenge of any kind to Marxist theory:

> Taken together, business opinion, the Democratic Party, the federal agricultural complex, and the farmer organizations explain the enactment and successful implementation of the agricultural adjustment program. The same factors served as conservative influences upon the AAA, ensuring that it addressed the problem of farmer prosperity without challenging the position of the dominant class interests within agriculture.[32]

Whereas Skocpol dismisses Marx as 'society-centred', Stepan makes direct reference to his analysis of Bonapartism in his analysis of state-society relations under military rule in Latin America. He notes that in every case analyzed (Argentina, Brazil, Chile and Uruguay) 'the bourgeoisie provided the social base for the new authoritarian regimes, whose first political acts were the use of the coercive apparatus of the state (located institutionally in the army) to dismantle and disarticulate working-class organizations'. He then claims that all four regimes 'began with periods in which the institutions of civil society were emasculated while the state enhanced its ability to pursue its own goals' (though without saying how these might or might not relate to class interests), and asks 'how much direct political (or, in extreme cases, economic) power are the state's bourgeois allies willing to abdicate in a brumairean sense in return for defensive protection?'[33] Given his other concerns in the essay he does not pursue the answer as methodically as he might. However, examination of the cases as he presents them does reveal a consistent answer: in every case, the bourgeois allies of the regime were willing to support authoritarian rule for as long as a threat of working-class militancy remained, and the regime appeared to have their general interests at heart. And once the bourgeoisie withdrew their support, return to civilian rule ensued fairly promptly. The Chilean case is dealt with in the most detail, and eventually reveals, to Stepan's satisfaction, the weakness of a structural Marxist perspective. He ascribes the ability of the state under Pinochet to implement its authoritarian project to the intensity of class conflict during the preceding period, and the threat of a recomposition of the Marxist opposition, providing evidence that among producer groups and the upper class in general there was widespread fear at the beginning of the 1980s of a possible return of the left to power, and widespread recognition of the need for long-term structural change in society and the economy if that possibility was to be ruled out for the future. On this basis he offers the following original contribution to Marxist theory:

> One might even go so far as to argue that the Chilean state represents a step beyond Bonapartism. Instead of exchanging the right to rule for the right to make money in the classic Bonapartist transaction, significant fractions of the Chilean bourgeoisie abdicated the right to rule and severely jeopardized their right to make money in the short run in the hope of preserving class privilege in the long run.[34]

Stepan has stumbled here on a central contention of a structural Marxist perspective, which does indeed go beyond Bonapartism: that the state must at times intervene against some of the interests of the bourgeoisie if the long-term prospects for accumulation are to be preserved. However, he manages to find reasons to dismiss such a perspective. Noting that such events are not in themselves unusual, he asserts that 'what is unusual about the Chilean case is that the state was able to persist in this strategy for almost a decade':

> The question raised by the Chilean case, then, was how long the state could continue to find support for a project that stood in objective contradiction to the requirements of local capital accumulation. The fact that it did so for as long as it did must be considered a strong challenge to theories of the 'capitalist state'.[35]

On the contrary, this must be considered the most bizarre argument ever mounted in defence of the superiority of a statist perspective over Marxism. Bonapartism itself lasted more than twice as long, and far from standing in objective contradiction to the requirements of local capital accumulation, the Chilean state project was intended to restore and preserve them. Stepan's own informants told him explicitly that a long-term period of authoritarian rule was necessary if their interests were to be protected. In any case, within a structural Marxist perspective one might well expect an authoritarian regime founded in a moment of grave weakness on the part of the bourgeoisie to succeed in overstaying its welcome for a while. It is not surprising, given the terms of the authoritarian constitution, that Pinochet should have survived in power through the 1980s. The Chilean bourgeoisie dispensed with him at the first moment which seemed to be consistent with the continued protection of their class interests against the proletariat.

The impression given by these two contributions is that the enterprise of 'bringing the state back in' is more fruitfully conducted within a Marxist frame of reference rather than in opposition to it. This is confirmed by a contribution from Skocpol's co-editors, Dietrich Rueschemeyer and Peter Evans, which avoids ill-informed polemics with Marxism, declines to pursue the will-o'-the-wisp of 'true autonomy', and draws heavily on Marxist theory in its examination of state intervention in the areas of capital accumulation and distribution. Rueschemeyer and Evans distinguish carefully between states in capitalist, pre-capitalist and peripheral capitalist social formations, follow contemporary Marxist analysis in noting the strict limits to the autonomy of any capitalist state, and generally explore real world variations consistent with an overall Marxist framework of analysis. Their judicious summary of the scope of their work makes it clear that their concern with the institutional requirements for state capacity supplements rather than replaces a broader theoretical analysis. They depict state intervention as seeking to enable 'capitalist political economies to foster economic growth and manage socio-economic conflicts', note that limits to its capacity to do so may arise from the internal structure of the state and from its relation to the class structure of society, and conclude as follows:

> The analysis here has focused on two propositions concerning the conditions under which these limitations may be overcome. First, in order to undertake effective interventions, the state must constitute a bureaucratic apparatus with sufficient corporate coherence. Second, a certain degree of autonomy from the dominant interests in a capitalist society is necessary not only to make coherent state action in pursuit of any consistent policy conception possible, but also because some of the competing interests in economy and society, even structurally dominant ones, will have to be sacrificed in order to achieve systemically required "collective goods" that cannot be provided by partial interests. Although our energies have been devoted primarily to modifying these propositions, they have remained substantially supported.[36]

There is of course room for constructive debate as to the implications of these propositions, and the kinds of theoretical frameworks within which they might best be developed. The first is as much Marxist as Weberian, as Skocpol and Stepan attest when they draw on Marx and Engels respectively on the state, while the second rests primarily on classical and contemporary Marxism. More to the point, given the arbitrary dichotomy set up by Skocpol between grand theory on the one hand and historically sensitive case study analysis on the other, it reflects a commitment to a theoretically informed *and* historically based method of analysis, a commitment which it shares with classical Marxism and the bulk of contemporary Marxism. It is only by bracketing Marxism with contemporary structure-functionalism and refusing to admit the existence of theoretically informed empirical analysis within the Marxist tradition that it is possible to sustain the illusion that the programme of *Bringing the State Back In*, where it is defensible, constitutes either a challenge to Marxism or an advance upon it.

The New Institutionalists

The 'new statism' has now largely given way to a 'new institutionalism' in which the emphasis upon the autonomy of the state has shifted to a more balanced analysis of its relations with society, or more broadly with its environment. Some of its concerns were foreshadowed by Krasner, in a 1984 review of recent writing on the state. He argued that in addition to its concern for the state as 'an actor in its own right', this saw politics more as a problem of rule and control than of allocation; emphasized institutional constraints on individual behaviour; saw current institutional structures as products of past conjunctures, and current paths of change as products of past choices; and rejected the view that structures exist because they perform certain functions in favour of a focus on disjunctures, and stress and uncertainty about the rules of the game.[37] For the new institutionalists, the polity is a relatively autonomous institutional sphere; institutions tend to persist over time; institutional codes and constraints invalidate interpretations of behaviour as rational maximization; change is path-dependent, hence not predictable; and as a consequence, the particular history of processes of change must be explored; and functional explanations for outcomes are ruled out. They focus on disparities between environmental and institutional change and between optimal and actual outcomes, and on the institutional shaping of behaviour, and see institutions as mediating between macro and micro phenomena in a complex manner which makes the tracing of simple invariant connections between them impossible. They seek to 'bring politics back in'; and a specific element in the treatment of politics as a relatively independent sphere is a continuing focus upon the state, as the most significant of all social institutions. However, the focus is generally explicitly on state-society relations, and views differ on the extent to which it is possible or appropriate to see the state as an actor. The objective now, it appears, is to 'get inside the state', and explore its internal structure and its complex links with various social actors.

At its best, the new institutionalism raises significant issues, but because it shares the statists' antipathy to 'grand theory', it proves unable to resolve them. Krasner's institutional perspective for the understanding of sovereignty illustrates the point.[38] His attempt to develop a rigorous analytical framework on the basis of the ideas of institutional persistence and path-dependency breaks down precisely because of his unwillingness to adopt *any* 'grand theoretical' framework. Institutionalization is defined as 'the tendency of behaviour, norms, or formal structures to persist through time', and Krasner argues that 'the basic characteristic of an institutional argument is that prior institutional choices limit available future options'. Thus 'while an institutionalist argument does not maintain that. . .rapid change never occurs', it does imply that such episodes are infrequent and are followed by long periods of either relative stasis or path-dependent change.[39] Here he draws an analogy with 'punctuated equilibrium' in evolutionary theory, which opposes to the Darwinian view a picture of long periods of stasis broken by rapid change in marginal, isolated subspecies, fortuitous adaptation, and a view of structure as primary and constraining, rather than permissive of continuous marginal change. Explanation must take into account both structures (institutions) and environmental incentives; change is difficult, as once established a particular institutional structure tends to maintain itself or channel future change; optimal adaptation is not always possible, as choices at one point in time limit future possibilities; historical origin and present utility may require different explanations, as structural features evolved for one reason may later be put to different uses; and explanation rather than prediction ought to be the primary objective of science.[40]

In Krasner's work, as among the new institutionalists in general, ideas regarding institutional persistence are generally far more fully elaborated than ideas concerning origins, or change. However, none treats institutions as permanent. In each case, we are dealing with a cycle, in which lengthy periods of institutional persistence are broken by rapid change in which old institutions disappear, and new ones originate. Here lies the theoretical problem at the centre of the new institutionalist approach. Until the concept of institutional persistence is located in a broader theoretical framework, it is impossible either to decide whether it reflects successful adaptation or resistance, or whether it challenges or confirms functionality; equally, it is impossible to explain the periods of rapid change which do occur. It remains arbitrary at a macro-structural level. This implies a need to explore not only the roots of institutional persistence, but also its relationship to underlying forces for change, and the conditions under which it will be overcome. In other words, it implies the need for a theory of history. In the absence of one, Krasner cannot move from the idea of institutional persistence to an explanation of change over the longer term; and he admits as much when he notes that his model lacks any mechanism to parallel the role of allotropic speciation in 'punctuated equilibrium' theory. He can explain equilibrium, but not punctuation. In contrast, Marxism does of course have a theory of history, famously laid out in the Preface to *A Contribution to the Critique of Political Economy*, and one, what is more, which envisages and explains long periods of path-dependent development, interspersed by episodes of rapid change. Krasner's development of the idea of institutional persistence reveals the need for something like it, and suggests that the new institutionalists have yet to produce a coherent theoretical framework.

If at best the new institutionalism confirms the need for an integration of 'grand theory' and detailed empirical investigation, at worst it is simply a retreat from statism. This is best reflected in Skocpol's introduction, written jointly with Weir and Orloff, to *The Politics of Social Security in the United States*. This approaches the history of social provision in the United States from an 'institutional-political process' perspective, and in doing so departs from earlier statist arguments:

Many of the puzzles about American social politics left unresolved by. . .alternative theoretical persuasions. . .can be addressed anew from what we shall call an 'institutional-political process' perspective. This approach examines state formation and the state's institutional structure in both societal and historical context. Political struggles and policy outcomes are presumed to be jointly conditioned by the institutional arrangements of the state and by class and other social relationships, but never once and for all. For states and social structures are themselves transformed over time. And so are the goals and capacities of politically active groups, in part because of ongoing transformations of political and social structures, and in part because of the effects of earlier state policies on subsequent political struggles and debates.[41]

This 'post-statist' approach rejects abstract, ahistorical, single-factor or generalizing styles of explanation, but does not claim explanatory primacy either for the state in particular, or for institutions in general. It opts instead for the anodyne concept of 'joint conditioning': rather than a new theoretical framework, it is a decision not to have one at all. In presenting it, Weir, Orloff and Skocpol reject in turn approaches based upon *economism*, the *logic of industrialism, culture*, and *class politics*. These approaches are considered separately, and dismissed on narrow grounds in turn, with no effort to assess either the general claims or potential of each individual approach, or their joint explanatory potential. Elements of each are then combined into a new descriptive synthesis, to which nothing is added. Thus

the historical particularities of U.S. state formation, *when understood in relationship to capitalist economic development, urbanization, and transformations of liberal values*, explain the distinctive rhythms and limits of American social policy making more effectively than do socioeconomic or cultural processes abstracted from the institutional contexts of national politics (emphasis mine).[42]

The institutional-political process perspective collapses here into a statement of the need for an awareness of historical particularity in the analysis of particular historical situations, with no *theoretical* force behind it; its institutional element consists of the assertion that institutional change cannot be explained without reference to institutions. It is neither a coherent theoretical framework, nor an explanation, but rather a descriptive synthesis which borrows from the different explanations which have previously been assessed serially and found wanting, giving no clue as to the theoretical principles upon which explanations should be constructed. Not surprisingly, after all the talk of new approaches, it turns out to be perfectly compatible with class analysis. A footnote informs us that the institutional-political process perspective

is not shared by all the contributors to this volume, but the editors believe that the arguments of all the papers fit within this frame of reference. Several contributors also explicitly develop analytical insights consistent with perspectives that emphasize capitalism and class relations.[43]

This candid admission rather gives the game away. As it lacks any theoretical content of its own, the institutional-political process perspective must import some from outside. As it happens, while Weir, Orloff and Skocpol touch on various elements of Marxist argument in their dismissal of approaches based on economism, the logic of industrialism, class politics and culture, they do not consider the potential of a holistic Marxist approach attentive to the issues of accumulation, class struggle and ideology. This would provide an integrated perspective on the issues they dismiss separately then bring together into their own synthesis under the descriptive categories of economism/logic of industrialism, class politics, and culture. As far as Marxism is concerned, they proceed by considering elements of a complex whole in isolation, and rejecting them in turn as one-dimensional, only to present as superior a synthesis of those same elements, stripped of any theoretical content.

An example of the same technique on a much grander scale can be found in Hall's study of post-war economic policy in Britain and France, with its focus on the institutional logic of the process of economic intervention in the industrialized democracies. Hall emphasises 'the institutional relationships . . . that bind the components of the state together and structure its relations with society', adding that the concept of institutions refers to the 'formal rules, compliance procedures, and standard operating practices that structure the relationship between individuals in various units of the polity and economy'.[44] However, as his study develops, the scope of the 'institutional' framework expands to include major organizational or structural variables of an all-embracing kind: 'the organization of labor, the organization of capital, the organization of the state, the organization of the political system, and the structural position of the country within the international economy'.[45] His institutionalism operates on two quite distinctive levels, and incorporates at the second level five major macro-structural variables which encompass the state and the entire social, political and international environment within which it operates. This treatment of all micro-structural and macro-structural elements relating to the state *and* its environment as 'institutional' simply produces a return to a familiar macro-structural style of analysis, with very little that is distinctively 'institutional' about it. The illusion of novelty is created, however, as by Weir, Orloff and Skocpol, by an initial review and rejection of *functionalist* (system) theory, *cultural, public choice, group* (pluralist or class), and *state-centric* approaches, and a subsequent reincorporation of elements of each into a descriptive synthesis. He follows Weir, Orloff and Skocpol in declining to consider an integrated Marxist perspective as an alternative to his own, choosing instead to allocate Marxists variously to the functionalist, cultural and group theory categories. Marxism is then rejected as functionalist in its treatment of accumulation and legitimation, and teleological in its positing of a superordinate 'system' with a status beyond that of the institutions themselves. This portrayal of Marxism, made possible only by an arbitrary scattering of different Marxist approaches between different analytical categories, and a one-sided reading of the work of Poulantzas, provides the cover he needs to present a thoroughly Marxist argument throughout his account, and pass it off as institutionalist.

This is clearest in his handling of the French case. Here he not only adopts a straightforward structural Marxist approach, but also reintroduces the functionalism that had earlier been dismissed:

> We might summarize the role of the French Plan by saying that it served two basic purposes. Its primary task was the modernization and reorganization of the nation's productive apparatus. In that respect it was the centre-piece of a strategy of state-led growth. This entailed a measure of economic triage, letting the more inefficient sectors of French industry die – in some cases from exposure to the global market – and strengthening the sectors with apparent competitive potential in manufacturing and agriculture. However, this kind of activity inevitably generated social dislocation and resistance. Accordingly the Plan also served a second purpose – to prevent social conflict – a task that was accomplished in three ways: by masking individual loss with the veneer of common interest, by presenting industrial execution as economic euthanasia, and by tying present sacrifice to future gain. These functions were especially important in such a fragmented society.[46]

He then follows the logic of structural Marxism, depicting with striking faithfulness in his account of French planning a state that is actually able to foster accumulation and maintain legitimacy. The French state, on Hall's account, was able to take the lead in both economic restructuring and the building of consent. It was able to eliminate inefficient industry and promote new sectors, masking individual loss with the veneer of common interest, and tying present sacrifice to future gain. It was able, in other words, to develop, impose and win support for a long term strategy of economic restructuring aimed at fitting France for a leading place in an increasingly competitive world economy. This was not bound to happen, of course, but Hall has no problem with the fact that it did, or with the resort to functionalist arguments to 'explain' it. In addition, the logic of the comparison of the French and British cases rest squarely on the issue of relative autonomy. In Britain, Hall argues, it was the rule for industry to be asked to rationalize itself, while behind the motif of indicative planning in the French case there lay 'an apparatus with the capacity to put real pressure on private sector actors to conform to the government's economic strategy'.[47] He later goes to some lengths to differentiate his concept of *étatisme* from the Marxist concept of relative autonomy, on the grounds that the latter term was 'originally intended to describe the independence of the state vis-à-vis capital. *Etatisme* refers to a more general kind of independence and power relative to a broader range of social actors'.[48] The distinction is valid, but entirely irrelevant, as Hall's account of the decline of French planning in the 1960s and 1970s does revolve exclusively around the French state's growing closeness to capital, and the resulting weakening of the ability to deliver accumulation and legitimacy. He argues that as industrial planning succeeded, the state grew closer to large firms in the most advanced sectors in the periods of the Fifth and Sixth Plans, creating a new joint elite while simultaneously the producers' association, the CNPF, was taken over by the large modern exporting firms who were the big beneficiaries of planning. Its new leaders virtually wrote the Sixth Plan, and the government 'appeared to have abdicated responsibility for socioeconomic management to one segment of industry'. The state lost legitimacy because 'the ability of the public to regard the state as an independent entity was eroded by the increasingly close connections between the representatives of capital and the state, which the planning process encouraged'.[49] The concept of *étatisme* is no doubt different from that of relative state autonomy, but here it functions strictly as a decoy.

Failing to advance on Marxism, Hall falls short instead. He fails to apply to France the 'institutional' approach introduced in his discussion of Britain and in his closing comparative essay – in particular as regards the organization of capital, and the situation of France in the international economy. Had he pursued the analysis, elements which he addresses separately would come together in a single coherent argument: France, more than most other leading Western economies, emerged into the mid-twentieth century with a relatively large peasantry and fragmented bourgeoisie in which small capital had a particularly prominent role. Determined to put the French economy on a level with its international competitors, the leaders of the French state embarked on a programme of planned industrialization. Responding to changes in the French economy and in the international market, the planning process came to concentrate on the largest and most advanced exporting firms. This was essential if the process of accumulation was to continue; but it had negative effects for legitimation. Hence planning was undermined by the contradictions it generated. The virtue of a holistic perspective of this kind is that it reveals the structural constraints arising essentially as a consequence of France's late industrial modernization in a global economy increasingly dominated by large multinational corporations. Without it, it is impossible to decipher the significance of state penetration of the private sector, or private sector penetration of the state, with which Hall is greatly concerned.

The significance of this analysis, beyond its direct implications for the status of Hall's argument, is that it confirms the conclusions reached above with regard to the indeterminacy of an institutionalist perspective if it is not set in a broader macro-structural theoretical framework. Hall's intuitive analytical strategy illuminates the issue with painful clarity. At exactly the point where his micro-level institutionalism, focussed on 'formal rules, compliance procedures, and standard operating practices' loses explanatory power, he switches to a macro-level institutionalism which turns out to be an integrated Marxist perspective informed by class and structural logic. As he appears unaware of the nature of this break in his argument, and unable in consequence to draw full benefit from it, there could be no more compelling demonstration of the need for a broad macro-structural theory, and the ability of Marxism to provide one.

Finally, I turn to a quite different strain of institutionalism, which has developed under the influence of rational choice theory and methodological individualism, exemplified here by Margaret Levi's *Of Rule and Revenue*.[50]

Levi focusses on individuals (rulers) rather than structures (states), and offers the central hypothesis that 'rulers maximize the revenue accruing to the state subject to the constraints of their relative bargaining power, transaction costs, and discount rates'.[51] Her theoretical framework emerges out of and breaks with a Marxist perspective, and she is precise as to the manner in which it does so. She argues that the Marxist tradition provides 'the best guidance for determining the most significant macro-level variables affecting a political economic system', and notes that her central perspective has some affinity with classical Marxism in that

> dilemmas of predatory rule are consistent with the primary contradiction of economic development as put forward by Marx and Engels: The property rights that serve the dominant interests of society come into conflict over time with innovations in technology and economic organization and with the new and powerful classes these innovations create.[52]

However, 'the theory of predatory rule differs from the classical Marxist approach in its focus on rulers rather than on the dominant economic class'; by eliminating the emphasis on class as the primary historical actor and undertaking instead the investigation of individuals, it gains more general application. In sharp contrast to the other institutionalists reviewed here, she adopts an uncompromisingly 'statist' perspective, albeit at the level of the ruler as individual, and claims universal applicability for her 'theory of predatory rule': state actors have interests of their own; they are not 'simply handmaidens of the dominant economic class or other influential actors. They will act in their own interests when and if they can'; rulers are predatory in that 'they try to extract as much revenue as they can from the population'.[53]

Levi asserts that by down-grading class from a prime mover to a variable among other variables she broadens the scope of her theory, but in doing so she glosses over the fact that if the theory is proposed as universal, class, and the rise of capitalism, become variables which make no difference. Whatever the historical context, rulers continue to maximize revenues, subject to structurally invariant constraints. The model is intended to have universal validity, from ancient Rome to contemporary Australia: to be applicable to all rulers and all societies in which the raising of revenue occurs, be they elected prime ministers or absolute monarchs, modern capitalist economies or ancient empires. I shall suggest here, taking the case study of the 1799 English tax reform as illustrative, that on her own evidence it does not apply to any capitalist society. Far from being a successful generalization which supplants Marxism, the theory of predatory rule is an over-generalization which confirms the wisdom of the historicity of Marxism. In its effort to be universal, it obscures the particular logic of capitalist society that a Marxist analysis captures.

A simple Marxist hypothesis to pose against Levi's universalizing logic is that as societies become more fully characterized by capitalist relations of production, and more subject to the logic of capitalist accumulation, the taxation policies of rulers are likely to change to reflect the new logic of social reproduction, the class alliances supporting them, and the structural implications of their stances with regard to accumulation and legitimation. This makes more sense of the imposition of income tax in Britain in 1799 than Levi's own account is able to do. She claims that it 'demonstrates that even rulers reluctant to maximize revenue are compelled to choose policies that increase returns to the state',[54] but a close analysis suggests that it does so in a way that supports a structural Marxist interpretation over her own.

The circumstances in which William Pitt the Younger introduced income tax were exceptional. Costly wars had put the state under severe fiscal pressure. Mounting national debt repayments were eating increasingly into what revenues were available. The American colonies had been recently lost. Napoleon, at the head of the new fighting machine that had emerged in the wake of the French Revolution, declared war at this juncture. Levi explains that

> Those in Parliament shared the popular consensus that French aggression posed a particularly severe risk. They feared that the French would strip Britain of her commercial advantages and that French radical ideologies would incite an already restless British populace to rebellion. Landed interests sensed a threat to their own social and material well-being and were generally willing to cooperate to repel the enemy.[55]

The introduction of income tax clearly reflected the logic of class interests, as related to the twin issues of accumulation and legitimation. Whatever Pitt's 'own' interests were, they do not seem to have differed from those of the societal groups Levi persistently presents as the source of 'constraints' on the predatory ambitions of rulers. In fact Levi rounds off the study with the observation that

> Pitt's personal aims were neither to build a bigger state nor to extract all the revenue that could in principle be extracted. He believed in a limited state that carried out its limited responsibilities efficiently. After all, he was a self-professed follower of Adam Smith. . . .War compelled Pitt to become a revenue maximizer. He sought the income tax because it was the most lucrative available means for producing revenue. However, he came to this policy reluctantly. The logic of institutional change – the necessary evolution of the state to meet new demands within a changed economy – required that, whatever his personal goals, he, as chief executive, maximize revenue to the state.[56]

This statement alone comprehensively refutes her claim to have produced a superior analytical alternative to Marxism. It flatly contradicts the central organizing claim of the theory of predatory rule, as it shows that Pitt's 'personal' aims were *sacrificed* when he moved to maximize revenues to the state. But as the preceding argument has made clear, although Levi is silent on the point here, war was seen as necessary to preserve the developing capitalist system. Pitt's acceptance of the need to make war on France was perfectly consistent with Smith's doctrines with regard to the role of the state – whose liberalism specifically endorsed the state's responsibility for national defence – and with the view that the state should normally minimize its revenue demands. Pitt did not consistently seek to maximize revenue. On the contrary, his attitude to revenue-raising varied directly, on this account, in accordance with the requirements of the developing national capitalist economy. Here as elsewhere, the case study suggests that revenue maximization is a feature of "abnormal times", and a sign of crisis. This suggests in turn that Levi is as much in need of a theory of history as the new institutionalists reviewed above, but less likely to see the need because of her determination to present her argument as good for all times. She does acknowledge at one point, as a limitation of the model, that 'the analysis of ruler behavior becomes considerably more difficult in modern polities or where rulers are a collection of individuals rather than a single individual'.[57] There is a simple reason for this. In modern (capitalist) polities, rulers have no personal or macro (systemic) reasons to give priority as a rule to the maximization of revenues. Forms and levels of revenue raising, and patterns of expenditure, will vary in accordance with the logic of class struggle and capitalist reproduction. Where rulers develop an interest in the maximization of revenue for personal gain, we are in the realm of delinquency, as we were, on Levi's account, in late Republican Rome.

Conclusion

In their different ways, Krasner's attempt to provide a framework for institutional analysis, Weir, Skocpol and Orloff's attempt to establish an institutional-political process perspective, Hall's attempt to provide an in-stitutional analysis of British and French economic development, and Levi's attempt to formulate a universal theory of predatory rule, all end in failure. They do so, like the statists and just as ironically in view of their self-conscious antagonism to Marxism, in ways which suggest the strength of a Marxist perspective. This is in almost every case a consequence of two simple errors. The first is the polarisation of theory on the one hand and history on the other, as in the rejection of grand theory in favour of historically situated case studies, and the treatment of Marxism as functionalist and teleological, which rules out the possibility of a dialectical *theory of history*, and recognition of Marxism as one such theory. The second is a failure to approach Marxist commentaries on the state in the context of the wider corpus of Marxist theory, from which they cannot be detached. A decade ago, when contemporary Marxist theory was much in vogue, it was impossible to pretend that classical and contemporary Marxism had not addressed the issue of the state. Hence the recognition of these debates, distorted though it is, in the work of the first new statists. Ten years on, intellectual fashions have changed, memories have faded, and Marxism can be ignored or caricatured with greater ease. However, the shelf life of competing theories appears to be shorter with each new candidate. The works reviewed above fail to establish a viable alternative to Marxism, and the most intellectually substantial of them – Skocpol's *States and Social Revolutions*, Krasner's *Defending the National Interest* and his institutional perspective on sovereignty, and Levi's *Of Rule and Revenue*, precisely because they make the most serious effort to do so, point the way most clearly back to Marxism.

NOTES

1. A. Stepan, *The State and Society: Peru In Comparative Perspective*, Princeton, 1978, p. xi.
2. *Ibid.*, pp. 17–18.
3. *Ibid.*, pp. 19–24.
4. S. Krasner, *Defending the National Interest: Raw Materials Investments and US Foreign Policy*, Princeton, 1978, p. 12. In what follows, I summarise a fuller discussion in P. Cammack, 'Bringing the State Back In?', *British Journal of Political Science*, 19, 1989, pp. 269–274.
5. *Ibid.*, pp. 332–3.
6. *Ibid.*, p. 333.
7. T. Skocpol, *States and Social Revolutions: A Comparative Analysis of France, Russia and China*, Cambridge, 1979, p. 13.
8. *Ibid.*, pp. 7, 13.
9. *Ibid.*, pp. 25–6.
10. *Ibid.*, pp. 26–28.
11. *Ibid.*, pp. 27–8.
12. *Ibid.*, p. 30.
13. E. Nordlinger, *On the Autonomy of the Democratic State*, Cambridge, Mass., 1981.
14. *Ibid.*, pp. 47–48.
15. *Ibid.*, p. 119.
16. *Ibid.*, p. 175.
17. *Ibid.*, pp. 175–180.
18. M. Löwy, 'The Poetry of the Past': Marx and the French Revolution', *New Left Review*, 177, September–October 1989, p. 114.
19. *Ibid.*, p. 289.
20. *Ibid.*, p. 286.
21. Skocpol, *States and Social Revolutions*, pp. 47 and 99.
22. K. Marx and F. Engels, *Manifesto of the Communist Party*, in K. Marx, *The Revolutions of 1848*, ed. D. Fernbach, London, 1973, p. 71.
23. Skocpol, *States and Social Revolutions*, p. 60.
24. *Ibid.*, pp. 174–5.
25. *Ibid.*, p. 205.
26. K. Marx, *The Eighteenth Brumaire of Louis Bonaparte*, in K. Marx, *Surveys from Exile*, ed. D. Fernbach, London, 1973, p. 237.
27. *Ibid.*, p. 243 and pp. 244–5.
28. P. Evans, D. Rueschemeyer and T. Skocpol, eds, *Bringing the State Back In*, New York, 1985. I summarise and extend here arguments developed in P. Cammack, 'Bringing the State Back In?', *op. cit.*
29. T. Skocpol, 'Bringing the State Back In: Strategies of Analysis in Current Research', in Evans, Rueschemeyer and Skocpol, eds, *Bringing the State Back In*, p. 6.

30. *Ibid.*, p. 5.
31. *Ibid.*, p. 13.
32. K. Finegold, 'From Agrarianism to Adjustment: The Political Origins of New Deal Agricultural Policy', *Politics & Society*, 11, 1982, p. 25.
33. A. Stepan, 'State Power and the Strength of Civil Society in the Southern Cone of Latin America', in P. Evans et al., eds, *Bringing the State Back In*, p. 318.
34. *Ibid.*, p. 324.
35. *Ibid.*, p. 324.
36. D. Rueschemeyer and P. Evans, 'The State and Economic Transformation: Toward an Analysis of the Conditions Underlying Effective Intervention', in P. Evans, et al., *Bringing the State Back In*, p. 68.
37. S. Krasner, 'Approaches to the State: Alternative Conceptions and Historical Dynamics', *Comparative Politics*, 16, 2, 1984, pp. 224–5.
38. S. Krasner, 'Sovereignty: An Institutional Perspective', *Comparative Political Studies*, 21, 1, April 1988.
39. *Ibid.*, pp. 71, 74.
40. *Ibid.*, pp. 79–80.
41. M. Weir, A. Orloff and T. Skocpol, 'Understanding American Social Politics', in Weir, Orloff and Skocpol, eds, *The Politics of Social Security in the United States*, Chicago, 1988, pp. 16–17.
42. *Ibid.*, p. 17.
43. *Ibid.* ft. 29, p. 17.
44. P. Hall, *Governing the Economy: The Politics of State Intervention in Britain and France*, Cambridge, 1986, p. 19.
45. *Ibid.*, p. 259.
46. *Ibid.*, p. 163.
47. *Ibid.*, pp. 54, 162.
48. *Ibid.*, ft. 1, p. 288.
49. *Ibid.*, pp. 171, 176–7.
50. M. Levi, *Of Rule and Revenue*, Berkeley, 1988.
51. *Ibid.*, p. 2.
52. *Ibid.*, pp. 34, 38.
53. *Ibid.*, p. 3.
54. *Ibid.*, p. 123.
55. *Ibid.*, p. 131.
56. *Ibid.*, p. 143.
57. *Ibid.*, p. 39.

THE WELFARE STATE:
TOWARDS A SOCIALIST-FEMINIST PERSPECTIVE

LINDA GORDON

The conservative renascence of the 1980s in the US and elsewhere signifi-cantly reduced public provision, most notably in the areas defined as 'welfare.'* In the 1980s continuing deindustrialization combined with cutbacks in welfare spending and a regressive tax policy sharply increased inequality and poverty and many of their attendant sufferings – illness, drug and alcohol addiction, violence in both public and private spaces. In response, many socialists, feminists, and other Leftists have joined with a broader spectrum of progressives to defend the welfare programmes, admittedly puny, that we now have and to advocate new ones on a similarly stingy and stigmatizing model.

Such a defence is vital – one would have to be inhumane not to feel compelled to support campaigns for the immediate amelioration of misery at a time when homeless people are freezing to death in the streets of New York, when 90% of drug users applying for rehabilitation programmes are turned away for lack of places, when aid to single mothers is never high enough to raise them and their children out of severe deprivation. Still, one damaging effect of these new political alignments has been to suppress a Left discourse about what 'welfare' ought to be like. The conservative mood places the Left on the defensive with regard to many political issues, not just welfare, and defensiveness tends to squelch the visionary, 'utopian' dimension of socialist thought. But designs for welfare in its modern meaning are particularly truncated in the socialist tradition. Western Marxist socialism has never devoted much energy to imagining and designing ideal welfare programmes. The core notions of socialism imply that welfare as we know it – the 'dole' or various means-tested programmes – need not exist. In

---

*Welfare, of course, means, at least in the US, public provision for the poor; in fact, the US government gives much more to the rich and the middle-class, through loans for college education, subsidies for highway and airport construction, subsidies, mortgage programmes, and tax policies that favour wealth and capital over income.

fact, the implications of recent feminist thinking suggest that, short of a purely communist set of arrangements, such a hope may be futile, because reproductive responsibilities towards children, the aged, and the disabled may always leave some citizens less able to contribute to production than others. A nonstigmatizing welfare programme is thus essential to sexual equality, unless and until we get a complete eradication of the sexual division of labour. Moreover, as feminists have argued, a valorization of nurturing, caretaking labour, is basic to constructing a noncompetitive, nonmilitaristic society, and the right kind of welfare policy could contribute to that development of new values. Very few voices today offer a truly democratic perspective on welfare policy. Socialists ought to turn their attention to elaborating a vision of a good and possible society that includes public provision.

Beginning such a discussion is not impossible even in these times of defensive politics. The current liberal politics of defending social services creates openings to a socialist discourse about welfare. For example, political mobilization against welfare usually occurs through anti-tax initiatives, especially in the US where relatively low taxes reflect and reproduce hostility to the public sector. Defence of welfare requires defence of the entire principle of public provision, of attending to 'the needs of strangers.' The growing need for welfare in capitalist society demonstrates the failure of the wage-labour system. The much discussed growing 'underclass,' if such exists other than as a pejorative term for the poor – i.e., as a criminal, violent, and irresponsible group – is above all a group that has lost confidence in wage labour as a reliable means of living. Welfare rights movements, moreover, transcend this loss of faith; their assertion of an entitlement to state support challenges the notion that only waged employment 'earns' one a livelihood and roots their claims to aid in other, noncapitalist, values.

To a considerable degree, socialist discussion of welfare policy is emerging from among feminists. This should not be surprising because welfare has in some sense always been a women's issue. Women constitute the majority of the recipients and the providers of 'welfare.' In modern society, welfare appears as an extension of the traditional caretaking, nurturing roles of women. In the US women were disproportionately (that is, in relation to their overall political power) influential in the development of welfare programmes. Moreover, the greater part of the need for welfare arises not merely from 'natural' events such as death or disability, not merely from the failure of the wage-labour system to provide, but specifically from the failure of the family-wage system, that highly gendered arrangement in which breadwinning men are supposed to provide for all their dependents.[1]

Despite the essential implication of gender in welfare needs and programmes, most of the liberal and Left discussion of this problem today continues without an adequate gender analysis.[2] This is a seriously weakening limitation. It may be precisely a feminist perspective on welfare that can make the difference between an analysis that simply calls for more generosity in existing programmes, a recommendation that cannot prevent the influence of welfare in reinforcing inequality, and a genuinely transformative vision. With these purposes in mind, I offer here a brief introduction to the new feminist scholarship about the welfare state, after reviewing briefly the gender-blind scholarship to which feminists are responding.[3] It is no doubt a particular reading of that scholarship, weighted towards that which offers historical as well as theoretical insight, and towards that which reaches the US, where feminist scholarship on this topic is just beginning. Although women's studies began earlier in the US and have proliferated more than in many other countries, on this topic we are retarded in comparison to the greater quantity of scholarship from other countries.[4] Behind this slowness lie the relative lack of class consciousness in the US and the relative weakness and, even more important, low visibility of the US welfare state in comparison to its European counterparts – because of its decentralization through a federal system, and because of the mystification accomplished through labelling as 'welfare' only some of those state programmes which contribute to citizens' well-being. Also contributing to the disinterest of US feminist scholars has been the tradition of hostility to the state which marked the women's liberation movement here, influenced as it was by the New Left. Happily, in this area the discussion has been more international than on other topics of interest to feminists. Unfortunately, the segregation between feminist and nonfeminist thinkers has not been overcome; I should like this essay to contribute in some small way to that goal.

The Gender-Blind Welfare-State Scholarship

Most scholarship about the welfare state simply does not use gender as a category of analysis (by contrast most does understand welfare to reflect and form the class system).[5] Some of the more recent historians of the US welfare state, such as Robert Bremner, James Patterson, Walter Trattner, John Ehrenreich, David Rochefort, and Michael Katz, do notice and specify women's particular welfare situation at times, but they do not consider it a major organizing principle of the system.[6]

The omission of a gender analysis distorts our understanding of the welfare state through many levels. Sometimes it obscures the existence of a policy altogether, especially if the policy is not spelled out at a general level but emerges from the intersection of many governing rules. One author, for example, recently concluded that the US has no policy towards pregnancy,[7] a mistake that results from the tendency to perceive women's reproductive activity as 'natural,' from failure to understand that policy is as much constructed by denials of needs as by meeting them, and, because of the nature of the state in the US, from the difficulty of identifying policy that is constructed of the practices of private employers, educational institutions, medical insurance carriers, town, country, state, and federal taxation, employment, welfare, and family law. For example, an examination of US policy towards pregnancy would have to consider the period in which pregnant women were excluded from certain jobs, such as teaching, and the evolution towards a standard that no longer considers pregnant women as symbols of or stimuli for immorality; the fact that US employers today provide virtually no paid and few unpaid maternity leaves; the fact that public funds will often pay for childbirth but not for abortion.

Without examining the impact of gender relations, many of the vagaries and inconsistencies of US welfare policy cannot be explained. The US has several levels of welfare, some of them – such as old age insurance – so privileged in relation to others that they are never considered 'welfare'. One source of this system of differential treatment was political pressure from employing groups to maintain low-wage labour forces, but since the labour force was hierarchically segregated along race and gender lines, so too were the welfare programmes. Another source of this differential treatment is our gender system, including norms that women, especially mothers, should be primarily domestic and supported by men. But these gender norms were contradicted by class norms, for the charity and welfare establishment expected poor mothers to earn. Thus for the entire 20th century, US national and local policy in aiding single mothers has been ambivalent and even contradictory, never supporting these women adequately but condemning their employment outside the home at the same time. The failure of several decades of 'workfare' programmes (efforts to encourage or coerce single mothers to find employment) can only be explained in terms of fundamental ambivalence on the part of legislators, welfare professionals, and voters about whether public support of single mothers is better or worse than sending mothers into the labour force. As waves of recent welfare reform have tried to get Aid to Families with Dependent Children (AFDC) recipients to 'work' – i.e., take wage-labour employment – the lack of gender analysis obscures the labour-market sex segregation that makes it difficult for women to get jobs that provide even as good an income as welfare provision. Lack of gender analysis has also hidden the fact that even identical welfare programmes would have different meanings and consequences for women, especially mothers, who already do the vast majority of parenting and housework labour, which must then be added to whatever wage work they do. Assumptions about masculinity have equally affected the welfare system, as it has been mainly unthinkable for able male welfare recipients not to work, while welfare workers made it a priority to protect men's egos from the damage of being unable to support a family.

Moreover, gender distinctions helped create the meanings of welfare. In an insightful study of German welfare history, Heide Gerstenberger showed that just as welfare rested on a worthy/unworthy distinction, so it helped define the bounds of the 'respectable,' drawing a circle that excluded those who needed help.[8] There has been too little examination of the gender sources of the stigma attached, both for men and for women, to receiving welfare.[9]

Since so many women's major work is taking care of children, it has been harder to define, perhaps, whether single-mother recipients are working or malingering; since their singleness usually involves an appearance of sexual freedom, the sexual double standard is easily exploited to label them immoral. Definitions of 'respectability' have been deeply gendered, and there appears to be some sexual as well as sexist content to taxpayers' hostility to independent women. For example, in my own recent study of the history of family violence, I found that although social work agencies accepted in theory a deserving/undeserving distinction which put widows in the former and illegitimate mothers in the latter category, in practice they did not necessarily treat the widows better than the 'immoral' women. This was because in practice *any* female-headed family seemed to them to threaten immorality.[10]

Even more fundamentally, lack of gender analysis obscures the *roots* of poverty, the inequitable distribution and production that create the need for welfare programmes in the first place. Much of US welfare expenditure goes to Aid to Families with Dependent Children, a programme founded on the principle that the norm is for mothers and children to be supported by men; that norm is, of course, the product of our particular sex/gender system – it is not a biological or divine given. A different sex/gender system might require men and women to share in child care and in earning; yet another might assume that the state should take all responsibility for the financial support of children. The sex/gender system is responsible for women's low wage rates and segregation in low-status jobs.

The contemporary discussion of the underclass in the United States is dulled by lack of a gender analysis. 'Underclass' is of course a vague and highly ideological term used in a variety of ways: stirring up fears of crime, supporting the 'war' on drugs, but also uncritically mixing into this amalgam hostilities to minorities, single-mother families, taxes, and welfare provision in general. There are serious and answerable questions about whether there is a shift among the very poor towards more criminal, self-destructive, exploitative, sexually irresponsible behaviour. It is difficult in any case to examine a topic about which there is so much hysteria, but lack of sex distinctions makes the discussion even more murky. Criminality, drug business, sexual and physical violence are overwhelmingly male; more, they are associated specifically with assertions of masculinity. When women participate in these behaviours it is usually as followers of men, a pattern associated precisely with one sense of femininity, as being both nurturant and loyal to men. Thus it is reasonable to hypothesize that this kind of increasing underclass, if it exists, is associated with crises of gender identity. Meanwhile many women, particularly single mothers, are often included in generalizations about the underclass even though they do not engage in violent or criminal behaviour; they are so categorized either because they are welfare recipients or because they are single mothers, making of 'underclass' just another rhetorical device in the attack on social provision and depriving us of categories which might illuminate specific problems.

Not only problem definitions, but also their solutions, have been gendered. Most welfare programmes have been designed to shore up male-breadwinner families or to compensate – temporarily – for their collapse. But welfare clients must work to collect their entitlements, and women do a disproportionate amount of this work too. Medical aid, aid for the disabled, programmes for children with special needs, indeed educational institutions altogether assume that women will be available to make it possible for the aid to be delivered: to drive, to care, to be at home for visits, to come to welfare offices. Just as in the market economy women translate between the paycheck – that is, money as an abstract token of exchange – and the meeting of material needs of their families – for example, buying the food, cooking it, cleaning so that new food can be cooked the next day – so too in the 'welfare' economy women translate between the entitlement and the actual giving of nurture.[11]

Blindness to gender exists in a sometimes contradictory but nevertheless mutually reinforcing relation to ignorance of the racial bases of the modern welfare state. This is particularly true in the US, where economy and government have been from the beginning of the state organized around Black subordination and the expropriation of Indians and Mexicans. The assumptions and priorities which guided the welfare system here, since the 17th century, have been as fundamentally white as they have been male. The vision of republicanism that underlies both US resistance to public welfare programmes and the design of those programmes was based not only on 'manly' definitions of dignity and independence, but also on co-existence with a slave society, with black servitude as a foil against which (white) citizenship and self-respect were defined. In the New Deal period, for example, the exclusion of African–Americans from welfare benefits was not peripheral to the new federal programmes but a fundamental part of their construction, part of the basic political realignment that created the New Deal.[12] Most good-quality welfare programmes were designed as emergency wage-replacement provisions for those accustomed to (at least) upper-working-class wages. For different reasons and in different ways, virtually all but white men were excluded from these jobs and thereby from the better welfare programmes.

The relation of the welfare state to both gender and race as fundamental social divisions is mutual. These divisions have helped create the need for welfare by creating poverty, and then shaped its nature and distribution, but the welfare programmes in turn have influenced the nature of the divisions. The situation of women and of minority men has been affected, for better and for worse, by the structure of the welfare state. Indeed the very meanings of femininity, masculinity, Blackness and other racial stereotypes in the US today derive in part from the shape and administration of these programmes. The exclusions and limits of unemployment insurance, which thereby force many onto general relief or AFDC, create negative attitudes about the high levels of minority unemployment, for example. The definition of masculinity as breadwinning and independent is reinforced by the assumption, long present in AFDC, for example, that men should be responsible for the children of the women they live with. The consensus about women's normative domesticity has been shaped in a double-binding way by the structure of AFDC (keeping women at home but inadequately supported, thereby forcing them into the underground wage labour market, but declining to provide for child care).

Similarly contradictory is the rhetoric that welfare represents deplorable 'dependence,' while women's subordination to husbands is not registered as unseemly. This contradiction should not be surprising, for the concept of dependence is an ideological one that reflects particular modes of production. For example, in traditional societies only men of substantial property were considered independent, and not only women and children but all men who worked for others were considered dependents. Only in the modern era, where wage labour became the norm for men and voting rights were extended to all men, did employed men begin to be 'independent.' Women, for whom wage labour was not the majority experience until recently, and whose earnings are on average much less than men's, continued to be considered as dependent. Indeed, women's dependence (e.g., their unpaid domestic labour) contributed to men's 'independence.' Only in this century has the term 'dependent' begun to refer specifically to adult recipients of public aid, while women who depend on husbands are no longer labelled as dependents (except, of course, for purposes of the Internal Revenue Service). There is also a class double standard for women: the prosperous are encouraged to be dependent on their husbands, the poor to become 'independent.'[13] Public dependence, of course, is paid for by taxes, yet it is interesting that there is no objection to allowing husbands tax exemptions for their dependent wives. The anti-dependence ideology then penalizes those who care for the inevitably dependent – the young, the sick – who are, of course, disproportionately unpaid women and low-paid service workers. In fact, the entire discourse about dependence masks the evident interdependence of vast numbers of the population in modern societies.

The gendered design of welfare programmes is by no means simply a matter of male policy-makers keeping women subordinate. Few scholars have noted the disproportionate influence of women in envisioning, lobbying for, and then administering welfare programmes, especially at the state and local levels where most programmes are located. This is not only a matter of giving recognition where it is due, although that is in itself important to compensate for patterns of systematically depriving women of credit for their work. It also requires incorporating the fact that women have often been influential in campaigning for welfare provisions that turned out to be quite discriminatory against women, as in the case of protective legislation or AFDC itself. An analysis of women's activism requires understanding the complex relation that women, especially reformers, have had to conventional gender and family arrangements – often seizing upon what is beneficial to women in those arrangements, often distancing themselves from and seeking to control the needy quite as much as did men, often negotiating delicate compromises hoping to shift slightly the sexual balance of political and economic power.

Meanwhile, theoretical debates about the nature of modern welfare states have been similarly impoverished by the lack of gender analysis. Among historians two rather polarized perspectives competed throughout much of the mid-20th century. One is affectionately known to those who use a British model as Whig history,[14] although the American Talcott Parsons was an able advocate of it. Jill Quadagno characterizes this view thus: 'As industrialization proceeds, it. . .reduc[es] the functions of the traditional family and. . .[dislocates] certain categories of individuals whose labor becomes surplus – the very young, the old, the sick, and the disabled.'[15] Quadagno is here correct to leave out women, for the theories she is describing do so. And yet without women the theory is mushy, to say the least. These lost 'functions' of the 'traditional' family were mainly women's labour, and modern welfare systems do not in fact replace them with anything except differently organized women's labour: women are the main workers in the welfare system, still badly underpaid, performing labour that the current tax system could not support if living wages prevailed; and women continue to do the work of consuming welfare, always vastly underestimated – waiting in lines, making phone calls, filling out forms, submitting to interviews and questioning, scrimping when cheques are late, begging help and favours when cheques are inadequate.

The task of placing welfare developments into a *longue durée* story of progress was done best by T.H. Marshall, a sociologist who sought to justify the British welfare state. He constructed an influential theory of the evolution of citizenship rights, arguing that 'social' citizenship, what US President Franklin Roosevelt called 'freedom from want,' was a third stage following the guarantee of political citizenship, i.e. the vote. But Marshall's theory did not theorize women's citizenship, ignoring the contradictions of women's dependence on the male wage. As Gillian Pascall has argued, according to Marshall women's marital dependency should be called feudal because it is an ascribed rather than an achieved status, a relic that subverts his theory of the development of citizenship rights.[16] Marshall's periodization is contradicted by the history of women's relation to the state. His stages of citizenship (first due process rights, then political rights, or the franchise, then social citizenship, or welfare entitlements) only describe the male experience; throughout the world women won important 'social' rights from the state *before* they got the vote. Indeed, for many poor women, the earliest relation to the state was as a recipient of relief.

This Whig view often assumed a kind of gradual progress that specified no agent, other than sympathetic and wise legislators. A social-democratic version specified organized labour as the agent,[17] but this was rarely argued *historically*. Most of these arguments were based on static sociological operations that correlated welfare programmes with union membership or some similar index of labour strength; few offered an actual historical narrative of union campaigns for welfare programmes. Moreover, without taking gender into consideration, none of this scholarship is correct. In the US and probably elsewhere as well, organized women, feminist and nonfeminist, devoted a higher proportion and sometimes absolutely more energy to campaigning for welfare programmes than did unions, and in certain periods – for example, the first decades of this century – were more influential. These were largely elite women and their class and race assumptions marked the welfare system indelibly. Furthermore a gender analysis *of* trade union activity is needed, to determine which unionists made welfare high priority, and which programmes aroused the most union support.

Opposing the Whig interpretation were both Left and Right-wing criticisms of welfare programmes as controlling: suppressing individual freedom, weakening resistance, and/or distracting the citizenry from the fundamental issues of power. The Left version of this 'social control' argument views welfare provisions (like higher wages) as encouraging workers to accept the capitalist economy and the liberal governmental system, essentially trading political power for a higher standard of living.[18] This perspective has many problems but foremost is its hidden assumption that the workers making this bad bargain are male. Frances Fox Piven and I have both argued that working-class women, who received much less money from the welfare system, actually gained more power from it, because they could use different 'systems' against each other, e.g., welfare provision against domestic male-supremacy.[19]

Both the Whig and the social control perspectives, as Theda Skocpol has argued, tended to remove politics from consideration, and to render the state merely an abstraction or at best a homogeneous and passive tool of larger interests. In the last two decades there has been a renascence of theorizing about the state, particularly among Marxists,[20] and its richness has drawn some feminist theorists to appropriate this argumentation to welfare and gender issues. Ralph Miliband argued that the capitalist class, if it does not literally staff the state, nevertheless retains power to influence it from without.[21] But what has great explanatory power about class relations by no means works equally well for gender. If we attempt to insert gender into this model we meet trouble: it is difficult to specify what 'male' interests are, and if we argue that 'men' (a dubious category as a universal) have the preservation of women as their long-term interest and will therefore support measures at least to keep them alive, then the theory becomes so vague as to be not disprovable.[22]

Nicos Poulantzas met some of these objections with his functionalist view, arguing that direct participation of capitalists is not crucial in understanding state functions, but that the state is *objectively* bourgeois and *definitionally* committed to maintaining those values and structures. Here the state becomes abstract; it has no necessary connection with any particular capitalists at all but serves to retain unity among them (and to promote disunity among the working class).[23] Can gender be added to this model? It has indeed been argued that the maleness of the state comes not only from its personnel, but is embedded in its nature, in bureaucratic and hierarchical forms. And in fact Poulantzas' emphasis on unity would find more evidence if it were understood as a class and gendered unity. But to argue that the state objectively functions to maintain male dominance *either* suggests that women have never advanced their position, that we are no better off now than a century ago, which is patently counterexperiential; *or* defines male supremacy in such as way as to include all concessions to women, in which case the premise is tautological.

Some of those interested in gender analysis have been attracted to a conflict model of the state such as that suggested in Fred Block's class-struggle approach. He postulates a group of state managers, separate from capitalists; but the managers' fortunes depend on a healthy economy which, given the real alternatives available to managers, can only be capitalist. Block rejects the view that the state can become a tool of working-class goals, as in the social-democratic model of the welfare state, but he also rejects 'social-control' theories on the grounds that capitalists are usually far too short-sighted to trade concessions for long-term stability. Instead these concessions represent victories for workers; but in making them, managers accumulate more power for the state which then, in periods of working-class weakness, allows it to re-form these concessions into structures that support the economic as well as the political system.[24] Organized feminists, too, have won major concessions, only to have these reshaped in periods of feminist decline. But of course those concerned with gender must also consider the possibility that the group of managers, being male and being influenced by its maleness, is in that respect similar to the ruling group, also male. Furthermore, Block's theory involves a fairly economistic, mechanistic determination of when the 'working class' will be weak and when strong, and certainly there is no such model for predictions with respect to gender relations.

Among non-Marxist sociologists, 'state-centred' theories of welfare state development are most associated with Theda Skocpol who has argued for the influence of particular political configurations. (This model is less novel to historians and political scientists, for whom traditional scholarship has been 'state-centred.') Theoretically it is not difficult to acknowledge the importance of such political factors on policy development, and historians in particular welcome this directive to return to narrative, detailed, causal explanations. Unfortunately in Skocpol's own historical work, the notion of state 'capacity' is a bit circular: lack of state capacity is invoked to explain the failure to enact certain conceivable welfare programmes at certain times, even though such programmes are precisely what builds state capacity. Moreover her work redefines 'politics' narrowly as elite politics; she studies the decision-making processes of state and political party operators – bureaucrats and politicians – and tends to occlude evidence of non-elite, non-governmental activism.[25] Skocpol wavers in how much she claims for her politics-centred approach: to the extent that it calls for a more complex explanatory theory, adding political complications to simplified class models, it is evidently reasonable; but in other places, Skocpol seems to want to substitute politicians for social formations (such as class or gender or race), elite for mass politics, political conflict for social struggle; her work seems to erase the social movements of labour, the unemployed, the elderly, from the history of the New Deal, for example. Since there has been little previous acknowledgement of the role of organized women, or of social change with respect to gender, in the history of welfare programmes, here she is not erasing but merely continuing to paint around big blank spots.[26]

Most welfare scholarship, especially in the United States, presents itself as operating without ideology altogether. I am referring to the establishment network of primarily liberal poverty researchers, funded primarily by the government, who have made of poverty and welfare (or 'income transfers' as they are mainly called) a subfield of economics and quantitative sociology. Historian Michael Katz in his new book, *The Undeserving Poor*, offers a cogent critique and history of this intellectual work. Some of the increased government spending in the US 'poverty program' inaugurated under the Johnson administration went to research; between 1965 and 1980, annual federal spending on poverty research increased from $2.5 to $160 million (in current dollars). The poverty researchers created large data archives and began longitudinal studies in attempts to measure trends in poverty and to evaluate the impact of welfare programmes. Much of their data is extraordinarily valuable, and their findings usually supported welfare spending. But they redefined the issues technically, mathematically, so as to be the responsibility strictly of experts; in this procedure they both followed and contributed to the transformation of much of American social science into quantitative work highly vulnerable to government and foundation agendas. The conclusions of the poverty research establishment were offered as value-neutral, although efforts to secure and retain government funding, especially as government moved to the Right, meant the adoption of highly ideological categories, such as 'underclass,' 'broken families,' 'transmission of welfare dependency.' As Michael Katz puts it, 'the capture of the social science agenda by government combined with the capture of poverty research by economists to confine the scope of debate within market models of human obligation and interaction. . . . By narrowing their criteria for public policy to the relation between income maintenance and work incentives, liberals had ceded the debate before it began.'[27] This kind of empiricist work sometimes (although on the whole rarely) included gender variables, but its research procedures excluded the critique of existing systemic and individual power relations. Certainly it dampened public debate about the values which a welfare state might promote.

The New Feminist Scholarship

With the renascence of women's studies in the 1970s, feminist thinking turned to welfare. The lowest common denominator of this new work shows that the premise with which I (deliberately) began, that previous scholarship about welfare had been gender-blind, is too simple. However 'blind,' that scholarship was hardly disabled, for it functioned effectively to mystify and thus defend a gendered and unequal society. In exposing that defensive function, the new feminist scholarship about welfare moved through discernible stages, albeit they are not neatly consecutive and the 'progress' involves no consensus but disagreement. These 'stages' exist only as analytic categories, but perhaps useful ones.

First there was a great deal of work that demonstrated the *discriminatory* character of welfare programmes, and their function to reinforce sexist arrangements in domestic and public life.[28] In a rich article on the British poor laws in the 19th century, Pat Thane showed how the traditional distinction between the deserving and the undeserving poor was drawn for women in terms of their relations to men: widows were always deserving, deserted or unmarried mothers nearly always condemned.[29] In the US it was demonstrated that Social Security old-age insurance discriminates against women,[30] and how women have been excluded from unemployment compensation because of the kinds of jobs they do, for example.[31] Analysts learned to recognize policies where they seemed invisible, such as Irene Diamond's work on discrimination against women in housing.[32]

The critique of discrimination quickly developed into a *structural* critique of welfare, in what I consider a second stage of development of the feminist scholarship. A recent sustained example of this sort of approach is Mimi Abramovitz's *Regulating the Lives of Women*, the first book-length feminist analysis of the history of welfare in the US Abramovitz moves beyond concern with discrimination to demonstrate how welfare policy functioned to reinforce the entire social system of women's subordination, particularly their constriction within the family and dependence on men.[33] Barbara Nelson and Gwendolyn Mink showed that gender assumptions about women's dependence were part of the historical bases of welfare policy.[34] Several scholars have noted the existence of inequalities within the welfare system, most commonly described as a double standard between privileged and nonstigmatized programmes such as Old Age and Survivors Insurance (commonly called Social Security) and stingy and humiliating ones such as AFDC, but most have viewed these as class divisions.[35] Others, such as Hace Sorel Tishler, thought the mothers' aid payments were small because the group of 'dependent mothers' was insignificant in comparison to unemployed or injured men or the aged – an absolute myth based on the social invisibility of single mothers.[36] Several feminist scholars have interpreted these inequalities in gender terms.[37]

Nelson's work is part of a new school of analysis that sees welfare programmes as having the function not only of keeping women subordinate, but, perhaps more importantly, of supporting a whole social system. I prefer to call this system the family wage, since it rests on a familial organization in which the husband/father is supposed to be the exclusive breadwinner and the wife/mother responsible for the large quantities of unpaid domestic labour which are essential to every aspect of human life, including the continuation of a capitalist economic system.[38] Internationally, feminist analyses have noted that the only explanation that can make sense of seemingly contradictory welfare policies is their function to keep this system (women's economic dependence on men, men's monetary dependence on wages and personal dependence on women) in place. Many students of welfare policy, including Jill Roe writing about Australia, Hilary Land, Jane Lewis and Mary McIntosh writing about Britain, Mimi Abramowitz and myself writing about the US have argued this perspective.[39] Indeed, in England where family allowance programmes were adopted after World War II, the payments were originally made to male heads of families and women were able to collect them only after considerable feminist campaigning.

Making the family-wage assumptions behind welfare programmes even more pernicious is the fact that few men have ever *actually* been able to earn a family wage, that is, a wage large enough single-handedly to support a family. Full dependence on husbands has actually been a 'privilege' of a minority of women. Thus negotiations between women and welfare givers were often ritualized exchanges of fictional slogans, with both parties aware that women's likelihood of stable reliance on male wages is not great. Furthermore, women have been coerced by welfare requirements into following paths of action which are least conducive to achieving ultimate independence of welfare – by pursuing men instead of their own upward mobility, or by accepting low-wage, unskilled, part-time jobs with terrible working conditions instead of holding out for education, good quality child care, and better jobs.

The family-wage assumption on which the welfare system has been predicated expresses some of the economic assumptions of industrial capitalism. In this century government intervention to stabilize relations of production has been more widely accepted – as in workmen's and unemployment compensation, industrial health and safety laws, agricultural stabilization programmes, even labour relations acts guaranteeing union recognition, for example – while the domestic sphere remains ideologically 'private.'[40] In fact, domestic, reproductive life is indeed governmentally regulated, certain forms of it supported and others penalized. Michael Walzer has argued slightly differently: that in the US governmental regulation of distribution – i.e., welfare – is more accepted than is governmental control of production.[41] This is true ideologically only, because in fact there is extensive state control of production. The differences concern the degree to which such controls are mystified, and the distributional results of both – not only in cash benefits but in power. With respect to welfare, the ideology of the privateness of reproduction is itself an influence, and one disadvantageous to those who do reproductive work, for it undermines their formation of a sense of entitlement to public help.

In its most extreme form, women's responsibility for domestic, reproductive work has deprived them of citizenship. Carole Pateman has argued that in liberal theory, the first criterion for 'citizenship,' as that concept evolved, was some form of 'independence,' defined in terms of the characteristic male experience – for example, property ownership, bearing arms, self-employment. Hegel was one of many who found a way to acknowledge women's membership in the human and national community without attributing to them citizenship by viewing women as members of families, i.e., nonindependent members.[42] The very concept of modern citizenship (in contrast to that of the rights of the subject) arose along with the public/private distinction that ideologically separated women from public life. Of course women were by no means as effectively cut off from public activity as these abstractions would suggest, but were active political and commercial figures long before the beginning of legal citizenship entitlements in the 19th century. Nevertheless the view of women as private, noncitizens, added to the expectation that they should be the dependents of men, made it difficult to conceive that they should have entitlements to state support.

Some versions of these critiques of the welfare state looked more to its contemporary functions than to its original assumptions, and adopted and adapted the New Left social-control model. They reflect the antistatist, anti-expert, participatory-democracy values characteristic of the late 1960s/early 1970s women's liberation movement, originating in the New Left but also in individualist values and middle-class experience of many women's liberation theorists, and the anger of the welfare rights movement. A classic example was Barbara Ehrenreich's and Deirdre English's *For Her Own Good*, an indictment of physicians, psychoanalysts, child psychologists, and home economists for usurping women's traditional autonomous skills and then using their newly professional 'expertise' to control women's work and even identity.[43] Another is Alicia Frohman's analysis of day care. Following James O'Connor's *The Fiscal Crisis of the State*, which argues that such services function to regulate the labour market, subsidize the costs of production, legitimize the system ideologically, and provide social control, Frohman denies that day care programmes serve women in any way. Rather she relies on a reserve-army-of-labour theory to explain that such programmes emerge when needs for women's labour are paramount and contract at other times.[44] Others used social-control assumptions to challenge the

Whiggish view that the state functioned to protect the weaker social groups: for example, Diana Leonard Barker's article on the regulation of marriage argues that the primary effect of marriage law is to perpetuate the exploitative entitlements of the stronger spouse, the husband.[45] A more complex form of social control argument, and one that made many feminists uncomfortable, called attention to the role women reformers played in disciplining men, and to women's influence in definitions of 'respectability,' recognizing the socially conservative content of some feminist reform work.[46] Equally unsettling to a simple social-control model has been the evidence of women's *choice* in the family wage system – not only accepting it, but agitating for it. Patricia Tulloch, writing about Australia, concluded that care-giving was often women's chosen preference, notwithstanding its disadvantaged economic consequences.[47] (In scholarship outside the area of welfare – in labour history, for example – a great deal of evidence has accumulated that working-class married women would have preferred a family wage system had it been available, because they preferred a chance to devote themselves full-time to domestic labour.)

A common feminist theorization of the social control inherent in the welfare system was the notion of a public or state patriarchy as opposed to private, familial patriarchy. This perspective rested in part on the interpretations of Talcott Parsons, influential in the sociology of the family several decades ago, that family functions had been transferred to the state. Parsons and his predecessors such as W. I. Thomas had been positive about this transfer, for they believed that the state could provide experts who were needed to socialize citizens in our modern, complex societies; and indeed the strongest critique of this transfer-of-functions tendency came from those, Left, liberal, or Right, who sought to support a family erroneously identified as traditional and who did not notice, or mind, the suppression of women it entailed. Feminists, by contrast, attacked both old and new forms. Carol Brown argued that patriarchy is an umbrella system in which there are public aspects, controlled by men collectively, and private aspects, run by men individually. Since male-headed families are no longer needed to maintain the overall patriarchy, men's individual powers in familial matters have been increasingly delegated, so to speak, to the state.[48] Political theorist Zillah Eisenstein has conceptualized a 'capitalist patriarchal state.' States are patriarchal, she argues, because the 'distinction between public (male) and private (female) life has been inherent in the formation of state societies.'[49] She too describes a transition from husband/father's control to state control, but sees the nature of the social control of women as continuous and essentially similar.

The 'state patriarchy' analysis was extremely useful in pointing to the growing independence of some women from fathers and husbands, but its way of seeing the state did not hold up in the face of mounting historical scholarship about women and family. In the first place, this school of analysis relied on the feminist appropriation of the word 'patriarchy' from an older and richer historical usage. Deriving from the Greek, the first English usage, in the sixteenth century, referred to an ecclesiastical hierarchy. By the early seventeenth century 'patriarchy' was being used to describe a societal form whose organization was based on, and analogous to, a father's control over his family. It is of course logical that this meaning of the word developed precisely as patriarchal society was beginning to erode in the face of commercial capitalism and the individualist values it promoted. By using a word so filled with fatherly, familial, organic, fixed hierarchical relations to describe today's male supremacy, situated in a nonfamilial, inorganic, meritocratic society, we lose much of its power and nuance, and we mask significant historical change. In the second place, the emphasis on the continuity of 'patriarchy' obscures from view the gains of women, or, at best, represents them as an inevitable epiphenomenon of modernization or secularization rather than as the result of collective political struggle, i.e., of feminism.

Another feminist scholar of the welfare state, Eli Zaretsky, broke with the emphasis on the continuity of patriarchy and argued, to the contrary, the transformative effect of capitalism on gender, achieved through the public/private distinction. Following from the important insight that only in modern society do we find intense subjectivity and consciousness of private life, Zaretsky argued (like Abramovitz and Nelson and many others) that the welfare state served to reinforce, not to subvert, the private family. Indeed, the very inadequacies of welfare programmes grew from the reluctance of welfare agencies and their leaders to undermine the male-headed nuclear family.[50] As Zaretsky noticed, the form of the welfare state – bureaucratized provision for strangers – is public, but its content – individual family 'independence' and women's responsibility for childraising and domestic work – private; the result was an alienated public life and an alienated private life.[51] But while Zaretsky recognized historical change, he too argued primarily functionally, neglecting the political struggles over welfare policy and particularly the influence of organized women in the growth of welfare policies, the notion of the private, and the resultant alienation.

All these structural critiques of welfare policy, emphasizing social control, share a major limitation: they rely only on functionalist argumentation, focusing on the rationality of welfare programmes for those in power. This is a limitation, not a defect; functionalist analyses are often illuminating. But they assume that welfare policy is coherently beneficial to some group or groups. Thus they cannot explain its often contradictory, even self-defeating aspects. These emerge both from the fragmented and inconsistent goals of policy-makers – a complexity that could be fitted into a functionalist theory that was supple enough – but also, most importantly, from the fact that most welfare policies represent the jerry-built compromises which are the artifacts of political and social conflict – a dynamic that functionalism cannot encompass.

It is not surprising then that the major critique of this social control model came from scholars looking at welfare historically. Carole Pateman, for example, despite her insistence on the patriarchal nature of welfare, recognizes that dependence on the state may be preferable to dependence on individual men; since women do not 'live with the state' as they do with men, they are better able to make collective struggles about their entitlements.[52] Frances Fox Piven points out a remarkable and constructive contradiction in the welfare system: that this form of support for 'dependent' women has in fact made many of them 'independent' by giving them employment in the welfare system.[53]

At a certain point, the efflorescence of empirical, historical scholarship about welfare created in the US a third 'stage,' documenting *women's political activism and influence* in the making of that system. At first this work, unlike the critical theoretical work, was primarily celebratory, and rightly so. Historians, on the basis of archival research, uncovered a virtually lost history of women's leadership in welfare in the US, arising from such organizations as the National Consumers' League, the Women's Trade Union League, the National Association of Colored Women, and the YWCA. But much of the feminist critique of these Progressive-era liberal programmes was lost in this work. More recently, historians have begun to synthesize this recognition with a critical perspective. Paula Baker discussed the influence a women's political culture had on American politics by the early 20th century, thereby illuminating with historical specificity some of the previously unchallenged male aspects of the state, such as the fraternalism of political parties. She showed that women engaged in political activity long before they won suffrage, a point which adds to a growing theoretical understanding that we must enlarge what counts as politics and the political far beyond electoral activity.[54] Moreover, this women's politics fundamentally changed the nature of the US state. Baker concludes that in the Progressive era, reaping the harvest from their cultivation of a new kind of state responsibility, women's very successes permanently ended the separate male and female political cultures that had characterized the previous centuries of US history, a convergence that was by no means without costs for women. In the early 20th century middle-class men too began to take up the kinds of single-issue, extra-electoral agitating and lobbying campaigns around welfare issues and, indeed, soon came to dominate at least the leadership of this politics.

This history often suffers from class and race biases, recognizing as welfare activity only the contributions of elite white women. Let us consider these limitations one at a time, beginning with the racial. This blindness was not only a matter of undervaluing the history of minorities, but resulted from the very definitions of what constituted welfare and welfarist work, developed from the white experience. A more complex, non-exclusive historical understanding of welfarist work is beginning to emerge, especially about that of African–Americans thanks to the development of black women's historical scholarship; the histories of Asian–American, Hispanic-American, and Native-American women are also gaining momentum. The new historical scholarship suggests that women played a particularly influential role among African–Americans, as among whites, in providing for the public welfare, but with considerable differences in form and content.

White women's strategies were often based on the substantial political influence, economic resources, and social mobility which many had, relying on wealth and connections to lobby for legislation and win administrative power through jobs and appointment to committees and commissions. Minority women, especially women of colour, usually lacking influence on government at any level, had to turn to 'private' welfare provision. (Ultimately studying this activity may contribute to an expanded and developed theory of the state, as constituting more than government.) While white women were lobbying Congressmen, blacks were raising money in the most difficult way – collecting from the poor to help the poor – in order to create their own schools, hospitals, orphanages, pension programmes, health insurance.[55] The evident inadequacy of such provision made it necessary for minorities simultaneously to campaign for access to private and governmental white welfare institutions and programmes. Thus minority welfare activity was often indistinguishable from civil rights activity.[56]

Out of the minority experience also came different welfare priorities. Particularly influential was the fact that black women were more likely to be employed than white women, black mothers especially more than white mothers; statistically black women were less able and possibly less willing to depend on male wages than were whites. Minority women in general worked in very different jobs from whites, as domestics, agricultural labourers, and laundresses, for example. These limits and choices were partly shared by working-class and other poor white women, but there were also considerable cultural differences. African-American reformers were also committed to the family wage ideal, but minority women activists were considerably more likely than whites to accept women's and even mothers' employment as a long-term reality and to seek programmes that would make it easier, such as child care facilities or protection against sexual harassment. This history suggests how racially specific have been what whites regard as mainstream welfare proposals; how deeply our welfare debates have taken place within a uniquely white set of political, economic, and familial assumptions. Moreover, the white women's welfarist activity played a role in maintaining, even reinforcing, class and race exclusions. Their organizations remained all white, not only because they had little interest in or sensitivity to women in other circumstances, but because on occasion they acted to exclude black women. Equally important, the white vision of public welfare – aid to needy children, replacement of male wages for dependent wives, protection for working women in industrial and urban enterprises – took as given the structures that not only excluded blacks but confirmed them in subordination.[57]

For white, even working-class white, women, the history of their work for public welfare confirms the notion that they were struggling within a masculine state, leaving aside the issue of how that maleness was structured and expressed. Even poor, immigrant white women were often operating in cities in which their men were organized, albeit as vassals, into party politics. For black women it is not clear that this conceptualization – a male state – holds. The modifier 'white,' as in a white male state, was in fact far more than a modifier; it was an absolutely fundamental structuring principle.

Historians have more often recognized the influence in welfare policy of a class perspective – that of the charity workers who were the direct antecedents of today's welfare policy makers. Critique of class interests expressed in welfare policy has been the basis of many social-control interpretations. But sorting out class from racial/ethnic interests has been particularly difficult in US history; in the US the class 'otherness' of the objects of charity became by the late 19th century indivisible from an ethnic/religious/'racial' otherness because of the heavy immigration of southern and eastern Europeans coincident with peak rates of urbanization and impoverishment. Just as whiteness was so important a part of the development of upper- and middle-class consciousness in the US, so too was being 'American' as opposed to immigrant. The social-control interpretations emphasized discrimination against, and disdainful attitudes towards, immigrants; they have not analyzed the contribution of the native-born/immigrant relationship to the formation of the consciousness of the welfare reformers themselves. Thus even the class character of a welfare system will be more fully revealed by the growth of scholarship about minorities.

Scholarship that puts together class and race and gender differences in visions of and campaigns for social provision is even less developed. For example, the standard view regarding working-class attitudes to welfare in the welfare-state histories relies on the pronouncements of Samuel Gompers, national leader of the American Federation of Labor, in opposition to governmental programmes. The opinions of rank-and-file unionists remain unexplored, and evidence that union locals often supported welfare campaigns neglected. Working-class women, unionized and not, seem unlikely to have been faithful devotees of Gompers' anti-public welfare attitudes. No scholar has inquired whether racial minority workers had different views about welfare programmes. Welfare policy has also had a substantial influence on the class consciousness of the privileged classes. In the US today, the tendency of the great majority to call themselves middle class reflects a definition of that term as meaning, not 'on welfare'. This equation of labour with middle-class status is also gendered, for it denigrates domestic labour. Here too there is a class division however: poor women who are not employed are vulnerable to being labelled lazy and parasitic, while prosperous women who are 'only' housewives are not. But for all except the wealthiest women, fears of being alone and willingness to stay with difficult and often violent men are conditioned by the deprivation and humiliation that welfare brings.

These class, race, and gender structures have been constantly contested. A framework for understanding the historical development of the welfare state, if it is to have actual explanatory power, must keep in focus not only the powerlessness but also the challenges and occasionally power of the resistant and sometimes organized subordinates. The reform activity of white middle-class women is only one kind of activism. For example, the 'child savers' who sought to 'rescue' poor children in the industrial cities from poverty and mistreatment were perceived by the poor as child kidnappers; in Boston poor people called the Society for the Prevention of Cruelty to Children 'the Cruelty'. But their response was by no means simply resentment and refusal to cooperate, as the social-control theorists imagined. Many of the poor sought out the help of the SPCC, despite their understanding that it might take their children away, particularly women hoping to use the agency's power against the domestic tyranny of husbands.[58] In New York the Irish immigrant working class defined the threat of the child savers in religious terms, as Protestants trying to proselytize by stealing Catholic children and placing them in Protestant institutions and families. These immigrants managed to force upon the city the 'Children's Law' of 1873, which required that children be placed in homes of their own religious persuasion; and nuns, mainly working-class Irish immigrants, created Catholic children's homes as a means not only of fending off Protestant institutions but of aggrandizing their own power within the Church against the male hierarchy.[59]

Moreover, a scholarship that looks at conflict about welfare policy will recognize that the subordinates are not a homogeneous group. Within working-class, poor, and minority families and communities, there are power hierarchies. In response to the legacy of racism, too much US scholarship generalizes about African–Americans as if they were all homogeneously poor, thus failing to recognize sharp class differences among blacks. Similarly the rise of feminism led to generalizations about women as if all were equally subordinated and victimized. Scholarship that recognizes the intersections of gender, class, and race has at times yielded conclusions that are unexpected and, to some feminists, even threatening, for if women's power is to be recognized, their responsibility must be also; and not only distinctions but even relations of domination among women become influential. Nancy Hewitt's study of women's activism in 19th-century Rochester, New York, is a good example of feminist critique of the universality of sisterhood and the often dominant influence of women's class allegiances in their reform activity.[60] Paula Giddings and Rosalyn Terborg-Penn have documented the racist exclusionary practices of many white women's reform organizations.[61] Similarly, my studies of family violence revealed women charity and case workers as controllers of poor women, cast doubt on whether there were any distinctions between the approaches of male and female child protectors, and showed women 'clients' actively struggling against efforts to 'help' them by their wealthier, altruistic 'sisters'.[62]

Lisa Peattie and Martin Rein have offered a conceptual approach to welfare contestation that makes gender central, and their perspective is valuable and underrecognized. They develop a notion of claims (to goods, services, resources) that does not privilege wages but considers the wage form merely one variety of claiming. Industrial societies have, they argue, three realms within which claims are generated: family, economy, government.[63] These have different logics: family claims rest on assumptions of what they call 'solidarity'; wage claims on assumptions of exchange; and the basis of claims on government is precisely the subject of dispute. Women's methods of claiming have been based more on familial assumptions – not only kinship solidarity but acceptance of interdependence – because family work has been more important and wage labour less important in most women's histories. The Peattie/Rein approach rejects the dominant view of wages or 'earnings' as somehow naturally deserved, but tries to situate wages as one among several potentially legitimate claims for goods and services, such as those arising from kinship or friendship obligations or from a welfare system. Peattie and Rein's discussion has the particular value of identifying what has been a Marxist, liberal and conservative consensus in privileging the wage form as *the* means of providing for the citizenry and the implications of this assumption for welfare and for women: dependence on men, with welfare functioning to replace the male wage when it is not forthcoming. (Most feminists who have recognized and criticized this assumption have concluded from this critique that women were *only* victims, missing the mixture of women's support for the family wage system and their resistance to it, and especially missing women's successes.)

Peattie and Rein's concept of solidarity-based claims has something in common with the new discourse of 'needs.' Neither are based on principles of exact exchange or meritocracy. Both Marxist and conservative social critics have remained suspicious of needs as a base of political struggle, because they are so obviously constructed historically by hegemonic cultural and economic powers.[64] Feminists are beginning to examine how a 'needs' discourse can remain a democratic, oppositional one. The Italian sociologist Laura Balbo and American philosopher Nancy Fraser have recognized the importance of women in the creation of a 'needs-oriented culture,' and that women have gained thereby a position of unprecedented strategic political strength and public importance.[65]

But Peattie's and Rein's perspective, although coming from a very different intellectual tradition, has some of the weaknesses of Foucault, another interpreter of welfare measures. In his work on, for example, prisons, Foucault was a member of the social-control group of theorists; in other respects – notably in the work on sexuality – Foucault argues for a multiplicity of competing discourses constructing needs. The Peattie and Rein view of competing claims is like Foucault's view of swirling discourses, tending towards pluralism, suggesting at times an indeterminacy so total as to deny the possibility of identifying any particular structures of hegemonic power. (In fact at other times Foucault returns to a quite conventional Marxist view that specific discourses express the material relations of specific historical stages.) The historical evidence will not confirm such an open-ended, power-agnostic view. *Not* everything is possible at every historical moment. Just as definitions of poverty have changed as minimal standards of living grew, so too aspirations and expectations of entitlement have grown. One hundred years ago many single mothers accepted – albeit with agony and fury – that they might have to lose their children in order to secure support for them. Today single mothers feel entitled to raise their own children. This transformation of hopes, indeed of 'needs,' is an historical artifact, explicable through the study of social and political movements. Histories that trace only legislation and political alliances and explanations based on an abstract concept of 'modernization' are not adequate to chart such transformations.

Towards a New Welfare Scholarship
Although scholarship about the welfare state is proliferating, much of it does not yet fully break with the many ideological factors that have surrounded charity, 'relief,' the dole, and even social 'insurance.' These include not only perceptions of welfare recipients as blameworthy or pitiable in their 'dependence,' not only beliefs that the need for public aid is exceptional, a need that would disappear if the economy was properly flourishing, but also ideas about desirable gender and family arrangements. We can begin to specify the axes of analysis that a critical scholarship must include.

Since, as we have seen, welfare systems both reflect and support gender systems, and since so many welfare recipients are women, we cannot understand these systems without considering the overall status of women. Studies of welfare lack explanatory power if they do not include the surrounding context of options for women – for example, contraception and abortion; deindustrialization and the relative increase in low-wage, unskilled, service jobs; the masses of women now in higher education; the contemporary conservative and religious revival which threatens many women's rights and benefits. A scholarship attentive to gender must also recognize as distinctly male many behaviours and expectations usually perceived as universal.

An accurate welfare scholarship must not only incorporate racial and gender relations of power as fundamental, but must also register the agency of these subordinated groups in the construction of programmes and policies. It must recognize the 'relative autonomy' of the welfare state from direct control by a unified ruling group and register instead that the state is a complex, multi-layered and often contradictory cluster. Its welfare arenas contain conflict at all levels, from the Congress to the caseworker's cubicle. This means, for example, that recent welfare reform should be examined in the context of the decline of a welfare rights movement, and a lack of unity among welfare 'experts' about what should be the content of such rights if there are any. For example, the development of welfare 'rights' has been neglected by historians, and left to legal scholars, who examine not the social movements for welfare rights but their legal 'tracks'. These 'tracks' are ambiguous. Somewhere in the 20th century recipients gained some kind of legal claim to this 'welfare' and to judicial recourse if grants are denied without due process.[66] This recourse is of course mainly theoretical, since most welfare recipients by their very need for welfare are unable to mount suits to claim the rights. Moreover some scholars, notably those identified with the 'critical legal studies' movement, have taken a negative view of this rights discourse altogether, not only because the claimants are so often unable to make them real, but also because the claims are by nature individualized and individualizing, perhaps even antagonistic to collective action. An historical view belies that criticism, since there are many past instances of rights claims provoking, rather than dampening, collective militance. In the National Welfare Rights Organization during the late 1960s and early 1970s, the discourse that named AFDC a right was important in shaping not only the political potential of welfare recipients – their sense of themselves as citizens – but also their personal identities.[67]

This acknowledgement of the power of social movements should not diminish understanding of the powerful weapons of domination that welfare programmes put in the hands of controlling groups. Sophisticated studies of welfare will need rather a better specification of the balance between 'structure and agency,' that is, between the long-term economic and ideological patterns that organize societies and the more short-term influence of politically active elites and subordinates. More particularly this will require synthesizing structural and functionalist critiques of the operation of welfare programmes with histories of their development. It will require a rejection of determinist models of historical narrative which assume that final outcomes were somehow inevitable and that defeated proposals were *ipso facto* impossible;[68] it means writing history with foresight as well as hindsight, so to speak, from the vantage point of participants who did not already know the outcome. It also means more effort to bring into scholarship the actual experience of welfare recipients. This is especially important because of the domination of welfare scholarship by technocratic 'experts' who not only narrow their focus to microeconomic questions but who usually exclude all but quantitative questions. Radical academics are in a position to challenge this definition of scholarship.

Another need is the fuller integration of evidence about minority groups and the influence of racial attitudes and practices throughout the society. Such considerations must include the racial content of the design of welfare programmes, the ways in which the experiences of minority welfare recipients have been distinctive, and the relation of civil-rights and other minority activism to welfare demands. To the extent that we have made any progress in this area so far, it has been primarily about African–Americans and there has been a tendency to use the terms 'minority' and 'black' interchangeably. A racial analysis in turn suggests a needed advance in gender analysis: examining not only the relationships between women and other family members, and between women and the state, but among women as well. Women are not only divided by class, race, and other 'differences,' but may enter actual conflicts of interest with other women that directly affect their views on welfare policy. One obvious example has been the role of women as the employers of domestic servants, and the interest of the first group in maintaining other women's dependence on low wages. The concept of 'difference' does not capture what is at issue because it implies a pluralist multiplicity of stories which benignly coexist or interact; it may obscure relations of inequality, domination, and even exploitation among women.

Towards a New Welfare Politics

Gender-conscious scholarship on welfare is flourishing, but 'gender-blind' (or really, gender-obscuring) scholarship is also. This intellectual divide represents something about our historical moment: the women's movement produced a powerful feminist intellectual renascence, within and without the universities; but it has never been hegemonic and is now facing particularly sharp attack from conservatives and dismissal as impractical from liberals. This is to say that gender is also involved in welfare scholarship through the personal and collective transformations of many feminist scholars; and to say that this body of scholarship is inseparable from politics. The feminist critique of welfare reflects our own raised aspirations for ourselves and other women. But the steadily increasing inequalities, increasing particularly drmatically in the US, implicate women as well as men and often separate intellectuals sharply from the subjects/objects of our work. Thus while the conservative attack on social services places us on the defensive, academics are also farther than ever from the poor. Probably none of us in the US, however critical, can remain uninfluenced and unfrightened by the increasing alarm about the growth of an 'underclass;' few of us know how to sort out the real evidence of increasing violence, disease, and child neglect from a moral panic.

A good example of the resulting political confusion was the 1988 US welfare reform (the Family Support Act) which, among other provisions, mandates 'workfare,' requiring single mother welfare recipients to find employment. This legislation reflects a combination of conservative motives (tax-cutting, racism, hostility to single mothers and women's sexual and reproductive independence) with an acceptance of mothers' employment that most liberals and Leftists share. Indeed, the reform rests on an alliance between those who believe that employment and reliance on wages are on the whole strengthening to women and those who would use employment as a punishment for deviant women. Unfortunately the liberal as well as the conservative programmes are injurious to women, doing nothing to expand most women's choices beyond the alternatives of dependency (on men or the state) or inferior employment – underpaid, nonunionized, with poor working conditions. A democratic welfare reform will require a campaign against sex and race segregation in the labour force as well as against women's subordination in domestic life and labour. Thus the transformation of welfare into a nonstigmatizing, empowering system, one that encourages independence rather than dependence, must include a higher valuation of the work of child-raising and nurturance of dependents, an end to discrimination against women and minorities in the labour force, *and* a radical increase in employment opportunities overall.

This goal rests, too, on a redefinition of independence. We remarked above on how this notion described a male privilege, but we need also to question its very content as an ideal. The original meaning of independence, a word which appeared in English only in the 17th century, was: not needing to work for a living by having an independency, or competency – that is, a fortune. Since it was precisely such wealth that gave a man rights in early modern England, 'independence' also meant freedom. Later it evolved to describe the situation of a proprietor who owned everything he needed to live, such as land, tools, animals. In this pre-industrial and early industrial world, wage-earning meant dependence; it was a sign of the hegemony of capitalist political culture that wage-earning was redefined to mean the opposite, independence, thus denying or at least mystifying the abject dependence of workers on their employers. In this redefinition, women remained dependent, as non-wage-earners or lesser wage-earners, codified officially as dependents for tax purposes in the 20th century. Of course all these meanings are ideological, as all members of modern societies live in interdependence. Moreover the ideological functions support gender as well as class relations, justifying the undervaluing of unpaid reproductive labour and, through women's exclusive responsibility for it, the subordination of and disrespect for women. Thus a democratic welfare reform programme would include also a critique of fundamental social relations in capitalist society.

Clearly the articulation of a socialist-feminist welfare programme should be directed not only at other Leftists and other academics but also, somehow, at welfare recipients themselves. No serious reform seems possible in the absence of a strong movement of welfare recipients themselves, and it is hard to know what might bring that about. This is not, however, a good reason for silence or intellectual laziness among socialist-feminists with respect to welfare. Thinking and talking about these issues is a way of raising critical questions about our fundamental social organization.

NOTES

1. I have developed this point in my 'What Does Welfare Regulate', *Social Research* 55, 4, Winter 1988, pp. 609–30.
2. Oddly, this is less true of the conservative discussion. Commentors such as George Gilder and Charles Murray directly accuse feminism and resultant family breakdown as the source of welfare 'dependency,' and their goals explicitly include the maintenance of certain non-neutral gender patterns, especially the division of labour in the family. See Allen Hunter, 'Children in the Service of Conservatism: Parent-Child Relations in the New Right's Pro-Family Rhetoric,' University of Wisconsin Institute for Legal Studies Working Paper 2–8, April 1988, for references, especially George Gilder, *Wealth and Poverty* (NY: Basic Books, 1981) and Charles Murray, *Losing Ground. American Social Policy, 1950–1980* (NY: Basic Books, 1984).
3. This article appears, in another version, in my forthcoming anthology, *Women, the State, and Welfare* (Madison: University of Wisconsin Press, 1990).
4. There are already several collections of feminist articles on welfare from the U.K., Norway, and Australia, for example: Cora V. Baldock and Bettina Cass, *Women, Social Welfare, and the State in Australia* (Sydney: Allen and Unwin, 1983); H. Holter, ed., *Patriarchy in a Welfare Society* (Oslo: Universitetsforlaget, 1984); Jane Lewis, ed., *Women's Welfare, Women's Rights* (London: Croom Helm, 1983); Jennifer Dale and Peggy Foster, *Feminists and the Welfare State* (London: Routledge and Kegan Paul, 1986). In Britain a stronger radical social-work perspective has produced more feminist scholarship on social welfare. There are excellent books such as Gillian Pascall's *Social Policy. A Feminist Analysis* (London: Tavistock, 1986) and Elizabeth Wilson's *Women and the Welfare State* (London: Tavistock, 1977).
5. Jill Quadagno, 'Theories of the Welfare State,' *Annual Reviews in Sociology* 13, 1987, pp. 109–128.
6. Robert Bremner, *From the Depths. The Discovery of Poverty in the United States* (NY: New York University Press, 1956); James T. Patterson, *America's Struggle Against Poverty 1900–1980* (Cambridge: Harvard University Press, 1981); Walter I. Trattner, *From Poor Law to Welfare State. A History of Social Welfare in America* (NY: Free Press, 1974, 1984); John Ehrenreich, *The Altruistic Imagination: A History of Social Work and Social Policy in the United States* (Ithaca: Cornell University Press, 1985); David A. Rochefort, *American Social Welfare Policy. Dynamics of Formulation and Change* (Boulder & London: Westview Press, 1986); Michael B. Katz, *In the Shadow of the Poorhouse. A Social History of Welfare in America* (NY: Basic, 1986).
7. Patricia Huckle, 'The Womb Factor: Pregnancy Policies and Employment of Women,' in *Women, Power and Policy*, ed. Ellen Boneparth (NY: Pergamon, 1982), pp. 144–161.
8. Heide Gerstenberger, 'The Poor and the Respectable Worker: On the Introduction of Social Insurance in Germany,' *Labour History* 48, May 1985, pp. 69–85.
9. For example, Patrich M. Horan and Patricia Lee Austin in their 'The Social Bases of Welfare Stigma,' *Social Problems* 21 (1974), pp. 648–657, virtually ignore gender.
10. Linda Gordon, *Heroes of Their Own Lives: The Politics and History of Family Violence, Boston, 1880–1960* (NY: Viking/Penguin, 1988), chapter 4.
11. For examples, see Emily I. Abel, 'Adult Daughters and Care for the Elderly,' *Feminist Studies* 12 3, fall 1986, pp. 479–97; Laura Balbo, 'The Servicing Work of

Women and the Capitalist State,' in *Political Power and Social Theory*, ed. Maurice Zeitlin (Greenwich, Ct.: JAI Press, 1982), pp. 251–270). On women as translating between money and needs, see Batya Weinbaum and Amy Bridges, 'The Other Side of the Paycheck: Monopoly Capital and the Structure of Consumption,' in *Capitalist Patriarchy and the Case for Socialist Feminism*, ed. Zillah Eisenstein (NY: Monthly Review Press, 1979). pp. 190–205.

12. Jill Quadagno, 'From Old Age Assistance to Supplemental Security Income: The Political Economy of Relief in the South 1935–1972,' in *The Politics of Social Policy in the United States*, ed. Margaret Weir, Ann Shola Orloff, and Theda Skocpol (Princeton: Princeton University Press, 1988); Jerry Cates, *Insuring Inequality: Administrative Leadership in Social Security, 1935–1954* (Ann Arbor: University of Michigan, 1983); Harvard Sitkoff, *A New Deal for Blacks. The Emergence of Civil Rights as a National Issue: The Depression Decade* (NY: Oxford, 1978); Raymond Wolters, *Negroes and the Great Depression: The Problem of Economic Recovery* (Westport, CT: Greenwood, 1970); Wolters, 'The New Deal and the Negro,' in John Braeman et al. eds, *The New Deal: The National Level* (Columbus: Ohio State University Press, 1975).

13. Martha Ackelsberg, 'Dependency, Resistance and the Welfare State. Contributions and Limits of Feminist Theory,' in *Gender and the Origins of the Welfare State*,' Proceedings of Conferences at the Harvard Center for European Studies, 1987–88.

14. The first to apply the characterization 'Whig' to a view that the progress of representative government led inevitably to the welfare state was probably Asa Briggs in his 'The Welfare State in Historical Perspective,' *Archives Européennes de Sociologie*, II 2, 1961, 221–258.

15. Jill Quadagno, 'Theories of the Welfare State,' p. 112.

16. Pascal, *Social Policy*, p. 9.

17. Michael Shalev, 'The Social Democratic Model and Beyond: Two Generations of Comparative Research on the Welfare State', in *Comparative Social Research* (1983) 6, 315–51; Quadagno, 'Theories of the Welfare State,' p. 115.

18. This model is used by John Ehrenreich, *The Altruistic Imagination: A History of Social Work and Social Policy in the United States* (Ithaca: Cornell University Press, 1985).

19. Frances Fox Piven, 'Ideology and the State: Women, Power, and the Welfare State,' in Gordon, ed., *Women, the State, and Welfare*; Linda Gordon, 'Family Violence, Feminism, and Social Control,' *Feminist Studies* 12 3, Fall 1986, pp. 453–478; this point is also extremely well argued in a review of Gordon, *Heroes of Their Own Lives* by Ann Withorn, 'Radicalizing History: Writing about Women's Lives and the State,' *Radical America* 22 2–3, 1989, pp. 45–51.

20. In the following discussion I am indebted to Theda Skocpol's 'Political Response to Capitalist Crisis: Neo-Marxist Theories of the State and the Case of the New Deal,' *Politics and Society* 10 2, 1980, 155–201.

21. Ralph Miliband, *The State in Capitalist Society* (London: Weidenfield & Nicolson, 1969).

22. The difficulty in positing a homogeneous set of interests among men has been a problem for all theorizing about 'patriarchy' or male supremacy. This difficulty is one reason that I prefer an historical approach to conceptualizing male power, describing its actual operations in specific historical circumstances, examining class and ethnic groups among men as well as particular relations between men and women.

23. Nicos Poulantzas, 'The Problem of the Capitalist State,' in *Ideology in Social Science*, ed. Robin Blackburn (NY: Random House, 1973).

24. Fred Block, 'The Ruling Class Does Not Rule: Notes on the Marxist Theory of

the State,' in *Revising State Theory* . . *Essays in Politics and Postindustrialism*, ed. Fred Block (Philadelphia: Temple, 1987), pp. 51–68.

25. Theda Skocpol and John Ikenberry, 'The Political Formation of the American Welfare State in Historical and Comparative Perspective,' *Comparative Social Research* 6, 1983, pp. 87–148, for example.

26. Skocpol's *Protecting Soldiers and Mothers: The Politics of Social Provision in the United States*, forthcoming, may represent an improvement in her *oeuvre* in this regard.

27. Michael B. Katz, *The Undeserving Poor: From the War on Poverty to the War on Welfare* (NY: Pantheon, 1989), pp. 122, 138, and passim. See also Robert Haveman, *Poverty Policy and Poverty Research: The Great Society and the Social Sciences* (Madison: University of Wisconsin Press, 1987).

28. Sylvia Law, 'Women, Work, Welfare, and the Preservation of Patriarchy,' *University of Pennsylvania Law Review* 131 6, May 1983, 1251–1331; Joan Cummings, 'Sexism in Social Welfare; Some Thoughts on Strategy for Structural Change,' *Catalyst* 8, 1980, 7–34; Hilary Land, 'Women; Supporters or Supported?' in *Sexual Divisions and Society: Process and Change*, ed. Diana Leonard Barker and Sheila Allen (London: Tavistock, 1979), pp. 108–132; idem., 'Who Still Cares for the Family? Recent Developments in Income Maintenance, Taxation and Family Law,' in *Journal of Social Policy* 7 3, July 1978, 275–84.

29. Pat Thane, 'Women and the Poor Law in Victorian and Edwardian England,' *History Workshop: A Journal of Socialist Historians* 6, Autumn 1978, 29–51.

30. Gail Bushwalter King, 'Women and Social Security: An Applied History Overview,' in *Social Science History* 6 2, spring 1982, 227–232.

31. Diana M. Pearce, 'Toil and Trouble: Women Workers and Unemployment Compensation,' *Signs* 10 3, spring 1985, pp. 439–59.

32. Irene Diamond, 'Women and Housing: The Limitations of Liberal Reform,' in *Women, Power and Policy*, ed. Ellen Boneparth (NY: Pergamon, 1982), pp. 109–117.

33. Mimi Abramovitz, *Regulating the Lives of Women. Social Welfare Policy from Colonial Times to the Present* (Boston: South End Press, 1988).

34. Barbara Nelson, 'The Origins of the Two-Channel Welfare State: Workmen's Compensation and Mothers' Aid,' and Gwendolyn Mink, 'The Lady and the Tramp: Gender, Race, and the Origins of the American Welfare State,' both in Gordon, ed., *Women, the State, and Welfare*.

35. For examples: Katz, *In the Shadow of the Poorhouse*, pp. 238–39; James Leiby, *A History of Social Welfare and Social Work in the United States* (NY: Columbia University Press, 1978), p. 247; Samuel Mencher, 'Status and Contract in Assistance Policy,' *Social Service Review* 25 1, March 1961.

36. Hace Sorel Tishler, *Self-Reliance and Social Security 1870–1917* (Port Washington, NY: National University Publications, 1971), p. 142.

37. Nelson, 'The Origins of the Two-Channel Welfare State'; Diana Pearce, 'Welfare is Not *for* Women,' in Gordon, ed., *Women, the State and Welfare*; Nancy Folbre, 'Intergenerational Transfer and the Origin of Social Security,' unpublished paper, Population Association of America, 1987.

38. See my 'What Does Welfare Regulate?' *Social Research* 55 4, Winter 1988, pp. 609–630.

39. Hilary Land, 'The Family Wage,' *Feminist Review* 6, 1980, pp. 55–77; Jill Roe, 'The End is Where We Start From: Women and Welfare Since 1901,' in *Women, Social Welfare and the State in Australia*, ed. Cora V. Baldock and Bettina Cass (Boston: George Allen & Unwin, 1983), 1–19; Jane Lewis, 'Dealing with Dependency: State Practices and Social Realities, 1870–1945,' in *Women's Welfare, Women's Rights*, ed. Jane Lewis (London: Croom Helm, 1983), pp. 17–37; Mary McIntosh, 'The

Welfare State and the Needs of the Dependent Family,' in *Fit Work for Women* ed. Sandra Burman (NY: St. Martin's Press, 1979), pp. 153–172; Mimi Abramowitz, *Regulating the Lives of Women. Social Welfare Policy From Colonial Times to the Present* (Boston: South End Press, 1988), esp. chapters 1 and 3; Linda Gordon, 'What Does Welfare Regulate?'

40. Helene Silverberg, 'Women, Welfare and the State,' *Cornell Journal of Social Relations*, vol. 18, spring 1985, pp. 1–12.

41. Michael Walzer, 'Socializing the Welfare State,' in *Democracy and the Welfare State* ed. Amy Gutmann (Princeton: Princeton University Press, 1988), pp. 13–26.

42. Carole Pateman, 'The Patriarchal Welfare State,' in Gutmann, ed., *Democracy and the Welfare State*, pp. 231–260. See also her *The Sexual Contract* (Stanford: Stanford University Press, 1988). On issues of citizenship see also Susan Moller Okin, *Justice, Gender, and the Family* (New York: Basic Books, 1989).

43. Barbara Ehrenreich and Deirdre English, *For Her Own Good. 150 Years of the Experts' Advice to Women* (NY: Anchor/Doubleday, 1978).

44. Alicia Frohman, 'Day Care and the Regulation of Women's Labor Force Participation,' *Catalyst* 2, 1978, 5–17. She does not seem aware that Ruth Milkman has demonstrated that the reserve-army-of-labour hypothesis does not work for women, because the labour market is so sexually segregated that it has little flexibility to exchange women's and men's jobs. See Milkman, 'Women's Work and the Economic Crisis: Some Lessons from the Great Depression,' *Review of Radical Political Economics* 8 1, spring 1976, 73–97.

45. Diana Leonard Barker, 'The Regulation of Marriage: Repressive Benevolence,' in *Power and the State*, ed. Gary Littlejohn et al. (NY: St. Martin's Press, 1978), pp. 239–266.

46. Ann Douglas, *The Feminization of American Culture* (NY: Knopf, 1977); William Leach, *True Love and Perfect Union. The Feminist Reform of Sex and Society* (NY: Basic Books, 1980); Ellen DuBois and Linda Gordon, 'Seeking Ecstasy on the Battlefield; Nineteenth-century Feminist Views of Sexuality,' *Feminist Studies* 9 1, spring 1983; Linda Gordon, *Heroes of Their Own Lives: The History and Politics of Family Violence, Boston 1880–1960* (NY: Viking, 1988); Linda Gordon, 'Women and the Creation of Public Welfare, 1890–1945,' paper given at AHA/Smithsonian Institution conference on the Progressive Era, March 1988, unpub.

47. Patricia Tulloch, 'Gender and Dependency,' in *Unfinished Business; Social Justice for Women in Australia* (Sydney: George Allen & Unwin, 1984), 19–37.

48. Carol Brown, 'Mothers, Fathers and Children: From Private to Public Patriarchy,' in *Women and Revolution*, ed. Lydia Sargent (Boston: South End Press, 1981), pp. 239–67. Norwegian scholar Helge Maria Hernes conceptualizes this as a transition from private to public dependence; see her 'Women and the Welfare State. The Transition from Private to Public Dependence,' in Holter, *Patriarchy in a Welfare Society*, op. cit. U. S. Feminist philosopher Ann Ferguson makes a finer and somewhat different distinction between 'father patriarchy,' 'husband patriarchy' in the modern period, and 'public (capitalist) patriarchy.' See her 'On Conceiving Motherhood and Sexuality: A Feminist Materialist Approach,' in *Mothering. Essays in Feminist Theory*, ed. Joyce Trebilcot (Totowa, NJ: Rowman & Allanheld, 1984), pp. 153–182.

49. Zillah R. Eisenstein, *Feminism and Sexual Equality* (NY: Monthly Review Press, 1984), p. 89.

50. Linda Gordon, 'Single Mothers and Child Neglect,' *American Quarterly* 37 2, spring 1985, pp. 173–192.

51. Eli Zaretsky, 'The Place of the Family in the Origins of the Welfare State,'

in *Rethinking the Family. Some Feminist Questions*, ed. Barrie Thorne (NY: Longman, 1982), pp. 188–224.

52. Pateman, 'The Patriarchal Welfare State.'
53. Piven, 'Ideology and the State.'
54. Paula Baker, 'The Domestication of Politics: Women and American Political Society, 1780–1920,' *American Historical Review* 89 3, June 1984, pp. 620–47. On enlarging the notion of the political, see Linda Gordon, 'What Should Women's Historians Do: Politics, Social Theory, and Women's History,' *Marxist Perspectives* 3, fall 1978, pp. 128–136.
55. For overviews of this activity, see Paula Giddings, *When and Where I Enter. The Impact of Black Women on Race and Sex in America* (New York: William Morrow, 1984); Cynthia Neverdon-Morton, *Afro-American Women of the South and the Advancement of the Race, 1895–1925* (Knoxville: University of Tennessee Press, 1989).
56. Linda Gordon, 'Race and Class Divisions in Women's Welfare Activism,' forthcoming.
57. Gordon, ibid.
58. Gordon, *Heroes of Their Own Lives*.
59. Maureen Fitzgerald, 'Saints, Seduction, and Social Control: Irish Catholic Nuns and Immigrant Women in New York City, 1845–1900, dissertation in progress, Department of History, University of Wisconsin.
60. Nancy Hewitt, *Women's Activism and Social Change. Rochester, New York 1822–1972* (Ithaca, NY: Cornell University Press, 1984.)
61. Giddings, *When and Where I Enter*; Rosalyn Terborg-Penn, 'Discrimination Against Afro-American Women in the Woman's Movement, 1830–1920,' in *The Afro-American Woman. Struggles and Images*, eds. Sharon Harley and Rosalyn Terborg-Penn (Port Washington, NY: Kennikat Press, 1978), pp. 17–27.
62. Gordon, *Heroes of Their Own Lives*; and Gordon, 'The Frustrations of Family Violence Social Work: An Historical Critique,' *Journal of Sociology and Social Welfare*, XV 4, December 1988.
63. Lisa Peattie and Martin Rein, *Women's Claims: A Study in Political Economy* (Oxford: Oxford University Press, 1983), esp. p. 9 ff.
64. For the Marxist critique of needs talk, see Agnes Heller, 'Can "True" and "False" Needs be Posited?', chapter 5 in *The Power of Shame. A Rational Perspective* (London: Routledge, Kegan Paul, 1985).
65. Laura Balbo, 'Family, Women, and the State: Notes Towards A Typology of Family Roles and Public Intervention,' in *Changing Boundaries of the Political*, ed. Charles S. Maier (Cambridge: Cambridge University Press, 1987), pp. 201–219; Nancy Fraser, 'Struggle Over Needs: Outline of a Socialist–Feminist Critical Theory of Late-Capitalist Political Culture,' in Gordon, ed., *Women, the State, and Welfare*.
66. There is an interesting legal debate about *when* the rights claim emerged. Sylvia Law, 'Women, Work, and Welfare;' Rand E. Rosenblatt, 'Legal Entitlement and Welfare Benefits,' in David Kairys, ed., *The Politics of Law. A Progressive Critique* (NY: Pantheon, 1982), pp. 262–278; William H. Simon, 'The Invention and Reinvention of Welfare Rights,' *Maryland Law Review* 44 1, 1985, pp. 1–37; and Simon, 'Rights and Redistribution in the Welfare System,' *Stanford Law Review* 38 143, 1986, pp. 1431–1516.
67. Guida West, *The National Welfare Rights Movement. The Social Protest of Poor Women* (NY: Praeger, 1981).
68. For an egregious example of this kind of thinking see Daniel Levine, *Poverty and Society. The Growth of the American Welfare State in International Comparison* (New Brunswick: Rutgers University Press, 1988.)

INTELLECTUALS AGAINST THE LEFT:
THE CASE OF FRANCE

GEORGE ROSS

The French intellectual Left has undergone a startling conversion experience. Socialism, Marxism and virtually all other post-enlightenment visions of human liberation through political struggle remained prominent in French intellectual life until very recently, far longer, in fact, than in almost any other advanced capitalist society. Yet by the time of the 1989 *Bicentenaire* of the French Revolution, concepts like class conflict and revolution had completely vanished from Left political and intellectual discourses. In Perry Anderson's well-chosen words,

> In the three decades or so after the Liberation, France came to enjoy a cosmopolitan paramountcy in the general Marxist universe that recalls in its own way something of the French ascendancy in the epoch of the Enlightenment. The fall of this dominance in the later seventies was thus no mere national matter. . .Its consequences have been drastic. Paris is today the capital of European intellectual reaction.[1]

This essay will explore the substance and sources of this conversion. In Part 1 we will review the actual story of the changing ideas of the French Left intelligentsia. In Part II we will try to to connect these trajectories to underlying social and political trends. Here we will touch the heart of the story. Economic modernization brought substantial change to France's class structure, including, most importantly, a vast expansion in new middle strata. France's official Left, alas, proved quite incapable of adapting its own visions in ways which would have attracted critical Left-leaning intellectual segments of these strata. What happened was that the intelligentsia declared its theoretical independence from the official Left, with disastrous consequences for the Left itself.

I. Stories of French Left Intellectuals
There is a conventional way to talk about recent French Left intellectual thought. Put simply, Sartre failed to reconstruct French Marxism, Lévi-Strauss imposed structuralism, and Althusser failed to turn it in a Marxist direction. The field was thus left open for post-structuralism which gave way to neo-liberalism in the 1980s. We will review this story, but with an

unconventional twist. Rather than focussing exclusively on the 'greats' we will follow the trajectories of three specific types of intellectuals, the greats, to be sure, but 'artisanal' political sociologists and generational cohorts of young Left intellectuals in addition. The reason for this is that we can find no good reason to believe, in contrast to most intellectual historians, that elite intellectual thought consistently overdetermines other, less exalted, types of intellectuality.

The High Years of Gaullism

The Vichy period had destroyed the credibility of Right-of-Centre elite intellectualization, so that after Liberation reformist and Left-leaning *socialisant* notions dominated. The coming of the Cold War after 1945 further narrowed things around Communist ideas. Despite the crudely instrumental nature of the PCF's 'intellectual' positions the party's political strength gave it considerable power.[2] This manichaean Cold War situation came to an end in 1956. The PCF's unwillingness to undertake serious de-Stalinization and its support of the Soviet invasion of Hungary dramatically undercut its power to compel intellectually. In a new environment of peaceful coexistence and economic growth, official Communist thought appeared more and more inadequate to the task of accounting for a rapidly changing French society. Thus Marxism, which had briefly assumed immense importance in high Left intellectual life, came under siege.

Here our story really begins. None other than Sartre himself took up the task of revisionist reconstruction to defend Marxism. The very model of the modern intellectual titan, Sartre, manipulating a huge store of intellectual capital accumulated by the success of existentialism, remained an overpowering presence.[3] But it was neither the militant existentialist nor the Cold War fellow traveller who stepped forward at this point.[4] Instead Sartre offered the existential Marxism of *Search for a Method* and, above all, *Critique de la raison dialectique*.[5]

With Sartre thus in the lead, one major Left intellectual vector, stretching well into the 1960s, was an attempt to revise reductionist, mechanical and politically determined Cold War Marxism towards greater causal complexity and epistemological openness. Important journals like *Arguments* and *Socialisme ou Barbarie* were founded by ex-Communists and other *marxisant* thinkers. Their animators – Morin, Lefort, Lefebvre, Castoriadis, etc. – shared Sartre's basic concerns, if not his existentialist predilections.[6]

Despite Sartre's *patronage* and involvement, however, the quest for such an open-ended Marxism fell short. Michel Foucault's 1966 comment that the '*Critique de la raison dialectique* is the magnificent and pathetic effort of a 19th century man to think through the 20th century' was indicative of how younger intellectuals received Sartre's magnum Marxist opus.[7] Sartre's public prominence remained very significant, but more as celebrity and witness, ever eager to champion radical protests, than as a modernizer of Marxism.[8]

In similar vein, most 'lesser' post-1956 reformulators of Marxism, like the *Arguments* group, were quick to abandon the effort altogether.

As these attempts to reconstruct a new Marxism faded, a new 'great,' Claude Lévi-Strauss, armed with a new vision, structuralism, climbed to the top of the elite intellectual hill. Beginning the famous 'linguistic turn' by analogizing from linguistics into anthropology, Lévi-Strauss and his followers sought deep, transhistorical constants in human experience, buried structural 'languages' common to all social life. Structuralism, like Marxism, thus sought to decode social relationships and expose their basic logics. In contrast to Marxism, however, the logics uncovered by structuralism were so profound that they made history disappear altogether. Perhaps more important, proponents of structuralism were quick to denounce what they considered to be the anachronistic historicism in Marxism's focus on the connections between economic dynamics and social conflict. In its purest forms, in the master's own works, structuralism thus made Marxism look relative and ephemeral.[9] The structuralist movement thus 'defeated' the old mechanical Marxism of the PCF. More important, it blocked the claims of post-1956 'Independent' Marxism, of which Sartre's existential Marxism was probably the most important variety, to institutionalize a more subtle Marxist-humanist vision of the world. Of particular interest was the appeal – which was intellectually odd, given its broadsides against historicism – of structuralism to young, 'thirdworldist' intellectual activists.

Marxism responded in the person of Louis Althusser, who adopted much of the conceptual vocabulary of structuralism and attempted to graft it onto the body of Marxism itself. While the patient was on the operating table, Althusser and his acolytes created a 'structuralist Marxism' which, while attacking both Marxist humanism and Stalinist economism, managed to devise a 'history without a subject,' in the words of Pierre Grémion.[10] By burying social causality in deep structures like 'mode of production', the Althusserian turn undercut perhaps Marxism's greatest practical appeal, its purported capacity to lay bare the various motors of historical development and make them accessible to rational, progressive human action. The connection between the Althusserian reformulation of Marxism and real politics became ever more tenuous, leading eventually to a political and intellectual impasse.[11] Ultimately Althusserianism proved to be yet another Parisian fad which was well in retreat by the mid 1970s.[12]

Here we will abandon the familiar. French thought about state-society relationships, as in other societies, was also carried on by academic 'artisans' working within their disciplines. French political sociology, the 'artisanal text' we have chosen to explore, is no exception. As things gathered momentum after the Algerian War, many plants, if not 100 flowers, bloomed. Thus in the 1960s, there developed a number of *socialisant* sociological visions of state-society relations. Alain Touraine, but one example, worked towards a theoretical model in which class structuration and struggle were the key elements for understanding political behaviours and state actions in quite a *marxisant* way, at least in the abstract.[13] Pierre Bourdieu deployed a similar conceptual vocabulary in his earlier works on reproduction through education.[14] The important contributions of Serge Mallet, Pierre Belleville, Pierre Naville, André Gorz, Cornelius Castoriadis and others might be added.[15]

More generally, each sociological artisan developed different specific approaches and each developed visions which were profoundly different from orthodox Marxisms, PCF or other.[16] But the basic perception of a society unequally structured into conflicting classes determining political behaviours and state action persisted. Here what was interesting was the contrast between the flight of elite intellectuals into structuralism and artisanal persistence in the use of *marxisant* conceptual catalogues.

Looking at 'generations' of young Left intellectual activists – a particularly fruitful way of thinking about intellectual politics which French contemporary historians have developed in recent years[17] – provides yet a different map of the evolution of the Left intelligentsia during the high Gaullist years. The deeply segmented Algerian War generation of young Left intellectuals was nonetheless unified around one thing, its attitude towards the official Left.[18] Student and intellectual rejection of the war was much more strident and militant than this Left wanted to see.[19] The PCF was eager to protect de Gaulle and prospects for a post-war alliance of the Left and thus desired a moderate and circumspect anti-war movement. Its scornful and repressive responses to the budding radicalism of student protest meant that virtually all segments of the student movement came to a committed rejection of the PCF's theories and practices.[20] The complicity of French Socialism with the war itself meant that students saw nothing meritorious in the SFIO either. The more *marxisant* segments of the generation thus sought different 'vanguards' from the PCF along with a different, more muscular, Marxism.[21] Youth protest against the Algerian War was also an essential moment in the development of the Left Catholicism whose role would be so important in '60s and '70s France.[22]

The Algerian War and May '68 generations were intimately connected. May '68 had its own complex causes and logics, of course. The protest movement, sparked in large part by the day-to-day ineptitude of university administrations, Gaullist ministerial staffs and the police, had quickly to improvise structures and organizations, practically out of nowhere. The politically-proven cadres of the Algerian War generation were available for such tasks. This juxtaposition explains the May movement's strange combination of extreme libertarianism, even anarchism, and Marxist sloganizing. 'Imagination' was brought briefly to power, amidst some chaos, to the words of the *Internationale*. But those who coached the crowds in the words of Citoyen Pottier's very French poem, even though they could not agree among themselves *which* International was being referred to, were united about the one which was not. The Marxism of May, such as it was, was an anti-PCF Marxism.[23]

Entre Deux Mais: 1968–1981
Pure structuralism, triumphant among the *grands intellos* in the 1960s, was itself superseded in the 1970s by what Luc Ferry and Alain Renaut have labelled *La Pensée 68*, post-structuralist 'anti-humanism.'[24] Figures like Michel Foucault, Jacques Lacan and Jacques Derrida became the post-1968 kings of the intellectual hill. All shared a profound rebelliousness, though each in his own differing way. More generally, all were united by a common rejection of enlightenment thought with its historicist postulation of ever-progressing rationality and understanding. Marxism was but one target here.

Foucault, a Nietzschean and perhaps the most important post-structuralist in explicitly political terms, explored the genealogies of various human meaning structures as almost serendipitous historical creations which blossomed into long-standing oppressive realities. History, for Foucault, produced underlying discourses which shaped and constrained social behaviour, constituting power in the process, but in a virtually random way. 'Man' was dead, or so at least was the Enlightenment's integral subject moving bravely forward progressive step by progressive step. Enlightenment humanism, including its Victorian subsidiary, Marxism, was deemed parochial. Oppressive power, to Foucault, could not be localized in institutions and institutional complexes, but instead resided in the discursive constructs within which such institutions and complexes operated. One did not look to *the* state to see power in action, but rather to a 'micropolitics' of discursive definitions and constraints. Moreover, one could never be sure of what one saw, given that actors themselves were placed in – even constituted by – webs of discourses.

Resistance to oppressive power was essential, Foucault implied (and himself practised in a number of different ways, including activism on prisoners' rights issues and the Indochinese boat people).[25] But the historically serendipitous genealogy of discursive structures and the relativized position of actors – the subject itself constantly changed in accordance with its positioning in different discursive constructs – meant that resisters could never be sure what the appropriate object was, what they should aim to change and whether any set of specific actions would change things for better or worse.[26]

The Freudian revisionism of Lacan was analogous, dissolving Freud's concept of the subject and undercutting Freud's projected rationalist, if tragic, trajectory of psychodynamics, although here into a much more explicitly linguistic universe. Derrida, the Heideggerian, rigorously denounced the metaphysical cores both of humanism (with Sartre the main target) and of structuralism itself, proposing instead a hard-nosed deconstructionist hermeneutics in which the 'subject' again disappeared.[27] One could make analogous remarks about the nature of Lacan's and Derrida's rebelliousness to those made earlier about Foucault.

Taken together, all three – and we might include a number of other thinkers (Barthes, Baudrillard, Lyotard, Guattari, plus the influential feminists Kristéva, Cixous and Irigaray) clearly struck responsive chords in post-1968 debates. In the experience of many of the post-1968 generation, rebellious acts derived from rationalistic, enlightenment-derived schemas for political action, including those of the traditional Left, proceeded from a statist logic which missed the point of real domination. Changing things at state level through legislation would have but limited, perhaps perverse, effects. All of this resonated with post-structuralist thought. Protest was necessary, given the oppressiveness of reality. Yet the diachronic setting of such protest would be impenetrable and its outcome unclear.

If May 1968 and its aftermath brought the ascension of post-structuralism and post-modernism in elite intellectual circles, they had different effects on the 'artisan' sociologists. For them, there was no dramatic shift analogous to that from structuralism to post-structuralism. To Alain Touraine and his *équipe*, for example, May 1968 'proved' that the conflict relationships characteristic of 'industrial societies' were beginning to give way in France to those of 'post-industrial' societies.[28] Production-based conflicts over an economistic 'historicity' were being transcended by 'new social movements' and struggles over the 'programming' of society by new technocratic elites. Here the essential point was that the form of traditional *marxisant* arguments – arguing from class to politics – was maintained in order the better to argue against the usual *content* of such arguments, in particular against the more classical propositions of the official Left. The Bourdieu school likewise expanded its production on reproduction, with arguments which proceeded from class conflict to various types of behaviours, *via* use of Bourdieu's conceptual toolbox of cultural capital, habitat, 'field,' cultural investment, etc.[29] What happened in different realms of culture could only be understood in terms of the strategies of different classes either to maintain their superior positions or to challenge their relegation to inferiority.[30]

There was also a great expansion in stratification-based *marxisant* contributions from other, less strictly academic, sources. Later Eurocommunist and Euroleft reflections (like those of Nicos Poulantzas and Christine Buci-Glucksmann) were significant, for example.[31] Even *autogestionnaire* political sociology, whether associated with the Parti Socialiste Unifié (PSU) or the Confédération Française Démocratique du Travail (CFDT), tended to follow a neo-Marxist outline, rejecting, of course, statist correlations in the interests of decentralized class actions.[32] And as the 1970s – and the renaissance of the French Left – progressed, the effects of 'official' Left intellectualization made important contributions. The elaborations of State Monopoly Capitalism theory by the PCF's *Section Economique* and the Socialist Party's discussions about *le Front de Classe*[33] were examples.

The political intellectuality of the 'generation' of May was another story. The renaissance of ultra-Leftism was but one of its manifestations. There was also a plethora of autonomous 'new social movements' – feminism, regionalism, ecology etc., not to speak of the social movement energies incorporated into the PSU and the Left Catholic trade unionism of the CFDT. A 'new culture' side of much of the May generation, whatever specific trajectory one discusses – excepting, perhaps, the ultra-Leftists, is also worthy of mention. The conviction that social life, including sexual life, ought to be more relaxed, or at least different from what it had been before, was shared across political divides.[34]

The 1970s biographies of other segments of the '68 generation are different still. *Pace* Alain Touraine, French post-1960s 'new social movements,' including, most importantly, French feminism, upon whose trajectory we will briefly focus, never achieved the prominence of those in other advanced societies. At the precise moment when these movements arose, the official French Left, which had been out of power for decades, itself began to gather the steam which eventually brought it to power in 1981. Both the Socialists and the Communists, the major components of the official Left, were eager to coopt the energies of various post-1968 rebellious currents, including feminism. Moreover, both had a history of what one might call 'socialist feminism,' of raising women's issues in the context of a broader 'class' appeal. The new women's movement in France – along with virtually all of the other 1970s 'new social movements' – had therefore to choose between independence and integration into the official Left, which promised a certain amount of political effectiveness at the price of accepting 'socialist feminism.' The consequence of this situation divided and severely weakened the autonomous women's movement in France. Different fractions of the movement made different choices, but the 'vacuum cleaner' effect of the official Left parties was considerable. Those segments of the movement which remained outside the orbit of the official Left (and the unions, also important players) themselves rapidly divided into small competing groups whose internecine conflicts further undercut the movement's position.[35]

The *gauchiste* sequels of May 68 were different – here we will follow the trajectories of the Maoists. The passionate *encadrement* of Maoists and others like them in quasi-cult grouplets could not be sustained in an ever more indifferent environment. The feelings of self-deception and personal waste which followed contributed to the creation of an important community of apostates. The so-called 'new philosophy' was one manifestation of this apostasy.[36] From naive beliefs in miracle solutions to France's problems – whether proletarian revolution or *autogestion* – there first emerged anger that the world was refractory to such visions and then fury at the 'straight' Left which, in the 1970s, was capitalizing on French discontents using traditional political programmes and methods. A strange, extremely belated, discovery by the French intelligentsia of the unpleasantness of Soviet society and a

consequent wave of anti-Sovietism played an important role. By the mid-
1970s, the underlying direction which had emerged was that the politics of
the 'old' Left, embodied in *Union de la Gauche*, were both out of date and
dangerous.

The separation of important segments of the maturing *soixante huitard*
generation from official Left politics was thus reconfirmed even as the
justifications for this separation changed dramatically. The new perspectives
involved complete rejection of global social thinking plus strong anti-statism,
given the ties to post-structuralist thought and anarchism. Conviction grew
that decentralized and democratic, often non-political, movements below
central state level were the real bearers of progressive change in France – in
the jargon which was to come, 'civil society' was the locus of social creativity,
not parties and civil servants. Here, the ex-*gauchistes* rejoined other, more
autogestionnaire, segments of the 1968 generation.

In retrospect, the coming of *Union de la Gauche* in the 1970s was of great
importance for the 1968 generation. Not all of that generation gravitated
towards a radical scepticism of official Left ideas. A large group of *soixante
huitards* did find their way towards the two major parties of the Left.
By the early 1970s, the renewed Socialist Party offered young intellectual
militants new openings to do Left politics within a rapidly changing political
organization which might, in the medium term, confer large career rewards.
Large numbers of the 68 and Left Unity generations also joined the PCF,
motivated by a desire to combine militancy, passion and career similar to
that of their PS *frères-ennemis*.[37]

The most important characteristic of this incorporation of intellectuals into
the official Left was its partiality. Those who entered the PCF were rudely
removed at the end of the 1970s when the party's strategy changed. For their
part, those who joined the PS bought into it a profound contradiction between
the party's coalition setting and the social alliance needs to which it had to
respond. Opting for *Union de la Gauche* involved 'dealing' with the PCF
in order better to subordinate and weaken French Communism. We now
know how successful this choice turned out to be electorally. But *Union de
la Gauche* meant compromising with the PCF on programme and ideology.[38]
This meant a general PS outlook in the 1970s governed by the spirit of the
1972 Common Programme, a statist, *dirigiste* platform of reforms which many
intellectuals rejected.

The Success of Anti-Marxist Intellectuality: The 1980s
Fate marked the first years of the 1980s. In close proximity, a number of once
and would-be kings of intellectual Parisiana died – Barthes, Sartre, Aron,
Lacan, Foucault. Certain others (Althusser, after the murder of his wife,
even Derrida, despite his continuing American celebrity) fell into lengthen-
ing shadows. The death of Vincennes University, the symbol of post-1968
thought, was equally ominous.[39] Starting at the same point, post-structuralism

began to decline – even though its success as an export product to the English-speaking world kept such news from crossing the Channel and the Atlantic – wounded by ever more intense critical attack and changing political concerns. Socially, the post-68 moment of rebellion had ended. Economically, the post-war boom had collapsed into hard-nosed discussions of policy reevaluation. 'Boat people' washing ashore, the sequels of the Chinese cultural revolution, martial law and the repression of Solidarnosc in Poland, and the Afghan invasion, among other things, provided additional reasons to reflect on the various radical utopianisms of the 1960s. The rapid policy failure of the French Left after it came to power in 1981 furthered contributed to a newly sober environment.

By the turn of the 1980s, characteristic outlooks among elite Left intellectuals had changed dramatically. Something which we might label 'neo-liberalism with a human face' progressively took stage centre away from post-structuralism. Growing anti-statism fed a resurrection of liberal political philosophizing. There were, to be sure, distant lines of kinship between post-structuralism and an emergent decentralized individualism. Post-structuralism had made it unsound to reify the state as the key locus of oppression and the central fulcrum for progressive change. Still, post-structuralism had been intent both on identifying the roots of oppression elsewhere and in advocating resistance. And here the break occurred. The new liberalism, if also belligerently anti-statist, was infinitely less concerned with localizing sources of oppression and, more important, was anything but rebellious.

A number of different intellectual quests converged on the final results. The Marxist operation of reducing the separate dynamics of state and society to one set of causal variables and programming their reconciliation in a utopian, non-contradictory future had been disposed of earlier. To budding new liberals, the use of state power to reduce social oppression created new problems without alleviating those which statist strategies set out to resolve in the first place. In the new setting, elite intellectuals also found it less and less compelling to use deconstructive techniques to cast doubt on the very possibility of finding meaning in the social and political world. Thus it could no longer be a question of positing the constantly shifting, unpredictable but nonetheless omniscient oppressiveness of both state and society. The contradictions between these two things seemed, instead, to be permanent, and this was what was most important to confront. The conclusion was that one had to philosophize anew about relationships between state and society.

The underlying search, by the mid-1980s, was for the theoretical groundings of a polity where state power would be limited and circumscribed, allowing maximum space for democratic individualism while avoiding the undesirable atomizing aspects of Anglo-Saxon utilitarianism. It was a case of looking for America without Reagan and Adam Smith. To find it, there was first of all an Aron renaissance, which grew even more important following the great liberal's death. Aron once monumentalized, there then followed a massive reexamination of 19th century French liberalism – Constant, Guizot and, above all, Tocqueville.[40] Simultaneously there was busy translation from the English and American – of Karl Popper, Friedrich von Hayek and Hannah Arendt,[41] along with 1950s and 1960s reflections on pluralism and more recent liberal reflections on distributive justice, Rawls in particular.

There was striking new modesty in all this. Elite French Left intellectuals lost their traditional taste for global reflection on the nature of society per se. Instead, they turned to a preoccupation with what they perceived to be the eternal problems of all societies which, by definition, were unresolvable. The new issue was to find humane ways of living with their permanence. In consequence, generalizing conceptualizations which placed their makers in positions of critical externality to what existed – 'ideologies,' if you will – came to be regarded as intrinsically dangerous. What existed was fundamentally ineluctable, rendering effort to transcend it futile and hubristic. As two insightful critics noted, because politics could no longer change anything profound, political issues became technical '. . .it was up to politics to ensure the indispensable minimum of collective relationships, but real life lay somewhere else.'[42]

The situation of Left intellectual artisans also changed dramatically. First of all, there was a rapid deflation of artisanal confidence in neo-Marxist stratification-based models of politics, such that by the mid-1980s Marxist concepts had disappeared from the wordprocessors and bookshelves of French social scientists.[43] In more influential recent works, issues pertaining to social stratification and politics – Luc Boltanski's *Cadres*, for example – one finds a newly phenomenologized sense of the social construction of groups rather than reference to underlying social structures.[44] The centrality of politics itself declined. Alain Touraine, always a bellwether, wrote in 1987 that '. . .Politics seemed. . .[as late as]. . .1981, to be at the center and summit of social life. Now it is only a passage way between the problems of personal life and those of the international economic and military system. . .'[45]

If Left political sociology ceased being 'Left' in the older French sense of the term, no single coherent alternative replaced the 'old' class analytical orthodoxy. Nonetheless, here too there was also new reflection about 19th century French liberal republican political culture and its social bases, paralleling the rise of similar concerns in elite social theory. Tocqueville, retranslated from the American, often replaced Marx.[46] Quite as important, the increasing intellectual prominence of economists and economism erected a new language of constraint and refractory environments.[47] Underlying this, confidence in the state's capacity to reorient social behaviours, to coordinate the economy in equitable ways, to regenerate civic virtue, etc. disappeared. Much theoretical and methodological attention turned towards individuals and their calculations[48] – aided and abetted by evidence from opinion polls and election studies which showed a rise in individual, as opposed to class, orientations – and to the textures of non-political associative life.[49]

Throughout the 1960s and 1970s one got a different picture of intellectual movements and the forces behind them when one chose the prism of political generations of intellectuals rather than those of the *grands intellos* and 'artisans.' By the 1980s this was much less true. The trajectories of many post-1968 *gauchistes* towards liberalism was already quite clear prior to the 1980s, as was the virtual disappearance of 'new social movement' activists due to the vacuum cleaner effects of the Left in the 1970s. On the level of Left intellectual generations, by the earlier 1980s a 'certain Leftism,' *marxisant* or *socialisant,* statist and voluntarist about the uses of political power to change economy and society in a radical way, had disappeared. It was replaced in differing ways, of course, but there were common themes placing much greater weight on the importance of creativity and innovation in the social sphere together with much greater scepticism about the capacities of the state to promote social change. And, almost as significantly, the 'market' was rediscovered as a part of this creative social world rather than an appendage of politics to be manipulated by the state.

II Deconstructing French Intellectuals
Telling the story of French intellectuals in a more complicated way than it is usually told – by refusing to focus exclusively on the so-called 'greats' – does not make it any more uplifting from a Left point of view. More important, we have not yet uncovered the real plot. Intellectuals are creators, undeniably. Yet, to paraphrase an author no longer read in France, they create in social contexts not of their own choosing. We must therefore explore the contexts within which French intellectuals have worked in the past three decades. What have been the social *causes* of the cataclysm of Left thought in France?

The Limits of Sociology
We must first look at the data. The social settings of French intellectual life were well under reconstruction by the 1960s. A massive post-war demographic upturn had begun to affect French institutions, coinciding with the very high growth rates, changing lifestyles and shifting occupational patterns of the onrushing post-war boom. Employment in tertiary areas, those demanding higher educational attainment in particular, increased very rapidly: managers, bureaucrats and professionals practically doubled from 7.7% of the labour force in 1954 to 14.8% in 1968, while white collar workers grew from 10.8 to 14.8%.[50] Political changes, the coming of the Gaullist Fifth Republic after 1958 in particular, also played their role. The political aftermath of the Algerian War thus coincided with a dramatic increase in new middle strata occupations, in the numbers of young French people seeking higher educational credentials, and in the population being schooled more generally.[51]

Modernizing capitalist societies needed more educated people, more 'intellectual' workers in teaching, research and development and the production of new cultural objects (books, magazines, films, television programmes, advertising), more trained managers and bureaucrats, more social service workers. France, moreover, needed these new people rather rapidly, given the unusual speed of its modernization. And in France, they burst upon a society which still cherished pre-war cultural outlooks. Thus in the 1960s, French intellectual institutions, particularly those in education and research, expanded amidst chaotically changing rules, unpredictable expectations and careers, changing professional structures and shifts in the organization of knowledge itself. And while these things occurred, the Gaullist regime, which combined technocratic commitment to economic modernization, authoritarian attitudes towards movements in 'civil society' and a socially conservative coalition base, reacted to expressions of discontent as *lèse-majesté*. The burgeoning French middle strata were bound to be rebellious. The young felt such changes with greater intensity to the degree to which they were also living a huge intergenerational drama between the outlooks of their parents and their own understandings and expectations. Add to this the traditional *rite de passage* of student *militantisme* and the prodigious amount of intellectual Leftism the Algerian War years had fostered, and one has a good recipe for the social troubles of May–June 1968.

These structural trends continued through the 1970s. For every university student in 1960–61 there were four by 1980–81. In consequence, the numbers of teachers and researchers expanded and the percentage of new middle strata segments of the labour force continued to grow, if at a somewhat slower pace than in the 1960s. Aggregated, the labour force percentages of categories like 'liberal professionals and *cadres supérieurs,*' '*Cadres Moyens*' and '*Employés*' grew from 19.5 per cent in 1952 to 41.4 per cent in 1982. During the same period the official percentage of workers remained roughly the same (33.8 in 1952, 35.1 in 1982).[52] By the early 1980s, France's 'post-industrialization' had been more or less complete. One of the major factors for rising unemployment in the 'crisis' – beyond demographic pressures, continuing growth in female labour force participation and France's declining industrial competitiveness – was a distinct levelling off in tertiary sector job creation,[53] while changing economic circumstances also brought a squeeze on social service growth, public sector salaries and institutional overhead expenses.

The larger social composition of the French intelligentsia had thus changed rather dramatically. There was a congeries of groups whose work was 'intellectual,' a considerable mass with many common outlooks and practices who looked to the Parisian working intelligentsia for cultural guidance. The educational credential governing access to new middle strata jobs involved subjection to an important process of socialization.[54] Beyond a certain sense of cultural superiority opening them to the influence of intellectual and cultural trends and fads, many in these groups were attracted to the peculiar individualism which came with 'careers' as opposed to 'jobs.' This individualism created a propensity towards a moralistic politics of witness together with impatience with the cumbersome processes of more collectivist traditional Leftism. Moreover, while many, particularly those employed in the public sector, leaned to the Left in electoral terms, they often had quite practical reasons for doing so, sometimes the corporate outlook of a professional guild, for example – the behaviour of the teachers unions in the FEN were models here.[55] The inadequacy of public sector structures, schools and universities in particular, fed periodic crises, constant worries about finances and hopes for the great funding that Left electoral victory would bring. Moreover, by the later 1970s such groups had begun to feel economically insecure, along with much of the rest of the French population.[56]

These broader trends touched the particular situations of elite intellectuals as well. The traditional Parisian Left intellectuals had been the centre of a relatively small world, few in numbers, often recruited from a narrow social base and a small circle of elite schools and reasonably well connected with provincial 'troops' with similar backgrounds and values. By the later 1960s this world had changed out of all recognition. There were still important elite networks and cliques, to be sure. But there were also thousands of intellectuals spread over France who did not partake of them.[57] There might still be Sartres but the bulk of French intellectuals could not aspire to be or know one.[58]

What does our brief sociology tell us so far? Schematically, beginning in the 1960s there was an increase in the weight of new middle strata occupations in the labour force, particularly in the public sector, and an attendant modification of structures of cultural communications 'circuits' reflecting the increased weight in the French population of educationally-credentialised new middle class groups. As these processes moved forward – creaking and groaning, to be sure – the class structure of France was ultimately changed. One could no longer look at French society plausibly using a simplistic 19th century Marxian model – workers vs. capital and its appendages, with, perhaps, a few social oddments tossed in (intermediary 'categories,' as the PCF tried labelling them).

The new middle strata – particularly those in France's rather large public sector – brought with them their own peculiar ideological and political predilections. And at the centre of this congeries of new middle strata groups lay the intellectuals. Intellectual musings and theorizings about the sociopolitical environment, disseminated outwards through complex networks of esoteric intellectual production, Parisian cultural faddism, energetic and often quite lucrative publication empires and the electronic media, played an essential role in 'representing' these new groups, shaping them and socializing them politically.

The Primacy of Politics

These sociological 'facts' do not in themselves explain the evolution of intellectual thought and politics which we reviewed in Part I, however. To be sure, the new middle strata had their own needs and desires which called for new forms of political and ideological representation, and the massive presence of these groups was bound to change the ways in which French politics worked. But the precise nature of what ultimately emerged, in whose construction intellectuals played central roles, cannot be read out of new middle stratification itself. Social trends may help begin accounting for the general political instability of all kinds of intellectuals beginning in the 1960s, but they do not explain its more precise logics. We need another level of analysis.

Intellectuals do not create political ideas either for their private pleasure or in immediate response to their changing social structural positions. Rather their political ideas are produced primarily to influence a real political world dominated by those who actually 'do' politics, their organizations and institutions. And, conversely, what is thus 'done' by such political actors will be the central point of departure for the political thinking of intellectuals. Thus what statistical and institutional indices turned out to mean for French intellectual politics in recent decades can only be clarified by exploring the interaction between the outlooks of official political actors and the desires and needs of the emergent new middle strata. The real drama in the situation was to be found, therefore, in the complex interactions among the rapidly changing intelligentsia, broader new middle strata groups, and the official French Left.

At issue was whether France's official Left would prove itself sufficiently adaptable and politically astute to devise ideological and political forms to *incorporate* the bulk of new middle strata energy without fundamentally disrupting its own ongoing political logic. Was an effective working class-new middle strata alliance under the hegemony of the existing Left a possibility? If so, then the basic forms of the French Left's outlook and practices, *marxisant* and anti-capitalist suitably modified beyond traditional workerism to coopt new middle strata moralistic individualism, might have been preserved into a new period, economic changes notwithstanding. If such an alliance proved impossible, however, there was grave danger that the political and theoretical structures of nearly a century of Left practice in France would collapse.

To begin the more political analysis which we need let us restate the context of the Algerian War years. The point of departure of our story occurred at the point when the PCF's tenuous Cold War intellectual hegemony came to an end[59] largely because of the ways in which the party's policies on Algeria alienated radical student and intellectual anti-war activists. The Socialists, with their deep complicity in colonial warfare – one important Left Catholic labels SFIO politics in this period a *socialisme expéditionnaire*[60] – and their sordid domestic political record in the Fourth Republic, had little to offer either. In consequence, as of the early 1960s there existed little official Left space for the strong student and intellectual anti-war movement to occupy and influence. Thus, organized largely by Union Nationale des Etudiants Français (UNEF), the movement went ahead on it own, despite the indifference, hostility and active sabotage of the official Left.[61] The result was a generational break between major parts of the Left intelligentsia and official Left organizations.

In this context of generational break, the structuralist turn of 'high' thought plus attempts by non-PCF Marxists to regenerate a workable intellectual Marxism can be seen as efforts to found a progressive intellectuality independent of the PCF, with the burgeoning new intelligentsia the target constituency. Sociological 'artisans,' at the same time, were busily borrowing categories from *socialisant* political catalogues to describe the modernizing – and occupationally post-industrializing – France which official Left reflection proved unable to confront. These artisans were clearly more attuned to the evolving rhythms of French politics in the 1960s than were the *grands intellos,* and were trying quite hard to *influence* the evolution of French Left politics through their work at this critical juncture, hence the specific political vocabularies which they chose to employ. Among younger intellectual generations there was an even broader variety of independent Leftisms. There was considerable young activism in the PSU, overlapping the positions of the artisans. Then, given the decolonizing, national liberation, nation-building events of the time, there was also a wide variety of *marxisant* 'thirdworldisms.' Here, as with the 'artisans,'there was an intimate connection between political ideas and political strategies – however naive and far-fetched.

The official French Left, seriously weakened by the Cold War, Algeria and the change in Republics in 1958 was strategically lost in the early 1960s. This situation was clear to elite intellectuals, artisans and younger generations alike, who had thus concluded in their different ways that the official Left was both obsolete and non-responsive to new political concerns – new middle strata concerns. The practical politics of the situation, from the point of view of this broad cast of intellectual actors trying to play politics, were that the PCF seemed vulnerable to isolation and the non-Communist Left seemed ripe for major reconstruction.

At this point the key errors were made by the PCF. Had the PCF been more theoretically and organizationally adaptable, less wedded to a traditional *ouvriérisme* which could make no serious room for middle strata, and less attached to Stalinist organizational practices which allowed no space to initiatives not controlled by the party, things might have been different. Because they were not, the major loser in the situation was a PCF which was unable to see anything in the rise of independent Left intellectualism beyond anti-communism and the agitation of petit-bourgeois enemies.

In the 1960s, the PCF was confronted with fundamental changes in France's social map. The party's misperception of this critical situation, which called for new approaches to the burgeoning new middle strata,[62] created a self-fulfilling prophecy. By 1968, there thus existed a broad and determined network of anti-Communist Leftist intellectuals. Moreover, this divorce between the official Left and leading Left intellectuals was occurring in a context in which the broader intelligentsia, growing apace, was clearly engaged in an important 'Left turn.' And here our line of argument about the relationship between Left intellectuals and official Left politics rejoins our earlier discussion about the changing social setting of the intelligentsia more generally.

The key factor mediating structural trends and intellectual behaviours which best 'explains' Left intellectual trends in the 1970s is once again the relationship between the working intelligentsia and the official Left. Here strategic contradictions were involved. The official Left had changed, committing itself to *Union de la Gauche* – programmatic alliance between the Communists and Socialists. The Socialists had made an extremely shrewd strategic bet that by 'buying' a set of outlooks from the PCF – which came to be enshrined in the 1972 Common Programme – they would ultimately be able to undercut and marginalize French Communism. The coalition logic behind this was clear. In any intra-alliance competition between the Communists and Socialists, the Socialists, more moderate and legitimate, were bound to win out. There were two problems here, however. The first involved the internal problems of both official Left parties. The second was that this coalition logic was at odds with the social alliance logic needed to approach the bulk of the new Left intelligentsia which had little or no sympathy for Common Programme politics.

First let us turn to PCF and PS internal problems. Those parts of the post-68 and Left Unity generations who chose to enter the official Left, and which undoubtedly bore with them a considerable amount of energy and commitment to force on their respective parties theoretical and practical adaptation to France's changing social structure, faced a situation beyond their capacities to shape. Those who entered the PCF brought dimensions of the '68 experience with them and changed the party almost as much as they were changed by the party. The PCF's brief, and woefully incomplete, flirtation with Eurocommunism was immensely promising as a creative political approach to the new middle strata. But this only lasted until 1978–79. The PCF's dramatic strategic shift at this point involved nothing less than a return to the most schematic traditional workerism and the surgical removal of these intellectual generations from French Communism altogether.[63] It was rare, subsequently, for the ex-Communists who emerged from this horrendous episode to follow ex-gauchistes and autogestionnaires towards apostasy. Rather they became political orphans, people with very good ideas and no institutional place to express them.

The fate of the 1960s and 1970s Left intellectuals who aligned themselves with the various Socialist *courants* was different. To the degree to which the PS became a sophisticated machine to manufacture political careers they tended to fight out their various fractional battles inside the party, often using quite innovative and promising theoretical and political language. Prior to 1981, when the party finally came to power, such struggles could be justified in terms of their influence on the course of future Left governments. In fact, however, they were as much struggles between elite cliques as anything else.

Here lay the rub. The PS was the key Left political actor in the 1970s. Parts of the PS were undoubtedly sincerely and creatively devoted to developing a politics adequate to the task of adapting a traditionally social democratic discourse to the new needs of cross-class alliance presented by post-industrial occupational changes. But the real leadership of the PS, the clique of Florentine manoeuvrers around François Mitterrand, was committed primarily to coming to power. No doubt, this clique cared sufficiently about the nature of political discourse deployed by their Socialist Party to make their complex coalition strategy effective, hence a certain devotion to the programmatic outlook of *Union de la Gauche*. But reaching power and staying there was vastly more important than maintaining any specific political discourse, as the 1980s would show.

Next come contradictions between coalition and social alliance logics. We have discussed the evolution of post-'68 Maoists in Part I. Suffice it here to repeat that the hothouse sectarianism in these circles which emerged from the May events could not survive the refractory response of French society in the 1970s to conform to Maoist revolutionary fantasies. 1960s ultra-Leftism had always been anti-Communist and anti-Social Democratic. In the 1970s, given the collapse of sectarian dreams in a context of renewed traditional Left strength, many ultra-Leftists 'saw the light' and began preaching the evils of Marxism, Socialism and traditional Left politics more generally. It is quite unlikely that the official Left could have done very much to stop the hysterical outbursts of the 'new philosophers' and their friends, particularly because, in the complicated atmosphere of tightly fought electoral combat between Right and Left in the 1970s, these outbursts were an important source of aid to the Right. The real question for the official Left was to limit the damage, and here it did not do well at all.

Those advocating *autogestionnaire* politics, perhaps the largest and most influential political and intellectual sequel of 1968, in particular, found the Left's chosen 'Common Programme' strategy unpalatable. Post-1968 autogestion thought, stressing decentralized democratic social creativity embedded in a vague anti-statist, anti-traditional social democratic and, of course, anti-communist feeling, struck deeper roots in the PSU and the CFDT.[64] Autogestionnaire segments of the intelligentsia supported the Left electorally, but did not recognize their own political ideas and outlooks in the official political ideas of the Left in the 1970s.[65] PS strategists, François

Mitterrand in particular, quickly recognized the problem, and moved to include major parts of the organized autogestionnaire forces into the PS at the autumn, 1974 *Assises du Socialisme*. The PS thus made a commitment to autogestion, but the operation was not persuasive since Mitterrand immediately manipulated the PS's new autogestionnaires to his own ends in the party's complicated internal politics without really modifying the basic line of the party.

This missed opportunity had important consequences. Autogestionnaire parts of the post-1968 Left intellectual generation were never effectively integrated into the politics of the official Left. Thus as the official Left moved closer to power, a clear movement of ideological opposition to official Left politics crystallized around a 'second Left' with immediate roots in the decentralized rebellion of 1968. However, responding to the progressive extinction of rebelliousness, economic crisis after 1974 and the wave of intellectual anti-Sovietism of the later 1970s, this Second Left itself began to change its positions. Autogestion was decoupled from radicalism. The goal of transcending capitalism disappeared.[66] Autogestion, duly deradicalized, thus became an appeal to de-statize the Left, for decentralized bargaining as an approach to social problems of all kinds, for a revitalized 'civil society,' and for recognition of the utility, as a decentralized mechanism, of the market.[67] Considerable help in negotiating this turn to neo-liberalism came from the apostate ultra-Leftists we have already discussed.

This evolution was accomplished, in part, through the symbiotic fusion of the autogestionnaires with the largely pre-1968 Left intellectual generation of followers of Pierre Mendès-France. From their moment of glory in the mid-1950s onwards, these followers and collaborators of Mendès-France had opposed traditional *marxisant* Leftism as archaic, holding on into the 1970s to become strong advocates of technocratic centrism. Not 'socialist' in any conventional ways, they explicitly rejected notions of the transcendance of capitalism, recognized the centrality of innovative management and proposed a 'mixed economy' which acknowledged the market's limits and the role which remained for intelligent state intervention. Above all, they stressed the need for conscious and continual efforts to modernize France and rejected the lyrical, transformative and statist rhetoric of the Left Common Programme.

As we have earlier remarked, the lifestyles and size of the new intellectual middle strata had changed in ways which challenged the traditional Left. The actual politics chosen by these organizations for the 1970s seduced some Left intellectuals but not all. This situation 'opened' parts of the new middle strata to political influences from outside the official Left. For such groups *militantisme* and older types of 'engagement' gave way to a more synthetic cultural adhesion which political parties were either unable or unwilling to provide.[68]

Media entrepreneurs were quick to perceive the opportunities. *Nouvel Observateur*, a Mendesiste weekly, is the most interesting case. In the

1970s *Nouvel Obs* practically became a quasi-party, disseminating trendy cultural material – including a great deal of vulgarized post-structuralism – plus a shrewd combination of 'second Left' ideas to undermine the prevailing political discourses of the official Left.[69] *Nouvel Obs* was not alone, either. Concentrated efforts in the same direction by publishing houses – like Editions du Seuil – intensified the effects. Moreover, by the end of the 1970s *Libération*, an important daily newspaper, had come to play an analogous role as quasi-party for the 'new culture' segments of the post-1968 Left intelligentsia.

By the later 1970s new dialogues between parts of the Left intelligentsia and such commercially-oriented quasi-parties had been solidified. The explosion of intellectual anti-Sovietism occurred largely in such dialogues as did, more generally, the breast-beating, anti-enlightenment apostasy of the 'new philosophy.' The trials and tribulations of *Union de la Gauche* in 1977–78 provided new material about the evils of statism and the inherently manipulative nature of official Left ideas and apparata, as did the major internal crisis of the PCF after 1978.

By 1981, when the official Left finally came to power determined to implement its long-standing programme, an important impasse had thus been reached. Much of the intelligentsia, and many important intellectuals, voted to make this political success happen. At the same time, however, substantial parts of the Left intelligentsia were profoundly, and quite vocally, alienated from the Left's official politics. At first the Mitterrand regime tried to implement its Common Programme derived reformism only then to run aground on a totally unfavourable international economic environment. Then, after a brief moment of confusion, the PS, henceforth dominant on the official Left, completely changed the way it viewed the world. After 1981 the entire PS, including intellectuals of all generations and all fractional stripes, fell hostage to the experience of power. The administrative logic of state managers – which many PS intellectuals either were or had always wanted to be – supplanted the rhetoric of collective mobilization. And when, after 1982–83, François Mitterrand and parts of his government decided that the time had come to 'accept the mixed economy,' and 'modernize' France, PS intellectuals were obliged to follow.[70]

In March 1983 *Libération* rather cheerfully and ironically headlined that *Le Mitterrand Nouveau est arrivé*. The 'old Mitterrand' was a reformer who talked, at least, about the imperative of redistributing economic and political resources in France away from the wealthy and powerful to ordinary people. In 1981 he announced that '. . .by nationalizing industry [I am doing] what de Gaulle did in the realm of nuclear energy. I am endowing France with an economic *force de frappe*.' The 'new Mitterrand' talked about the need to increase profits, to allow the market to flourish, to accept the 'mixed economy,' to 'modernize' French industry and society in order to compete better internationally. The quest to change the domestic balance of resources in France through statist reforms had abruptly given way to a new crusade to free up the resources, primarily economic, necessary to increase the comparative effectiveness of French capitalism and to do so in a largely decentralized, market-centred way.

The rest of the 1980s demonstrated that the political and ideological conversion experience of the PS was definitive. The old outlooks of the official Left were denounced in confessionals that 'we could ever have thought such things.' In their place came a much more personalized political life. Ideologies were out. Policy talk became ever more economistic, riddled with 'realistic' portraits of the different structures of constraints which dictated reduced expectations and modest claims. Professions of ultimate value commitments, which had earlier been utopian socialist, turned into vague invocations of the need for solidarity, the right to difference, individual liberty, Europe's mission and the like.

The different strains of official Left politics in the two decades after the end of the Algerian War had never connected satisfactorily with important parts of the emerging new intelligentsia. By the later 1970s, as we have seen, much of the Left intelligentsia had developed sets of ideas which were independent of and different from those of the official Left. These ideas lived a thriving parallel existence in the more general universe of Left intellectualism in France, even if they did not impinge decisively on the evolution of official Left politics. In the 1980s, however, the situation was transformed. Left intellectuals and Socialist politicians came to accept *more or less the same ideas*. More interesting still, a goodly portion of these shared ideas had their origins in the intellectual 'second Left.'

The subtext? Policy failure after 1982–83 meant ideological and intellectual collapse for the official Left. Its old positions no longer worked either programmatically or inspirationally, to mobilize. Without some new presentation of self, the Socialists faced a political disaster. An ideological conversion experience was imperative to avoid political bankruptcy. The PS thus tried to repair its damaged political position by foraging through the ideological parts-bin of the moment. Some of its new ideas came straight from the vocabularies of state management itself – technocratic realism, proclamations of superior competence. Others came from the internationally ambient economism of the times. Many, however, came directly from pirating the vocabularies of the new middle strata groups which had earlier found the Common Program so rebarbative. The prevalent neo-Tocquevillean intellectual climate of the second half of the 1980s was in part the consequence, in part the cause, of this. In particular, the PS borrowed as much as it could from the storehouse of 'second Left' ideological and intellectual material which had accumulated outside the corridors of official Left power prior to the early 1980s. By this point, however, the ideas of these intellectuals had evolved away from the corrosive radicalism both of post-structuralism and *autogestionnaire* thought into the 'soft' liberal revisionism which now dominates both the Left political and intellectual scene.

Conclusions: The Moral Of Our Story?
By the end of the 1980s both the Left intellectual scene and the Left ideological scene in France had been completely transformed. Marxism was dead. Traditional social democracy was dead. Classes and workers had been removed from political discourse. Tocqueville was very much alive. A new individualism had emerged triumphant.

Part of our story ought to have been familiar. Our stress on French Communism's inability to respond creatively to changing social and political circumstances is hardly news. Our emphasis on the political unreliability of French socialism will startle few readers either. More generally, the official French Left failed to understand the changing context which it faced, but we knew this as well. We intended our discussion of these somewhat familiar matters as a prelude to further analysis, however. When the Left falls short, the consequences are usually great. But when the French Left fell short in recent decades, intellectuals played an essential, and quite negative, reorienting role in the ideological sphere of French Left politics. This is what we have tried to communicate.

Let us be blunt and somewhat old-fashioned. Post-structuralism in the 1970s was a form of thought appropriate to new middle strata which, given specific political circumstances and incessant propagandizing by intellectuals, became dedicated to a trajectory of destroying the socialist dream and establishing new middle strata ideological hegemony in French political life. Given the continuing power of French and international capitalism over the ultimate contours of political discourse, the latter goal was largely unattainable. It was the former which turned out to be most important, therefore, largely for the same reasons. The slippage of many of these same intellectuals into a microwaved reheating of John Locke and Alexis de Tocqueville in the 1980s was no accident. That enterprising bourgeois politicians and elite interest should seize the opportunity to manipulate this type of intellectualizing is not surprising at all. Nor is it surprising that the French Socialist Party, during one of its periodic balletic movements of ideological vacuity, should buy into it, even though it is quite shocking.

One thing is heartening. 'Soft ideology,' the end product of intellectual activism in France, convinces little and moralizes few. Neither post-structuralism nor neo-liberalism with a human face will provide anything more than a brief respite for a French capitalism faced with serious decline. The French people, like Molière's M. Jourdain in earlier times, have been force-fed a line that 'democracy is really wonderful, we already speak it and aren't we blessed?' They will eventually deconstruct this particular text and find it contradictory when they do, for democracy is precisely what remains to be built.

222   THE SOCIALIST REGISTER 1990

NOTES

1. Perry Anderson, *In The Tracks of Historical Materialism* (London, Verso, 1983), p. 32.
2. Jeannine Verdès-Leroux conveys a good sense of what PCF intellectualism was like in this period in *Au Service du Parti* (Paris, Fayard/Minuit, 1983).
3. On this period, see Pascal Ory and Jean-François Sirinelli, *Les Intellectuels en France, de l'affaire Dreyfus à nos jours* (Paris, Armand Colin, 1986), Chapter VIII. The Ory-Sirinelli *manuel* is a useful tool for our subject in general. On the PCF and its own intellectuals in this period, see Verdès-Leroux *Au Service du parti* and Michel-Antoine Burnier, *Les Existentialistes et la politique* (Paris, Gallimard, 1970).
4. Anna Boschetti's *Sartre et 'les temps modernes'* (Paris, Minuit 1985) provides a very useful sociology-of-knowledge review of Sartre's strategies. The problem of this, and other such analyses is that in their sociological reductionism they tend to overlook the importance of creativity. See also Annie Cohen-Solal, *Sartre* (Paris, Gallimard, 1985), for additional strategic information.
5. Paris, Gallimard, 1960
6. Here, for a good sampling of *Arguments*, see Christian Biegalski, ed. *Arguments/3, Les Intellectuels, la pensée anticipatrice* (Paris, Gallimard 10/18, 1970). See also Gilles Delannoi, '*Arguments*, 1956–1962, ou la parenthése de l'ouverture', *Revue Française de Science Politique*, February, 1984.
7. Foucault, cited (from *Arts et loisirs*, June 15, 1966) in Didier Eribon, *Michel Foucault* (Paris, Flammarion, 1989).
8. His support of the Algerian Rebels – here one should reread his preface to Fanon's *Wretched of the Earth* and his articles in *Les Temps Modernes* from the period, were very important politically as was his subsequent advocacy of *tiersmondiste* causes and perspectives and, later, various 1968-generation ultra-Leftists. Annie Cohen-Solal's biography reviews these matters with great care.
9. See Chapter 9 in *The Savage Mind* (Chicago, University of Chicago Press, 1966) for example.
10. On the Althusser crusade against Marxist humanism, see R. Geerlandt, *Garaudy et Althusser; le débat sur l'humanisme dans le PCF et son enjeu* (Paris, PUF, 1978). On structuralist Marxism more generally, see T. Benton, *The Rise and Fall of Structural Marxism* (London, Macmillan, 1984). The Grémion citation is from the excellent *Paris-Prague* (Paris, Julliard, 1985).
11. Here see Hervé Hamon and Patrick Rotman, *Génération*, Volume 1 (Paris, Editions du Seuil, 1985) for the full story.
12. Even if an 'Althusserian' generation of *normaliens* would become front-line actors in May 1968 and constitute the backbone of French Maoism thereafter. As Perry Anderson noted '. . .Even at the peak of its productivity, Althusserianism was always constituted in an intimate and fatal dependence on a structuralism that both preceded it and would survive it. Lévi-Strauss had peremptorily sought to cut the Gordian knot of the relation between structure and subject by suspending the latter from any field of scientific knowledge. Rather than resisting this move, Althusser radicalized it, with a version of Marxism in which subjects were abolished altogether, save as the illusory effects of ideological structures. But in an objectivist auction of this kind, he was bound to be outbid.' *In The Tracks*, op. cit, p. 38.
13. See, for example, Touraine's *Production de la Société* (Paris, Seuil, 1973).
14. See Bourdieu and J-C Passeron, *Les Héritiers* (Paris, Minuit, 1964).
15. Mallet and Gorz, each in his own way, was importing 'foreign' Marxism into France, particularly from Italy. See Serge Mallet, *Le Gaullisme et la gauche* (Paris, Seuil, 1964) and *La Nouvelle Classe Ouvrière* (Paris, Editions du Seuil,

1963); Pierre Belleville, *Une Nouvelle Classe Ouvrière* (Paris, Julliard, 1963); André Gorz, *Stratégie Ouvrière et Néo-capitalisme* (Paris, Seuil, 1964). Castoriadis continued, until just prior to 1968, to put out *Socialisme ou barbarie* and animate the S+B group which included a number of other important writers like Daniel Mothe. S+B, with a Trotskyist edge to its analyses, was explicitly anti-statist and *autogestionnaire* before its time. Important Left journals like *Les Temps Modernes* and *France Observateur* were willing regular vehicles for such ideas.

16. Touraine began to outline a schema of societal evolution which posited that classically Marxist notions of class and class conflict were at least a solid beginning towards understanding of political and state behaviour in 'industrial' societies, but that a very different set of class actors, goals and state-society relationships would emerge in the transition to 'post-industrial' society which was in the wings. Bourdieu, in strong contrast, presented no picture of the direction of history, instead positing a never-ending process of elite strategies to maintain predominance over popular groups in the multiplicity of arenas where 'reproduction' (of power, status, privilege) went on, presumably including the political arena.

17. See *Les Cahiers de l'Institut d'Histoire du Temps Présent*, No. 6, November 1987 for a good introduction. The IHTP *Bulletin Trimestriel,* No. 31, March 1988 provides an extensive 'generational' bibliography. Hervé Hamon and Patrick Rotman's massive, two volume *Génération* (Paris, Seuil, 1985 and 1988) popularized the notion and uncovered many of the problems which it posed. See also Jean-Francois Sirinelli, 'Le hasard ou la nécessité? Une histoire en chantier: L'histoire des intellectuels,' in *Vingtième Siècle,* January–March 1986 and Michel Winock, 'Les générations d'intellectuels' in *Vingtième Siècle,* April–June 1989 (this whole issue is devoted to the theme of generations.)

18. This is evident from the IHTP's marvellous set of essays 'La Guerre d'Algérie et les Intellectuels,' *Cahiers de l'IHTP*, 10, November 1988. To be sure, as political trends in the 1980s make painfully clear, there was a strong Right Wing side of this generation (Le Pen, et al, Occident, Ordre Nouveau and the like).

19. See Hervé Hamon and Patrick Rotman's excellent *Les Porteurs de Valise* (Paris, Albin Michel, 1979) for a thorough overview of this.

20. The PCF, persistently unable to cope with any mobilizations from the Left which it could not control, acted forcefully to constrain and denigrate UNEF, the national students' union which assumed the lead in anti-war activities, and other student protest vehicles. This left a profoundly bitter aftertaste for an entire generation of Left politicized students for whom anti-PCF Leftism became a virtual necessity. The effects of PCF policy were felt equally strongly by those young people who actually entered the PCF's youth organizations during the Algerian War. When tensions developed between these young people, drawn towards the protest activism of the moment, and the party leadership, the leadership responded by heavy-handed repressive tactics. The consequence of this was to create a generation of very able ex-Communist young intellectuals who, given their baptism under fire by the PCF's organizational harshness, became profoundly anti-PCF.

21. This sometimes led to Trotskyism (as in the trajectories of Alain Krivine and Henri Weber) and sometimes, prodded by identification with the FLN, to romantic involvement with other Third World revolutionary movements. Hamon and Rotman, *Génération* I do a wonderful job in showing this trajectory as well.

22. Thus the older Cold War pattern, typified by the trajectories of worker priests and fellow travelling Catholic unionists, of 'choosing the side of the party of the working class' would be largely broken. If one was a militantly reformist or revolutionary Catholic from this point onwards – and many young people were such – one had to seek out a different form of Leftist vocabulary and project from that of official Communism.

224 THE SOCIALIST REGISTER 1990

23. It was also frenetic in its search for a new, more viable and militant 'vanguard' for the *damnés de la terre,* whether Trotskyism, Maoism or role modelling on Che Guevara

24. Luc Ferry and Alain Renaut, *La Pensée 68: Essai sur l'anti-humanisme contemporain* (Paris, Gallimard, 1985).

25. See *Le Monde,* October, 13, 1989 for reportage on a conference on Foucault's politics, including his own political activities, the article by Catherine De La Campagne is particularly good. The recent journalistic biography of Foucault (*Michel Foucault,* Seuil, 1989), by Didier Eribon, talks a great deal about such things as well.

26. It is worth here reproducing Jean-Marie Domenach's commentary on this (Domenach was at the time editor of *Esprit*). 'Doesn't a system of thought which introduces both the constraints of the system and discontinuity in the history of the mind undercut the foundations of any progressive political intervention? Doesn't it eventuate in the following dilemma: Either acceptance of the system or else calls for 'wild' events, an eruption of external violence which is alone able to upset the system?' (Cited in Eribon, *Foucault,* Op cit, p. 190.)

27. For a summary of the social theories of Foucault and Derrida, see the David Hoy (Derrida) and Mark Philip (Foucault) chapters in Quentin Skinner, ed. *The Return of Grand Theory in the Social Sciences* (Cambridge, Cambridge University Press, 1985). On Lacan, see Sherry Turkle, *Psychoanalytic Politics* (Cambridge, MIT Press, 1981).

28. See Alain Touraine, *Le Mouvement de Mai ou le communisme utopique* (Paris, Seuil, 1968) and *La Société post-industrielle* (Paris, Denoel, 1969).

29. See Pierre Bourdieu, *Homo Academicus* (Paris, Minuit, 1985), published much later, but initially put together in the aftermath of May.

30. Bourdieu's actual conclusions were redolent of the Frankfurt School's pessimism about the eternalization of domination, but the neo-Marxist flavour of the argument was what counted. *Distinction*, published in 1979 (Paris, Editions du Minuit), is where this affinity is most obvious. See also *La Noblesse d'état* (Paris. Editions de Minuit, 1988).

31. Poulantzas' efforts in *Classes in Contemporary Capitalism* and *State, Power and Socialism* were, of course, very important not only in France, but in the 'theory of the state' debate in Anglo-Saxon countries.

32. In the aftermath of 1968, the CFDT very rapidly changed its doctrinal vision of the world from Left Catholic reformism to genuine radicalism, in the process adopting a commitment to 'socialist transformation' and belief in the class struggle. See, for example, Pierre Rosanvallon, *L'Age de l'autogestion.* Rosanvallon was at the time head of research for the CFDT. Guy Groux and René Mouriaux, *La CFDT* (Paris, Economica, 1989) Chapter 3 goes into considerable detail about this. The PSU, alas, is a much less chronicled body. See nonetheless Charles Hauss, *The New Left in France* (Boulder, Greenwood, 1978).

33. We have talked about such matters in George Ross, 'French Marxists and the New Middle Classes,' in *Theory and Society*, Winter 1978 and, more recently, 'Destroyed by the Dialectic: Politics, The Decline of Marxism and the new middle strata in France,' in *Theory and Society*, Fall 1987.

34. The discovery of Freud, via Lacan, of the post-May generation is undoubtedly connected with personal searches for different ways of organizing individual identity.

35. The best source on this subplot is Jane Jenson 'Ce n'est pas un hasard: the varieties of French feminism,' in Jolyon Howorth and George Ross, *Contemporary France*, 3 (London, Frances Pinter, 1989)

36. 'New Philosophy,' of course, accused big think social theory, the enlightenment

and Marxism as bearing 'totalitarianism.' It was more than coincidental that the new philosophers were granted an extensive public hearing during the runup to the 1977–78 electoral season (when the Centre-Right majority was in considerable danger). What made their splash even bigger was the objective collusion between the interests of the Right establishment in using the 'new philosophy' to undercut a rising Left and certain sectors of the Left itself which disagreed with the logic of Left Union.

37. PCF membership skyrocketed in the mid-1970s, with a large part of the new recruitment coming from new middle strata and intellectuals. The complex processes and battles around the 'Eurocommunization' of the party from 1973 to 1979 preponderantly involved intellectuals who were, to varying degrees, the bearers of propositions about inner-party reform involving greater internal democracy, attenuation of ties to the Soviet Union and the Soviet model, *autogestion* of a certain kind (decentralized movements for change) and changes in the PCF's theoretical mapping of the social world.

38. We have discussed these issues at great length in George Ross and Jane Jenson, 'The Tragedy of the French Left,' in Patrick Camiller ed. *The Future of the European Left* (London, Verso, 1989).

39. In fact, the faculty of Vincennes moved to St. Denis, where obscurity and neglect awaited it.

40. Rosanvallon, *Le Moment Guizot* (Paris, Gallimard, 1985); Pierre Manent, *Histoire Intellectuelle du libéralisme* (Paris, Calmann-Levy, 1987).

41. Popper's *Open Society and Its Enemies* was first translated into French, amidst much clamour, in *1979*.

42. Francois-Bernard Huyghe and Pierre Barbés, *La Soft-Idéologie* (Paris, Calmann-Levy, 1987).

43. Only Bourdieu, among well-known figures, persisted along such lines, after a fashion.

44. See Luc Boltanski, *Cadres* (Cambridge, Cambridge University Press, 1988).

45. *Le Monde,* October 8, 1987.

46. It is not uncommon to find Left-leaning sociologists in Paris these days lamenting that 'Bourdieu is all we have left.' And indeed the Bourdieu boutique, marred by considerable defections, can be seen to be the last remaining bastion of class analytical perspectives. This is not very comforting to the lamenters, however, given that Bourdieu's class analytical model is one of deep pessimism about change. What characterizes 'reproduction' over time, to Bourdieu, is that the upper classes always win.

47. On the fringes of this movement there also appeared a reborn phenomenological sociology, usually borrowing from American sources (Schutz and Heidegger via Garfinkel and Goffmann) skeptical of the endeavour of social mapping altogether.

48. Raymond Boudon's work is the leading source of this in French sociology. See, for example, *L'Ideologie* (Paris, Fayard, 1986). For a very good discussion of this approach see *Sur l'individualisme méthodologique,* eds. Pierre Birnbaum and Georges Lavau, (Paris, Presses de la Fondation des Sciences Politiques, 1986).

49. The mind-boggling devotion of contemporary French political science to polling and elections, almost to the exclusion of everything else, is extraordinary. The French – their political journalists and scientists (with the two categories increasingly overlapping) – have become the largest consumers of political opinion polling in the entire world.

50. Serge Berstein, *La France de l'expansion* (Paris, Seuil, 1989), p. 190. Chapter 6 of this book provides an excellent quick overview of socioeconomic changes from 1958 to 1969. The French census category for white collar workers – *employés* –

includes a large number of operatives, store clerks and the like. Even with these groups subtracted, however, growth was impressive.

51.	The total population of students nearly doubled between 1947 and 1968 (737,000 in secondary school in 1946, three million by 1963 and nearly four by 1968). 150,000 university students in 1955 had grown to 510,000 in 1967. While roughly one in twenty (4.4%) of 1946 students earned their *baccalauréat*, one in ten did so by 1959 (9.7%) and 16.2% by 1969. In 1952 there were 263,000 teachers at all levels, 615,000 by 1967 (1,200 university teachers in 1946, 8000 in 1959, 31,000 in 1969). 2,500 educational buildings were opened between 1965 and 1975, one for every school day.

52.	J. and G. Bremond, *L'Economie Française* (Paris, Hatier, 1985). These gross figures exaggerate the point about new middle stratification which we are making. One would have to go through sub-categories and subtract inappropriate groups, particularly in the 'employees' group. Even so, however, the change is impressive.

53.	In the boom years, rise in service sector employment had persistently compensated for declining agricultural and relatively static industrial job creation. This had ceased as of the 1980s.

54.	Bourdieu's *La Distinction*, whose data base stops in the middle 1970s, is crystal clear about these changes.

55.	See Véronique Aubert et al, *La Forteresse Enseignante*, (Paris, Fayard, 1985), especially Part IV, Chapter 3.

56.	The actual differences in outlook between public and private sector new middle strata groups has been explored in an important new book by François de Singly and Claude Thélot, *Gens du privé, gens du public (Paris, Dunod, 1989)*.

57.	The existence of a vastly increased number of academic and research intellectuals also fostered more professional and 'American' structures of intellectual association and peer evaluation. For individuals setting out on new careers in a progressively more fragmented world of knowledge and with much less of the universalistic *esprit de corps* that older intellectual elite status had conferred, the changing system established new gatekeepers over cultural creation.

58.	Technological innovations changed the contexts of intellectuality as well. Régis Debray and others make much of what they call 'mediacracy' and its effect on intellectual outlooks. A generic version of this argument might go as follows. Television, the massification of a new middle strata reading public (plus increases in literacy of other groups) and the consequent concentration of publishing together reconfigure the cultural products industry. In consequence the field of incentives within which many intellectuals operated was restructured. Television enhanced rapid turnover in intellectual modes and a shortening of historical perspective. In this setting, mass publishing controlled by a few large houses sought quick 'coups' which could be widely advertised and rapidly sold. Becoming a 'famous French intellectual' thus involved 'flexibilization,' to borrow a barbaric word from the economists. Aspirants had to write very quickly on very contemporary subjects in ways which would be accessible to wide audiences. Those who succeeded often had to work in a somewhat ephemeral world of current events and be prepared to change swiftly. The rewards for becoming this new kind of intellectual were very great, the argument went, thus many were tempted into careers which involved networking from, say, an academic point of departure, into regular writing for a newsweekly like *Nouvel Observateur* and into affiliations with important Parisian publishing houses. See Régis Debray, *Teachers, Writers, Celebrities: The Intellectuals of Modern France* (London, Verso, 1981); Régis Debray, *Le Scribe* (Paris, Grasset, 1980). For a succinct version of a similar argument, see Claude Sales, 'L'Intelligentsia, Visite aux artisans de la culture,' in *Le Monde de l'Education*, February, 1977. From a very different point of view, and on a much higher theoretical plane, see Raymond Boudon, 'L'intellectuel et ses publics: les singularités françaises,' in *Français, qui êtes-vous?* (Paris: Documentation Française, 1981). The best book on this Parisian world of interlocking cultural cliques is Hervé Hamon and Patrick Rotman, *Les Intellocrates* (Paris, Ramsay, 1981).

59. The PCF's hegemony over Left intellectuals was relative and limited, as well as temporally brief. Circumstances of the Cold War, in particular the willingness of French Socialism to assume the critical role of the pro-American pivot in majorities after 1947, a willingness which obliged the SFIO to jettison any serious reformist intentions, left the PCF de facto in control of Left legitimacy in general. This legitimacy, extended to intellectuals, was essentially *political*. The PCF was never able to develop a convincing theoretico-ideological posture and its Marxism was always a pastiche of Soviet ideas and homilies derived from French politics of the day. The party's political position may have compelled intellectuals to listen to it, whether to accept or reject it, but it provided few convincing ideas for intellectuals to deploy professionally. PCF hegemony was thus vulnerable to the change in the general political situation which occurred in the later 1950s.

60. The term is Michel Winock's, see *La République se meurt* (Paris, Seuil, 1978).

61. On UNEF see Alain Monchablon, *Histoire de l'UNEF de 1956 à 1968* (Paris, PUF, 1983).

62. Here there is a counterfactual model, of course. The Italian Communist Party, obviously different from the PCF in many ways, managed to change its approaches and its self-presentation to intellectuals and succeed much more in maintaining its plausibility and the salience of its ideas in the intellectual world.

63. We have talked about the dimensions of this shift in Jane Jenson and George Ross *The View From Inside: A French Communist Cell in Crisis* (Berkeley, University of California Press, 1985).

64. Pierre Rosanvallon's writings provide a bellwether for this very large segment of the intelligentsia. See *L'Age de l'Autogestion* (Paris, Seuil, 1976).

65. For a solid, if biased, overview of major parts of this *autogestionnaire* movement see Hervé Hamon and Patrick Rotman, *La Deuxième Gauche* (Paris, Ramsay, 1982).

66. An interesting document here is *Pour une nouvelle culture politique* by Pierre Rosanvallon and Patrick Viveret (Paris, Editions du Seuil, 1977).

67. The political evolution of Michel Rocard, the 'second Left's' spokesperson par excellence in the 1970s was exemplary. From leadership of the radical PSU after May, 1968, Rocard became the challenger of François Mitterrand's Common Programme 'archaism' in the name of a new 'realism' in 1978.

68. One could present a similar analysis about publishing houses.

69. There is a very good monograph on *Nouvel Obs*. See Louis Pinto, *L'Intelligence en action: 'Le Nouvel Observateur'* (Paris, Anne-Marie Métaillié, 1984).

70. The history of all this is recounted in Daniel Singer, *Is Socialism Doomed?* (New York, Oxford UP, 1988). It is treated somewhat more analytically in George Ross, Stanley Hoffmann and Sylvia Malzacher, eds. *The Mitterrand Experiment* (New York, Oxford UP, 1987).

DERRIDA AND THE POLITICS OF INTERPRETATION

ELEANOR MACDONALD

It is time for a political reading of the work of Jacques Derrida. Derrida's work, situated within a body of ideas variously described as postmodernism, poststructuralism, and deconstructionism, is important politically, in part because of a series of challenges that this body of theory generally and specifically presents to Marxism and feminism.

The first of these challenges consists in the relationship of the themes of postmodernism (and Derrida as a principal exponent of postmodern theory) to popular contemporary experience. It is the attunement of postmodern ideas to the experiences of cynicism and disillusionment, so common in the 1980s, that accounts in large part for its popularity. The 'optimism of the will' which Gramsci advocated for Marxist politics is absent from postmodern theory, as it is from much popular sentiment. The ability of postmodern theory to capture and express a popular mood of mistrust and defeatism therefore warrants consideration by Marxists and feminists. A second challenge of Derrida's work is that it cuts into the heart of many of the salient debates within Marxism, and within socialist feminist theory. To some Marxists and feminists, Derrida's work appears to provide a potential resolution to some of those debates, and raises the possibility of transcending them, through an alternative understanding of how we interpret reality, an understanding which seems ethically compatible with some of the concerns that those debates have raised.[1] Yet, despite the appeal that Derrida's work has found among Marxist and feminist scholars, the resolution that he offers is fraught with problems and contradictions which raise suspicions about its usefulness for political change. Finally, Derrida's approach to Marxist and feminist debates presents yet a further challenge insofar as it portrays a certain relationship between ethics, truth, and power, which is at odds with the classical understandings of Marxism and feminism. The challenge that Derrida presents to us at this level is a fundamental one, one which confronts us with a renewed demand to interpret reality in a way which can empower us to change the contemporary experiences which his work so well describes.

Locating his work politically requires more than categorizing him as either

Marxist or anti-Marxist, feminist or anti-feminist. Although Derrida himself claims that he is a Marxist, it is obvious to any reader that his work does not fit neatly into the usual designations of either Marxism or feminism.[2] Instead, I will argue that understanding the politics of Derrida's work, and understanding its implications for Marxism and feminism requires that we take seriously the challenges it presents to our interpretations of the world, and appreciate the circumstances in which those challenges have become insistent. Only then will we be able to confront the politics that both produce and are derived from postmodern theory.

Derrida and Postmodern Experience

The themes of Derrida's work are reflected in 'postmodern' theory generally, (including the work of Michel Foucault, Jean Baudrillard, Jean-François Lyotard, and Gilles Deleuze) with the label 'postmodernism' coming to suggest a variety of ideas, including both a radical continuation of modernism's rejection of all traditional beliefs, as well as a rejection of modernity's sense of itself as 'progressing' beyond those beliefs into some higher truths. Before analyzing Derrida's philosophy in order to see precisely how it accounts for its principal themes, it would be useful to describe those themes, and to suggest how they may resonate with features of contemporary experience.

A central theme which is present in postmodern thought, and which underwrites Derrida's theory, is a deep suspicion of power, and of the way in which power seems necessarily to corrupt. The optimism of the Left, in its aspirations for power, and indeed in its faith in the prospect of the withering away of the state, can only be held in scorn by postmodernists. Their cynicism is a result of the belief that power has its own mechanisms, which are not subject to the desires and determinations of those who are 'in power'. Instead, the structures of power itself will determine, if not the precise activities of those in power, then at least the effects of those activities. Those effects will be a reduction in individuality, in spontaneity, and in independence. Increasingly, the direction of all institutions and practices of power will be towards normalization and conformity.

Postmodern theorists, like feminists and Marxists, speak from an ethical resistance to this view of power. In Derrida's case, this resistance comes from a view that power enforces sameness, that it attempts to deny and withstand differences as they appear between different people, and among different interpretations at a given point in time and across time, historically. The political practices of representation would necessarily impose a structure of 'sameness'; i.e. representatives are supposed to fix in one location and time those who elect them. So what Derrida's work would seem to prescribe is the most radical form of democracy, one without representation, and therefore one in which even individuals' representations of themselves would be drawn constantly into question.

Unlike feminist and Marxist theories, therefore, Derrida seems to base the desire for democracy not on collective identities, and barely on the notion of identity at all. Moreover, at a fundamental level, his work denies the possibility of democracy ever being achieved, not only because of the radical requirements which his theory proposes, but because this desire for democracy can only fuel resistance, and cannot be 'powerful'. Power, per se, is anti-democratic.

What is apparent from this description, and what perhaps accords with contemporary postmodern experience, are these two features. First, that power cannot be trusted, that it does not matter who is in control. And secondly, that collective identities cannot be fostered in trust, that individuals are unable to represent their own interests, even to themselves. Derrida's theory reflects the experiences both of individualism and of powerlessness, experiences which Marxism and feminism attempt to counter.

A similar set of suspicions informs the Derridean view of ethics. It is clear enough, at least in a close reading, that Derrida speaks from an ethical position, that he genuinely engages in his work in order to deconstruct, and hopefully disengage from systems of domination. Yet the ethics which inform his work are not something which he develops in his theory. He can, for example, demonstrate the 'false' nature of representation, and reveal the 'truth' of non-identity, of the inability to represent anything (in language or in politics) as it actually is. This 'truth' then corresponds to an ethical position, in which he sides with the underdog, the oppressed, the powerless. But the oppressed, it seems, deserve his support, simply because they have no power. In other words, there are no inherent qualities of political underdogs to which he can attribute value, other than their existence as underdogs, as marginal to the power system. Obviously, this leaves all questions of values and ethics terribly undertheorized.

Nevertheless, several features of Derrida's ethical position deserve emphasis for their apparent correlation with popular experience. First, Derrida's consideration of ethics, like his theory of power, allows him to capture the popular sentiments of futility and powerlessness. His view of ethics serves to underline the degree to which the present system is felt as stable and unchanging, and as oppressive to the powerless. The oppressed are oppressed because the system will inevitably reproduce oppression. In addition to capturing this sense of the futility of ethical practices, Derrida's view of ethics also demonstrates that the social structures of power are not justified by a common perception that the powerful are necessarily better people. On the contrary, contemporary culture, and postmodern culture, find the powerful to be no better, and possibly much worse than the oppressed. Because there are no standards for evaluating values or ethics, postmodern thought can hold that mass culture and any values and ethics which arise in it, are as valid as any alternative. That is, the values and ethics of popular culture are valued not because they are popular or democratic, but because there are no standards for judgement which would permit ethical or value superiority to emerge. Finally, what is valued in his theory is the process which Derrida calls deconstruction. This process involves taking apart and analyzing the components of all previous thought, beliefs, and values, in order to discover within all of them the same tendency to try to become powerful through following certain practices which permit them to declare that they are accurate representations of reality. Through revealing this tendency, deconstruction shows the deception and the misrepresentation of reality on which all representation is premised.

The combination of Derrida's theory of ethics and theory of power leads to another theme of postmodern thought and experience, and that is the limited place that is given to freedom. There are no grounds for choice of action, and no way in which action can be made more effective through the theory. There is even a vague suspicion that whenever it is effective, then it may also become part of the normalizing and totalizing practice of power, and therefore that all effective action would have to be unethical. If freedom could be exercised ethically, then it is only through the highly intellectual practice of deconstruction. This theme of postmodernism too, appears to correspond well to people's actual experience of a lack of freedom in their lives, and the general despair that a different political system, or the possibility of acting politically in concert with others, could provide greater freedom in their lives. Most fundamentally, however, Derrida's deep concern with 'interpretation' serves to emphasize a common feeling that the world is becoming increasingly difficult, even impossible to comprehend. Even if we do not concur with him that all language is deceptive and dissembling, the sentiment that some language certainly is, is a strongly felt one and a frequent one in our lives. The challenge to interpret the world in a way which is both empowering, and in some way ethical, is becoming increasingly difficult.

The themes of postmodernism, its suspicion of power, its despair about a way in which ethics and power could be brought together, the lack of grounding for values or ethical positions, a bleak outlook on freedom, and a suspicion of all interpretation are among the most resonant themes in contemporary political experience. They are, as well, themes which Marxism and feminism have sought to combat. The challenge to rearticulate an optimism for politics and a trust in interpretation is an immense one, and must start with an ability to interpret in the hope of changing the very experiences that Derrida and the other postmodernists describe.

Derrida and Interpretation

The resonance of postmodernist thought at the popular level today finds many Marxists and feminists in tow. Although we may be committed to political change, we are hardly immune from the despair that change may never happen, or such change as may come to pass may never be enough to create the society which we are working for. The pessimism and hopelessness of postmodern theory have particular appeal for intellectuals, for whom at least Derrida seems to reserve some ethical space (although this space is severely limited in its effectiveness). But many intellectual feminists and Marxists have also found appeal in Derrida's work for other reasons, specifically the promise of Derrida's theory to surmount some of the basic conflicts which have emerged in Marxist theory and in socialist feminist thought.

The conflicts which have emerged, and which persist, for Marxists and for feminists, can be depicted in terms of problems of interpreting experience in order to change it. How, for example, can the experiences described in the first section of this paper, the experiences of futility and despair concerning political action, be understood in order that they can then be altered? And what is the relationship between interpreting those experiences accurately, and actually being able to change them?

For Marxists, the problem of interpretation has been encountered in the debates concerning ideology and social change.[3] It is a central thesis of Marxism that human subjects cannot immediately understand the reality in which they are enveloped. Classical Marxism demonstrated that while the immediate level of experience could not be certain, attention to the deeper structures latent in that reality would reveal both an accurate understanding of phenomena and also reveal the internal processes of change. But the ensuing debates within Marxism have revealed inconsistencies and a certain vagueness in some of the early formulations.

For Marxists who stressed the power of human agency, ideology could be overcome through the practice of class struggle combined with Marxist theory. They have assumed that at some level, separate from ideological influence, workers have access to experience which would correspond to the truths revealed by Marx. But after a century in which the working class of capitalism has been mostly unmoved by analyses of their continuing 'false consciousness', the appeal of this approach has worn thin. It is increasingly difficult to argue that there are realms of experience untouched by ideology, which provide unmediated truths to those who look for them. And, if Marxism offers simply another ideology, then how can it be guaranteed that it is the 'correct' one or that it would emerge the more powerful in a competition among ideologies.

Structuralist Marxism offered one alternative to the fading trust in human agency. The 'scientific' approach of structuralist thought demonstrated that humans did have access to a type of knowledge which would reveal reality, and at the same time explain the processes of ideological formulation and promulgation. But structuralism has been properly criticized for the ease with which it transposed all of the problems of the subject onto another level (where it then proceeded to ignore their problematic status). Society is granted its ability to occlude subjective understanding; subjects are understood as constituted ideologically by the society and thereby mystified by it. But the 'scientific' autonomy and vision of the structuralist who sees beneath this cannot be explained by the theory itself, and the macro-subject of the economy which propels society forward appears to be divorced anyway from any connection to human agency or knowledge which would inform it. The interpretation which structuralist Marxism offered was limited by both its inability to explain its own recourse to correct interpretations which were generally unavailable, and at the same time, made the necessity of interpretation rather redundant to a society in which change was principally a property of the structures themselves. History, it appeared in the theory, had already been written, and interpretation was mostly incidental to it.

While many of the debates over interpretation within Marxism have focussed on this pole of agency vs. structure, the debates within feminist thought have had a different content, and have centred more on the question of foundation. Feminism, too, has had to explain the deep roots of sexist beliefs within society, and the concomitant experience of sex oppression. And it has had to explain the complicity of women in their own oppression, for which some of Marxism's understandings of ideology have occasionally appeared useful. Socialist feminists have had the additional task of explaining how capitalism reinforced and bolstered women's oppression, while not reducing women's oppression to the capitalist form of production, nor ignoring the real exploitation of all workers. More recently, feminist theory generally has been criticized heavily for universalizing its assumptions about women's oppression, and for not recognizing that the experiences in which the theory has been grounded have been only the experiences of white women.[4] There is an irony in this criticism. Feminism, which has had as a principal part of its critique of society the universalization of male experience as human experience, has been forced to confront its own tendency to universalize from a narrow and specific set of experiences. Feminism is now challenged with the task of trying to articulate common grounds for a feminist interpretation of reality, and for a women's movement aimed at freeing women from oppression, while simultaneously trying to be sensitive to the lack of commonality in women's experience of oppression, and in the forms of oppression that women face. The result has been a movement towards a celebration of women's differences, and a caution against the formulation of collective identities. Even the use of the term 'woman' has been declared problematic.[5] Recent debates within feminism have concerned just this question: how to create a common struggle without imposing commonality across class, race, sexual orientation, location, culture.[6]

Derrida's work does not explicitly enter into these debates in Marxism or feminism, but the turn to his work witnessed in recent Marxist and feminist writings suggests that he has had some impact on them.[7] This impact can best be explained by concentrating on the central theme in Derrida's work, the problem of interpretation. Through examining Derrida's theory of intepretation, we can see the way in which it intersects with, and proposes a resolution for the conflicts in Marxist and feminist thought.

Meaning, according to Derrida, is a result of an originary 'differance'. 'Differance' is a play on the French verb 'différer' which has two meanings: both 'to differ' as in to distinguish, and 'to defer' as in to postpone, or put off. Derrida uses this term to highlight an originary condition of meaning, that it is always part of a system of making distinctions, and of referring beyond the object in its temporal and spatial existence. The 'a' in differance is significant, because it can only be seen when the word is written; it cannot be distinguished in sound from the word 'difference' with an 'e'.[8] Derrida makes this distinction, which may seem facile, because he is making a point about language generally, and about the order of language. The system of language is what we use to understand the world, and the traditional belief about it has been that language is, in some way, able immediately to reflect the world in words, and that it is secondary to that which it reflects. The relationship between writing and speech acts as a metaphor for this. Speech has been considered to be the major part of language, and writing its subordinate partner. Writing has been historically believed merely to reflect speech, hopefully to be an accurate enough account of speech, just as language's relation to the world has been understood as a mere reflection, an accurate enough account. And what Derrida finds significant in these hierarchies is the assumption of immediacy in the representation of the world in language, and particularly in speech. Speech, he says, is considered to be the dominant partner in language largely because the presence of the speaker is equated with the supposed presence of meaning in language's relation to the world.

Derrida's point regarding how to discover the basis of meaning is that these traditional beliefs must be inverted. First of all, he states that language does not reflect the world; it conditions and creates all the meanings that we find in the world, and we have no access to any interpretation of the world that is separate from language. Secondly, writing is a more accurate metaphor for this condition of language than speech is. Writing makes clearer both the absence of the speaking subject, and of the referent or object. And this absence is crucial to any understanding of interpretation, since words of necessity contain meanings and references which are unintended by the subject, and which extend beyond the object. Words and language, when examined, spill forth these 'traces' of other meanings, or 'supplements' which indicate the way in which interpretations actually exceed reality, not (as was traditionally thought) fall short of it.[9]

All meanings, therefore, and all interpretations of reality, are what Derrida calls 'texts'. The use of the term 'text' is deliberately extended to include not only written works, but also all ideas, beliefs, practices, and even institutions. The extension of the notion 'text' was designed, according to Derrida, to put into question the traditional divisions between texts, on the one hand, and reality on the other.[10] It was to spoil this separation so that we would come to see the degree to which we have no access to reality other than through our sets of interpretations and beliefs. Interestingly, the word 'texte' in French is also the word for 'script', and therefore emphasizes the degree to which language predetermines our actions in and our relation to the world. Further, we should examine those 'texts' to disclose the ways in which they participate in dissembling their own relation to reality.

The process of reading texts for their moments of dissemblance is what Derrida calls 'deconstruction'. Derrida's own work is focussed on the deconstruction of the major works of Western philosophy. In these works, he suggests, the structures of Western thought have been laid down and eloquently defended. Key among these structures are certain beliefs about interpretation of the world. These beliefs depend upon the ideas described above, that language is secondary and inadequate to reality, and that therefore interpretation always falls short of what it attempts to understand.

Derrida's inversion of these beliefs is not intended as merely an exercise in logic. It is also ethical and political. He sees the referential aspect of language, and its subordinate relationship to reality, as intrinsically totalitarian. This totalitarianism is due to the drive for interpretation to refer immediately in a complete, sufficient way to reality. The drive to interpret the world is also, he thinks, a drive to control it, and to form of the world and our relation to it, a closed totality. Derrida inverts the relationship of interpretation to the world to show both the impossibility of interpretations of the world ever being complete and immediate in relation to their objects, and also to demonstrate the dangers of attempting to achieve a total, seamless interpretation.[11]

The relationship of this theory of interpretation to the impasses described in Marxist and feminist thought should now begin to be clear. In the Marxist debate between structure vs. agency, the structuralists give an analysis of ideology which separates knowledge from the process of social change, without fully explaining their own privileging of 'scientific' knowledge as non-ideological. The humanists retain faith in the importance of human agency in class struggle, and in the capacity for understanding experience in a way which will fuel that struggle. Derrida's theory of interpretation is reminiscent of structuralism in its denial of human agency, and therefore serves as a critique of humanist Marxism's confidence in human perception, experience, and action. All we have access to, according to Derrida, are interpretations of the world which are necessarily already distorted and untrue. Moreover, our actions in the world are less significant than the powerful nature of the relationship of language to reality which predetermines our understanding of the world, and even predetermines the possibility of changing the way in which power operates. While some of these features of his thought may resemble structuralism, Derrida's theory is emphatically also a criticism of structuralism. Because of his theorization of 'the trace' and 'the supplement' which imply that there is always an excess, and an unpredictability in any system, he can criticize the ways in which structuralism works always with the idea of a closed totality, in which the structure, or form, is always theorized as being completely adequate to the content which it shapes.[12] There is a random quality which Derrida reintroduces to the debates in structuralism, an unpredictability to all structures. So, in the structure vs. agency debate, Derrida attempts a resolution by abandoning both structure and agency, thereby drastically limiting the explanatory value of the theory. Given his beliefs about interpretation, the loss of an explanatory function for theory is, in fact, his point.

Derridean interpretation has a different, but also interesting, relationship to the struggles and concerns of feminist theory. As feminist theorists attempt to theorize without any stability in any of the concepts they use, even the concept of 'women', they move quickly into an affinity with the non-universalization, and non-foundationalism of Derrida's work.[13] The choice, increasingly, is to pursue only those studies which are extremely specific in their attention to the class composition, race, culture, location and sexual orientation of those who are studied. Increasingly, the emphasis adopted in feminist writing is to emphasize the differences between women's experience, rather than the similarities. This development marks an important transition in feminist thought, for which Derrida's work initially appears to provide theoretical confirmation. His insistence on difference, and on the non-representability of differences, justifies a stance toward which feminism was already moving. The difficulty for feminism of transposing that understanding of difference into collective struggle is not, however, a difficulty for which Derrida's work, with its suspicion of collectivities, offers a solution.

Some of the appeal of Derrida's work, then, for Marxists and feminists is the way in which his ideas intersect, at an intellectual level, with the theoretical dilemmas of Marxism and feminism. For feminists, his work offers a theorization of the treacherous problems of interpreting and representing difference. For Marxist theorists, the rejection of the structure vs. agency problematic can come as a relief to what seemed like an insurmountable impasse between different versions of theoretical foundations. In both cases, the acceptance of Derrida's ideas is facilitated by the sense that his work shares many of the ethical sensibilities of Marxism and feminism, in particular a resistance to all forms of domination and oppression.

Interpretation and Experience

Although Derrida's work can be understood as having a certain appeal, at the popular level, in its sensitivity to contemporary experience, and at the intellectual level, as a way of approaching feminist and Marxist problematics, the contradictions and limitations of his work confound any direct application of it to politics or to progressive political theory. The contradictions between progressive politics and Derridean philosophy emerge around several themes. These problems can be recognized in the undertheorization of ethics in his work, in certain logical contradictions in his presentation of the 'truth' of 'differance', and in the implications of his theory for interpreting power. In each case, a serious difficulty in Derrida's work has to do with the distance that the notion of 'text' imposes on his analysis.

This difficulty can be witnessed first, for example, in his theorization of ethics. Despite Derrida's apparent political alignment with the left (broadly understood) and with the oppressed generally, there is no clear motive to his analysis why this value system should be so. Instead, what we find is an analysis of the oppression that exists in philosophical dualisms (such as nature/culture, reason/passion, subject/object, masculine/feminine). In each case, according to the form of interpretation which has been predominant in Western culture and language, the lesser term in the dualism will succumb to the former. This is because Western thought has privileged those terms which offer the possibility of mastery of the world through interpretation and representation of the world in language. It was always in the 'lesser' term of the dualism that one could sense the chance for subversiveness, for escape from this desire for mastery, or the impossibility of it. Derrida's inversion of the dualisms of philosophy, and his valorization of these lesser terms, is designed to restore that knowledge of the impossibility of mastery. And he demonstrates its undesirability as well in the movement toward 'totalitarianism' which is implicit in the privileging of those terms. There is, however, no reason why one side of a philosophical dualism should be celebrated over another; both of them can be deconstructed equally, to show how the existence of one is dependent upon the existence of the other, and to show that they are most dependent on the way in which meanings generally belong to a system of domination in language. The theory of deconstruction reveals how the lesser term of the dualism is repressed within the system; it brings the form of that repression to light. But no value belongs to that term. What deconstruction demonstrates is the necessity of both terms, and the inevitability of the privileging of the dominant term in all language and representation.

It is clear from this that the hierarchy of philosophical dualisms stays undisturbed despite deconstruction's revelation of the internal interdependency of its terms. What is obvious as well is that Derrida's attention to texts, and to the functioning of texts, as the root of oppression, distances his work from the understanding of oppression beyond intellectual questions of interpretation. Oppression only appears as such, within his work, when it is a question of meanings, and interpretations which are denying other meanings, or which are being hidden themselves. There is no opportunity to evaluate interpretations or meanings, much less to condemn oppressive practices, other than through the limited operations of deconstruction. There is no place to understand oppression, other than as interpretive oppression.

The limitations placed on theorizing ethics are equally evident in the untangling of Derrida's theorization of the truth of 'differance'. Under the process of deconstruction, Derrida demonstrates how all texts reveal their participation in 'the metaphysics of presence' (i.e. in the unfounded assumption that language is complete and adequate in the present with what it refers to). As a result, the meanings that come to light through deconstruction are not arbitrary or random; they are predetermined by a truth that deconstruction has discovered. Accordingly it seems that Derrida is advising that the workings of 'differance' should be understood, recognized, valued, because they contain a certain accuracy about the world. What Derrida appears to be doing, in this case, is not dismissing all logic and rationality (as he is sometimes purported to do), but registering an alternative form of rationality and logic. What is curious is that in many ways, this logic of Derrida's (the 'logic of the supplement' or the 'logic of deconstruction') parallels the 'metaphysical logic of presence' which it is supposed to replace.[14] What is the logic of deconstruction if not Derrida's own attempt to get through to some sort of truth behind meaning, albeit a truth that declares the near impossibility of accuracy of meaning? When Derrida indicates that our interpretation of the world requires that we suspend belief in our interpretations to some degree, and that in doing so we should attend to the play of language, the differences that emerge and tend to be suppressed in our attention to objects, the contingency and arbitrariness of all our attempts at meaning – what is this if not some reference to some real correspondence between thought (his thought) and its objects (the real relationship we have to the world).

Several features of this logic are clearly troubling, to put it mildly. First, there is the issue of its own dissemblance. If deconstruction is a logic which depends upon some correspondence with reality, then how can it account for its own self-presence, or immediacy, while renouncing the possibility of either? And if it does accept that at some level it constitutes a reflection of the world which is primary and determinate, then surely it would have to concede that the same logic (the metaphysics of presence) which it denounces would also have to be capable of acknowledging this foundation, or even ultimately arriving at this realization itself.

Secondly, there is the problem of the theory's inability to move outside of itself. Deconstruction, discovered, appears to be stuck at rediscovering itself. Despite Derrida's insistence on the importance of a lack of closure, his work reiterates the same general ideas, no matter which texts it explores. The revelation of the truths buried in the text, and the repetitive undermining of each text's self-assurance of presence amounts to the discovery and elaboration of a system whose logic does appear closed.

A third difficulty in accepting this logic as a political logic arises from its tendency to leave the existing system in place. The radical nature of deconstruction seems very quietistic when one realizes that the political impulse within it dictates only the practice of deconstructing texts. And in that deconstruction, discrimination among or between texts (except concerning the degree to which they they reflect the 'logic of the supplement') appears impossible.

If texts are understood to be interpretations of reality, Derrida's theory makes it clear that every text which claims an interpretation, is in fact a misinterpretation of reality. There is an irony involved here. Derrida's claim is that reality can only be misinterpreted, and the particular ways in which it is misinterpreted constitute a form of totalitarianism. Specifically, a misinterpretation which claims not to be, which claims to be a true and complete representation of reality, is a form of totalitarian belief. And additionally, a misinterpretation which claims only to be a partial explanation of reality, and which, in doing so, participates in the movement toward a total explanation (historically, structurally, etc.) would also participate in totalitarian politics. Only a misinterpretation which claims its status as such, and which considers itself to be (or knows itself to be) creative of reality could be anti-totalitarian. (This willing, conscious misinterpretation would be one way to account for Derrida's portrayal of his own work.) But the creative aspect of interpretation, in this case, would not involve control or predictability. The interpretation deconstruction offers of reality (or more logically, the specific misinterpretation it provides – since accurate interpretation has been declared impossible) could be anti-totalitarian only in the sense that it understood itself to be excessive to, and extensive beyond reality, and without any intentional or predictable control over reality. And the irony is that if only this form of 'misrepresentation', and non-deliberative dissemination of texts is anti-totalitarian, then all that practically separates this form of misrepresentation from previous ones is one's consciousness of it, since the theory predetermines that both will be misrepresentations, and both will produce effects over which they can have no intentional control. Politics, it appears in this analysis, could occur only in the mind. And to intend anti-totalitarianism is never necessarily to produce it.

This irony is a direct result of the reduction of all experience to texts, and therefore of all political theory to interpretations of texts, or better put, interpretations of interpretations. Truth is withheld by Derrida and reserved for those who speak from a specific vantage point, which allows them temporarily to step outside the representational system and view both its roots and its downfall in the originary condition of 'difference'. Moreover, the truthfulness of any interpretation is separated from experience. Experience is reduced completely to interpretation, such that there is then no basis why any interpretation would be believed over any other. The accuracy or truthfulness of various interpretations of experience can never be measured, since experience itself is not permitted in a theory which exclusively concerns itself with texts.

These considerations of the problems with Derrida's theory of ethics and his theory of the truth (of the originary condition of 'differance' and its necessary distortion in language and representation) make it evident that both theories have implications for his theory of power. It should be clear in a political reading of Derrida that truth (if truth is 'differance') is continually undone by power. Power is on the side of deception. Meaning is meaningful only within the belief in the 'presence'of meaning. Therefore, all intentional practices, and the exercise of power on the basis of certain understandings of the world, with a view to changing it, must always participate in the construction of, and desire for, 'totality'. Language and practice which retain faith in the possibility of interpretation are always, according to this theory, totalitarian. This view of power is not only profoundly negative, but it also suffers from an inability (parallelling the difficulties with his views of truth and ethics) to distinguish between one form of exercise of power and another. The exercise of power which would meaningfully desire to create a society of equality and freedom is as subject to deconstructive criticism as the most restrictive military state. In the theorization of power, the problem again appears to be that Derrida's interpretation is limited to the interpretation of other interpretations, and we are caught in a circle of texts.

Interpretive Challenges

From the preceding discussion, it should be apparent that Derrida's work does not, in fact, provide the solutions which are required for the theoretical dilemmas raised in Marxist and feminist thought. What an examination of his work does do (and this is where it may be politically valuable to pay attention to it) is introduce further challenges to our theorization and interpretation of reality.

One challenge that Derrida offers is a call for a reinterpretation of our understanding of texts. His extension of the notion of texts to the point where they are coextensive with all experience is clearly flawed. Taken to this extreme, the analysis of texts loses all contact with reality, except some originary reality of the relationship of language to the world. Yet his work does serve to draw attention to the importance of the interpretive moment in all experience. It raises questions concerning the reasons why some interpretations or meanings do have more resonance than others, and it suggest the necessity of investigating areas which Derrida leaves untouched, such as areas where interpretations are nebulous and changing, where their political effects in practical terms are made clear, or areas where force supersedes interpretation. Answering this challenge requires introducing again the sticky questions of ideology, and inquiring into social relations and institutions. In order to discover the relationship between interpretation and reality, more than 'texts' are needed; one must attempt to evaluate interpretations of reality based on what they reveal and conceal, what they put into effect, and what they inhibit. To accomplish this, what may in fact be required is a criticism of the structure/agency debate in Marxism, and the attempt to move toward some of the directions taken by feminist theorists, that is, theorizing with a sensitivity to a higher degree of contextualization, the necessity of relating and linking different forms of ideological mystification, and types of oppression, and a general caution against the effectiveness of any grand theory, such as Marx's theory of capital, in adequately interpreting specific historical circumstances. What this means for Marxists is that the foundational character of the 'economic' realm, and the corollary privileging of the category of 'class' in political analyses, must be continually drawn into question as a sufficient programme for useful political interpretation.

Another challenge, therefore, must be for Marxists and feminists to restate the relationship between power, truth and ethics. In Derrida's writing, truth is aligned with ethics, but in such a way that the powerlessness of the ethical position is assured. The need to understand power, and understand the empowerment that is possible in a truthful interpretation of reality, offers a particular challenge in present political circumstances to feminist theorists, in our attention to real differences among women and the necessity for a common struggle which does not deface those differences.

Finally, Derrida's work presents a challenge to interpret popular experience in an empowering way. One problem with most of Marxist theory of ideology is that it tended to deny, either by attributing it to 'false consciousness', or by the 'non-scientific, ideologically interpellated' consciousness that structuralism identified, the validity of most people's experience of their lives. Feminism, also, has been accused of this in its interpretation of women's reality, based on a very limited understanding of what most women experience. Ironically, postmodern thought with its denial that experience is anything but metaphysical, and with its denial that there is experience that is separate from interpretation, has directed more attention to those experiences, even while denying that that was its intent. It may be that Derrida, for all of his denial of experience, has expressed most eloquently the general sense of futility and despair about the possibility for good social change. Specifically, his theory may be felt to be most accurate in its interpretation of the relationship between power and ethics; people experience that what is right is also relatively powerless. What is frightening in his depiction of the experience of futility is his confirmation of it, his portrayal of powerlessness as a truthful account of the human condition, rather than as contingent to particular historical and alterable circumstances. Part of the challenge of Derrida's work, then, is to reinterpret these experiences of reality in order to give more space for, and more sensitivity to people's real sense of powerlessness. Can we find a way to transform that understanding into one which is empowering? That is the real challenge for Marxists and feminists today.

NOTES

1. See for example Gayatri Chakravorty Spivak, 'Speculations on Reading Marx' in *Post-structuralism and the Question of History*, ed. Derek Attridge, Geoff Bennington and Robert Young, Cambridge University Press, 1987, p. 35.
2. One of Derrida's references to himself as a Marxist can be found in James Kearns and Ken Newton 'An Interview with Jacques Derrida', *The Literary Review*, 14 (18 April – 1 May 1980), p. 22.
   'Though I am not and have never been an orthodox marxist, I am very disturbed by the antimarxism dominant now in France so that, as a reaction, through political reflection and personal preference, I am inclined to consider myself more marxist than I would have done at a time when Marxism was a sort of fortress.'
3. A useful summary of the debates concerning ideology in Marxism can be found in Jorge Larrain, *The Concept of Ideology*, London: Hutchinson and Co., 1979.
4. For an introduction to these debates, see Hazel Carby, 'White Women Listen! Black Feminism and the Boundaries of Feminism', *The Empire Strikes Back*, Birmingham: Centre for Contemporary Cultural Studies, 1982; Valerie Amos and Pratibha Parmar, 'Challenging Imperial Feminism' *Feminist Review*, 17, Autumn 1984; Michele Barrett and Mary McIntosh, 'Ethnocentrism and Socialist-Feminist Theory', *Feminist Review*, no. 20, Summer 1985, pp. 23–47; Carolyn Ramazanoglu et al. 'Feedback: Feminism and Racism – Responses to Michele Barrett and Mary McIntosh', *Feminist Review*, 22, Spring 1986; Kum-Kum Bhavnani and Margaret Coulson, 'Transforming Socialist Feminism: The Challenge of Racism', *Feminist Review*, 23, Summer 1986; and Jane Lewis, 'The Debate on Sex and Class', *New Left Review*, No. 149, Jan.–Feb. 1985, pp. 108–124.
5. For an example of these arguments, see Michele Barrett, 'Introduction to the 1988 Edition', *Women's Oppression Today: The Marxist/Feminist Encounter (Revised)*, London: Verso, 1988.
6. See Floya Anthias and Nira Yuval-Davies, 'Contextualizing Feminism – Gender, Ethnic and Class Divisions', *Feminist Review*, No. 15, Winter 1983, pp. 62–75; and Elly Bulkin, Minnie Bruce Pratt, and Barbara Smith, *Yours in Struggle: Three Feminist Perspectives on Anti-Semitism and Racism*, New York: Long Haul Press, 1984.
7. See Gayatri Chakravorty Spivak, *In Other Worlds: Essays in Cultural Politics*, London: Methuen Press, 1987; Meaghan Morris, *The Pirate's Fiancée: Feminism, Readying, Postmodernism*, London: Verso, 1988; Chris Weedon, *Feminist Practice and Poststructuralist Theory*, Oxford, 1987; Michael Ryan, *Marxism and Deconstruction: A Critical Articulation*, Maryland and London: Johns Hopkins Press, 1982; Derek Attridge et al. (ed.) *Poststructuralism and the Question of History*, Cambridge: Cambridge University Press, 1987; Linda J. Nicholson, (ed.) *Feminism/Postmodernism*, New York and London: Routledge, 1990.
8. For a close formulation of 'differance', see 'Difference', *Margins of Philosophy*, trans. Alan Bass, Chicago: University of Chicago Press, 1982, pp. 1–27.
9. Jacques Derrida, *Of Grammatology*, trans. Gayatri Chakravorty Spivak, Baltimore: Johns Hopkins University Press, 1976.

10. Jacques Derrida, 'Living On/Border Lines', *Deconstruction and Criticism*, New York: Seabury Press, 1979, pp. 83–84.

> 'What has happened, if it has happened, is a sort of overrun that spoils all these boundaries and divisions and forces us to extend the accredited concept, the dominant notion of a 'text', of what I still call a 'text', for strategic reasons, in part – a 'text' that is henceforth no longer a finished corpus of writing, some content enclosed in a book or its margins, but a differential network, a fabric of traces referring endlessly to something other than itself, to other differential traces.'

11. Jacques Derrida, *Positions*, trans. Alan Bass, London: Athlone Press, 1981, and *Of Grammatology*, trans. Gayatri Chakravorty Spivak, Baltimore: Johns Hopkins University Press, 1976.
12. See Jacques Derrida, 'Force and Signification' in *Writing and Difference*, trans. Alan Bass, Chicago: University of Chicago Press, 1978.
13. See Spivak, Weedon, Morris, op. cit.
14. Derrida discusses the 'logic of the supplement' in 'Structure, Sign and Play in the Discourse of the Human Sciences', *Writing and Difference*, trans. Alan Bass, London: Routledge and Kegan Paul, 1978, pp. 278–293.

SHOULD A MARXIST BELIEVE IN
MARX ON RIGHTS?

AMY BARTHOLOMEW

I

The question I have posed – should a marxist believe in Marx on rights? – is instigated by the debates in the literature over Marx, marxism and rights. In 1982 Alan Buchanan was able to write, in his widely acclaimed book *Marx and Justice*, that Marx's view of civil liberties and political rights 'has been neglected'[1]. Things have changed considerably since 1982. There have been a number of attempts recently to establish and evaluate Marx's position on civil and political rights[2]. For example, Steven Lukes, Drucilla Cornell and William McBride have engaged in a debate in the pages of *Praxis International* over the status of rights in Marx's thought and marxist theory[3]. What the proper question is has itself been an important part of the exchange. Lukes asks 'can a marxist believe in rights?' He clarifies his question by indicating that he really means to investigate whether a commitment to rights is consistent with the 'central doctrines essential to the marxist canon'[4]. Upon an analysis which directs its attention to the 'marxist tradition', he concludes that a marxist cannot be consistent and 'believe in rights'. One way to address Lukes would, of course, be to challenge the notions of 'central doctrines', 'marxist canon' and 'marxist tradition'. In his response to Lukes, William McBride does this well, arguing that the notion of a canon 'connotes an essential rigidity' which is neither plausible nor helpful[5], since marxism is indeed an internally diverse and contested terrain. While I too want to reject the notion of a marxist canon for all substantial purposes, asking what Marx thought of rights has the more limited potential of destabilizing what tends to be treated as the *received* canon, which provides the basis of Lukes' answer to the question[6].

Drucilla Cornell insisted in response to Lukes that the more pertinent question is whether a marxist *'should* believe in rights?' I am sympathetic to Cornell's version of the question. One virtue it has is that it extracts us from the straightjacket which Lukes wishes to impose on us by narrowly securing the boundaries of the tradition he is willing to call marxism, and then requiring us to walk gingerly in its footprints in order to be politically correct, or 'consistent'. Despite the fact that I think Cornell's question is the more pertinent one, pertaining as it does to the strategic questions we must get on with, her question does not mark out clearly enough what I take to be the *double* nature of the issue.

The question 'should a marxist believe in Marx on rights?' is intended to raise the double nature of the problem of rights for those working within the marxist tradition by indicating that the problem is composed of; first, establishing and evaluating Marx's position on rights and, second, asking how contemporary marxists should treat the question of rights.

I originally intended to proceed directly to the second part of the problem, as it seemed very much the more important one. I was prepared to accept the rather widely-held opinion amongst scholars that Marx *rejected* rights[7]. Therefore, because I want to support rights, my ready answer was: a marxist should *not* believe in Marx on rights. Yet, there is certainly a strand within contemporary marxism that has been supportive of rights[8]. So, I was prepared to argue that what counts is using marxist methodologies and, above all, relying upon socialist commitments in order to support, argue for and reconceptualize rights. But on some reflection, it seems to me that both aspects of the problem are important to consider. My attention, here, will be overwhelmingly on the first part of the problem both because of the importance of offering a different reading of Marx to that which is prevalent today; and, because, on the basis of this different reading, contemporary marxists will be better able to chart a course which is grounded, but not stuck, in Marx's texts.

Marx's work, especially 'On the Jewish Question' and 'Critique of the Gotha Programme,' has provided the analytical hints that have framed today's discourse within some strands of marxism regarding rights[9] and especially the assessment outside of marxism[10] regarding marxism's capacity and inclination to 'take rights seriously'. Several recent interpretations of Marx share a broadly similar reading of his position on rights, although they differ on the consequences they draw from this reading. In important treatments of the issue, both Buchanan and Lukes insist that Marx was 'scornful' of rights, and that he rejected them[11]. The American Critical Legal Studies critique of rights – an influential 'school' in North American radical academia – has been consistently hostile to rights; or scornful of them. And, much of that critique finds support in Marx's comments on, or attitude toward, rights[12]. Finally, in developing their 'post-liberal' socialist strategy, Samuel Bowles and Herbert Gintis argue there is little sustenance to be had in Marx's treatment of rights, choice and freedom:

> Marxism's discursive structure lacks the fundamental theoretical vocabulary to represent the conditions of choice, individual liberty, and dignity, and hence cannot fully address the problem of despotism. . .the Marxian theoretical lexicon does not include such terms as freedom, personal rights, liberty, choice, or even democracy.[13]

But is this sort of reading clearly sustainable? My contention, in constrast with Bowles and Gintis, is that, at least with respect to freedom and democracy, and the rights, both personal and political, which are crucial to them, we need not leave marxism, and that those who argue like Lukes that a 'marxist cannot believe in rights' are misguided. The simplest support for my claim is that despite the fact that Marx did not evince a particularly strong commitment to rights, neither did he 'reject' them. Moreover, marxism can be 'rethought' in such a way as to weave rights commitments more firmly into its theoretical lexicon. And my final contention is that this can be accomplished without moving particularly far away from Marx himself. In fact, I shall argue that by relying upon Marx's understanding of, and commitment to, the development of 'rich individuality' and self-development entailed in the notion of 'human emancipation' – commitments which have not been adequately attended to in the contemporary debate over Marx, marxism and rights[14] – a basis may be found in Marx's work in which to ground a positive commitment to rights. Moreover, a commitment to rights is, in fact, consistent with many of Marx's other commitments in addition to rich individuality, including the development of working class capacities and socialist political strategy.

It is important to emphasize from the outset that the project of recon-structing Marx's views on rights is important for several reasons, but it is not important as an exercise in marxist fundamentalism. I do not accept that even if Marx and the 'marxist tradition' had rejected rights, a contemporary marxist could not believe in rights. Clearly, we should care what Marx said, just as we care what any other major social theorist said. And, as 'marxists' there must obviously be some degree of agreement – what that degree is, of course, is properly a matter of lively debate. But it is necessary to distinguish between textual fundamentalism, which is to be rejected, and serious study and evaluation. The development and reconceptualization of rights in the marxist tradition may benefit by a groundclearing exercise which supports the argument that Marx did not reject rights, especially since the ideas of rich individuality and self-guided self-development have not had a high profile even within the contemporary marxist literature which is sympathetic to rights.

The analysis presented here will emphasize the pertinence of individuality, setting aside for the most part the relationship between rich individuality, class capacities and rights, as well as the way in which capitalist social and economic relations founded on private property both influence and stunt individuality. Partly because the treatments of Marx which take him to reject rights typically ground their conclusions on the link between rights and individualism, I believe this is where we might most usefully begin in order to clear the way for a more substantial analysis.

Finally, the rights to which I direct my attention are individual civil and political rights in the main. I focus on these rights for several reasons. First, they are the ones to which Marx attended. Second, Marx was particularly critical of the 'rights of man'[15], or personal rights. This position needs to be reevaluated. Third, if a case can be made for such individual civil and political rights within marxism[16], there is no barrier to arguing for collective social and economic rights. These rights are also crucial to the development of a democratic socialist political project.

II

It is one thing to say that Marx was 'scornful' of rights and rejected them and quite another to say that he was critical of, and unevenly committed to, them. I will briefly dispute the first interpretation, and defend and assess the import of the second.

The conclusion that Marx rejected rights even within capitalism typically draws upon Marx's pointed criticisms of the 'so-called rights of man,' calling them merely the 'rights of egoistic man', the 'right of the *circumscribed individual*', of the 'isolated monad'[17]. Attention is also drawn to his sarcastic criticisms of the Eisenach faction of the German Social Democratic movement in 'Critique of the Gotha Programme.' There, Marx criticized the party's reliance, in its political platform, on such 'pretty little gewgaws' as democratic rights[18] and argued that the party should abandon the 'ideological nonsense' of 'bourgeois right'[19]. Finally, insofar as Marx can be read as suggesting that communism would be a society beyond rights (because it would eradicate the circumstances which make rights necessary), this is taken to indicate a rejection of rights *tout court*[20].

This is a reading of Marx that is overly simplistic. And, it has the damaging consequence of laying the groundwork for insisting that a marxist cannot, or at the very least should not, 'believe in rights'. A better reading is that Marx did not reject rights *per se*. Rather, as will be demonstrated, Marx's treatment of rights is critical, differentiated, underdeveloped and, in more than a few instances, ambiguous.

In 'On the Jewish Question' Marx distinguishes between the 'rights of man' and the 'rights of the citizen.' He *does* roundly criticize the *rights of man*, which he believed were found 'in their most authentic form' in the French and American declarations of rights. According to Marx's distinction, the rights of man included freedom of conscience and religion, equality, liberty, security and private property[21]. He argued that none of these rights 'go beyond the egoistic man, man as he is, . . .that is as an individual separated from the community. . .'; that the only 'bond they admit between people is natural necessity, need and private interest. . .'; and, that they both reflect and are (re)constitutive of competitive, egoistic, atomistic individuals who view the community and others as potential enemies. Correspondingly, Marx complains that none of the rights of man address or embrace communal or social concerns, human sociality or species being[22].

But Marx provides a rather different view of *citizens' or political rights*, and political emancipation in general. As distinct from the rights of man, citizens' rights, in Marx's schema, included political liberty, civil rights and democratic participation rights. Marx's comments made in this regard are far less hostile. He is critical of citizens' or political rights for, among other things, not touching the real distinctions of status, wealth and ownership in civil society, and for being subordinate to the 'rights of man' such that the 'political community' is 'a mere means to maintain these so-called rights of man'[23]. Yet, he praises them in these terms: they 'can only be exercised if one is a member of a community. Their content is *participation* in the *community* life, in the *political* life of the community, the life of the state. They fall in the category of *political liberty*, of *civil rights*. . .'[24]. He argued that political emancipation, which entails the realization of political *and* civil rights, 'certainly represents a great progress', despite the fact that it is severely limited[25]. One year before writing 'On the Jewish Question' Marx argued that the importance of those 'liberals. . .who have assumed the thankless and painful task of conquering liberty, step by step, within the limits imposed by the constitution' should be recognized[26].

To be sure, Marx did seem to believe communism would be a society beyond the circumstances of rights, as most of the commentators suggest. So, what are we to make of all of this? Obviously, Marx provides no 'theory' of rights; indeed, he undertakes few sustained considerations of them. This adds considerably to the difficulty in determining how to assess the comments he does make. There are, nevertheless, a number of indications that these are not the statements of one who is consistently and utterly opposed to rights; who rejects them, or is 'attacking the very concept' of right[27] as Lukes and Buchanan insist.

First, it is quite clear that Marx was more than marginally supportive of citizens' or political rights; both in terms of restricting the freedom of the state and in providing some participatory rights which permit and encourage certain forms of collective action. According to Marx, while these rights are not sufficient and constitute nothing like human emancipation, the rights of the citizen under capitalism are desirable. His complaint about the subordination of these rights to the 'so-called rights of man' only serves to support the conclusion that he viewed participatory or citizens' rights as worthy of support. We should recall as well that Marx supported freedom of speech, dissent and organization as well as the universal franchise both because he admitted the possibility of achieving socialist transformation through the vote and, perhaps more importantly, as a 'school of development'[28]. Hence, to argue that Marx rejected rights as such is simply not supportable.

Second, although Marx was extremely critical of the rights of man entrenched in the French and American rights documents which he reviews, this does not indicate conclusively that he was hostile to rights in principle. This is clear enough when we bear in mind that Marx was supportive of citizens' rights. It is not even clear that he is rejecting all formulations of liberty, equality, security or property, or 'personal rights', insofar as he directs his criticisms to specific formulations of these rights. The fact that Marx complains that none of the rights of man *go beyond* egoistic man would seem to be significant. One of his complaints is that they *only* recognize private interest. This is not an objection to rights. Rather, it is an objection to a particular set of rights – a set of rights which recognizes exclusively 'egoistic man'.

Did Marx, however, reject personal rights because they express individualism or, what may be a rather different thing, because they reinforce individualism by separating 'man from man' and individuals from the community? It is often taken to be the core of Marx's complaint about the rights of man that they reflect individualism[29]. The conclusion which tends to be drawn is that Marx rejected rights because they have an individualistic frame of reference. Yet, given his support for individual citizens' rights, this position is, in fact, difficult to sustain. Moreover, this conclusion is based on a failure to appreciate Marx's own distinction between *egoistic*, atomistic individualism and rich individuality[30]. The latter is a specific type of individualism of which Marx was not at all critical, but of which he was remarkably supportive. Marx's complaint, therefore, is better understood as pertaining to the actually-existing rights of man, which he argued emerged from and contributed to a *particular* form of individualism – bourgeois individualism – rather than a complaint about rights because they are individualistic in their form. Moreover, the sort of rights about which Marx complains are those which he asserts are limited to egoistic, competitive, individualism; those which are '*wholly* preoccupied with his private interest and acting in accordance with his private caprice'[31].

If we consider the right to liberty, the French Declaration of 1793, which Marx cites, provided: 'Liberty is the power which man has to do everything which does not harm the rights of others'[32]. Since Marx makes it clear when discussing citizens' rights that he takes political liberty against the state to be important, his criticism of liberty understood as one of the rights of man is better treated as a criticism of its particular articulation rather than as a criticism of the general concept of liberty. We might suppose that had liberty been expressed in a manner to provide a right to refuse work which is exploitative, hierarchical and the like, or if it had been interpreted to mean that no one must sell her labour power to another – that is, had it been expressed as what C.B. Macpherson calls counter-extractive liberty[33] – Marx's estimation of liberty might have been quite different. In fact, his objection to the relations which obtain within civil society is that the individual 'acts simply as a private individual, treats other men as means, degrades himself to the role of a mere means, and *becomes the plaything of alien powers*'[34]. This would seem to indicate that he supported the general value attached to negative liberty – non-coercion and being treated as an end rather than a means.

This does, however, leave the considerable difficulty of assessing Marx's criticism of this formulation of liberty as having the effect of separating man from man and individuals from the community because of the 'boundary marker' character of personal rights. The point can be made in one of two ways. As I have argued, Marx's overarching argument seems to be directed at the rights of man as a bundle: 'none of the supposed rights of man, go beyond the egoistic man. . .'[35]. This may suggest that Marx would not have objected to the rights of man provided they were more fully articulated with rights that recognize and reinforce human sociality. If this is not what is intended, and it is certainly difficult to discern whether it is, then we may have to concede that Marx valued too little the right to liberty and other 'rights of man' because of their imputed character as boundary markers – i.e. as reinforcing the separation of man from man. The question whether the personal rights such as liberty and privacy can be conceptualized in a way which would not contribute to atomistic, egoistic individualism, but would contribute to rich individuality, is obviously a crucial one and will be taken up in the conclusion.

Even if we accept that Marx supported citizens' rights and that he was not in principle hostile to personal rights, we are still left with three further problems. First of all, the literature vigorously supports the contention that Marx rejected the need for rights under communism. This reading has resulted in a variety of attempts to construct a basis for supporting rights in communism[36]. I accept both the interpretation and the criticisms which are directed at Marx on this point. What has not been explored, however, is the flip side of this contention. If it is correct that Marx believed rights would not be necessary under communism – because rights function as a partial corrective to a deeply deficient society and are not, therefore, necessary in one that is free of these deficiencies – his position on rights within capitalism is better interpreted as critical, certainly not endorsing all of them, but accepting *some* as partial, albeit inadequate, 'correctives'. We can take support for the position that if Marx believed communism was a place lacking class conflict and lacking a state in the coercive sense of the word at least, then either he did or should have supported the rights in capitalism which protect people against the existing state and capital (e.g. the right to strike). Notably, when he argues against the Eisenach's proposition that the party should strive for the 'free basis of the state' he suggests he did:

> It is by no means the aim of the workers. . .to set the state free. . .Freedom consists in converting the state from an organ superimposed upon society into one completely subordinate to it, and today, too, the forms of state are more free or less free to the extent that they restrict the "freedom of the state"[37].

And this sentiment is, in fact, reiterated throughout Marx's work. He denounced state intrusions into freedom of the press, speech and dissent, the right of organization and freedom of association, and generally supported rights which 'limited and restrained the independent scope of the executive power' in addition to supporting rights which enhanced 'popular control from below'[38].

Marx's criticism of abstract, equal right in 'Critique of the Gotha Programme' is often taken to be one of the most important indications that he rejected rights. Here we come to the second problem. In the course of a criticism of the Programme's principle that 'the proceeds of labour belong undiminished with equal right to all members of society', Marx complains that equal right in this formulation is nothing but 'bourgeois right'. He argues that 'Right by its very nature can consist only in the application of an equal standard. . .' and complains that this equal right is 'a right of inequality in its content like every right' since, with the application of an equal standard, people are 'taken from one definite side only'[39] while other attributes, needs, social contexts, relationships and the like are ignored.

There is some dispute in the literature whether Marx is limiting his discussion to equal rights in this passage, or whether this is an objection to rights *per se*. For the sake of argument, I am willing to read this as an objection to the generally abstract character of rights. Even on this interpretation, however, it is not self-evident that this admittedly serious criticism of the 'nature of right' entails the necessary conclusion that Marx therefore rejected right. In fact, he goes on to argue that, while to avoid the defect of unequal results right itself would have to be unequal rather than equal, such problems are 'inevitable' in the early stages of communism, and only in higher stages of communism can the 'narrow horizon of bourgeois right be crossed in its entirety'[40]. A plausible interpretation is, therefore, that Marx was critical of the abstraction characteristic of right, entailing as it does the application of an equal standard imposed with regard only to the action or attribute in question. This criticism itself requires serious study as it has embedded within it a number of potential problems. But what is important for the present argument is that to criticise rights on this basis does not necessarily imply a rejection of rights within capitalism. Marx recognizes, and perhaps makes too much of, the limitations on the form of rights within capitalism. But he does not indicate that they are, therefore, to be rejected. Moreover, insofar as equal results are clearly not the only thing Marx was concerned to value, his criticism of right as entailing unequal effects does not necessitate the conclusion that he rejected rights.

But what about Marx's criticism of the Gotha Programme for the party's reliance upon rights talk or rights discourse? This is the third problem. A distinction must be drawn here between his criticism of rights talk and demands in party rhetoric and platform, and his support, which we have seen, for the use and pursuit of rights in concrete political struggles. In 'Critique of the Gotha Programme' Marx states that the party's political demands contain nothing beyond the old democratic litany familiar to all: universal suffrage, direct legislation, popular rights, a people's militia, etc. They are a mere echo of the bourgeois People's Party. . .[41].

And he chastizes the party for failing to deal with the 'revolutionary dictatorship of the proletariat' necessary to socialist transformation. Once again, the phrase 'nothing beyond' does not unambiguously signal a rejection of all recourse to rights demands. Rather, it might suggest that that which fails to go beyond democratic demands is judged insufficient.

It must be said, however, that Marx was not generally supportive of the use of rights discourse or demands in party rhetoric and political platform. There are a number of reasons for this beyond the textual ones already canvassed. One important reason is the assumption of a universalistic working class with always-already present objective interests with consequently little or no need to dress its demands in the illusion of universal interests as the bourgeoisie did with rights talk, according to Marx, in order to mask the particularity of its interests. As well, this rejection of rights talk is premised upon a rather crude version of materialism in 'Critique of the Gotha Programme,' which counterposes a 'realistic outlook' with an ideological one based upon demands for rights. It seems to ignore that the working class's material interest in socialism is a necessary but not sufficient condition for its attainment. But when put in context, that is in relation to why he bothered to write the critique of the party's programme in the first place, it is obvious that he believed that what the party argued *mattered*: going all the way back to 'The Communist Manifesto' we see that for Marx it is parties that organize the proletariat into a class[42]. So, the vulgarly materialist cast of his argument in the Critique would seem to belie the fact that he sees the party's role as a necessary condition for the realisation of workers' material interests in socialism.

Marx's failure to develop an analysis of language and ideology which goes beyond a reductionist account[43], did not only severely limit his ability to analyze the potential of rights discourse; but also unnecessarily polarized the issue as one between objective interests and the political capacity to realize them. The problem for Marx is that rights language is typically universalistic; it does not, therefore, represent class interests specifically. What he needed to attend to here, but did not, is that political organization to turn the proletariat into a class is enhanced by rights such as freedom of association, the right to strike, vote and the like. By failing to articulate the distinction between rights and rights talk, his objection to the discourse of rights is carried so far as *to appear* to undermine his own, concrete support for citizens' rights – including the vote, association and the like. All of this has had the effect not only of laying the groundwork for a subsequent vulgar marxism, but of confusing generations of theorists to this day. While this is a feature of Marx's analysis which should not be accepted by contemporary analysts or strategists, his suspicion of the use of *rights talk* remains a point apart from his position on rights.

It is notable that in addition to his support for actual rights elsewhere, in 'The Communist Manifesto' Marx supports the use, in political struggle, of 'weapons' provided by the bourgeoisie generally. Marx argues that the bourgeoisie is:

Compelled to appeal to the proletariat, to ask for its help, and thus, to drag it into the political arena. [It] therefore, supplies the proletariat with its own elements of political and general education, in other words, it furnishes the proletariat with the weapons for fighting the bourgeoisie.

And the role of the party is partly to encourage the people to 'use, as so many weapons against the bourgeoisie, the social and political conditions that the bourgeoisie must necessarily introduce. . .'[44]. This would seem to include political emancipation and the rights that go along with it, even if it does not include recourse to rights discourse. When coupled with Marx's support for the franchise and political rights in general, his support for the Chartists, his defence of freedom of speech, as well as his support for struggles around concrete rights, like the Ten Hours Bill, the conclusion that must be drawn is that Marx supported the pursuit of legal reforms in the nature of rights victories, always cognizant that these were limited, and potentially limiting, victories. He did not, however, appear to approve of communist parties' reliance on 'bourgeois ideology' and the universalistic language of rights.

Even upon a limited review, therefore, we come not to the simple conclusion of marxism's contemporary commentators and critics, but rather to a more complex one. I have tried to support the argument that Marx did not reject rights. He provides pointed criticisms of them and raises hard questions; but there is little, if any, indication that he rejects them as 'deontological commitments' (Lukes), as based upon property conceptions or as linked to individualism *per se*. The contention that he did not reject them is pertinent because so many scholars today act as if he did, and use that interpretation to shun either rights or marxism itself.

However, Marx's treatment of rights *does not* provide anything like an adequate basis for those who wish to elaborate on them in socialist political theory and political strategy. He did not provide analytical support for abstract rights. Even more damagingly, he did not clearly and unambiguously argue for the necessary but not sufficient character of personal rights, such as liberty and privacy. This was not his project, and as a result we must acknowledge that Marx was not particularly committed to elaborating the principles of right.

There are, to be sure, other reasons for Marx's criticisms of and lack of serious commitment to rights beyond those that can extracted from the passages canvassed. That Marx viewed rights as a result of a particular constellation of social forces and that he did not develop an especially penetrating analysis of ideology must be counted as two important reasons for this. Bowles and Gintis are quite correct, therefore, that Marx did not establish the ground for rights as an integral part of his 'theoretical lexicon'. Despite instances where he supported rights, he was not, and much of the intellectual tradition in general has not been, particularly attentive to, or enthusiastic about, grounding them theoretically and analytically as part of the socialist project. This *is* a crucial problem. But it is a problem of a different order from the one that is more typically argued. And, as I shall argue in the next section, to assert as Bowles and Gintis do that Marx provides no vocabulary of freedom or choice is misleading. The problem with Marx in this regard is not that he rejected rights, individuality, freedom or choice. Rather, it is that he undervalued the potential contribution of rights to the development of rich individuality, freedom and choice which he strongly supported.

III

Marx articulated and was fully supportive of a notion of rich individuality, connected individuality within community, as is attested to by Marshall Berman's brilliant recuperation of Marx's aspirations for self-guided, self-development and creativity[45]. Coupled with Marx's attention to the substantive basis of freedom is his persistent attention to individual self-development through self-guided activity within the community, and to responsible agents capable of remaking their world through collective and individual efforts. We have here some of the elements for developing a far richer conceptualization of the individual, the community, freedom, choice and rights than is available within the scope of liberalism. Something of Marx's commitment to the individual can be seen by commencing with the remarkably individualistic vision of communism in *The German Ideology*, where Marx so famously envisions it as a place where 'nobody has one exclusive sphere of activity, but each can become accomplished in any branch he wishes. . .[I can] hunt in the morning, fish in the afternoon, rear cattle in the evening, criticise after dinner, *just as I have in mind*. . .'[46]. From this vision we move to the endorsement of communism as a society in which 'the free development of *each* is the condition for the free development of all'[47]. And finally: 'only in community with others has each individual the means of cultivating his gifts in all directions; only in the community, therefore, is personal freedom possible'[48].

It would appear that a rejection of rights by some contemporary marxists, such as many of those in Critical Legal Studies, on the basis that they embody individualism is too simplistic and is not in keeping with Marx. There is in Marx not only a language of, but an abiding commitment to, the individual, to self-guided, self-development and freedom which is strong and rich. And it is not just richer than liberal treatments; it is also richer than the conceptualizations in many contemporary marxist pro-rights positions, such as those found in Thompson and Hall. The commitment to a form of individualism which entails liberation and creativity, not just liberty, has been all but neglected in contemporary marxist pro-rights positions[49]. Yet, it is precisely this commitment which Marx articulates.

While Marx viewed rich individuality – real, substantive freedom, participation, equality, and self-development – as attainable only within communism, both the aspiration and the contradictory basis for it lay, in Marx's view, with the 'new fangled men' produced within capitalism which at one and the same time constrains the energy and sociality implicit within it[50].

Might rights, then, contribute in any meaningful and positive way not just to the development of class struggles and capacities, but also to the development of rich, socialist individuality and democratic socialism? It is clear that Marx saw citizens' rights as containing the possibility for participation in community. But there are other rights which may also contribute to a movement intent upon 'ridding itself of all the muck of ages and becom[ing] fitted to found society anew'[51].

In addition to their institutionalized formal status as 'trumps', or 'enforceable claims of individuals or groups'[52], rights are important in another sense: as cultural commitments which pervade and cross society, discourses and social practices. In both senses, rights are a basis for the development of rich, active, creative, individuality. While many existing rights may also encourage atomism and egoism, this is not a characteristic which is naturally and necessarily inscribed into their status as rights, or even as individual rights. Rather, the content and cultural meaning of a right may best be understood as the crystalization of past victories and defeats. The extent to which a right expresses and reinforces one rather than another form of individualism depends on the struggles and demands that are, and have been, made around, within and through it. The important issues are, therefore, how to conceptualize and fight for individual, as well as collective, rights which contribute to democratic socialist objectives. I take a few of these objectives to be diversity, plurality, choice and even privacy.

Privacy, and the 'rights of man' in general, or personal rights, have received little support and analytical elaboration even in contemporary marxist treatments of rights[53]. As we have seen, Marx supported rights which contribute to participation and self-direction or, as C.B. Macpherson has defined it, 'the ability to live in accordance with one's own conscious purpose. . .'[54]. The problem in Marx is that he underestimated the potential role of personal rights in contributing to self-direction, participation and creativity. As we have also seen, Marx supported political liberty. His treatment of personal liberty and personal rights as boundary markers vis-à-vis the community is more ambiguous. But, notwithstanding Marx's ambiguity here, a strong case can be made that self-development, participation and creativity require 'negative liberty'. In order to realize self-directed self-development, one must first be free of the strictures of others. This points towards an answer to the question posed in the last section of the paper: can the personal rights such as liberty and privacy be conceptualized in a way which would not contribute to atomistic, egoistic individualism, but would contribute to rich individuality? At least some boundary marker conceptions are necessary, but are clearly not sufficient, to realizing the fuller concept of liberation and creative self-development. The proper conceptualization of personal rights, and negative liberty itself, is, of course, a matter of debate. Macpherson has perhaps made the case most persuasively for the Left that the breadth of negative liberty must be wide enough to encompass the non-deliberate, as well as deliberate, interference of others. Macpherson calls this counter-extractive liberty. For present purposes, the important point is to argue that negative liberty broadly defined is necessary to, but not sufficient for, a marxist conception of liberation.

One particularly problematic aspect of Marx's treatment of rights arises from what Jean Cohen has called his pre-modern conception of the desirability of dedifferentiating the public and private spheres[55]. This has led not just to the dismissal of rights as unimportant in the future as a protection against state intrusion, but as well to a reluctance on the part of contemporary marxists to rethink and reinvigorate a democratic private sphere. It is one of the contributions of the 'post-marxist' literature to draw our attention to the question[56]. If we take the vexing case of privacy[57] it is not, however, at all clear that marxism cannot and should not support a reconceptualization and valorization of the private. A socialist conception would not be the anxious privatism that dominates the current conception of privacy. Rather, a socialist privacy right would require a reconceptualization of, and a material commitment to, among other things, *freely chosen private spaces*; not ones where I just happen to be stuck by virtue of my class, gender and race or other source of a relative lack of power. This would require, amongst other things, a commitment to resources to make the choice meaningful. Freely chosen privacy may conflict with Marx's emphasis on the dedifferentiation of private and public spaces and may conflict with his view of the negative consequences of rights as boundary markers. But it *is* congruent with, and probably necessary to, free self-development. Private space is one of the places where the 'rich I' may get nourished with sensuality, free time, freedom from other gazes. But in order for privacy rights to contribute to personal and collective liberation, not just to liberty, privacy must exist along with vital socialist public spaces where diversity, plurality and difference are permitted and encouraged, as Rosa Luxemburg so clearly recognized long ago – not to mention democratized relations of production and socialised property relations.

If it is a socialism which values *this*, then the abstract character of rights about which Marx appears to have been so critical (and the work which draws from his analysis *is* unremittingly critical[58]) will also have to be reassessed. Abstract rights, by virtue of their abstract quality, mark out a realm of 'basic equality' of respect such that asserting a rights claim 'implies the existence of a similar claim' for other members of society[59]. Or, to state the point slightly differently, as Martha Minow has put it: 'This form of discourse draws each claimant into the community and grants each a basic, if minimal, equality to participate in the process of communal debate.' It encourages an 'equality of attention'[60]. It is on the basis of the abstraction, that freedom of expression, for example, permits and encourages, in principle if not in practice, diverse expressions, dissent, the shockingly new to flourish. Under this ideal, expression is judged not on a substantive basis of whether or not it is useful speech or 'correct' expression. This abstract form of freedom is crucial to the socialist project as it is only on the basis of being their own arbiters of what is valuable, what is decent, what is progressive, determined through the process of public debate and struggle that, as both Marx and Luxemburg recognized, the subordinate classes are capable of transforming themselves into a ruling class, and one with democratic and pluralistic aspirations and capabilities. Moreover, to draw on and extend another radical woman's position, if I can't dance as my creative spirit moves, I don't want the revolution. Even more to the point perhaps, if I can't dance as my creative spirit moves, the revolution, the success of which is dependent upon the full creative energy and inspiration of individuals as well as classes, probably doesn't need me.

There are undoubtedly important insights in Marx's critique of abstract rights. Formal rights do not even out or even attend to unequal access to rights (such as unequal ability to take advantage of freedom of expression) and do produce unequal outcomes where they are applied in situations marked by substantive inequality in the first place. However, as I have argued above, there is an important democratic consequence which flows from abstract rights. Moreover, supplemental principles can be conceived and demanded which give abstract rights more equal content and consequences. Thus, the abstract quality typical of rights does not logically preclude the adoption of substantive content principles. Many liberal democracies have, for example, developed limits to spending on political campaigns, and this has not been undertaken as an exception to free speech, but rather as a condition of its more equal attainment. And this raises an important point for contemporary marxist analysis: Marx showed a certain insensitivity to the variations of rights forms and articulations across time and space in capitalism. While this may be understandable enough given the period in which Marx worked, it is not so easily dismissed in the analyses of contemporary marxists.

Reconceptualizations of and struggles for more egalitarian and substantive visions of rights and the commitment to abstract rights principles can be expected to go only so far, however, within the property and social relations which obtain under capitalism. But the essential point is that struggles for rich individuality and the contribution of rights to those struggles may increase peoples' capacities, even as a thriving socialist politics is crucial to the potential for achieving rich, rather than atomistic and egoistic, individuality. This is not at all to imply that rights conceptions are sufficient to constitute rich individuality. Rather, they are one way of laying a cultural and legal groundwork for it; a groundwork which is necessary, but not sufficient.

A socialist 'belief' in rights does not necessarily entail a naive belief in their instrumental effectivity. Rather, it entails a recognition of their role in encouraging and reinforcing a political culture which is attentive to and, at best, respectful of individuality. In turn, this political culture affects and infuses social practices. This highly general notion does not imply that the existence of bills and charters of rights necessarily infuses political culture with rights commitments or that even when they do, other goals might not be considered more important and will, sometimes, trump rights. Nor does it guarantee that these goals might not sometimes be nefarious ones. Finally, it does not suggest that this is the only way to build a political culture which respects individuals and promotes socialist individuality. Rather, it indicates that social commitment to rights principles depends upon historical circumstances, practices and the like and that rights have been an important way of asserting and infusing important commitments (imperfectly) into social practices. The practices which may be said to be influenced by rights commitments include those of the state, of social movements, including the trade union movement, and of civil society itself.

Rights are conceptualized in this tradition neither as inalienable, nor as based upon trans-historical human nature. Rather, as McBride suggests, they are 'the conventional products of collective human action and decisions'[61]. While pitched at a high level of generality, this sort of understanding of rights is useful for emphasizing that rights are not natural, but are socially constructed and contestable. And this point is relevant not just in terms of thinking about the possibilities for expanding rights, but in terms, as well, of collectively determining whether, how and when to undermine or renounce particular rights, such as private property rights. That rights are the products of human action underlines that we are in no way forced to a position of respecting or protecting all of them simply by virtue of their contemporary status as rights within capitalism.

A commitment to take rights seriously by socialists highlights one large problem; it is the old problem of means and ends. What does one do in a socialist transformation? The issue of rights, here, is connected to, but is not coextensive with, constitutionalism. It is not so much a matter of working through legal channels, nor even of following legal rules as it is developing and sustaining a set of socialist ethics which should include, but is clearly not exhausted by, an ethic of rights. Insurrectionary politics must be considered with regard to rights commitments[62]. Equally, in considering reformist or constitutionalist transformation, we do not evade the problem of rights. Part of the 'problem' here is entailed in the universality of rights. What, then, about the rights of counter-revolutionaries? Of capitalists and the enemies of socialism? Perhaps just as problematic, what about the rights of socialism's supporters which may have to be encroached upon in the name of restraint and restructuring of the economy? Does one violate their freedom of association? The commitment to rights does not take us very far in terms of providing specific answers to these very general questions. What a commitment to rights does do, however, is suggest that the answer to the question, how much may one encroach upon the rights of others, demands at the very least this answer: as little as possible congruent with the importance of realizing the objective to be secured by that encroachment. This answer resides, it should be stressed, less in the formal application of the rules laid down than it does in the cultural commitment to rights. Thus, the commitment does not entail the conclusion that we never limit or even deny rights. Rather, it indicates that each limitation and denial must be justified and if not abhorred at least undertaken with the recognition that an accumulation of limits and denials chips slowly away at the culture which sustains respect for the protections and entitlements we call rights.

All of this of course raises a host of problems which need to be addressed by socialists. A reconsideration of *which* rights are valuable as abstract rights is necessary. When and on what bases should we fight for concrete and collective rights? Systems for supplementing abstract individual rights with substantive and concrete rights must be considered. The constitutive effects of rights and rights struggles on class and social movements' struggles in capitalism must be seriously explored. And, crucially, questions involving the relationship between socialist transformation and rights must be addressed far more seriously than has been done so far. One of the pressing issues involves the assessment of the utilization of rights discourses and rights strategies in ways which may empower progressive social movements and create the conditions for counter-hegemonic socialist struggles.

To articulate, demand and fight for socialist conceptions of the rights of persons, citizens' rights and social rights is crucial. But it is only by being comfortable with the realm of right as marxists that we can begin to argue for and conceptualize socialist approaches to rights; individual and collective, civil, political, economic and social. This may benefit by steps such as those taken here in terms of groundclearing and reemphasizing Marx's commitment to rich individualism. Given the current propensity to read Marx as rejecting rights and individualism of all types, the exercise of rethinking Marx and marxism is not unimportant. By emphasizing not only class, class struggles, exploitation and the like, but also giving a higher profile to rearticulating rights consistent with and supportive of socialist goals we will have come a great distance. For one thing, such an exercise begins to address the deeply felt suspicion with regard to the status of the individual within marxism. It is, moreover, prefigurative of a socialism committed to diversity, plurality and the rule of law. Secondly, it gives us a way of combatting the liberal, and especially neo-conservative, conceptions of the individual, choice and freedom; conceptions which have been successful in asserting atomistic, consumerist individualism. Finally, it requires serious consideration of socialist tactics, as much in terms of socialist political strategy in the present as socialist transformation in the future. Such a rethinking may, in sum, contribute to the development of political theory which is in aid of socialist political strategy – precisely what any analysis with marxist aspirations should do.

NOTES

I would like to thank Leo Panitch for his substantive and critically important contribution to this article. Even more than usual given the unconventional interpretation put forward here, the typical caveats apply. Thanks also to Marc Cezar who has substantially contributed to my understanding of rich individuality.

This paper was originally given at the 'Marxism Now: Traditions and Difference' conference, sponsored by *Rethinking Marxism*, Amherst, Massachusetts, 30 November – 2 December 1989.

1. Allen E. Buchanan, *Marx and Justice: The Radical Critique of Liberalism* (Totowa N.J.: Rowman and Allanheld, 1982) 50.

2. Without attempting to list exhaustively the recent contributions, in addition to Buchanan, ibid, see the contributions listed in note 3 and; Steven Lukes, *Marxism and Morality* (Oxford: Oxford U. Press, 1987); Alan Hunt, 'The Future of Rights and Justice,' 9 *Contemporary Crises* 309 (1985); and, Jeremy Waldron, 'Karl Marx's "On the Jewish Question"' in Waldron, *Nonsense Upon Stilts: Bentham, Burke and Marx on the Rights of Man* (London: Methuen, 1987).

3. Steven Lukes, 'Can a Marxist Believe in Rights?' 1 *Praxis International* 334 (1982); Drucilla Cornell, 'Should a Marxist Believe in Rights?' 4 *Praxis International* 45 (1984); and William McBride, 'Rights and the Marxian Tradition,' 4 *Praxis International* 57 (1984).

4. Lukes, *Marxism and Morality* 66. It is not entirely clear throughout his argument what Lukes takes to be the doctrines which are essential to the marxist canon. The most likely candidate is that marxism is a form of consequentialism; that is, it is 'a theory which judges actions by their consequences only.' *Marxism and Morality*, 142.

5. McBride, 'Rights and the Marxian Tradition,' 60.

6. Lukes concludes that a marxist cannot believe in rights initially on the basis of a review of Marx. According to Lukes, because marxism views rights as 'expressive of the egoism of bourgeois society', and approaches rights as 'unwarrantably abstract and decontextualized', rights are not supported in the tradition. *Marxism and Morality* 70, see 60–70.

   Lukes also argues that a marxist cannot believe in rights because marxism does not and cannot take the limitations imposed by rights seriously. He argues that marxism is consequentialist, and therefore anti-deontological. Deontological theories 'standardly hold that it is sometimes *wrong* to produce the best outcome overall, and *right* not to do so, by imposing 'side-constraints' or 'agent-centred' restrictions. . . .It therefore comes as no surprise that marxism is deeply and unremittingly anti-deontological. . . .' *Marxism and Morality*, 142.

   It should be noted that Lukes also maintains that Marx was not sufficiently supportive of rights. It is one of the central claims of this paper that we must distinguish between the claim that Marx *rejected* rights and that he was insufficiently attentive to and supportive of them. Marx did not reject rights. But, Lukes is correct that he did not value them highly enough. To argue that Marx did not reject rights also entails arguing against Lukes that Marx (as a 'marxist') must have been deeply anti-deontological. The entire cast of Marx's discussion of rich individuality discussed in the final section of this paper suggests he was not anti-deontological.

7. Waldron is one of the few who do not take this position. See Waldron, 'Karl Marx's "On the Jewish Question"' in Waldron, *Nonsense Upon Stilts*.

8. Some of the most notable are Stuart Hall, *Drifting into A Law and Order Society* (Amersham, Buckinghamshire: Robendene Ltd., 1980); Ralph Miliband, *Marxism and Politics* (Oxford: Oxford U. Press, 1977); Leo Panitch, 'The State and the Future of Socialism' in Panitch, *Working Class Politics in Crisis: Essays on Labour and the State* (London: Verso, 1986), and 'Liberal Democracy and Socialist Democracy: The Antinomies of C.B. Macpherson,' *Socialist Register 1981*, Ralph Miliband and John Saville eds. (London: Merlin Press, 1981); Nicos Poulantzas, *State, Power, Socialism* (London: New Left Books, 1978); E.P. Thompson, *Whigs and Hunters: The Origin of the Black Act* (New York: Pantheon Books, 1975), and *Writing by Candlelight* (London: Merlin Press, 1980); and Mike Davis and Sue Ruddick, 'Los Angeles: Civil Liberties between the Hammar and the Rock' 170 *New Left Review* 37 (1988).

9. See for example, Bob Fine, *Democracy and the Rule of Law* (London: Pluto Press, 1984); and Staughton Lynd, 'Communal Rights' 62 *Texas Law Rev.* 1417 (1984).

10. See for example, Buchanan, *Marx and Justice* and Lukes, *Marxism and Morality*.

11. Lukes, *Marxism and Morality*, 27. Buchanan concludes that Marx 'is attacking the very concepts of the rights of man and of civil and political rights. . . .' *Marx and Justice*, 67–68.

12. Peter Gable, for example, states that rights are 'exactly what people don't need' in 'Roll Over Beethoven' 36 *Stanford Law Rev.* 1 at 33 (1984); and Gabel, 'Book Review' 91 *Harvard Law Rev.* 302 (1977). Also see Duncan Kennedy, 'Critical Labor Law Theory; A Comment' 4 *Indus. Rel. Law J.* 503 (1981).
    For a useful discussion of the CLS's indebtedness to (a particular reading of) Marx, see Ed Sparer, 'Fundamental Human Rights, Legal Entitlements and the Social Struggle: A Friendly Critique of the Critical Legal Studies Movement' 36 *Stanford Law Rev.* 509. For a critique of CLS's critique of rights, see Amy Batholomew and Alan Hunt, 'What's Wrong with Rights?' unpublished manuscript, 1989.

13. Samuel Bowles and Herbert Gintis, *Democracy and Capitalism: Property, Community and the Contradictions of Modern Social Thought* (New York: Basic Books, 1986) 18–19 and 20, emphasis mine. They elaborate:
    'Classical Marxism is theoretically antidemocratic in the same sense that any political philosophy that fails to conceptualize the threat of state authoritarianism and the centrality of privacy and individual liberty to human emancipation, provides a haven for despots and fanatics.'
    Unlike the CLS, Bowles and Gintis insist that radical social movements have typically used the discourse of liberal rights in their struggles and that rights provide radical democratic resources. In my estimation, Bowles and Gintis are correct on this point.

14. In *Marxism and Morality* Lukes provides a useful discussion of Marx's view of emancipation, freedom and the individual. My argument is that he miscalculates the potential within marxism for connecting these commitments and rights.

15. Marx's gender-specific language is reproduced throughout this paper when relying upon his discussion and concepts. To rewrite Marx would be both inappropriate in the context of the specific project at hand and would 'cleanse' his analysis in a misleading way.

16. I argue that individual rights are necessary to protecting and promoting pluralistic, democratic socialism. Positions like Staughton Lynd's which reject individual rights and promote 'communal rights' are inattentive to the need to link individual interests with communal ones, and to protect individual interests from at least some communally desired ends. See Lynd 'Communal Rights'. Lynd suggests: 'if we desire a society in which we share life as a common creation and genuinely care for each other's needs, then this rhetoric [of individual rights] which pictures us as separated owners of our respective bundles of rights, stands as an obstacle' (1419). He argues that we must, therefore, displace the property basis of rights. Hence his support for communal rights which do not 'require a choice between our own well-being and the well-being of others' (1421). This undermines at least one important aspect of rights. Rights are 'trumps' or 'side constraints'. Even positive rights, rights to something, such as entitlement rights, rely on rights language in order to emphasize that even if the entitlement comes into conflict with 'the well-being of others', or their perceived well-being, it is to be honoured prima facie.
Note as well that the property-based aspect of individual rights is not self-evidently contradictory to marxism. Marxism does not oppose all property. It calls for the communal ownership of productive property.

17. Karl Marx, 'On the Jewish Question' 40, emphasis in the original. All references to 'On the Jewish Question', 'Critique of the Gotha Programme' and Marx and Engels 'Manifesto of the Communist Party' are taken from Robert C. Tucker, ed. *The Marx-Engels Reader* (New York: W.W. Norton, 1972).

18. Marx, 'Critique of the Gotha Programme' 395. Marx criticizes the party for articulating democratic demands that 'contain nothing beyond the old democratic litany familiar to all: universal suffrage, direct legislation, popular rights etc. . . . They are the mere echo of the bourgeois People's Party,. . .They are all demands which,. . ., have already been realised. But one thing has been forgotten. . .all those pretty little gewgaws rest on the recognition of the so-called sovereignty of the people and hence are appropriate only in a democratic republic.'

19. This is in the context of complaining about the party's reliance on equal right and fair distribution: 'what a crime it is to attempt. . .to force on our Party again, as dogmas, ideas which in a certain period had some meaning but have now become obsolete verbal rubbish, while again perverting. . .the realistic outlook [within the Party] by means of ideological nonsense about right and other trash so common among the democrats and French Socialists.' 'Critique of the Gotha Programme' 388.

20. Buchanan, *Marx and Justice* and Lukes, *Marxism and Morality*. Note that McBride disputes this in 'Rights and the Marxian Tradition.' Lukes states: 'Marx and Engels scorned "the faith of individuals in the conceptions of Recht"' *Marxism and Morality* 27. I take this to be equivalent to stating that Marx scorned rights.

21. Marx, 'On the Jewish Question' 38–40.

22. Marx, 'On the Jewish Question' 41.

23. Lukes, *Marxism and Morality* 27–28. Marx criticises, therefore, their lack of priority and vigorousness.

24. Marx, 'On the Jewish Question' 39, emphasis in the original.

25. Marx, 'On the Jewish Question' 33.

26. Cited in Waldron, 'Karl Marx's "On the Jewish Question"' 121.

27. Buchanan, *Marx and Justice* 67–68.

28. Miliband, *Marxism and Politics* 76–81.

29. See for example Lukes, *Marxism and Morality*; Buchanan, *Marx and Justice*; and Lynd 'Communal Rights.' Similarly, Eric Hobsbawm states, 'Marx was not only indifferent to "rights of man"' but strongly opposed to them, since they are essentially individualistic.' *Workers* (New York: Pantheon, 1984) 304–305.

30. Waldron defines atomism as a conception of individuals as 'free of any essential dependence on others,' *Nonsense Upon Stilts* 128. Abercrombie, Hill and Turner mark out individuality as a concern for each person's uniqueness. For social theories which support individuality 'society should be arranged so that individual qualities and differences can be recognized and individual talents developed. Self-development is a prime virtue.' Nicholas Abercrombie, Stephen Hill and Bryan S. Turner, *Sovereign Individuals of Capitalism* (London: Allen and Unwin, 1986) 79. That Marx supported rich individuality will be argued in part III of this paper. Also see, Marshall Berman *All that is Solid Melts into Air: The Experience of Modernity* (New York: Simon and Schuster, 1982).

31. Marx, 'On the Jewish Question' 41, my emphasis.

32. Marx 'On the Jewish Question' 40.

33. C.B. Macpherson, 'Berlin's Division of Liberty' in Macpherson *Democratic Theory: Essays in Retrieval* (Oxford: Clarendon Press, 1973) 95.
    To take the example of security, had it been expressed as the right to be free from state interference, rather than being defined as society's obligation to protect property and individuals, which Marx takes to be 'the concept of the police' (41), his estimation may again have been quite different.

34. Marx, 'On the Jewish Question' 32.

35. Marx, 'On the Jewish Question' 41.

36. See for example, Alan Hunt, 'The Future of Rights and Justice.'

37. Marx, 'Critique of the Gotha Programme' 394.

38. Hal Draper, *Karl Marx's Theory of Revolution, Volume 1: State and Bureaucracy* (New York: Monthly Review Press, 1977) 297. At 304, Draper quotes Marx denouncing the British government for passing a law which regulated assembly in public parks: '"This regulation carefully kept hidden from the London press destroyed with one stroke of the pen one of the most precious rights of London's working people – the right to hold meetings in parks when and how they please. To submit to this regulation would be to sacrifice one of the people's rights."'

39. Marx, 'Critique of the Gotha Progamme,' 387.

40. Marx, 'Critique of the Gotha Programme,' 388.

41. Marx, 'Critique of the Gotha Programme,' 395.

42. Marx and Engels, 'The Communist Manifesto'. For an elaboration of this point, see Leo Panitch, 'Capitalism, Socialism and Revolution: The Contemporary Meaning of Revolution in the West' *Socialist Register 1989* Ralph Miliband, Leo Panitch and John Saville eds. (London: Merlin Press, 1989).

43. See Bowles and Gintis, *Democracy and Capitalism* for an important and accessible discussion of language; and, Herbert Gintis, 'Communication and Politics: Marxism and the 'Problem' of Liberal Democracy,' 50–51 *Socialist Review* (1980) 189; Stuart Hall, 'The Toad in the Garden: Thatcherism among the Theorists' in *Marxism and the Interpretation of Culture* Cary Nelson and Lawrence Grossberg eds. (Urbana: Univ. of Illinois Press, 1988), and 'The Battle for Socialist Ideas in the 1980's,' *Socialist Register 1982* Martin Eve and David Musson, eds. (London: Merlin Press, 1982).

44. Marx and Engels, 'The Communist Manifesto' 343, 362.

45. Berman, *All that is Solid Melts into Air*. For the fullest elaboration of rich individuality and emancipation, see Bertell Ollman, *Alienation: Marx's Conception of Man in Capitalist Society* second edition (Cambridge: Cambridge U. Press, 1976).

46. Karl Marx and Frederick Engels, *The German Ideology* (Moscow: Progress Publishers, 1976) emphasis added,53.

47. Marx and Engels, 'The Communist Manifesto' 353, emphasis added.

48. Quoted in Berman, *All that is Solid Melts into Air* 97.

49. See however, Charlie Leadbeater, 'Power to the Person' *Marxism Today* October 1988, 14 who argues for the development of a concept, and politics, of socialist individuality. Also see C.B. Macpherson, 'Berlin's Division of Liberty'. Some feminists have contributed useful interventions in this area as well. See especially, Virginia Held, 'Liberty and Equality from a Feminist Perspective' in Neil MacCormack and Z. Bankowski eds. *Enlightenment, Rights and Revolution* (Aberdeen: Aberdeen Univ. Press, 1989).

50. See Berman, *All that is Solid Melts into Air* 109. In 'The Communist Manifesto' 347, Marx and Engles argue: 'The abolition of bourgeois individuality, bourgeois independence, and bourgeois freedom is undoubtedly aimed at.' And: 'In bourgeois society capital is independent and has individuality while the living person is dependent and has no individuality.' This suggests a recognition of other individualities.

51. Marx and Engels, *The German Ideology* 60.

52. Martha Minow, 'Interpreting Rights: An Essay for Robert Cover,' 96 *Yale Law J.* (1987) 1860, 1866.

53. Cornell, for example, attends only to participation rights. Cornell, 'Should a Marxist Believe in Rights?' Stuart Hall and E.P. Thompson do not attempt to reconceptualize them, just rehabilitate them. The latter was certainly necessary. However, we must now go further.

54. Macpherson, 'Berlin's Division of Liberty' 109.

55. See Jean Cohen for a defence of the argument that this is pre-modern. Jean L. Cohen, *Class and Civil Society: The Limits of Marxian Critical Theory* (Amherst, Ma: The U. of Ma. Press, 1982). Also see John Keane, *Democracy and Civil Society* (London: Verso, 1988) 61–64.

56. See in particular, Bowles and Gintis, *Democracy and Capitalism* and Jean Cohen, *Class and Civil Society*.

57. In the radical legal and feminist literature, it has been commonplace to denounce the 'public-private distinction' for insulating the so-called private sphere from scrutiny of a desired kind. All too often, the argument has been made that the problem is privacy itself, rather than the particular forms which privacy has taken under particular social conditions.

58. See for example, Mark Tushnet, 'An Essay on Rights' 62 *Texas Law Rev.* (1984) 1363.

59. Martha Minow, 'Interpreting Rights: An Essay for Robert Cover,' 1874, n. 52.

60. Minow, 'Interpreting Rights: An Essay for Robert Cover,' 1877, 1879. For another treatment of abstraction see Waldron, 'Nonsense Upon Stilts? – A Reply,' in Waldron, *Nonsense Upon Stilts*.

61. McBride, 'Rights and the Marxian Tradition' 69.

62. See Norman Geras, 'Our Morals: The Ethics of Revolution,' *Socialist Register 1989*, Ralph Miliband, Leo Panitch and John Saville eds. (London: Merlin Press, 1989).

LIBERAL PRACTICALITY AND
THE US LEFT

JOHN BELLAMY FOSTER

There is a large left constituency in the United States but it is mainly invisible, lacking any central organizational basis in the society as a whole. The partnership of the state and capital operates relatively smoothly in comparison to other advanced capitalist societies. Consequently, the dominant organs of power have been able, with considerable success even in times of crisis, to project a hegemonic 'consensus' from above that has left a majority of the population marginalized, effectively removing them from meaningful participation in the polity. The chief tenets of this hegemonic consensus are: (1) 'America' is an essentially classless society in which Emerson's 'infinitude of the private man' is a working reality. (2) 'The genius of American politics' lies in its rejection of all closed ideological systems, hence the lack of fundamental controversy over values.[1] (3) The political sphere is an equilibrium of freely competing pluralist interests. (4) Conquest of the natural-technological frontier through the growth of private enterprise will allow for steady improvement in the human condition with no alteration in the already ideal social relationships. And (5) America is the leader of the Free World.

Given such a definition of 'America,' it is possible to contend without too much fear of exaggeration that Ralph Ellison's metaphor of the 'invisible man' applies not only to African–Americans, but also in certain respects to Hispanic Americans, Asian Americans, American Indians, women, the poor, gays, radical environmentalists, socialists and almost the entire working class; while the term 'America' itself symbolizes US dominance over Latin America, and hence the subordination of the third world.[2]

In this hegemonic construction of reality, everything that does not fit the preferred self-image of possessive-individualist society is systematically excluded from view and all ideas outside a narrow – and, it would appear, still narrowing – spectrum are declared unAmerican. US left intellectuals, most of whom were products of the rise of the new left in the 1960s, have increasingly arrived at the conclusion that they have no alternative but to exploit the contradictions of the dominant liberal democratic ideology from a position located inside that ideology, as a means for advancing the interests of the 'other Americas.' Such a strategy, however, invariably involves employing the form of thought and language that C. Wright Mills called 'liberal practicality,' the worst aspects of which are a refusal to view society as an organic whole, and a 'democratic theory of knowledge' in which 'all facts are created equal.'[3]

Concrete manifestations of this growing recourse to liberal practicality within the US left can be seen in such devices as: (a) the notion that the discourse of liberal democracy, if simply broadened and extended, provides the basis for a form of socialism; (b) the utilization of social contract metaphors outside of any realistic consideration of power relations; (c) the proliferation of timid blueprints for the rebuilding of America; (d) the insistence on attacking corporations rather than capitalism; (e) the reliance on nationalist thinking that downplays US capitalism's historic role as an imperial power; (f) the presentation of social struggle entirely in terms of a plurality of social movements; and (g) the calls to 'liberate theory' by decentring the concept of social class. Underlying all of this is the mistaken assumption that by constantly toning down its demands and adopting what Mills referred to as the 'vocabulary of motive' of liberalism the left will somehow be able to persuade the powers that be to compromise their own interests.[4]

To be sure, these developments are not unique to US radicalism but are similar to recent reformist tendencies emerging within the European left during a period of widespread conservative ascendancy. It is therefore not surprising that the arguments of those US left thinkers who in the era of Reagan and Bush have most fervently embraced liberal practicality as a way of advancing radical ideas are not easily distinguishable from what Ralph Miliband has aptly termed 'the new revisionist spectrum' in Britain under Thatcher.[5]

Nevertheless, the contributions of US radicals must be viewed in a slightly different light from those of their European counterparts. The lack of any socialist or even social democratic organizational structures of any significance in the society, and the extraordinary weakness of the US trade union movement, means that it is perhaps inevitable that many dedicated radicals will be drawn within the circle of the liberal debate for no other reason than the seemingly pragmatic one that it appears to be the only game in town. Hence, it is much more difficult in a one-dimensional US than in a relatively two-dimensional European context to characterize a shift toward liberal discourse in and of itself as 'revisionist' or even 'reformist' in character. In making concessions (sometimes unknowingly) to the hegemonic ideology, therefore, many US radicals are doubtless simply trying to be practical and realistic, as these terms are overwhelmingly defined by vested interests within US society. Still, the thesis of this essay is that socialist intellectuals can fulfill their responsibility to the working class – the great mass of society – under these circumstances only to the extent that they speak the truth and openly employ the socialist language of class, power and anti-capitalist struggle; thereby avoiding the political, moral and ideological pitfalls of timidly entreating capital on the basis of its own preferred discourse of liberal practicality.[6]

For the left to give way to liberal ways of defining reality in this particular historical juncture, moreover, would represent not only a failure of nerve and imagination, but also would constitute an unconscionable abandonment of popular forces in their hour of need. Thus while numerous left intellectuals have been engaged in making concessions to liberal forms of practicality, the actual class struggle in the United States has heated up, with economic restructuring and market fetishism constituting the basis of a continuing right wing assault, and the Rainbow Coalition (or Jackson phenomenon) representing perhaps the first signs of a nascent mass-based class struggle from below aimed at the state in more than half a century. At such an historic moment any attempt to embrace liberal thinking would be a retreat from the very possibility now offered of breaking out of the ideological straightjacket that dominates US politics.

I. C. Wright Mills and the Critique of Liberal Practicality

In order to understand the full implications of the 'discursive strategy' now favoured by many leftists – which involves adopting liberal language and ways of interpreting reality in preference to traditional socialist discourse as a means of advancing radical ends – it is useful to begin with a detailed look at the critique of liberal practicality presented by C. Wright Mills at the height of the early Cold War defeat of the socialist left. Following the successful McCarthyite assault on the left in the first decade following the Second World War, socialist political and intellectual activity in the United States, which had been rekindled for a time during the Great Depression and New Deal, virtually disappeared from the social landscape – outside of the dogged resistance of a handful of independent radicals. These were the years that Daniel Bell glorified in terms of 'the end of ideology' and that Mills characterized as the time of the great 'American celebration.'

Significantly, it was during this period of conservative ascendancy, that Mills was to emerge as perhaps the single greatest critic of 'liberal values in the modern world' that the United States had produced since the time of Thorstein Veblen.[7] In this regard it is crucial to understand that, contrary to what some have supposed, Mills' well-known studies of class and power in such works as *The New Men of Power*, *White Collar* and *The Power Elite* do not sum up the extent of his intellectual achievement. Rather these studies carry their full impact only when seen in terms of his larger, lifelong critique of the liberal creed, in which he was primarily concerned with demonstrating the institutionalized powerlessness of individuals on the lower levels of the pyramid of power, and the various ideological means through which this fact remained concealed from a majority of participants in the class struggle.

At the core of Mills' thought therefore was a critique of the poverty of contemporary mainstream social science, traceable to both the shallowness of liberal discourse, and the cultural default of the intelligentsia. 'The ideals of liberalism,' Mills observed, 'have been divorced from any realities of modern social structure that might serve as the means of their realization. Everybody can easily agree on general ends; it is more difficult to agree on means and the relevance of various means to the ends articulated. The detachment of liberalism from the facts of a going society make it an excellent mask for those who do not, cannot, or will not do what would have to be done to realize its ideals.'[8] Despite its dominant place in the vocabulary of advanced capitalist society, the liberal creed, Mills argued, no longer represented a progressive vision – as it had in the heroic era of the rising middle classes. Instead, it had been reduced to little more than an empty rhetoric divorced from any meaningful theory of historical agency. 'If the moral vision of liberalism is still abstractly stimulating,' he wrote in *The Marxists*,

> its sociological content is weak: its political means of action are unpromising, unconvincing, unimaginative. It has no history of man in society, no theory of man as the maker of history. It has no political program adequate to the moral ideals it professes. Twentieth-century liberals have stressed ideals much more than theory and agency. But that is not all: they have stressed going agencies and institutions in such ways as to transform *them* into the foremost ideals of liberalism. . . .[Liberalism] is much more useful as a defense of the *status quo* – in the rich minority of nations, and of these nations before the rest of the world – than as a creed for deliberate historical change. . . .To the world's range of enormous problems, liberalism responds with its verbal fetish of 'Freedom' plus a shifting series of opportunistic reactions.[9]

As early as 1939 Mills had noted that, 'Vocabularies socially canalize thought.'[10] Hence, it was the liberal vocabulary itself, through its inability to relate its ideals to a realm of social practice realistically conditioned by existing social structures, that could be blamed for much of the confusion of cause that characterized mainstream social science in general. The result was the growth of a form of thought that ironically was at its very best when dealing with isolated individuals, disconnected values and scattered problems.[11]

'So far as orienting *theories* of society and of history are concerned,' Mills wrote in his famous 'Letter to the New Left,' 'the [liberal] end of ideology [outlook] stands for, and presumably stands upon, a fetishism of empiricism. . . .Thus political bias masquerades as epistemological excellence, and there are no orienting theories.'[12]

Rather than a genuine theory of society or a conception of human agency one merely finds a celebration of blind drift. '[I]n the "organic" metaphysics of liberal practicality,' Mills observed in *The Sociological Imagination*, 'whatever tends to harmonious balance is likely to be stressed' and the dogma of 'principled pluralism' is replaced for the supposed dogma of 'principled monism.'[13] Underlying this emphasis on 'a pluralist confusion of causes' emanating from scattered milieux, moreover, is the presumption that larger structural questions simply don't matter since society is governed by a balance of interests derived from the atomistic competition among individuals and groups, uniquely reinforced by the 'checks and balances' built into the US constitution. 'Not wishing to be disturbed over moral issues of the political economy,' Mills wrote with respect to the pluralist theory of liberal democracy, 'Americans cling to the idea that the government is a sort of automatic machine, regulated by the balancing of competing interests. This image of politics is simply a carry-over from the official image of the economy: in both, an equilibrium is achieved by the pulling and hauling of many interests, each restrained only by legalistic and amoral interpretations of what the traffic will bear.'[14] In short, 'the liberal "multiple factor" view,' Mills observed, 'does not lead to a conception of causation which would permit points of entry for broader types of action, especially political action.'[15]

This can be sharply contrasted to the more holistic approach inspired by Marx. 'To come to terms with marxism,' Mills wrote,

> whether that of the young Marx or of yesterday's Moscow slogan, forces us to confront: (1) every public issue of the modern world; (2) every great problem of social studies; (3) every moral trouble encountered by men of sensibility today. Moreover, when we try to observe and to think within the marxist point of view, we are bound to see these issues, problems and troubles as inherently connected. We are forced to adopt an over-all view of the world, and of ourselves in relation to it.[16]

Marx thus represented the antithesis of liberal practicality as described by Mills. Indeed, the mood and style of contemporary liberal discourse – its concentration on the piecemeal problems of isolated milieux – could be seen as a more or less conscious abandonment of the challenge raised by Marx.

> Intellectuals accept without scrutiny official definitions of world reality. Some of the best of them allow themselves to be trapped by the politics of anti-Stalinism, which has been a main passageway from the political thirties to the intellectual default of the apolitical fifties. They live and work in a benumbing society without living and working in protest and in tension with its moral and cultural insensibilities. They use the liberal rhetoric to cover the conservative default. They do not make available the knowledge and sensibility required by publics, if publics are to hold responsible those who make decisions in 'the name of the nation.' They do not set forth reasons for human anger and give it suitable targets.[17]

This default of the intellectuals, Mills added, was frequently justified in terms of a kind of 'crack-pot realism.' 'Crack-pot,' in his sense, because of its narrow conception of reality and its mere acquiescence with the main drift of social events. Behind this form of practicality, in fact, lay a kind of opportunism.[18]

In sharp contrast to this, Mills quoted John Morley as saying, 'It is better to bear the burden of impracticableness, than to stifle conviction and pare away principle until it becomes hollowness and triviality.' Mills never forgot Hume's dictum that one cannot, in principle, derive what ought to be from what is.[19] This warning of the danger of 'cultural default' in an environment ideologically conditioned by the crackpot realism of liberal practicality constituted the most important intellectual legacy of C. Wright Mills to the new left generation of intellectuals that was to follow.

II. The Growth of Tactical Liberalism

Most of the radical intellectuals who were drawn into the left in the 1960s did so at a time when the main drift of society seemed to be in that direction. But when a conservative tide followed in the 1970s and '80s, many simply concluded that the best way to cope with the narrowing political and ideological climate in which they found themselves was to refuse to 'name the system,' in the hope that the ideological space could thereby be won to advance radical ends;[20] others eventually came to suggest that the best strategy was to replace a socialist orientation with a more up-to-date 'post-liberal' one. Once again left intellectuals, commonly refused 'to set forth reasons for human anger and give it suitable targets.'

The Idea of Postliberal Democracy

One form of this emerging post-liberalism is evident in the fashionable view that the true meaning of liberal democracy can only be found in a form of radical democracy that would extend the democratic principle beyond the state to the family, army, factory and office, thereby breaking down the artificial walls that separate the public and private realms within capitalist social formations. This is seen as representing the essence of what was worthwhile in the socialist project, while remaining consistent with a radical reading of liberal democratic ideology itself. Scarcely original, this approach has nonetheless been dressed up in the 1980s in startling new clothes, discernible in the works of important left theorists like Samuel Bowles and Herbert Gintis.

Taking their cue from such writers as Gareth Stedman Jones, Ernesto Laclau and Chantal Mouffe, Bowles and Gintis have thus sought to advance a new 'prefigurative discourse' of 'postliberal democracy' as an alternative to both liberal democracy and Marxism. On the subject of liberalism and Marxism they write: 'Whatever internal coherence these traditions possess derives more from their status as systems of communication than from their substantive propositions about how the world works or ought to work.' The liberal lexicon, Bowles and Gintis tell their readers, is strong with respect to its insistence on the need for democracy, freedom, liberty, personal rights and pluralism but weak in its failure to recognize issues of exploitation and community. In contrast, they assert, the Marxian theoretical lexicon does not include such terms as freedom, personal rights, liberty, choice, or even democracy. . . .The Marxian commitment to democracy even where it is most heartfelt as in the writings of Rosa Luxemburg and Nicos Poulantzas, is thus without firm theoretical roots. This commitment can disappear as quickly as it has appeared in the post-Stalin era and nothing in Marxian discourse per se will remain to mourn its passing. Classical Marxism is theoretically anti-democratic in the same sense that any political philosophy that fails to conceptualize the threat of state authoritarianism, and the centrality of privacy and individual liberty to human emancipation, provides a haven for despots and fanatics.[21]

Indeed, Bowles and Gintis go on to claim that Marxism: (1) 'accords no status to the private at all'; (2) treats state domination and patriarchy as 'unimportant or epiphenomenal'; (3) sees capitalism as fundamentally corrosive of patriarchy; (4) rejects a truly democratic ontology through recourse to a 'productivist' discourse inherent in the labour theory of value; (5) lacks the indispensable theory of individual action based on the learner/chooser distinction that liberal theory itself provides; (6) promotes a simple 'expressive theory of action' that sees individuals as mirrors of larger social structures; (7) has a simplistic notion of language that sees it as a mere 'conduit' for thought; (8) dismisses the discourse of rights as 'essentially privatistic'; and (9) consists of a discourse that is neither hegemonic nor related to the way in which change is articulated by modern social movements.[22]

It is significant that none of these charges – all of which are obviously open to debate – are provided with any substantive backing in Bowles and Gintis' book. Nor do they examine Marxist theory as it has actually developed in an historical context of class struggle. Rather, all of the above charges are said to be derived from a straightforward analysis of the discursive structure of Marxist thought. Nowhere in a book that is largely devoted to supplanting Marxist theory as a critical outlook, do Bowles and Gintis make even the slightest attempt to analyze the concrete thought much less the words of any single Marxist theorist. Rather, they simply extract isolated quotations – without any concern for the original context. For example, Marx is quoted briefly in order to highlight his criticism of the French 'Rights of Man' in *On the Jewish Question* – with the implication that he simply rejected out of hand the bourgeois discourse of rights – without even the slightest examination of his overall argument, in which he pointed beyond political to human emancipation. Hence, Bowles and Gintis treat Marx as a theorist who saw the discourse of rights as 'inherently individualistic,' while ignoring the fact that in the very work cited he had critically transformed 'the philosophy of right' in ways that pointed to the necessity of the liberation of whole classes at the bottom of society. Similarly, Bowles and Gintis repeatedly claim in their book that Marxism is 'theoretically antidemocratic,' both in its discursive structure and because it does not include in its analysis a thorough critique of state despotism. No doubt, the argument is implicitly backed up by the extremely poor performance of post-revolutionary societies in this regard.

272 272 THE SOCIALIST REGISTER 1990

272 THE SOCIALIST REGISTER 1990

Such criticisms are not made explicit, however; and innumerable Marxist criticisms of the post-revolutionary societies, and the whole history of Marxist writings on democracy are simply ignored.

The enormous confusion that Bowles and Gintis generate by simply focusing on discursive practices, outside of any analysis of material struggles, can be seen in the fact that they actually go so far as to insist that, '[L]iberalism gives us the discourse of social change whereas Marxism gives us the theory of social change. Social change itself, however, is opaque to both liberalism which does not recognize that its discourse developed through class and other collective struggles and Marxism, which misconstrues what these struggles were for.'[23]

Doubtless, many people accustomed to historical materialist reasoning will find this statement bewildering. By what form of logic is it possible to contend that 'Marxism gives us the theory of social change,' while at the same time saying that it 'misconstrues what these struggles were for'? Can the theory of social change and the true motives for change be so easily separated? Doesn't this contradict the most elementary understanding of the relationship between theory and practice? Similarly, how could liberalism possibly fail to recognize that 'its discourse developed through class and other collective struggles,' while nonetheless knowing 'what these struggles were for'? Is it really possible to know the cause(s) of struggle without knowing who it is that is doing the struggling?

Still, questions of logic aside, the point that Bowles and Gintis are trying to make seems sufficiently clear. Namely, that the class struggles portrayed by Marxist theory were fought not for socialist ends, but for the ends, such as the extension of personal rights, envisioned by a liberal discourse, which was nonetheless innocent of theoretical or historical insight into class struggle. For Bowles and Gintis, then, the problem of social analysis seems to be one of incorporating the essentials of a Marxist theory of collective struggle into a predominantly liberal discourse – in order to create a new, prefigurative discourse of postliberal democracy. 'Our conviction,' the authors of *Democracy and Capitalism* write, 'is that elements of the now-dominant liberal discourse can be forged into powerful tools of democratic mobilization which, if successful, is almost certain in the long run to burst the bounds of the liberal discourse itself.' Thus, for example, these authors speak of the 'de-gendering potentials of liberal discourse.'[24]

Further, Bowles and Gintis straightforwardly admit that, 'Our choice of terms reflects a recognition of the hegemony of liberal democratic discourse as the virtually exclusive medium of political communication in the advanced capitalist nations and the profoundly contradictory, malleable, and potentially radical nature of this discourse.' Such discourse of course consist of words. 'Lacking an intrinsic connection to a set of ideas, words, like tools, may be borrowed. Indeed, like weapons in a revolutionary war, some of the most effective words are captured from the dominant discourse.' Why then, they ask, should those dedicated to radical change insist on substituting 'unprecedented' words for 'familiar' ones? The liberal discourse of rights is the central lexicon of past and present and future social change. Consequently, the realization of the vision of postliberal democratic discourse 'requires no fundamental shift in social dynamics.'[25]

Bowles and Gintis repeatedly emphasize that this new postliberal discourse is not just another form of accommodation with capitalist reality.[26] The 'visionary-historical' changes that it identifies belong instead to that broad historical tradition of radical democracy represented not by socialism as such, but by the legacy of the levellers, *sans culottes*, Chartists, agrarian populists, feminists and the supporters of workers' councils.[27] Like all of these earlier popular calls to mutiny, postliberal democracy is free of Marxism's inherent weaknesses, for the simple reason that it derives its sole meaning from the democratic imperative to 'transport' the lexicon of personal rights as conceived by liberal theory to the realm of the market, where narrow property rights now predominate.[28] By organizing our understanding in this way, Bowles and Gintis tell us, it should be possible to create a fuller democracy in which both individuals and groups – in the language of game theory – 'have trumps to play.' Or as they go on to state in language that reverberates with a kind of Emersonian optimism: 'In contrast to traditional liberal doctrine, which supports a society of acquisition based on the exchange of property claims, postliberal democracy is a vision of a society based on learning governed by the exercise of personal rights. It presents a profound reorientation of our normative grid, an inversion of the relationship between human development and economic organization. This allows economic activity to be considered not as an end but as a means toward democratically determined human development.'[29]

The trouble with this outlook is that not only does it rest upon a profound obfuscation of the social problem, but it also represents an extreme case of the 'declassing of language.'[30] If we are to believe with Bowles and Gintis that discourse is the key to social struggle, then we are confronted with the fact that the prefigurative discourse that they have chosen in the name of radical pluralist democracy would be considered radical in no country in the advanced capitalist world except the United States. To speak simply in terms of extending the realm of personal rights to the realm of the market is to ignore the fact that the conceptions of personal and property rights within liberal theory are mutually reinforcing, and that at the heart of it all lies a system of class and state power.[31]

Indeed, it is this question of the mutually reinforcing nature of class and state power that is most conspicuously absent from Bowles and Gintis' analysis. They treat the political sphere in advanced capitalism as a realm of freedom and right which merely needs to be extended to the private sphere and deny any central importance to the fact that liberal democracy is itself implicated in a system of class exploitation. Since liberal democracy is the product of the struggles of all social movements, not just those of the bourgeoisie, it can therefore be turned against capitalism itself. In order to make this argument convincing, however, Bowles and Gintis try to elude other, more critical conceptions of liberalism, in which the class context stands out more clearly. This is most obvious in the criticisms that they level at C. B. Macpherson:

> Where he [Macpherson] has treated liberalism as an ideology justifying capitalist exploitation, we see it as a contradictory discourse providing effective tools for radical anticapitalist movements. Further, unlike Macpherson, we emphasize the 'rights' components of liberal discourse – derived from the partitions of social space and agency that characterize it – rather than its utilitarian aspect. Utilitarian reasoning is important only in liberal economic theory, we believe, and even there it cannot justify capitalist property relations. Finally, we do not share Macpherson's conviction that 'market principles' and scarcity itself bar the development of a 'fully democratic society.'[32]

In other words, Bowles and Gintis systematically downplay those aspects of liberalism having to do with (1) its role as an ideology justifying capitalism, (2) its character as a philosophy of possessive individualism, and (3) the limitations with respect to democracy inherent in its commitment to market principles. So systematically in fact do these theorists insulate their conception of liberalism from any association with 'possessive individualism' that they can hardly be said to be emphasizing – as they repeatedly claim – the 'contradictory' aspects of liberal discourse at all. A contradiction, after all, has two sides. Hence, a proper exploration of the contradictory nature of liberalism would force these theorists to analyze the ways in which liberalism itself reinforces capitalism; not simply the ways in which it can be used to promote freedom at capitalism's expense.

All their emphasis on the transportation of discourses to new sites notwithstanding, it is difficult in truth to see how postliberal democracy, as envisioned by Bowles and Gintis, differs greatly from some of the more progressive and developmental visions of liberal democracy itself. Certainly, it represents no advance on – and perhaps even a step back – from certain versions of liberal thinking, such as that of Hobhouse. The strategy that they seek to advance is not simply a disguised form of social democracy, since Bowles and Gintis are sharply critical of the social democratic emphasis on the role of the state.[33] Yet, it shares some of social democracy's weaknesses, being premised on a series of accomodations between capital and labour (beginning with the democratization of the workplace to make workers more productive) which will eventually lead on to the capitalist, like the feudal lord, becoming 'superannuated.' Their 'optimistic scenario of a no doubt tumultuous encroachment by economic democracy on the economic prerogatives and ideological hegemony of capital' avoids social democracy's statism, but shares all the evasions and illusions of social democratic gradualism.[34]

An exaggerated faith in the power of liberal rhetoric, coupled with a belief in the autonomous character of such rhetoric vis-à-vis capitalist economic and class relations, has led Bowles and Gintis to the conclusion that a radical democratic movement can use liberal words to enhance the possibilities for meaningful social change.[35] Such views seem to reflect a naive conception of discourse in which the language of liberalism is no longer connected to the hegemony of a particular class, but has somehow become – what liberalism has always claimed to be – the universal language of society.

One cannot deny that Marxist theory – which is certainly in a state of crisis – could use a great deal of 'revising' and updating to make it more applicable to contemporary situations. And in this sense it has something to learn from the kind of appeal to the individual in which liberalism excels.[36] Reality is, however, much more complex and contradictory than such an analysis would suggest. A particular discourse is, as Mills emphasized, a vocabulary of motive that must be *situated* within a definite context of social practice. Liberalism, as presently constituted, is more than simply a collection of words. It is a means of engendering motives and actions and represents a specific type of practicality – liberal practicality – tied to a definite power structure.

The Call for a New Social Contract
A related if somewhat more modest, recourse to liberal practicality on the left is to be found in the reliance on the concept of 'social contract' as a means of justifying reform. With the transition from feudalism to capitalism 'the contract – to work, to sell, even to live in marriage – took pride of place.'[37] Hence, the demand for a 'new social contract' between capital and labour – deploring capital's abandonment of the previous social contract as a result of the economic crisis of the 1970s and '80s – is a convenient way of pleading progressive causes. Martin Carnoy, Derek Shearer, and Russell Rumberger therefore open their book, *A New Social Contract*, with the words:

> There is a crisis in America. To move forward we must have a new social arrangement between all of us living here – employees and employers, women and men, white and nonwhite, those with high and low incomes, young and old, working and retired. The eighteenth-century philosopher Jean Jacques Rousseau called this arrangement a 'social contract.' We never sign it, but we believe in it. When this belief degenerates, society does not work anymore. It becomes time for a new contract.[38]

Yet, in contrast to the powerful way in which the social contract concept was employed by Rousseau and other Enlightenment thinkers to raise issues of sovereignty and class in a bourgeois revolutionary context, its current use obtains its meaning from the relatively shallow quasi-corporatist notion that by breaking its previous social contract with labour capital has engaged in class warfare alien to a properly functioning, mutually beneficial democratic order where such struggle has no place. As such it becomes a way of avoiding central questions of social agency and social power.

Moreover, it is doubtful whether it is particularly meaningful to speak of a social contract in this sense when describing US reality – which is obviously quite different from the reality of a social formation like Sweden. The fact of the matter is that the harsh conditions that capital was able to impose on labour during the 1940s and '50s represented not so much a new 'post-war accord' as a crushing defeat for those wishing to defend the 'New Deal formula.' Summing up just one aspect of this counterattack during the early Cold War or McCarthy era, David Montgomery has noted that,

> The 1947 amendments to the Wagner Act, which were known as the Taft-Hartley Act, banned sympathetic strikes, secondary boycotts, and mass picketing. They required elected union officers to sign affidavits that they were not members of the Communist Party, and they outlawed political contributions by unions. Perhaps most important of all, they authorized the president to seek injunctions ordering strikers to return to their jobs, and they made unions legally liable for damages if their members struck in violation of written contracts. In effect, the only union activity which remained legal under Taft-Hartley was that involved in direct bargaining between a certified 'bargaining agent' and the employers of the workers it represented. Both actions of class solidarity and rank-and-file activity outside of the contractual framework were placed beyond the pale of the law. . . .Since 1947 successive court rulings (especially those of the 1970s) have progressively tightened the legal noose around those historic forms of working-class struggle which do not fit within the certified contractual framework.[39]

If there was a 'social contract' with organized labour in this period it was an exceedingly one-sided one – requiring the expulsion of the radical unions from the CIO, and finding its complement in the general McCarthyite attack on the left. Nor should it be forgotten that such a social truce – to the limited extent that it can be said to have existed – was connected to obvious failures of the trade union movement with respect to the organization of the South and Southwest, and to the differential treatment of peoples of colour and women. Viewed from this standpoint, the immediate post-Second World War period was characterized not so much by a new social compact between labour and capital as by the successful imposition from above of a divide and conquer strategy designed to break up the popular alliances that had constituted the material foundation of the New Deal in its later years.

Notwithstanding these weaknesses of the social contract argument, however, its appeal to progressives trying to construct a defensive strategy in the face of constant assaults from the right is considerable. Hence, even such good radical economists as Bennett Harrison and Barry Bluestone continue to root their analysis in an exaggerated notion of the 'post-war accord.' In fact, these theorists actually go so far as to deny what they oddly call 'the conventional wisdom'; namely, 'that business departed en masse from Roosevelt's [full employment] agenda when it discovered that the unique international position of the United States after 1945 offered seemingly limitless opportunities for profitable growth, without any sort of government planning.' Proof to the contrary – that capital stuck to its side of the 'social contract' – can be found, Harrison and Bluestone contend, in the passage of the Employment Act of 1946. However, this contention is difficult to reconcile with the undeniable fact that this Act was a dead letter even before it was passed. As Bertram Gross, who not only drafted but helped to administer this piece of legislation has pointed out in his book *Friendly Fascism*, 'the idea of guaranteeing human rights was ruthlessly stricken from the bills finally enacted as the Employment Act of 1946 and the Full Employment Balanced Growth Act of 1978. In place of human rights to useful paid employment came a whole series of ceremonial rights in which the operational definition of full employment soon became "whatever level of official unemployment is politically tolerable." Over the years this level constantly rose. . . .'[40]

It is true of course that US workers benefited considerably from the prosperity that characterized the early years of US hegemony. And to that extent there was a partial cessation of hostilities. Yet, their institutionalized gains during this period were remarkably small. The US welfare state remained the most underdeveloped in the advanced capitalist world, and workers had little in the way of a safety net to fall back on when prosperity waned.

It is not just that an overemphasis on the so-called 'post-war accord' is bad history. To argue, as Harrison and Bluestone and other dedicated leftists have, that the 1980s represented a great-U-Turn away from a viable social-contract capitalism, which must be corrected through a second U-Turn and the creation of a new social contract, is to embrace a perspective that owes much of its power to persuade to its conformity to the theory of balance characteristic of liberal practicality. Thus Harrison and Bluestone place their greatest emphasis on the need to swing the pendulum 'back toward a better balance between unfettered free enterprise and democratic planning.' 'In reality,' as one critic of their work has correctly observed, 'labor will be able to articulate the anti-capitalist strategies needed to break with the dependence, degradation and inhumanity in which it is now entrapped only by acknowledging the irreconcilable nature of its conflict with capital.'[41]

A rejection of a class struggle perspective for one that emphasizes the writing of social contracts as the key to social change would make some sense only if one were to assume either that such contracts do not themselves reflect fundamental relationships of class and power in society, or are based on a kind of 'countervailing power' in which the various parties are constantly engaged in creating some sort of equilibrium. Otherwise such an emphasis only serves to veil the real power relationships in society. In this regard it may not be entirely out of line to recall that a wily French slave trader once named one of his slave ships *The Social Contract*.[42]

Blueprints for Better Management

Under the influence of the industrial policy debate it has also become commonplace for radical political economists to advocate modest 'blueprints' for economic development and democratic change. Martin Carnoy, Derek Shearer, Samuel Bowles, David Gordon, Thomas Weisskopf, and Michael

Harrington are among the left intellectuals in the US to contribute such plans. One characteristic of these blueprints is that they consist of policies, modelled after the experience in Sweden and elsewhere, with which almost all progressives would agree as constituting desirable short-term goals. Yet, such policies are presented as their own object and are used to close the analysis (typically at the very end of a book), rather than as a means of opening up a discussion of the actual class revolt that would be necessary to achieve even these limited objectives.[43] Hence, the issue of class confrontation is usually avoided, and the proposals are mainly crafted in ways that suggest the possibility of creating a better capitalism – rather than attempting to transform the system. Yet, the hard truth, as Miliband and Panitch contend, is that 'those people on the Left who do want Swedish or Austrian-style social democracy, but who reject a confrontation with capital as too "extreme", are simply refusing to face reality. In the conditions of "late capitalism". . .radical reform inescapably entails such a confrontation.'[44]

What is at issue here is a strategy that points beyond simple reform or accomodation, and toward the concrete formulation of a radical reform strategy with a potential mass base in the here and now consistent with the goal of long-term societal transformation, or what Raymond Williams and others have called 'the long revolution.' For the left to involve itself in 'the presentation of more or less elaborate schemes for dealing with what are seen as our most pressing ills' while allowing its proposals to be entirely governed by the need of the profit system is to operate, as Harry Magdoff and Paul Sweezy argue, under a set of illusions borne of wish-fulfillment about the nature of power in advanced capitalist society, with damaging consequences for a 'long revolution' dedicated to nothing less than 'deconstituting the present structure of power.' Pointing to the example of the Works Progress Administration during the Great Depression, in which jobs were created to fit individuals 'where they were and as they were,' Magdoff and Sweezy argue that this embodied an anticapitalist logic, from which more general lessons can be drawn. According to this perspective the left should concentrate its effort on advocating those kinds of fundamental reforms that while meaningful in a present-day context, in the sense that they represent class defences for the oppressed, are nonetheless clearly anticapitalist in character, consistent with a strategy of long-term social transformation.[45] Such a strategy, moreover, demands a class struggle perspective rooted in the needs of those at the bottom of society – what Marx called 'the political economy of the working class' as opposed to 'the political economy of capital' – and not simply the drawing up of blueprints for better management designed to appeal to enlightened members of the dominant class with its 'bottom line' accounting.[46]

For example, the problem of the federal deficit can be approached on the revenue side from a socialist standpoint by advocating higher taxes on the wealthy. But instead of simply pushing for a resumption of effective taxation of corporate incomes the left should raise the issue of a general tax on capital assets – even at the considerable risk of questioning the legitimacy of private property itself – backing this up with the kinds of arguments in relation to efficiency introduced by a theorist like Michal Kalecki.[47] Meanwhile on the spending side, the class and imperial composition of state spending can be questioned – particularly where the military is concerned. Hence, the goal of the left should be wherever possible to promote a *different* logic from that which drives capital itself.[48] The hegemony of private property is not simply a given fact, but a process of struggle in which the boundaries are constantly being changed. And the movement to contain, repel and even defeat this logic represents a continuum of anticapitalist, socialist struggle.

Anticorporate vs. Anticapitalist Strategies

An elaboration of this general approach has been provided by Prudence Posner Pace, who distinguishes the 'anticapitalist' strategy of thinkers like Magdoff and Sweezy from the 'anticorporate' strategy of certain radical theorists – Samuel Bowles, Thomas Weisskopf and David Gordon constituting, according to Pace, the 'outstanding spokespeople.' The anticapitalist strategy requires that 'the measure of a program should be whether (1) it is consistent with a theoretical framework in opposition to capitalist relations; (2) it is accompanied by an educational process which ties it to broader social questions; and (3) the process of struggle consciously attempts to separate the participants from the values and ideas of the capitalist class.'

In contrast, the anticorporate strategy is quite different since organizationally its goal is not one of forming a movement of people dedicated to opposing the unbridled hegemony of the capitalist class, but rather to 'modify corporate functioning so that it is less top-heavy and undemocratic, and thereby becomes productive enough to meet people's needs.' For anticorporate thinkers, Pace explains, the 'major emphasis is on the demonstrating how democratic reforms (in the workplace, investment, and in managerial decision-making) could restart the engine of capitalism.' Because their focus is on the corporation, and not the system itself, she points out,

> those who put forth these kinds of proposals do not have to address the dual nature of the state. They are free to alternate between an 'anti-statist' community control stance and the demand, for example, that the federal government underwrite union organizations (because unions are good for productivity). Their main concern is whether their proposals are 'politically persuasive and economically feasible,' and for this reason they do not address the problems of ideology and the education of people away from the dominant ideas and values of the society.[49]

So far has the US left departed from a clearly articulated anticapitalist strategy, in fact, that the very question of whether or not to 'name the system' – i.e. to adopt an outspokenly anticapitalist strategy – has been a persistent source of controversy among radicals. The main fear is that, as Hans Koning has observed, 'A word like "capitalism" contains secret enzymes which stop up the ears of most Americans listening or even drive them into semantically induced hysteria.'[50] Still, while one may struggle to invent a new language of class struggle, one cannot simply avoid the question of the system – say by attacking corporations rather than capitalism – without doing serious damage to the quality of the argument.

The Retreat from Internationalism

Such an unwillingness to confront the system can also be found in the foreign policy debate as it affects US radicals. Given the US imperial role, it is perhaps not surprising that a loose anti-imperialist orientation has frequently constituted the common thread in the organization of the grass roots left. Nevertheless as the memory of the Vietnam War has receded and as the decline of US hegemony has come more to the fore it has become increasingly frequent for radical intellectuals in the US to construct arguments in terms that emphasize national competition irrespective of its effect on international solidarity. National industrial policy proposals are therefore advanced by progressives in the name of national competition, with barely a glance at the conditions in the third world. Nor are internationalist commitments as strong among US socialists as they once were. Despite continued popular resistance to US interventions in Central America, left publications in the US, with certain notable exceptions, have backed off from any serious discussion of imperialism as a *system* (the global face of monopoly capitalism), and have tended to treat it as a mere *policy* – or not at all. Serious theoretical studies of imperialism, as opposed to the mere development of the world economy, have become unfashionable even in Marxist circles.

Thus it is not surprising that considerable confusion is exhibited on issues like the third world debt crisis and the newly emerging competition of South Korea and Taiwan (to say nothing of Japan). Rather than lending support to Cuba's stance that Latin American nations – as victims of a long history of superexploitation imposed in large part from without – should band together in order to default on their loans (advice which the ruling classes in these countries are of course loath to follow) many radical political economists, with their eyes glued to the financial exposure of the largest US banks, have succumbed to the wish to be considered responsible in the terms in which this is understood by the powers that be, and have simply urged greater foreign assistance to these countries along with more favourable debt rescheduling to make it easier for them to repay their debts. One result of this is that radical political economists have offered solutions that have soon proven excessively moderate even when judged by the actions of conservative Latin American governments themselves.[51]

Worse still, many left thinkers in the US increasingly seem to be less concerned about imperialism than about waning US competition and a kind of imperialism-in-reverse. Robert Heilbroner, for instance, has raised the spectre of '. . .a capitalist periphery combining high technology and low wages to extract surplus from a defenseless capitalist core. . . .Capitalism

would remain the dominant regime, but it would be the nascent capitalism of
the newly industrializing countries, now generalized across the face of Asia,
South America, and into strategic parts of Africa and the Near East.'[52]

The significance of this argument, which Heilbroner apparently presents
quite seriously, lies in the exaggerated fears that it portends for those looking
out from the centre of the capitalist world system.

In this kind of deindustrialization and imperialism-in-reverse scenario
that has become increasingly prominent within the left in the advanced
capitalist world, neither imperialism nor the relative stagnation of capitalism
in recent decades are central to the analysis. Instead, it is simply assumed
that the dynamism of the 'technological gale of creative destruction' (to use
Schumpeter's phrase), when coupled with the role of international capital,
will undermine the traditional core-periphery relationship – so that formerly
imperialist nations will have no choice but to abandon their traditional open
door strategies, and limit the excesses of the international system. Not to do
so, Heilbroner leads us to believe, would result in the fall of the capitalist core
in a manner analogous to the Roman Empire.

Such an overemphasis on a 'defenceless' capitalist core imperilled by a
rising periphery is quite irresponsible from a socialist standpoint, given
the harsh reality of imperialism and dependency as currently experienced
by the lower classes among third world populations. In this respect, it is
worth keeping in mind that, to quote the latest World Bank development
report: '[I]n Africa and Latin America hundreds of millions of people have
seen economic decline and regression [in the 1980s] rather than growth and
development. In some countries in Latin America real per capita GNP is less
than it was a decade ago; in some African countries it is less than it was twenty
years ago.'[53] Confronted with this dire situation, all references to the 'Latin
Americanization of the US economy' through the agency of multinational
corporations – while doubtless capturing a part of the truth – seem more than
a bit out of place.[54]

Social Movements vs. Class

All reversions to liberal practicality ultimately involve a retreat from class.
Nowhere is this overall conservative drift in left thought borne out more
clearly therefore than in current fashions in the analysis of social change,
where it has become commonplace to replace the concept of social class with
social movements. Thus Richard Flacks, in an argument that criticizes both
the Marxian emphasis on class struggle and the Millsian notion of the power
elite for failing to perceive the actual pluralist roots of US society, argues that
this democratic pluralism reveals itself through the social movements that
periodically challenge centralized power. These movements, he contends,
'are themselves the primary vehicles of democratic restructuring in America.'
Moreover, Flacks goes on to add that, 'My argument suggests that *in the
United States the movements themselves have played many of the political*

functions that a labor party would have played had one been successfully formed.'[55]

In this view it is neither necessary to articulate the social struggle in class terms, nor to rely on the building of a labour party, since the social movements themselves provide the basis for democratic restructuring and a new electoral advance. Speaking of the need for unity among these diverse movements Flacks writes: '*The main political goal of social movements is to turn the national government into a vehicle for social democratization.*' Moreover, he argues that this can be accomplished by a 'new public philosophy' emanating from grassroots social movements, and constituting the core of a new Democratic majority.[56]

Drawing the reader's attention back to Robert Michels' 'iron law of oligarchy,' Flacks argues that the main fault of what he calls the US 'ideological left' has been its susceptibility to 'elitist' and 'vanguard politics,' which have led it to overlook the true importance of those very pluralistic social movements that have constituted the main agencies of radical social change in the US. Attempting to drive this point home Flacks observes:

> C. Wright Mills' depiction, in *The Power Elite*, of American society in the fifties failed to even glimpse the sixties and the scope and intensity of mass intervention in history that succeeded the mass apathy of the fifties. His elitist perspective helped clarify the structures of established power, but it tended to blind him with respect to the potentials for history making available for the powerless. Yet his style of thought and the content of his critique have tended to characterize the articulated understanding that most American leftists have of how society works.[57]

In contrast, Flacks would have us believe that US society is elitist at the top and pluralist (in its social movements) at the bottom. Moreover, any theory that overemphasizes the role of the power elite or the ruling class is partially responsible for blinding us to the spontaneity and democracy that characterizes social movements close to the level of everyday existence.

This argument – especially where Mills is concerned – is not particularly convincing. This is not only because the latter was so aware in his writings of the role of social movements in making 'available the knowledge and sensibility required by publics,' but also because there is no reason to think in 1990, over three decades after the publication of *The Power Elite*, that Mills fundamentally overestimated the weight of the control exercised from the top in US society. Thus the current left fashion of emphasizing the pluralism of US political culture could easily be criticized from a Millsian point of view as a reversion to the theory of balance characteristic of liberal practicality rather than an accurate description of contemporary reality.

In any case, Flacks' emphasis on social movements as the sole constituent element of struggle in the US, while clearly representing a progressive outlook, seems a step backward when compared to the shift toward a more unified class politics already discernible in the Rainbow Coalition or 'Jackson phenomenon.' It is important to remember, as Vicente Navarro has pointed out, that 'other countries with less powerful social movements [than the US] but with solid class instruments (social democratic, socialist, and Communist parties) have better rights for minorities, women, and workers, and more protection for the environment than we do.'[58]

Indeed, the main lesson that grew out of the later phase of the civil rights movement, perhaps the single most heroic 'new social movement' to develop in the advanced capitalist world in the post-Second World War period, was that a poor peoples' movement that is to continue to advance must eventually evolve from a question of rights to a question of power – from political to human emancipation. And this requires a shift in the nature of the organized struggle toward class politics. As Martin Luther King indicated to his staff in 1967 '[W]e have been in a reform movement. . . .But after Selma and the voting rights bill [in 1965] we moved into a new era, which must be an era of revolution. I think we must see the great distinction here between a reform movement and a revolutionary movement.' By 1968, shortly before his assassination, he was publicly stating that, 'We are engaged in the class struggle.'[59]

In the women's movement too self-organization of working class women, disproportionately confined to household, service and part-time labour, may be the key both to reversing the rapid decline of US trade unionism and reviving socialist feminism. Thus, as Johanna Brenner has emphasized,

> [T]he counterposition of feminism and marxism, of the feminist movement to the trade union movement, appears particularly absurd. Feminism as a mass reform struggle with radicalizing potential cannot be renewed on the basis of its old middle-class constituencies but depends on the rebuilding of working-class self-organization. . . .Without the capacity, *in practice*, to take on the limits set by the demands of capital accumulation in a period of increasing international competition, feminism will continue to be vitiated of its radical potential, capitulating to the right, and unable to mobilize broad layers of women. . . .The fate of feminism as an actual *movement*, then, is tied to the fate of trade unionism and other forms of collective resistance to corporate capital.[60]

For all that can be said of the 'new social movements' in areas such as anti-racism, feminism, ecology, etc., the fact remains that their power to reshape society will be critically dependent on the extent to which they can connect their struggles to that of the 'old social movement' of organized labour – albeit in ways that will radically transform the latter. And when the problem is viewed in this way it becomes obvious that the greater part of the common ground and common strategy is to be found in the realm of class. Indeed, it is precisely this kind of unified labour based movement, particularly if activated by a socialist consciousness, which still remains the main spectre – the one that 'must above all be contained, repelled, and, if need be crushed' – from the standpoint of those chiefly concerned with maintaining the existing order; and it is at this antagonist that the class struggle from above is therefore to this day mainly directed.[61]

Liberating Theory

Nevertheless, numerous radicals continue to oppose a framework that finds the strategic common ground for the struggle of the oppressed in the reality of class. Perhaps the most debilitating concession to liberal practicality among US left intellectuals in recent years has grown out of the call to 'liberate theory,' closely associated with the work of such 'libertarian socialists' as Michael Albert, Robin Hahnel and Lydia Sargent.[62] As Albert puts it, 'Marxism opens our eyes about the ills of capitalism, but it also fosters continued sexism, aggravated homophobia, continued racial and ethnic strife, increased political authoritarianism, and a post-capitalist economy that subjugates "traditional workers" to "intellectual workers". . . .And it does this at the level of theory and practice.'[63] Frequently attacking all Marxist thinkers for being 'economic monists' in their focus on class, Albert and his colleagues point to the need for a 'complementary holism' that, in the name of providing a theory suitable for activists engaged in diverse social movements, stresses the equal importance of four interacting 'spheres' of oppression: community, kinship, authority and economy.

This, however, is little more than a radicalized version of the fallacy that Mills referred to as 'the democratic theory of knowledge' in which 'all facts are created equal.' 'Is it not evident,' Mills asked, 'that "principled pluralism" may be as dogmatic as "principled monism"?'[64] Arguing in terms reminiscent of Mills in this respect, Michael Parenti has responded to Albert's criticisms of Marxism by pointing out that,

> Instead of the primacy of class Albert offers 'four defining spheres': economics, community, kinship and authority, which permeate each other with equal effect. Regrettably, he gives us no evidence of having undertaken the kind of historical study that would invite us to embrace his fourfold model and discard the works of Marx, Engels, and all the later Marxist writers. Instead, we are left to wonder, why only these four 'spheres' and not others? Why renounce Marxian 'monism' for Albert's quadrupalism? If four causes are less reductionist and economistic than one, might not ten be better than four? Why hold back with the diversity of our causalities? At one point he himself hints that there might be more than four basic forces in history when he says there are '(at least) four'. . . .Albert has dished up what Engels called the 'devil's brew of eclecticism,' a plurality of equipotent causalities that float ahistorically in social space.[65]

None of this, it should be emphasized, is meant in any way to suggest that Marxism is actually 'monist' in orientation or that it systematically excludes other forms of oppression – racial, ethnic, gender, national or cultural – in favour of a 'narrow' class theory, as writers like Albert erroneously contend. Rather as Manning Marable has put it, focusing on the interrelationship between race and class,

> Racism, sexism and forms of social intolerance such as homophobia, are powerful forces within American society. Factors of culture and kinship are vitally important in providing the character and ideological composition of a social class or nationality. But within a capitalist social formation, the factors of material life and more specifically the struggles generated by the existence of the market and the exchange of labor for commodities prefigure all other social relations, including racial relations. In other words, the history of Black America cannot be explained satisfactorily by focusing solely on race or class factors. Yet it is class which has set the range of human options and possibilities, from the expansion of the transatlantic slave trade to the development of an urban reserve army of labor to repress wage levels

for all working people. C.L.R. James' formulation of the problem was as follows: 'The race question is subsidiary to the class question in politics, and to think of imperialism in terms of race is disastrous. But to neglect the racial factor as merely incidental is an error only less grave than to make it fundamental.'[66]

It is this central strategic role played by class in the historical construction of capitalist society – including the role that capitalist *class* rule has played in the formation of capitalism's doubly and triply oppressive racial and patriarchal configurations – which makes class the most important common ground for all movements emanating from fractions of the working class (the great majority of society) forced to confront the system in terms of power. What is needed at present, according to this conception, is not a democratic theory of knowledge but a rainbow understanding of the working class.

III. The Historic Moment

As we enter the 1990s the political reality of the United States is beset with contradictions more severe than at any time since the 1930s. On the surface, the political climate of the country is shaped by the realignment that took place in the 1980s associated with the rise of the New Right party system, in which the Republican party – in continuous control of the executive branch since 1980 – is in a hegemonic ideological position vis-à-vis Democratic party interests. Beneath the calm surface suggested by these recent voting patterns, however, is a society torn by contradictions born of class struggle, in which there exists a potential for mass political rebellion that would threaten conservative political elites and tear the mask off the US ideological system for all to see.

Viewed solely from an internal political angle, there are two reasons for believing that the United States may possibly be on the brink of a new historic moment. First, the US has witnessed a fairly steady, long-term decline in voter participation, which in the 1988 presidential elections dropped to about 49% of all eligible voters. These losses in voting participation have been suffered disproportionately by the Democrats and represent to a large extent the underprivileged members of society. This 'party of non-voters,' as the leading theorist of political realignment, Walter Dean Burnham, has continually emphasized, is the natural constituency for social democratic politics; a constituency that an increasingly conservative Democratic party, although still representing the more enlightened wing of capital, has largely abandoned. The Republican political dominance of recent years has therefore rested to a considerable extent on the lack of enthusiasm that both the working and non-working poor have demonstrated for the moderate, centrist strategy of the Democrats, and thus on the declining voter participation of millions of marginalized individuals at the bottom of society.[67]

The single greatest political threat to the status quo was represented by 'the Jackson phenomenon' in the 1984 and 1988 election campaigns; itself a response to years of crisis and economic assault on the subaltern strata of society coupled with the political default of the Democrats. Starting out from a solid base within the African–American community, and thus emerging out of the most self-conscious mass movement of the oppressed in the United States today, Jackson articulated a class politics new to the post-Second World War US. Not only did Rainbow Coalition politics threaten the divide and conquer strategy vis a vis the working class that the US capitalist class has so effectively wielded over the course of its history, but it continually broke through the ideological quarantine imposed on class politics and threatened to reintroduce millions of non-voters back into the political arena by addressing at least some of their genuine needs. Constituting both a force outside of the Democratic party and able to use the facilities of that quasi-public institution to advertise and advance its cause, the Jackson campaign threatened to alter fundamentally the nature of politics – making increasingly visible all of those who have politically disappeared within the society, and making the conservative default of the Democrats obvious for all to see. This represented the beginnings of a crucial unravelling of the internal Cold War political order; an order that requires for its coherence the imposition of an ideological straightjacket that leaves a majority of the population not only invisible, but effectively voiceless and optionless as well.

Whether or not the Rainbow Coalition itself will be the means by which this contradiction is played out in the future is of course less certain than that the contradiction will continue to haunt the established order in the US. Indeed, the unstable nature of the political alignment of forces, as the country enters the final decade of the twentieth century, becomes all the more evident when viewed against a background consisting of the dramatic decline of the Cold War political order from without, the waning of US hegemony and growing world economic instability. There is ample reason both on the domestic and international planes therefore to believe that a new decade of political and social instability may be in the offing.

What is the responsibility of the left under these circumstances? It is what it has always been: to advance a politics of truth; to avoid easy compromises; to address the immediate and long-term needs of the mass of the population and of those who suffer the most severe forms of oppression; to search for the common ground of that oppression; to resist ideological claims that 'we are all in the same boat' in this society; to reject what Mills called the 'crackpot realism' that makes the status quo into a kind of inescapable second nature and closes off the future; to fight market fetishism. In short, to avoid making what Raymond Williams called 'long-term adjustments to short-term problems.'[68] The only thing that has changed with the crisis of Cold War liberalism is that it has become more important than ever to resist liberal practicality, if new historic opportunities to advance a socialist practicality dedicated to the cause of undivided humanity are not to be lost

– and if we are to make our uncertain way forward once again. Indeed, only when the issue is addressed in terms of responsibility, rather than in terms of short-term victory or defeat, does it become possible to alter the balance of forces in favour of those whose need is best served by a long revolution. And it is this perhaps more than anything else that constitutes the essence of genuine socialist practicality in our time.

NOTES

1. David Marr, *American Worlds Since Emerson* (Amherst: University of Massachusetts Press, 1988), p. 3; Daniel Boorstin, *The Genius of American Politics* (Chicago: University of Chicago Press, 1953).
2. Ralph Ellison, *The Invisible Man* (New York: Random House, 1982).
3. C. Wright Mills, *The Sociological Imagination* (New York: Oxford, 1959), pp. 85–6.
4. C. Wright Mills, *Power, Politics and People* (New York: Oxford, 1963), pp. 439–52.
5. Ralph Miliband, 'The New Revisionism in Britain,' *New Left Review*, 150, March/April 1985, pp. 5–26.
6. See Ellen Meiksins Wood, *The Retreat from Class* (London: Verso, 1986).
7. See C. Wright Mills, 'Introduction,' in Thorstein Veblen, *The Theory of the Leisure Class* (New York: Mentor, 1953).
8. Mills, *Power, Politics and People*, p. 189.
9. C. Wright Mills, *The Marxists* (New York: Dell, 1962), p. 29.
10. Mills, *Power, Politics and People*, p. 434.
11. See Mills, *The Sociological Imagination*, esp. pp. 85–86
12. Mills, *Power, Politics and People*, pp. 251–52.
13. Mills, *The Sociological Imagination*, p. 86.
14. C. Wright Mills, *The Power Elite* (New York: Oxford, 1957), p. 242; cf. C. B. Macpherson, *Democratic Theory* (New York: Oxford, 1973), pp. 78–80.
15. Mills, *Power, Politics and People*, p. 536.
16. Mills, *The Marxists*, pp. 30–31.
17. C. Wright Mills, *The Causes of World War Three* (New York: Simon and Schuster, 1958), pp. 126–27.
18. Mills, *The Causes of World War Three*, p. 87.
19. *Ibid.*, p. 94; Mills, *The Sociological Imagination*, p. 77.
20. This has been a recurring strategy of the US left most clearly articulated by the early leadership of the Students for a Democratic Society. See the chapter 'Name the System' in Todd Gitlin, *The Sixties* (New York: Bantam, 1987).
21. Samuel Bowles and Herbert Gintis, *Democracy and Capitalism* (New York: Basic Books, 1986), pp. 15, 19–20. See also Ernesto Laclau and Chantal Mouffe, *Hegemony and Socialist Strategy* (London: Verso, 1985); Gareth Stedman Jones, *Languages of Class* (Cambridge: Cambridge University Press, 1983).
22. These nine points are to be found, respectively, in Bowles and Gintis, *Democracy and Capitalism, op. cit*., pp. 18, 23, 110–11, 229n, 18, 146, 160, 153 and 62.
23. *Ibid.*, p. 25.
24. *Ibid.*, pp. 175, 107.
25. *Ibid.*, pp. 209, 153, 185 and 179.
26. *Ibid.*, p. 203.
27. *Ibid.*, p. 8.
28. *Ibid.*, p. 105.

29. *Ibid.*, pp. 4, 178.
30. See the Marxist historian John Foster's brilliant refutation of similar arguments in the work of Gareth Stedman Jones: 'The Declassing of Language,' *New Left Review*, 150, March/April 1985, pp. 29–45.
31. Wood, *The Retreat from Class*, *op. cit* ., pp. 140–45.
32. Bowles and Gintis, *Democracy and Capitalism, op. cit* ., p. 233n.
33. *Ibid.*, p. 179.
34. *Ibid.*, pp. 212–13.
35. On the autonomy of discourse see *Ibid.*, pp. 161–62.
36. In this respect there is much to be learned from Sartre's *Search for a Method* (New York: Vintage, 1963).
37. Michael E. Tigar and Madeline R. Levy, *Law and the Rise of Capitalism* (New York: Monthly Review Press, 1977), pp. 211–12.
38. Martin Carnoy, Derek Shearer and Russell Rumberger, *A New Social Contract* (New York: Harper and Row, 1983), p. 1.
39. David Montgomery, *Workers' Control in America* (New York: Cambridge University Press, 1979), pp. 166–67.
40. Bennett Harrison and Barry Bluestone, *The Great U-Turn* (New York: Basic Books, 1988), p. 84; Bertram Gross, *Friendly Fascism* (Boston: South End Press), p. 144.
41. Harrison and Bluestone, *op. cit* ., p. 20; Michael Dawson, 'The Myth of the Great U-Turn,' *Monthly Review*, 41 (3), July/August 1989, p. 84. For a critique of the way in which the social contract concept has been employed by radical Fordist theorists see John Bellamy Foster, 'The Fetish of Fordism,' *Monthly Review*, 39 (10), March 1988, pp. 14–33.
42. Tigar and Levy, *Law and the Rise of Capitalism, op. cit* ., p. 254.
43. See the excellent piece by Kim Moody, 'Going Public,' *The Progressive* 47 (7), July 1983, pp. 18–21.
44. Ralph Miliband and Leo Panitch, 'Socialists and the "New Conservatism,"' in Ralph Miliband, Leo Panitch and John Saville, eds, *Socialist Register 1987* (London: Merlin, 1987), 511.
45. Harry Magdoff and Paul M. Sweezy, 'The Responsibility of the Left,' *Monthly Review* 34 (7), pp. 1–9; Sheldon Wolin, 'The People's Two Bodies,' *Democracy* 1 (1), January 1981, p. 24.
46. On the political economy of the working class see Michael Lebowitz, 'The Political Economy of Wage Labor,' *Science and Society*, 51 (3), Fall 1987, pp. 262–86.
47. For an elaboration of this particular argument see John Bellamy Foster, *The Theory of Monopoly Capitalism* (New York: Monthly Review Press, 1986), pp. 128–59; Edward Nell, *Prosperity and Public Spending* (Boston: Unwin Hyman, 1988), pp. 244–47.
48. See Michael Lebowitz, 'Social Justice Against Capitalism,' *Monthly Review* 40 (1), May 1988, pp. 28–29.
49. Prudence Posner Pace, 'On the Responsibility of the Left,' *Monthly Review* 36 (1), May 1984, pp. 49–53.
50. Hans Koning, *Nineteen Sixty-Eight* (New York: W. W. Norton, 1987), p. 116.
51. See for example Debt Crisis Network, *From Debt to Development* (Washington D.C.: Institute for Policy Studies, 1986).
52. Robert Heilbroner, 'The Coming Meltdown of Traditional Capitalism,' *Ethics and International Affairs* 2, 1988, pp. 72–73.
53. World Bank, *World Development Report, 1989* (New York: Oxford University Press, 1989), p. 6.
54. See Richard Barnet and Ronald E. Muller, *Global Reach* (New York: Simon and Schuster, 1974).

55. Richard Flacks, *Making History* (New York: Columbia University Press, 1988), pp. 252–53.
56. *Ibid.*, pp. 260–61.
57. *Ibid.*, pp. 210–11, 252.
58. Vicente Navarro, 'The Rainbow Coalition and the Challenge of Class,' *Monthly Review*, 39 (2), June 1987, p. 24.
59. David Garrow, *The FBI and Martin Luther King* (New York: Penguin, 1981).
60. Johanna Brenner, 'Feminism's Revolutionary Promise,' in Miliband, Panitch and Saville, *Socialist Register 1989 op. cit* ., pp. 253–54; Dana Frank, 'Labor's Decline,' *Monthly Review*, 41 (5), October 1989, pp. 48–55; Joan Acker, 'Class, Gender, and the Relations of Distribution,' *Signs*, 14 (3), Spring 1988, pp. 480–83.
61. Ralph Miliband, *Divided Societies. Class Struggle in Contemporary Capitalism* (New York: Oxford, 1989), p. 114.
62. See Michael Albert, et. al. *Liberating Theory* (Boston: South End Press, 1986).
63. Michael Albert, 'Green Marxism!?,' *Zeta Magazine* 2 (3), March 1989, p. 35.
64. Mills, *The Sociological Imagination*, *op. cit,* p. 86.
65. Michael Parenti, in 'Socialist Ecology Roundtable,' *Zeta Magazine* 2 (7–8), pp. 145–46.
66. Manning Marable, in *Ibid.*, pp. 146–47.
67. Walter Dean Burnham, *The Current Crisis in American Politics* (New York: Oxford, 1982), pp. 289–313.
68. Raymond Williams, *Resources for a Journey of Hope* (London: Verso, 1989), p. 317.

INTELLECTUALS AND TRANSNATIONAL CAPITAL

STEPHEN GILL

The problem posed

It has become a commonplace in discussions of the international political
situation during the 1970s and 1980s to argue that socialism, defined both
in terms of a series of doctrines and arguments as well as social movements
and political parties, has been on the defensive. Socialism has appeared to
retreat and move towards a position of intellectual retrenchment in the face
of the onslaughts of the restructuring of capital and the social relations of
production on a global scale. The changes which have taken place have helped
to reinforce the positional advantage of the dominant ideologies within the
capitalist system. This has appeared to shift the terrain of contestability
in prevailing political discourse to the right, with the ostensible return to
dominance of ideologies of *economic liberalism*, and cold war (at least for
much of the 1980s). This has been linked to the neo-liberal advocacy of
the reconstitution of state power to restore a more hospitable world-wide
investment climate for capital, especially financial capital.

One way to explain these complex changes may be to explore how policy
is made at the interface between domestic and international aspects of
rule within and between the major capitalist states. To date, most Marxist
analysis has mainly concentrated on the former. Where work has analysed
the international dimension of this question, it has generally been from
the viewpoint of classical theories of imperialism or from world systems
analysis (both discussed and criticised below). However, little empirical
work, using primary, rather than secondary sources, has been carried out
on the transnational aspects of the formation of classes and strategies of rule
by internationalist fractions of capital and the state apparatus.[1]

This essay cannot deal with the vast range of evidence needed to explain
these issues with any degree of plausibility. However, it will examine one
necessary aspect of any approach to understanding such complex questions.
It attempts to do this through an investigation of the way in which leading
fractions of the bourgeoisie of a range of major capitalist nations have
sought, and under certain conditions have succeeded in, international co-
operation in the co-ordination of policy. A part of this process entails the
epistemology, ideology and techniques of policy conceptualisation and elite

interaction. A framework within which these aspects of elite and ruling class consciousness come together on a transnational basis is in what can be called, in Gramscian terms, ideological apparatuses, both formal (e.g. the OECD) and informal (e.g. the Trilateral Commission). The development of strategic consciousness is part of a much wider process of elite interaction which is aimed at the synchronisation and possibly the synthesis of conceptions of the world political economy, and of domestic rule. This needs to be understood as an ongoing process under conditions of rapid global change. This is a necessary prerequisite for a series of initiatives which have sought to establish the hegemony of internationally-oriented fractions of capital.

The normative or subjective dimension of the power of capital involves, for example, the salience and political effectiveness of ideas and theories concerning the desirability and necessity of private capital accumulation as the source of wealth, well-being, growth and prosperity. In broader terms, it encompasses the primacy of ideas based upon possessive individualism, rather than collectivist views concerning the constitution of society. Material dimensions of capital's power involve the privileged access to or control over certain state capacities as well as the more basic control over the means of production. At the international level, this dimension includes the scale, scarcity and mobility of private transnational capital *vis-à-vis* the state, 'national capital', and much organised labour. However, the two dimensions are only analytically separate, since much depends upon the consciousness and mobilisational capacities of capital, state and labour, and the perception of leaders and led of the 'limits of the possible' which may inhere in a range of situations, and which may constrain action.[2]

The developments of the past 20 years are, of course, by no means straightforward. They include contradictions, even for those interests which appear to have benefited most from the global conditions of the 1970s and 1980s. For example, as some of the more far-sighted intellectuals associated with such interests have been swift to point out, the rising power of large-scale, international-mobile capital has gone with global macroeconomic instability and the perversity of a situation where capital has been drained from many of the most needy economies to the most powerful, helping to cut dramatically living standards and thus contributing indirectly to the bleak outlook for economic development in many parts of the world.[3] A side-effect of this depressing economic atmosphere is its pernicious contribution to further environmental depredation and ecological catastrophe, although the record of most of the Communist states in this regard has been even more appalling and catastrophic. Nevertheless, contradictory aspects of international market forces, allied to myopic policies on the part of private and public international banks, from the point of view of international capital, undermine the long-term investment climate and the future prospects for more stable accumulation on a world-wide basis.

Prevailing Orthodoxies and Alternative Visions
The prevailing orthodoxy of the ruling forces is based on the doctrine of economic liberalism, with its stress on efficiency and competition and the primacy of the private sector in economic and social life. Its international perspective is drawn from a synthesis of 'transnational' liberalism and neo-realism.

There are two distinct vantage points from within this perspective. These are, respectively, 'pure' and 'compensatory' liberals.[4] The former, drawing on the inspiration of the likes of F. A. von Hayek, sees the market as a spontaneous human institution, a source of vitality, motivation, progress and wealth; as such, the state's role should be to act as a nightwatchman, protecting market freedoms or creating the conditions for competitive markets to prevail on a world-wide basis. Much of the thinking of this strand was associated with the market-monetarist policies which were widely pursued during the 1970s and much of the 1980s. This is a position which has been recently strongly associated with the short-term and often speculative interests of financial fractions of capital, as well as with some Reaganite cold warriors at the political level.

'Pure' liberalism is, however, intellectually and politically countervailed by 'compensatory' liberalism, which, like most radical writings in political economy, makes more allowance for market imperfections and the externalities generated by free market forces: thus, *à la* Keynes, the market should be steered to protect capitalism from its own tendency tc self-destruct. This viewpoint has been associated with a range of centrist forces over the last two decades. It emphasises a longer-term, more productivist vision, which is heavily critical of the neglect of the social, ecological and political aspects of development of 'pure' liberalism. Compensatory liberals have therefore frequently attacked the wildcat free-marketism of the first Reagan electoral coalition of 1980 using this type of argument. The social democratic variant of this line of denunciation, one which shares many of the assumptions of the 'compensatory' perspective but which is more welfarist in emphasis, is represented in the activities and proposals of the Brandt, Palme and Brundtland Commissions.

At any one moment, of course, the actual policy stance of a particular country will depend on a balance of political and material forces, and intellectual influences. In the first Reagan administration, for example, economic policy shifted towards the 'pure' position, although it had substantial Keynesian elements (e.g. big budget deficits). From the mid-1980s onward, however, US policies have gravitated back to the more 'compensatory' viewpoint of the East Coast Establishment, and have become more congruent with the international orientations of centrist parties in Western Europe and with those of the Japan Liberal Democratic and Socialist Parties. This is the general position taken on the world economy by the bulk of the most strategically and politically conscious members of the international establishments', and the majority of Trilateral Commissioners.

At the international level, this type of stance implies ongoing co-operation with allies and the co-ordination of economic (and where possible politico-strategic) policies. Underlying this point of view is a view of changed international conditions, quintessentially represented by Robert Keohane and Joseph Nye's concept of 'complex interdependence'.[5] This concept implies a vision of international relations where military-security definitions are given less prominence than in the traditionalist *realpolitik* concepts of international rivalry and order, so that a range of other social forces – ecological, economic, technological, cultural – and the transnational interactions they are bound up with, create a more complex structure of international relations, with no clear-cut hierarchy of foreign policy issues. In traditional terms this means that the 'high politics' of security may fall from the summit of the international agenda. The 'actors' involved in this structurally new situation include not only governments, but also transnational companies, international organisations and non-governmental organisations and networks.

Taken together, the theory and practice of this constellation of forces which comprise the perspective (theoretical, practical and material) of 'compensatory' or 'transnational' liberalism (i.e. conducive to the long-term and politically stable growth in the structural power of transnational capital) can be said to be dominant in the global political economy. Its frame of reference largely sets the international agenda and informs the policies of many states and international organisations. This is to say that it has allies drawn from the ranks of the dominant factions in the centrist and right-wing political parties and elements within the state bureaucracies of the major capitalist countries and in key international organisations. It also has adherents from the ranks of privileged elements of organised labour in both the metropolitan and developing capitalist countries. Moreover, we have now arrived at a moment in history where some Western political leaders and capitalists are speaking of the urgent need for a new 'Marshall Plan' for Eastern Europe and an 'Okita Plan' for the Third World (Saburo Okita was the master-mind behind much of Japan's post-war economic planning).[6] The goal of these initiatives would be to widen the ambit of this constellation or bloc of forces to encompass the globe politically. I call this constellation a transnational historic bloc, since it is rooted in material as well as ideological structures which have global reach, and which are strongly associated with the political programme of transnational capital.[7]

Such a transnational bloc then, is a synergy of powerful elements at the level of ideas, institutions and material forces, and, for much of the 1980s, has only been significantly countervailed by either the 'pure' liberal vision of speculative financial capital, or by other more nationalist and security-oriented forces of the centre and right, for example those associated with the United States' security complex, which pressed in the late 1970s and early

1980s for renewed policies of Cold War *vis-à-vis* the USSR. By contrast, the prevailing elements of transnational capital would wish to open up the Soviet and China trades, integrate these countries gradually into international capital and exchange markets, and thus begin to subject them increasingly to the rule of capital. This transnationalist goal has, for example, already been made clear in the strategies of the IMF, the Paris Club, by most western governments and by the private banks in the management of the Third World debt crisis as it affects Latin America and the larger debtor countries. Despite the limitations and hesitations concerned with this process, it represents an important moment in the development of a collective strategic consciousness on the part of financial fractions of capital in the 1980s.[8]

The need for the left, and its allies, to move swiftly on the questions and challenges of the 1990s is indicated by the fact that the prevailing forces in the global political economy are already well aware of the potential of many counter-hegemonic movements, and will undoubtedly begin to develop strategies so as to co-opt them. This possibility was recently suggested in an article which appeared in the American Establishment journal *Foreign Policy*. Its author stressed that the prevailing political forces in the West and in Japan had better pay attention to and come to terms with the changes which are now taking place in the Third World, so as to channel their development in the future:

> The great cultural upheavals of the twentieth century – rapid population growth, urbanisation, the advent of modern technology and the spread of Western commercialism – have stretched and often dismantled traditional Third World religious, tribal and village organisations already gravely weakened by the impact of colonialism. In the resulting organisational vacuum a new generation of grass-roots groups has steadily, albeit unevenly, risen up since mid-century with particularly impressive growth over the past two decades. Driving this growth have been stagnant or deteriorating economic and environmental conditions for the poor, the failure of governments to respond to basic needs, the spread of new social ideologies and religious doctrines, and the political space opened up in some countries as tight fisted dictators have given way to more permissive political systems – even nascent democracies.[9]

Theorising the International and the Global
One reason why Western socialists have not transcended an inward-looking metropolitanism may be because of a failure of orthodox socialist theory, if not of socialist vision. For whatever reasons, during much of the last two decades, many socialist perspectives on international relations have failed to develop in such a way that they are able to capture adequately the nature of global transformations. This is perhaps because many recent writers have been constrained by the dominant heritage of earlier theories of imperialism. The classical theories of imperialism – inspired by Lenin, Bukharin and Hilferding – were developed at a period when interaction between nation-states, acting in a militarist-mercantilist way to further the interests of their own monopoly capital, seemed to be the primary manifestation of international conflict.[10] These classical theories, developed earlier this century, may thus imply

an inability to conceptualise important questions in global terms. Most classical views have a tendency to reify the interstate system, seeing *national* capitalist classes and states as particular and relatively fixed configurations in a wider system of permanent inter-imperialist rivalry and crisis. Such views counterpose the forces of socialisation and the expansion of capital on a world scale (that is a world market which unifies the globe) with the national class structures and identities which politically divide it – at least until working class forces triumph on a world scale. In this view, international co-operation between capitalists is, in the long-term, theoretically impossible.

An appropriate inference to draw is then, that classical theories have in-built theoretical limitations when applied to present-day capitalism. This is now a more complex and politically flexible transnational system. Moreover, it is a system where the identification of a nation-state with the material interests of its own 'national capital' is more problematic. In economic terms, this system is increasingly constituted by a deepening interpenetration of capital, both functionally and geographically. This reflects both changes in consumption and production patterns, increasing flows of foreign direct investment within the golden triangle of metropolitan capitalism, and the intensifying integration of international financial and capital markets under the aegis of the Bretton Woods system. At the political level, there is a policy interdependence which is the counterpart to the economic internationalisation processes, as well as more integral, and more organic alliance structures binding the major capitalist nations together under American leadership, although the decline of the Cold War may begin to erode a primary military justification for this.[11]

None the less, there are often, as I have noted above, considerable divisions between and among more internationally-oriented and nationally-oriented class fractions and associated political constellations. Given the long peace and relative prosperity of the post-1945 period in the capitalist core – in contrast to the international instability and militarism for much of the earlier part of the century – the centripetal forces noted above have had a cumulative if uneven structural impact on the system. Of course, these forces were accompanied by cut-throat competition in the recessionary conditions of the 1970s and 1980s, which is likely to intensify in the 1990s. In addition, some have argued that the phenomenal internationalisation of financial capital since the late 1960s is leading or has led to the apparent delinking of production from the monetary and exchange structures. Others suggest that the system is becoming less and less stable and is losing any claim to legitimacy and moral credibility. The crashes of the late 1980s and the gyrations of international capital and exchange markets are taken as evidence for this. On the other hand, the management of the October 1987 crash, the handling of the 1982 Mexican crisis, and the ongoing containment of the debt crises of the 1980s may be taken as evidence of vastly enhanced surveillance and managerial capacity at the international level, in contrast, say, with the

1930s. In other words, the contradictory dynamics of capitalism mean that centrifugal forces are always likely to be in tension with centripetal ones. The key question here is whether these contradictions can be politically managed, and if so, by whom and for what purposes?

What I am arguing, therefore, is that the post-war system cannot be accurately characterised in the terms used by the classical theorists: thus it is not simply 'ultra-imperialism' under a new guise: a shift from the hegemonic ultra-imperialism of American leadership to a more tripartite system of global management. Rather, these terms may be anachronistic because the system has novel elements, not least of which is the degree of institutionalisation and informal and formal communication which takes place at the elite level between the state managers and major capitalists in the biggest capitalist countries. In this context, I think it is fair to say that whilst there is no international capitalist class *per se*, there is an intersecting set of establishments drawn from these countries, who together with the leaders of international organisations are linked to twin processes we can call the internationalisation of the state and its social counterpart, the internationalisation of civil society. Whilst the primary determinants of the international policies of capitalist states are still to be found mainly at the domestic level, the process is becoming tendentially internationalised. What is implied here, therefore, is a set of processes which are helping to generate and partly to configure both political and socio-economic changes which are transforming the globe.

Moreover, it is worth remembering that Marxists have no monopoly of wisdom in theorising the international. The theories of international relations from the perspective of the Establishment and associated dominant fractions of transnational capital has a degree of plausibility and salience lacking in many Marxist writings. Drawing upon concepts of complex interdependence, international regimes (for example in money, trade, exchange rate management) and stressing the importance of international institutions, some of the better writing from the Establishment perspective reflects three possibilities in terms of the appreciation of contemporary conditions. First, they appreciate the possibility of the changes in the nature of the state and indeed in the structure of international relations, that is the significance of historical transformations (although their appreciation of the depth and nature of such transformations may be limited). Second, they reflect the capacity to conceptualise such transformations. Third, they reflect or imply a political programme to regularise or to contain the contradictions which exist at the global level between a politically divided and constituted world of different territorial units and sovereignties on the one hand; and on the other, the social forces which are transnational or global in nature, such as those of economy and culture. In other words in these mainstream, and hegemonic viewpoints, there is some sensitivity to the problems of history, space and time in their views of modern international relations, although their major theoretical weakness is the absence of a deeper understanding and therefore integration of the social dimension of economic and political co-ordination.

Similar criticisms can be made concerning a second and influential current in Marxist theories of international relations: the world systems theory of Immanuel Wallerstein.[12] Wallerstein's theorisation or model has already been criticised in the *Socialist Register* and elsewhere as representing a neo-Smithian Marxism, that is its major theoretical weaknesses relate to the model's concentration on exchange relations, and because of Wallerstein's perspective of development in a largely Euro-centric world-view.[13] A preoccupation was to assess the propensity to war amongst the major capitalist states, a prospect which in today's historical circumstances, looks somewhat remote (in contrast to the Third World where there have been over 160 wars since 1945 and inter-and intra-state violence often appears endemic).

In Bukharin's formulation of *inter-national* relations the conflict between capitalist states necessarily took the form of a mercantilist-militarism, its virulence reinforced by jingoistic nationalist ideologies, with each rival capitalist state forced towards conflict by the domestic imperatives of accumulation. We might here note briefly that the very term 'international' was coined in the last quarter of the nineteenth century. By contrast, now there are emerging a range of new alternatives in Marxist theorisations of international relations, such as the work of the French Regulationist School (of Aglietta and Lipietz), and that of the Dutch School based around the Amsterdam School of International Relations.

My way of approaching these questions is through social forces analysis. This takes as our basic units of analysis and constituting elements in international relations not nation states or an inter-state system, but sets of basic social forces (ideas, institutions and material capacities) which operate and interact at a number of levels: the level or the structure of production, that of state-civil society complexes and at that of particular, historically specific systems of world order. Under certain conditions these social forces may interact and fuse together to generate what Gramsci called historic blocs, at either the national or international level. This type of analysis, partly inspired by Robert Cox's reading, avoids conflating the different types of socio-economic structures in the world into the logic of a single world system comprising a core, periphery and semi-periphery.[14] The strength of the Wallersteinian approach, of course, is to theorise international relations from a global vantage point; its political shortcoming, however, is its determinism which dooms most of the world's populations to eternal peripheralisation and dependency. This perspective is associated with and was inspired by André Gunder Frank's early work. Much of the writing on dependency theory suggests policies of intellectual, economic and political delinking from the global capitalist system, at a time when communications flows and ecological problems have a growing global dimension. Under contemporary conditions this is the approach of the ostrich: instead of theorising dialectically the political possibilities for development and change from a more global vantage point, a narrow and rather exclusive national path is often prescribed.

The project of Trilateralism

As I have noted, in classical Marxist theories of imperialism, the analytical focus was the identification of the contradictions in the international relations of the advanced capitalist nations around the period of World War I, when capitalist production was organised on a primarily national basis, under the domination of 'monopoly capital'. Little systematic attention was paid to the development of the political economy implicit in the work of Gramsci, which allows us to develop a new form of historical materialism which can be applied to the constitution and development of international relations under contemporary conditions.[15] In this sense, some types of international order can be considered hegemonic, that is where a relatively stable congruence of social forces is sustained at the levels of production, state-civil society and world order. Examples of this are the *pax britanica* and the *pax americana*. By contrast the inter-war period of extreme international instability and conflict was non-hegemonic, with a lack of congruence at each of the three analytical levels.

We can use also this method to analyse and explain the activities of the Trilateral Commission, and what I would call the project of Trilateralism. This project has for its historical origins the crises of Western capitalism and of the post-war hegemonic order which began to manifest themselves in the late 1960s and early 1970s. The first thing to be said in this regard is that it would be erroneous to suppose or to accept what has become the conventional wisdom on both sides of the Atlantic and indeed in Japan, that the international power and hegemony of the United States declined substantially during the 1970s and 1980s; and that this thereby opened up the possibility of a disintegration of the post-war global political economy and its associated international economic order into something resembling economic blocs or spheres of influence as occurred in the 1930s. Rather it is my contention that the centrality of the United States in a global political economy has changed, partly due to the internationalisation of economic activity within the United States so that in some respects American centrality within the system of global capitalism has been re-emphasised. Thus many of the arguments concerning 'hegemonic decline', associated with writers such as Paul Kennedy, David Calleo and Robert Keohane are misdirected and erroneous.[16] Indeed, if we associate the capacity to dominate in the future with knowledge-based high technology industries, and if, as many analysts now suspect, the financial surpluses of Japan will begin to decline substantially during the 1990s, the prospects for sustained American international power are good. Indeed, American centrality in the global political economy is also associated with the widespread use of English, the lead the US has in global communications and in the media industries, and with US primacy in the global security structure, a fact underlined by the defensiveness and military retrenchment of Gorbachev's USSR. There is no obvious alternative hegemon, understood in the conventional terminology of international relations, although a reconstructed and more integrated EEC, with a much more developed and independent military capacity might, in the twenty-first century, become a candidate. However, this is to theorise the problem in terms of inter-state interactions, whereas the forces of transnationalisation make this simple identification between state and capital more and more problematic, even for Japan, the most clearly mercantilist and nationalist of the major capitalist countries.

An alternative theorisation might therefore be to say that the period in question can be best characterised as a 'crisis of hegemony', that is a crisis or transformation which involves a structural reordering of the post-war politico-economic system and with it the political consensus between the prevailing elements in the state and civil societies of the major capitalist nations. This system was politically constructed during the period of the *pax americana* after 1945. In other words the crisis in question is not a crisis in American power *per se*; rather, it is a change in the relationship between key social forces within the constitution of the global capitalist order, a change manifested in different ways in various societies.

Theorists of American decline point to the evidence that the USA is now the world's largest debtor and has become dependent on infusions of Japanese savings to finance its government activity. However, by late 1989 Bush was apparently embarking on a considerable reduction of US military expenditures in order to reduce the US fiscal deficit and to begin to construct the domestic conditions for tackling the problem of international macroeconomic imbalances. Bush and his Secretary of State, James Baker III, now stress more comprehensive co-operation with the major allies (especially Japan and West Germany), and a move towards an internationally defined reconstruction of the European political settlement. A large number of plans are currently emanating from government and business circles designed to rebuild Eastern Europe and the Third World politically and economically. Noteworthy here is that, in contrast to the Marshall Plan, both sets of initiatives imply the multilateralisation of financing with large contributions from US allies, especially Japan. In other words, these forces are conscious of the opportunities inherent in the new conjuncture in Europe and elsewhere and are engaged in theoretical-practical activity to shape the course of future events.

Trilateralism needs therefore to be understood as an ongoing set of processes and policy practices in this type of context. With its emphasis on the steering of the market and the need for compensatory and at times redistributive mechanisms and for some international planning as well as crisis management on a discretionary basis, it is a neo-Keynesian attempt to stabilise the global capitalist system in a period of rapid change. In this sense, the importance of the application of strategic (rather than purely technocratic) consciousness is stressed heavily in the Trilateral Commission's documents and publications.[17] Comprehensive global institutions, such as a world central bank, have yet to be endorsed. Instead, Trilateralists stress the strengthening of existing international organisations such as the OECD, the IMF and the World Bank, and the institutionalisation of co-operation, co-ordination and consistency of policy apparatuses so as to 'manage' interdependence. In an era of transformation, the aim is to provide a kind of political gyroscope in order to sustain stability amid transformations and contradictions which may have a centrifugal and destabilising impact upon the nature of the system. For such an effort to be possible, this involves consciousness and action at a number of different levels in the system: local, national, regional, global. The effort necessarily encompasses a wide range of questions: economic, political, cultural. These questions have been considered in terms of immediate problems of crisis management, and in terms of long-term structural developments.

The Trilateral Commission was created in 1972 by David Rockefeller. Rockefeller drew together a substantial group of eminent individuals from the United States, Western Europe and Japan to his home in Pocantico Hills in New York State's Hudson Valley. This group then consulted with leading elements at the most senior levels in their respective countries to see if there would be support for a new private international relations council, for the first time including the Japanese on a multilateral and co-equal basis. The immediate catalyst for the creation of the Commission was disquiet (or outrage) within internationalist circles both in the United States and overseas at the policies of the Nixon administration in the early 1970s. It has become a historical commonplace to suggest that these policies represented the repudiation of the post-war liberal universalism of the United States with respect to the international economic order, and a retrenchment of American economic policy in the direction of economic nationalism. The policies in question also directly and severely damaged important European and Japanese interests.

Private international relations councils of this kind have a long lineage. Chronologically, we can identify a number of different contexts in which these councils have emerged. The first of these is what might be called the Anglo-Saxon context, that is, councils originating in the late nineteenth century and continuing during the inter-war years, for example the Round Tables inspired by British imperialists like Cecil Rhodes. A second, Atlantic, context emerged after 1918 and more pervasively after 1945 as in the Bilderberg meetings and the Atlantic Institute. This was inspired by a mixture of the American currents of Wilsonian liberalism, the subsequent internationalisation of certain New Deal ideas, and their eventual fusion with the ideas of European supra-nationalists, federalists and functionalists like Jean Monnet, the founding father of the EEC. Similar but less influential groups also developed in the Pacific, after 1945, but these were more closely associated with the bilateral relations of the USA and Japan (e.g. Shimoda meetings in the late 1960s; the 'Wisemen's' Groups founded by President Carter and Prime Minister Ohira). During the 1980s these forums have widened to include other Pacific nations. The unique Trilateral context, however, forges together both Atlantic and Pacific flanks of this type of activity. The substantial weight and status of the individuals in these groups is reflected in the membership of the Trilateral Commission, as well as the Atlantic Institute (which has now broadened its membership to incorporate some Japanese). In the shadow of the Trilateral Commission we have seen the development of such forums in the Euro-Pacific context, after 1976, with the so called Hakone meetings.

The general purpose of these councils is to provide a politico-educational framework for the internationalisation of the outlook of political leaders drawn from each of these regions. They involve attempts to promote a kind of cognitive shift of outlook of members, away from a short-term, more nationalist viewpoint, towards a more cosmopolitan, long-term one. These councils generally have, as a point of origin, the energy and motivation of a single individual or small group of individuals with some political weight in internationalist circles. In various ways these founders were able to bring together diverse individuals and interests for what was seen as common purposes: they had an idea whose 'time had come' as well as the wherewithal to promote it effectively. In this sense the forging of diverse interests for a common civilisational purpose is the positive side of an elite ideological process. On the negative side these councils are vehicles for the absorption of political frictions between constituent elements: that is at a minimum they enable the understanding of conflicts of position and interest, and provide a channel of communication, as it were an early warning system for political threats to the cohesion of the alliances that such councils reflect and to a certain extent embody.

The way this is achieved, for example in the Trilateral Commission, is by bringing together diverse individuals from the USA, Canada, Japan and the EEC countries (except Greece), who communicate through different, but none the less commensurable academic traditions mainly drawn from liberalism, functionalism and neo-realist theories of international relations. This goal is pursued in a rather unique way, since these efforts combine the work of scholars, policy experts and politicians from each of these nations, to create some type of common vision of how the political economy works, what its key problems are, why these problems exist, how they may be approached collectively, and perhaps solved. In general, when looking at the membership of the Trilateral Commission and indeed some of the other institutions which have been mentioned, the interests represented are those of the internationally oriented

302 THE SOCIALIST REGISTER 1990

fractions of capital, their allies and associates in the state apparatus, and in the mainstream political parties of the centre. Younger, up-and-coming, future leaders are groomed under the guidance of the established partiarchs and policy intellectuals of high status and of considerable experience.

The Trilateral Commission is more than just a debating chamber or a gentlemen's dinner club (very few women have been members): it is, in Gramscian terms, an ideological apparatus with a range of dimensions to its activity. As has been mentioned, central to its purpose is to advance the process of the internationalisation of outlook of members. This is attempted by creating a forum (and many others exist) for the forging of a transnational political identity. More concretely, this is attempted through a series of meetings, research activities, consultations and social events. However, the most important of these activities are meetings, held over 3–4 days in rotation in each of the three 'regions' and involving between 200 and 250 of its members and other invited guests and observers (the latter usually drawn from staff members of the American National Security Council, foundations, sometimes from other governments and the establishment press). At these meetings, all addressed by the heads of state and government of the host nation, as well as senior cabinet ministers, the debates are intense. The debates focus upon immediate questions of crisis management, as well as longer term trends affecting the relations between these regions, and the rest of the world. The debates are organised around the task force reports, which are substantial pieces of research written by three to five experts drawn from each of the regions. The authors' work is carried out collectively with a larger group of theorists and practitioners in the task forces. Their objective, where possible, is to try and synthesise a collective position which can serve as the basis for potential agreement about certain types common problems or international questions.[18]

This kind of process is, however, relatively indirect with respect to the precise contours of policy. It is really designed to help set the agenda and to develop operative or practical concepts which can be applied in discussions and debates and policy considerations in each region. These efforts are better seen as part of an ongoing process of attempting to incorporate immediate and long term developments into the common framework of thought and, at least potentially, a common concept of action.

At this point it is worth stressing the types of intellectuals who are, and who are not involved in this process. Those excluded from the process are those who might be called the *literati* and, of course, members of the left-wing intelligentsia, as well as those of the far right or indeed neo-conservatives like Irving Kristol (who is mildly supportive of the Trilateral Commission) and Norman Podhoretz. Also largely notable by their absence are the extreme free marketeers of the Hoover Institution, or some elements of the Adam Smith Institute in Britain. The types of intellectuals – what Gramsci called organic intellectuals – are involved because of their ability to combine theoretical and practical aspects of their activity, and to articulate these within the major discourses which I have mentioned above. They are also chosen because they sit in prominent positions within wider intellectual networks, and partly because of their vantage point from within a particular discipline.

A good example of the latter is Samuel P. Huntington, one of the authors of a very controversial Commission report, *The Crisis of Democracy*.[19] Huntington became President of the American Political Science Association in 1987, he is also the Director of the Harvard Center for International Affairs, and has served in a number of governments. Another Commissioner, Kinhide Mushakoji is a former President of the International Political Science Association. In other words, Commission intellectual networks are based on an international circle of theorists and policy specialists who are often at the summit of their discipline and who usually direct major academic institutes. Many of these theorists are also important practitioners who have held high political office. Examples of such figures include Zbigniew Brzezinski, Henry Kissinger and Saburo Okita. Other major political leaders have also written important Trilateral Commission publications, such as Yashuhiro Nakasone and Valéry Giscard d'Estaing.[20]

Commission networks are associated with high powered research institutes such as the Brookings Institution, (to a lesser extent) the American Enterprise Institute, the Institute of International Economics, the British Policy Studies Institute, and the Royal Institute of International Affairs in London, and its counterparts in other Trilateral nations. They are also associated with major American Ivy League Universities, with the ultra-prestigious Tokyo and Harvard Universities having many members. The Commission's intellectual networks also encompass important theorists from international economic organisations, such as the IMF and the World Bank, and from the OECD. American academics are very influential in framing the approaches of the Commission, but they are by no means the only important element. All in all the intellectual activity of the Commission is a truly transnational enterprise. As has been noted many members of the Trilateral Commission have had an important role to play in the framing of policy in each of its member countries, since many members hold or have held high political office (with the UK being a partial exception during the Thatcher years). It is well known that Trilateral Commissioners filled virtually all senior positions during the Carter administration, less well known that Trilateral Commissioners have also been influential in the (second) Reagan administration, and also in the Bush administration, with President Bush himself an ex-member.

Whilst American members are probably the most influential, Trilateral Commissioners have filled a significant number of high offices in other countries. For example in Japan, three members, Nohubiko Ushiba, Kiichi Miyazawa and Saburo Okita, have all at one time or another held the Foreign Ministry portfolio, and each has been an important figure in the shaping of post-war Japanese foreign economic policy. Indeed Saburo Okita is the architect of a major Japanese initiative designed to recycle Japanese capital overseas to help deal with the debt crisis during the 1990s. This initiative, encouraged from within the Trilateral Commission during the mid-1980s, is currently being more widely discussed and debated, and is now called the Okita Plan.[21] Other important figures have included Lord Carrington, former Secretary General of NATO, and a host of others drawn from each of the member countries. All in all Commission members have been directly or indirectly involved in the making and co-ordination of the foreign and economic policies of most of the Trilateral member countries since at least the early 1970s.

Corporate networks and affiliations are at the highest levels of blue chip corporate capital and in major international banks, other financial concerns, insurance companies, media and telecommunications/informatics, agribusiness, aerospace and some military-industrial and trading companies. Some of the affiliations are listed below, but it is worth mentioning here that in some countries there is a substantial interchange and rotation between the government, bureaucracy and corporate sector, as well as between academia and think-tanks and government. This phenomenon is well-known and documented in the US case and increasingly so in Japan.[22] Because of the processes of the internationalisation of production and exchange, as well as through the aegis of international organisations and in private councils like the Trilateral Commission, these networks have gradually begun to internationalise, particularly as the post-war generation of Japanese leaders is now slowly giving way to a second generation. Much of this more recent generation had some if not all of its post-graduate education abroad, usually in the American Ivy League schools, or at their educational counterparts in Europe, such as the London School of Economics, Oxford, or the University of Paris. This enables senior Japanese to communicate and interact more effectively than was the case even 10 years ago.

The Commission has discussed virtually all important questions of international relations which have surfaced since its inception in 1973. The issues which the Commission has addressed have concerned the political management of global economic forces in a period where it was widely assumed that the power of the United States, the hegemon of the system, has been in substantial relative decline. In this sense it is argued that a sharing of responsibilities, amongst the Trilateral nations, is necessary, to generate fruitful forms of co-operation and the possibility of an enduring political coalition which provides the means to place some rational control over global economic forces. As a number of the examples cited earlier in this essay indicate, this is by no means straightforward. In the early phases of the Commission's existence, Commissioners were generally pessimistic about the international outlook as well as preoccupied with the domestic problems of 'governability' within each of the regions, more so in Europe than in the United States or in Japan. Part of this problem concerned the managerialism implicit in the Trilateral outlook: given the apparent politicisation of a range of groups and movements at the domestic level in their own countries, leaders were politically constrained from having the autonomy to pursue the necessary policies, in Trilateral terminology, to 'manage' global interdependence. However, the recessions of the 1980s were crucial in rolling back these 'ever increasing expectations' of change both within the Trilateral nations and from the Third World challenges. A key 'governability problem' for the 1990s from this perspective is to place some control over the forces of international financial integration so that they can be channelled to allocate resources on a more 'rational' basis.[23]

To recapitulate: the origin of Trilateralism in the early 1970s was connected to the attempt at the renovation and reinforcement of the post-war politico-economic order (and what might be termed its associated civilisational project). Historically this has been associated with the *pax americana*: a system which involved the construction of the Bretton Woods economic institutions, American led military alliances, and the politico-economic reconstruction of liberal democratic capitalism in North America, Japan and Western Europe (and more broadly in the OECD regions). It encompassed, of course, the defence of this system and its values from communist and nationalist challenges, both internal and external. Trilateralism also implies that the increasing equality of economic capacity between the major capitalist regions should be matched by a redistribution of rights and obligations amongst its national members. In particular, Japan and West Germany, given their economic power, should play a more equal and political role in the councils of the alliance, and, for example, have more voting rights in the IMF and the World Bank.

The term transnational historic bloc seems appropriate to describe what Trilateralism is intended to give rise to. This is because the term historic bloc encompasses class formations and conscious initiatives (emanating from the dominant forces of what Kees van der Pijl aptly called the 'Lockeian heartland' of the system), that is it implies much more than the interaction of political and economic elements from different nations.[24] Gramsci's concept of historic bloc suggests that associated social forces are at least potentially able to fuse their identities and interests, more deeply and more extensively (i.e. within the golden triangle of metropolitan capitalism, and the wider world order). The term also suggests the leadership of vanguard elements of transnational capital – as a class force – in a process designed to incorporate and engage other powerful elements drawn from the states and civil societies of the OECD countries, and where possible to enlarge its membership as nations 'graduate' economically and politically (e.g. by allowing South Korea to join the OECD). This 'vital core' is seen as a point of anchorage for the wider world system in an era of transformation.

At the centre of these endeavours is a fraction of the capitalist class drawn from those corporations and companies which can be included as members of the *Fortune 500* biggest banks and corporations. Significant corporate moguls who have been important members include Giovanni Agnelli (Fiat), Akio Morita (Sony), Otto Wolff von Amerongen. Top American bankers such as Arthur Burns, Paul Volcker and Alan Greenspan have at one time or another been senior members. In 1986, for example, the Commission had members who were in very senior positions in the vast majority of the biggest 100 companies in a *Wall Street Journal Survey*.[25] All top 10 companies had members, 16 of the top 20, 27 of the top 40. Commissioners were directly associated (by personal citation of primary employment, based on Commission membership lists) with at least 60 of the top 100 manufacturing corporations in the world. They were also associated with 9 of the top 10, 18 of the top 20 and 25 of the top 30 banks; 9 of the top 10, and 14 of the top 20 of the world's largest insurance companies. Given the massive appreciation of the Japanese yen since this date, and given that all of Japan's major corporations and banking conglomerates and trading companies are associated with the Commission, it is possible that the proportion in the top 100 has now increased.

By implication, what I have called a transnational class fraction is itself partly mobilised by developing its consciousness and solidarity in international organisations of various kinds, such as the IMF, the World Bank, and OECD, as well as in their day-to-day business and leisure activities associated with transnational corporate activity. This class fraction is also heavily associated with other private international relations councils. These would include the Bilderberg meetings (which started in the early 1950s) the Atlantic Institute (which started in the early 1960s) and the Saltzburg Seminars on multinational enterprise (which began in the late 1960s). It is also involved with and is partly influenced by the research endeavours of think-tanks and philanthropic institutions or foundations such as those of Ford, Mellon, Carnegie, and Rockefeller. The key term which helps to capture the social interactions and processes absorbed here is that of the Establishment. The membership of the Trilateral Commission – about 350 people – consists of intersecting elements of the domestic Establishments of its member countries (drawn from the USA, Canada, the EEC – except Greece – and Japan), and as such can be said to form the outline of an international Establishment. Such an Establishment mirrors aspects of the emerging global civil society. It also reflects the fact that the self-perception of many individuals associated with forums such as these is both conservative (although centrist) and public spirited.

Organisations like the Trilateral Commission, in fact, appear to be more moderate and reasonable by virtue of the fact that there are also more right wing, free-market oriented institutes and networks, associated with the Mont Pelerin Society, the American Heritage Foundation and in Britain the Adam Smith Institute. However these more right-wing groups have been less effective, both in terms of their total capacity to mobilise intellectual and political resources on a transnational basis, and in terms of the degree to which they have been able to set the agenda for public debate at the international level. Whilst it is true that the Reagan administration and Thatcher in Britain have been influenced by some of these latter groups, this is much less the case with respect to Western Europe and Japan, and indeed, as has been noted, the new Bush administration in the United States seems more in tune with the moderate 'centrism' of Trilateralism than was its predecessor, with some overlap between the second Reagan administration and the Bush administration in this regard.

This trilateralist perspective and bloc may also be contrasted with 'pure liberalism' and with nationalist blocs which take different forms in different countries, where for example labour may combine with more 'national' fractions of (productive) capital, as well as with elements in the security complex. Such nationalist coalitions tend to argue for neo-mercantilist policies and protection against more dynamic and threatening forms of international competition. More generally this type of formation normally would oppose an uncontrolled or too far-reaching an internationalisation of the domestic economy, primarily for reasons of social welfare and/or for national security purposes. Thus the question of the hegemony of transnational capital is bound up with a struggle at a number of levels.[26] In this context the United States is crucial, both because of its centrality in the world capitalist system, its vast domestic market, and partly because of the policy consequences of the potential clash of perspectives between, for example, smaller firms and banks geared to production and services for the domestic market (strongly represented in Congress) and transnational manufacturing corporations and banks (who often find allies in the Executive Branch and the bureaucracy), as well as between the foreign policy and economic perspectives of the liberal internationalists and the military-strategic intellectuals associated with the US security complex.

Conclusion

My conclusion is implicit in much of my exposition. I have argued that both the dependency/world systems and classical traditional theories of imperialism and world systems theory have, therefore, severe shortcomings which undermine their capacities to think through creatively the emerging political possibilities and the contours of an agenda for transnational action. As such it can be suggested that they fail to meet the criterion of contemporary relevance. The prospects of a 'brave new world' (some would call it a dystopia) of global capitalism and the imperatives of a range of other global forces require a re-examination of theory and a search for either a reformulation or generation of new concepts and approaches which can begin to capture, at least theoretically, the changes which are actually taking place and the logic of their future trajectory. In other words whilst mainstream international relations theory, drawn principally from the liberal and to a certain extent realist traditions, is making progress on the task of conceptualising contemporary transformations, the two dominant sets of approaches from within Marxism have lagged behind.

A major problem with the dominant Marxist theorisations lies in their inability to grasp transformative aspects of the contemporary situation. As such, and at the risk of over-generalisation, I would suggest that they are unable to theorise the possibilities for the synergy of a range of progressive forces across as well as within national boundaries. Such a theorisation is vital so as to give general direction to a counter-hegemonic project which is sensitive to a range of concerns for not only the material aspects of class struggle, but also questions of culture, communication, gender and ecology.

NOTES AND REFERENCES

1. Exceptions are K. van der Pijl, *The Making of an Atlantic Ruling Class* (London, Verso, 1984); S Gill, *American Hegemony and the Trilateral Commission* (Cambridge, Cambridge University Press, 1990).

2. S Gill and D Law, 'Global Hegemony and the structural power of capital' *International Studies Quarterly*, (1989–90), Vol 33.

3. C F Bergsten *et al*, *Conditions for Partnership in International Economic Management* (New York, Trilateral Commission, 1986); S Ogata *et al*, *International Financial Integration: the policy challenges* (New York, Trilateral Commission, 1989).

4. These terms are used by R D Mckinlay and R D Little in *Global Problems and World Order* (London, Pinter, 1986).

5. R O Keohane and J S Nye, *Power and Interdependence* (Boston, Little Brown, 1977).

6. F G Rohatyn, 'Monnet, Not Mao, Had the Vision the East Needs Now' *International Herald Tribune*, 21 November, 1989; Saburo Okita, 'Policy Approaches to the Problem of Development' in L Emmerij (ed.) *One World or Several?* (Paris, OECD, 1989). The Okita Plan continues the logic of the Brady Plan (which itself assumed that the Japanese would foot most of the bill). It entails recycling Japan's massive balance of payments surpluses in three roughly equal portions of up to US $30 billion per year, allocated respectively to domestic demand growth; to supply capital to the USA and the other major industrialised economies; and to supply capital for development assistance. The Japanese intend to double development assistance from US $25 billion to US $50 billion in the period 1988–92, after cancelling debts of about US $ 5.5 billion to Asian and African developing countries following the 1988 Toronto summit.

7. Gill, *American Hegemony and the Trilateral Commission*; R W Cox, 'Gramsci, Hegemony and International Relations: an essay in method', *Millennium* (1983), Vol 12.

8. A somewhat different strategy is emerging for sub-Saharan Africa where the problem is being viewed as one of basic solvency and a fundamental collapse of state capacities. The Brazilian situation has been viewed, for example, as a

crisis of liquidity, and debt restructuring should be geared to Brazil's eventual return to 'normal' participation in international capital markets after it has made the necessary adjustments in macro-economic and other policies.

9. A.B. Durning, 'People, Power and Development', *Foreign Policy* (1989) pp. 67–8.

10. these theories and their limitations are ably discussed in A Brewer, *Marxist Theories of Imperialism*, (London, Routledge, 1980).

11. S Gill and D Law, *The Global Political Economy: Perspectives, Problems and Policies* (Hemel Hempstead and Baltimore, Harvester-Wheatsheaf/Johns Hopkins University Press, 1988).

12. I Wallerstein, *The Capitalist World-Economy* (Cambridge, Cambridge University Press, 1979). Other world systems writers who are immune to my criticisms are Giovanni Arrighi and Christopher Chase-Dunn.

13. See for example, P Worsley, 'One World or Three? A Critique of the World-Systems Theory of Immanuel Wallerstein' *Socialist Register*, 1980.

14. R W Cox, *Production, Power and World Order: social forces in the making of history* (New York, Columbia University Press, 1987)

15. See Cox, 'Gramsci, Hegemony and International Relations'; Cox, *Production, Power and World Order*; Gill, *American hegemony and the Trilateral Commission*, pp. 41–56.

16. D P Calleo, *Beyond American Hegemony: The Future of the Western Alliance*, (Brighton, Wheatsheaf Books, 1987); R O Keohane, *After Hegemony: Cooperation and Discord in the World Political Economy* (Princeton NJ., Princeton University Press, 1984); P Kennedy, *The Rise and Fall of the Great Powers*, (London, Unwin Hyman, 1988). For my criticisms of these and other arguments concerning American decline, see S Gill, 'American Hegemony: Its Limits and Prospects in the Reagan Era' *Millennium*, (1986) Vol 15; S Gill, 'The Rise and Decline of Great Powers: the American case' *Politics*, (1988) Vol 8; and Gill, *American hegemony and the Trilateral Commission* pp. 57–88.

17. For a full list of references to Commission publications see the appendix to Gill, *American hegemony and the Trilateral Commission*

18. For a full survey of agendas and activities see Gill, *American Hegemony and the Trilateral Commission*, pp. 122–201.

19. M Crozier *et al*, *The Crisis of Democracy* (New York, New York University Press, 1975).

20. See V Giscard d'Estaing, Y Nakasone and H Kissinger, *East–West Relations* (New York, Trilateral Commission, 1989).

21. See note 6 above.

22. In Japan, an entire cohort of bureaucrats retires when a member of a younger 'class of. . .1934, 1947, 1956', etc., (at the Faculty of Law, University of Tokyo) reaches the uppermost echelons of the bureaucracy (e.g. becomes Vice-Minister). This is to allow the seniority principle to stay inviolate, since no one should be commanded by someone younger than himself. Most of the retiring bureaucrats then find senior jobs in industry, banking, etc., that is they usually go to sectors they have been administering. In this light it is important to remember that in educational background and career pattern, senior Japanese bureaucrats are generalists. Bureaucrats carry much prestige and weight with them into the private corporate sector, the bulk of whose leadership is drawn from the graduates of the Faculties of Law and Economics at the University of Tokyo, widely known as 'Todai', an academic institution whose status, social centrality and prestige is unmatched: its role would be approximated in the US system if all the Ivy League schools were merged into one big, ultra-elite school. Thus the elite linkages between state and private sectors vary from one system to the next,

in horizontal and vertical terms, as well as intensity: Japan being more integrated and centralised than the USA.

23. Ogata *et al*, *International Financial Integration*
24. K van der Pijl, 'The Socialist International and the Internationalisation of Capital' Paper to the *International Studies Association*, annual conference, London, 28 March-1 April, 1989.
25. 'Global Finance and Investment', Special Report. *Wall Street Journal*, 29 September, 1986.
26. For example, between labour and capital, and between national and international blocs of forces, each possibly corresponding, broadly speaking to more 'productivist' and 'financial' fractions of capital. However, in most cases the most meaningful determinant of support of capital and labour for protection or openness, mercantilism or liberalism is the degree of its industry/sector/firm's international competitiveness.

WHY ARE WE STILL SOCIALISTS AND MARXISTS AFTER ALL THIS?[1]

ARTHUR MacEWAN

At the beginning of the 1990s, Marxist socialists in the United States are on the defensive. The turmoil in the Soviet Union and Eastern Europe and the massacre in China have been widely accepted as demonstrating a final failure of socialism. In the United States, the very long period of economic expansion, ignoring our repeated predictions of recession, seems to undermine Marxist analyses of the self-contradictory nature of capitalism; the expansion is all the more significant because it has come along with conservative policies, the rejuvenation of the market, and all that. It is easy for one to react, as much of the public has, to these recent developments with the conclusion that socialism and Marxism are dead and that capitalism will be increasingly triumphant.

These objective factors have a counterpart in intellectual life. Among left academics during the 1980s, there has been increasingly important opposition to Marxism. While at times this opposition keeps the name of Marxism, the rejection of basic propositions of Marxism (even most liberally defined) is so thorough as to make the rubric meaningless. Sometimes this intellectual development goes under the title of 'post-Marxist analysis' and at other times its adherents call themselves 'analytic Marxists.' What is important, I think, is to recognize that the people who make up this movement are leftists; this is not just a new variant of rightist attacks or a renewal of 'the god that failed' movement.

Yet there are those of us who continue to identify ourselves as socialists and as Marxists. Among us are those who have simply stuck their heads in the sand or who, like any religious zealot, are not bothered in their faith by facts. Those of us who think we do not fall in either of these categories have an obligation, to ourselves as well as to the broader community, to explain why we are still socialists and Marxists after all this.

The unsatisfactory responses

There are numerous unsatisfactory responses that we have provided to the developments of the 1980s. I think that if we are ever going to develop a satisfactory rationale for our position, it is first necessary to clear these weak (or wrong) arguments out of the way. Let me consider a few important examples:

1. The Soviet Union (or China, or Poland) never was socialist anyway. Many of us have been clear all along that what was going on in those countries was contrary to the goals of Marxists and socialists, and their crises should bring us a sense of satisfaction not a sense of defeat.

This response, however, ignores the fact that the great majority of the people in the United States – and, indeed, in the world – identify these countries as socialist and Marxist. For them, if not for us, the crisis in the USSR, the rise of the opposition in Poland, the increasing importance of the market in Hungary, and the repression in China are all signs of the failure of socialism. We are tarred with the same brush, our protestations to the contrary notwithstanding.

Furthermore, at the very least, experiences in these countries certainly do demonstrate the difficulty of trying to organize economic life in a highly centralized manner without recourse to the market as a coordinating mechanism. In a democratic social and political environment, there may be hope for planning. But the idea – held by many of us – that economic planning is a technically simple exercise, well, that is an idea whose time has passed. Also, these experiences certainly show that doing away with the capitalist markets as the mechanism of income distribution and establishing a more equal distribution of income is insufficient to assure a decent, democratic political structure. And without a democratic political structure, it is unlikely that income equality can be maintained.

The real issue here, however, is that, regardless of how we describe the social systems in this group of countries – William Hinton's use of the fascist label for the Chinese leadership may be quite reasonable[2] – we have to face up to the fact that they were created by people who embraced Marxism and socialism. It was, moreover, generally not a cynical or opportunistic embrace, as, for example, is the case when our own officials claim to be democrats and supporters of human rights. Lenin, Mao, and the others were as much Marxists and socialists in their beliefs as are any of us. So if we deny – as I would – that their efforts have led to something that should be called 'socialist' we are only left with the difficult question: why is it that our efforts will lead to something better?

2. The long expansion in the United States cannot be counted as a success for capitalism. Growth in the Reagan-Bush era has been slow growth and it has been devastating for people's well being, as income inequality has substantially increased. Moreover, the success of capitalism cannot be measured by the experience of a single country, since each country is tied in as part of an international system. Internationally, the crisis of capitalism in the 1980s matches in degree that in Eastern Europe; consider, for example, the devastation of living standards in much of the third world. Finally, the expansion is very precarious, built as it is on a mountain of debt, and the day of reckoning will surely come.

All of this is true and important, but it doesn't solve the problem. Part of the problem lies with popular consciousness in the United States, and that popular consciousness is a piece of the reality we must face. Also, we must own up to the fact that, while we may be able to explain the length of the expansion after the fact, very few of us expected it to last this long. We have, as the joke goes, predicted eleven of the last five recessions.

As to the devastating impact of the expansion on people both within the United States and in the third world, while this fits well with Marxist analysis, it raises another problem. Why is there so little resistance? Marxism, after all, does not just say that the lot of the masses will grow worse; it also says that the masses will do something about it. In the United States, while Marxists may take some intellectual satisfaction in the fact that things are getting worse (please don't miss the irony!), the lack of any growing opposition – indeed, there is what one might call an acquiescence by much of the labour movement – hardly gives any support to our analyses or our politics.

I do think capitalism is in a mess, that it is going through a crisis, and that we need to explain this to whomever will listen. But the problems for Marxism are still there.

3. Recent developments among left intellectuals should not be taken as a serious challenge to Marxism. These people are simply responding to the rewards of academia. They are taking the anti-Marxist course because in doing so they gain promotions, the acceptance and praise of their bourgeois colleagues, grants, and prestige.

This explanation may be true in particular cases (though I have no individual in mind when I say this), but it simply begs a new set of questions: why have we been failing in our efforts to sustain a Marxist culture that would provide a basis for people to resist the attractions of academic success? What happens to a Marxism that is so thoroughly enmeshed within and dependent upon academia?

Furthermore, regardless of why left intellectuals challenge Marxism, their challenges raise important questions about aspects of the Marxist paradigm. Many of us do not deny the validity of some of their criticisms, but at the same time we have not reconstructed Marxism in a way which would obviate those criticisms. In any case, why is it that many people have taken these criticisms, added them together, and found Marxism wanting? While others of us stick with Marxism in spite of its problems?

Self-criticism

Having rejected these unsatisfactory responses to the current crisis of socialism and Marxism, I want to present what I think are some elements of a better response. An effective defence of Marxism rests on its positive elements, the reasons why it provides us with an effective way to understand what is going on in the world and thus gives us a foundation for political work. An effective defence of Marxism also rests on a recognition of its limits. So to begin with,

I think we had better approach the matter with an attitude of self-criticisms. We will not be a in a position to bring ourselves out of this crisis unless we recognize our own weaknesses.

For example, we – and here I mean virtually all currents on the left in the US – have not developed a reasonable response to the development of Communism. We have been apologists; we have been rabid anti-Communists; we have been ostriches; and we have committed many other sins. But we have not done the job.

Or on the question of the US economy, we have almost universally underestimated the capacity of capitalism in this country to maintain itself. We have seen recession, if not depression, around every corner. Focusing our attention on the system's failures and its degradation of the lives of millions, we have generally ignored or obscured the extent to which others – and certainly not just capitalists – have attained tremendous material gains. With each new economic upsurge and with each political triumph of conservative forces, we are left gaping.

We have also ignored many weaknesses in Marxist theory. In particular, we often try to maintain that the lack of democracy in the Communist countries has nothing to do with Marxism. One line of argument that supports this separation of Marxism from the evils that have been committed in its name begins with the claim that in the writings of Marx – and, for that matter, also in the writings of Lenin – there are repeated calls for more democratic processes, for better representative systems, and for extensions of direct democracy.[3] This is all very well, but with Marxism, as with any other set of ideas, we need to go beyond the explicit statements on democracy and attempt to figure out the relation between the whole theory, the whole set of ideas, and democratic practices. Moreover, Marxism is something bigger than Marx, and bigger than Marx and Lenin. Reference to good ideas contained in the classics will no more absolve Marxism of its sins than reference to the Bible will wipe away the Inquisition.

A more substantive, historical defence of Marxism in light of the experience in Communist countries lies in the fact that Marxist movements have come to power in parts of the world which have been economically underdeveloped. This underdevelopment has, furthermore, been associated with political backwardness – a lack of capitalist democracy, a lack of parliamentary forms, and a lack of legal oppositional activity. Under these circumstances, the struggle for power – for example, in the Soviet Union – was organized in a highly centralized manner that did not allow the development of democratic experience within the struggle. When Marxists then did attain state power, the conditions of underdevelopment led them to give primary attention to production. Lacking a political movement with well-developed democratic experiences, production needs led to a top-down system of economic organization and a thorough erosion of the possibilities for building democracy – which meant, of course, a thorough erosion of the possibilities for building socialism. (This argument can be elaborated by reference to the hostility of the imperialist powers. Ironically, if the 'imperialist threat' argument is made well, I think it undermines rather than supports Marxist movements. If socialist movements are forced to resort to dictatorial practices antithetical to socialism when faced with an imperialist threat, then I see no alternative to the conclusion that socialist movements will always end up being antithetical to socialism! For the imperialist threat will always be present – or at least until socialism is a world-wide system.)

The historical argument has a great deal of legitimacy. However, historical conditions are not the whole story; if they were there would be little point in conscious political action. The historical conditions can make the situation more or less favourable, but our own political practice has a lot to do with how things turn out. Consequently, we need to look more thoroughly at our Marxism – the set of ideas which forms the basis for our political practice – and see how it encourages or hinders the achievement of our goals.

As examples of what I mean, I want to point out two flaws in Marxism, not fatal flaws but factors that can lead us to work contrary to our goal of expanding democracy. One of the central contributions of Marxism, as I shall argue below, lies in its focus on the conflict between workers and capitalists that emanates from the 'point of production.' The particular Marxist understanding of class relations based in production has given coherence and force to anti-capitalist struggles. At the same time – and this is the first of my two flaws – it has created a tendency for Marxists to view all other social conflicts as theoretically secondary and practically of lesser importance than worker-capitalist struggles.

As a result, Marxists have often viewed the organization of the state, whether in capitalist or post-revolutionary societies, as a subsidiary issue. In the one case, there is a tendency to believe that if capitalists are in control of production, political procedures – bourgeois democratic rights in particular – cannot be very meaningful. In the other case, if workers are in control, then there is little need to worry about political procedures. Of course when the tendency is stated in such bald terms, few Marxists would subscribe, and many would simply dismiss such beliefs as perversions of Marxism. The problem is that Marxism has regularly given rise to such 'perversions,' and I think we can see their origin in the extreme emphasis we have given to the 'point of production.'

Seeing everything in terms of worker-capitalist conflict around production has also limited Marxists' ability to contribute to struggles which have a multi-dimensional foundation. Part of the reason why Marxists have often relegated issues of feminism and race to an auxiliary position has been that so many of us are white males. Yet another reason lies in our theory, which identifies the central issue in peoples' lives as their class position, defined by their role in production – and for us, like almost everyone else, until very recently 'production' has not meant production in the home. In post-revolutionary societies and in revolutionary movements in capitalist societies, women and racial minorities have often been told to wait while the 'main struggle' around production solves everybody's problems.

The extreme emphasis on class and the point of production affects more than our views on race and gender. When people – who are, to be sure, mostly workers – are engaged in struggles away from the point of production, Marxism has not had much to offer. The needs of people as consumers has had little role in our analysis. Only recently have Marxists begun to address environmental concerns. It is widely perceived that people on the left must decide whether they believe class struggles are paramount or whether the struggles of new social movements are paramount. Marxism has, unfortunately, contributed to this perception, or misperception, by building a theory with a uni-dimensional focus.

A second flaw, or weakness, in Marxism that I want to point out derives from the fact that Marxism, true to its 19th century roots, has always seen the advances of production as the well-spring of human progress. Whatever its faults, capitalism has been, according to Marxism, a historically progressive system because it has revolutionized the forces of production, advanced our control over our environment, and created the potential for human freedom. This is all very well. But when we transfer our admiration for the accomplishments of capitalist history into policy prescriptions we run into trouble. As we have subordinated other struggles to class struggles, we tend to subordinate other avenues of progress to progress in production.

Within advanced capitalist societies, we often promote, or at least accept, a politics that demands a continual expansion of production. In the advanced countries, for example, we push the worthy demand of full employment and generally support Keynesian expansionary policies over conservative efforts to 'restrict inflation.' In the poor regions of the world, we attack capitalism for inhibiting productive advances, and we call for more rapid economic growth. The programmes we advocate have direct benefits, and they also strengthen workers as a class in struggles with capital. Yet when we adopt this 'productionist' politics, we generally fail to confront the bourgeois rallying cry that 'more is better', and we allow distributional issues and other goals to be pushed aside.

When Marxist forces have taken power in post-revolutionary situations, they have invariably placed central emphasis on the expansion of production. Of course these situations have always been ones in which capitalism had failed to accomplish its historic task, and socialists seemed to have had little choice but to follow a path of socialist accumulation. However successful this socialist accumulation has been, it has generally resulted in the subordination of other socialist goals, such as equality, the liberation of women and the creation of a humane work environment.

The real difficulty is that Marxists should be aware that economic welfare does not lie in attaining more and more products. As long as we live in a world of great inequality, we will invariably be frustrated in our efforts to advance through expanding the output of goods and services. 'Our needs and enjoyments,' Marx pointed out, 'spring from society; we measure them, therefore, by society and not by the objects of their satisfaction. Because they are of a social nature, they are of a relative nature.'[4] The experiences of the last 200 years – in post-revolutionary and capitalist societies – underscore the point, making it clear that more and more products do not meet our 'needs and enjoyments.' Yet, Marxism has been plagued by 'productionism' for decades.

I think Marxists'productionism and our uni-dimensional emphasis on class struggle at the point of production have contributed to the erosion of democracy in post-revolutionary societies and have limited the progress of revolutionary movements in capitalist societies. Of course neither leads in some automatic way to anti-democratic, dictatorial practices. Stalinism – in either its bloody form or its more common authoritarian and bureaucratic form – is not the necessary outcome of Marxism. It will help us avoid Stalinism, however, if we bring the flaws of our analysis to the fore and try to do something about them. We have, to be sure, moved far from the dogmatic era when Stalinism dominated so much left thought, but we still have a long way to go. I am just reminding us all that we can only move forward after we recognize the limits of what we have done and then approach things with a good deal of humility.

The strengths of Marxism
In order to move forward, we need to spend some time figuring out just what we mean by Marxism, just what it is we are defending. Marxism involves both a political commitment and an analytic approach that is connected to the political commitment. Together they comprise what is, somewhat grandly, referred to as a 'world view.' While I like the concept of a 'world view' because it implies a holistic approach to things, at the same time we should reject the idea that Marxism is 'totalistic,' that it provides an answer to everything. If, for example, we try to move from Marxist analysis to an understanding of sexuality, we will probably not get very far. (Certainly one aspect of self-criticism by Marxists should be a delineation of the limits of what we can do with our Marxism.)

Political Commitment
I think we should start by setting out the political commitment component of Marxism. When we are in a 'scientific' mode, we like to claim that our politics flows from our analysis, from our understanding of history. In fact, there is a dialectic between our political commitment and our analysis, and, if we are to be frank, we will recognize that, at least in part, we came to our analysis as a means to justify and support our political position. There is nothing wrong with this, but it is useful to recognize it.

In the modern history of capitalism, a commitment to Marxism has meant a commitment to serious opposition. By and large other forms of radical opposition have been either marginalized (even more than Marxism), or have been easily coopted and absorbed, or both. As Marxists we are committed to a rejection of capitalism, 'root and branch.' We do not seek to fix up the system; we seek to replace it with something different.

By emphasizing the oppositional stance of Marxism, I do not want to revive the stale revolution-versus-reform discussion. I never viewed that discussion as particularly useful, because in most of the instances where we in the United States are confronted with practical political options the revolution-reform choice is irrelevant. Revolution is not on the immediate agenda. The problem therefore is how do we push for reforms and what reforms do we push for that will challenge the system, lay the groundwork for structural change, bring about some desirable immediate gains, and also put us in a better position at a time when revolution – a fundamental and thorough-going change in the nature of our social system – becomes a realistic possibility.[5]

So how do you tell the difference in terms of commitment between the Marxists and others who also want change? How do you tell that the Marxists are the 'serious opposition?' Well, often in the short run you can't tell. There is no neat dividing line between 'reformist reforms' and 'revolutionary reforms.' But over the long run, it is a question of how we position ourselves in relation to society's institutional structures. A Marxist opposition does not ask simply the questions: will this reform make things better? will it improve people's lives? Instead, a Marxist opposition, having identified various reforms that might make people's lives better, goes on to ask: which of these reforms will provide a basis for further change? which challenges, in some way, how the system normally works? which provides more people with power to continue changes in the future? For example, consider the matter of environmental destruction. A programme for cleaning up rivers and waste dumps and having business pay for the clean-up is certainly a reform that would improve people's lives. But a Marxist programme would focus at least as much on prevention as on clean-up and payment, and would stress that controls on business decisions about investment and production are the most effective method of prevention. Of course, public control on these business decisions is a direct challenge to the prerogatives of capital.

Moreover, in addition to the content of reforms, it matters how reforms are accomplished. A Marxist way of doing things is one that relies primarily upon mass mobilization and popular organization, instead of working through 'existing channels.' When, for example, the Sierra Club hires skilled lobbyists to persuade Congress to pass laws limiting air and water pollution, they may achieve some desirable results. When, however, those same results are obtained by effective community organization and popular protests, they have a larger impact. Such activity teaches the participants to rely on their own power, and it gives them organizational experience and democratic practice. This sort of strong oppositional stance, this Marxist way of doing things empowers people for further change.

Having identified Marxism with an oppositional stance, I must add that, while this is the case in the United States and much of the rest of the world, it is certainly not the case in those countries where Marxism has been adopted as official ideology. In calling ourselves Marxists we run the risk of establishing a barrier between ourselves and people who are our allies in many other places. I think it is a risk we should take, but we should not ignore it.

Analytic Approach

The other part of the Marxist world view is our analytic approach, our understanding of the world that provides a basis for our politics. I will not attempt to distill *the* essential features of Marxism. I suspect that for different people, finding themselves in different situations and with different primary concerns, the essential features of Marxism may differ. I do want to explain some of the ideas that I have found important to my own Marxist analysis. For me, working as an economist, it has involved three central concepts: the labour theory of value; the theory of accumulation; and theory of crisis. However, the reader will discover that the meanings I attach to each of these concepts is not universally accepted among Marxists!

The labour theory of value is an explanation of the social relations that emerge from the capitalist production process. Its primary usefulness in my view is as a *qualitative* theory, as a description of the production process – the value creation process – that goes a long way in helping us understand the basic conflict of capitalist society. The crux of the theory is that workers enter into employment by selling their capacity to work, their labour power, to the capitalists. The capitalists are then faced with the problem of getting the maximum amount of work done, labour, out of this labour power. Moreover, having bought the labour power, the capitalists have the formal right to control and direct it as they see fit. Because the capitalists own what the labourers produce, they are able to make a profit insofar as they are able to get labour to produce a value that exceeds the wage.

This view of the capitalist production process implies that workers and capitalists are necessarily in conflict with one another over two issues, control of the work process and the distribution of income. While real wages may rise as the system grows – the basis for the claim that workers share an interest in the expansion of capitalism – the conflict over control and distribution cannot be eliminated as long as one group of people is employed for wages by another group. The significance of this conclusion depends on the point that control over one's work and equality of income distribution are very important factors affecting people's economic welfare. I will not try to establish this point here, but its essential role in the Marxist argument is worth noting.[6]

The labour theory of value, then, leads to the conclusion that a fundamental conflict between workers and capitalists is endemic to capitalism. That conflict may be alleviated, but it cannot be eliminated within the confines of capitalism. If all we got from the theory were this conclusion, I think it would be important. It would provide us with a well-reasoned foundation for anti-capitalist struggle, a strong ideological basis for our oppositional activity. But in fact we get a lot more from the labour theory of value.

The Marxist view of work has often been dismissed with the claim that it applies only to the harsh conditions of an early era of capitalist development. It involves, according to the criticism, a 'galley slave' view of work and also fails to see the changing living standards that have affected so many workers in today's world. It would be folly to claim that Marxists have been innocent of over-statement and over-simplification in our rhetorical attacks on capitalist work. However, the labour theory of value should lead us away from such errors, for it does not focus on the absolute level of workers' incomes and the degree of physical hardship that they face. In giving emphasis to the control of work and the question of income distribution, the theory provides a firmer basis for our politics. (Still, our rhetorical flourishes have some basis in reality. Throughout the third world – certainly a part of the modern capitalist system – as well as within the richest centres of the wealthiest countries, absolute poverty and physically degrading work are widespread.)

The labour theory of value also gives us an understanding of production that is very useful in developing the case for socialism because it gives us a basis to reject the notion that capitalism has provided the most productive technologies. Adversaries of socialism are fond of the argument that capitalism has already provided us with the best – that is, most productive – way of doing things. So, they claim, to take authority away from capitalists and place it in the hands of workers would either make no difference in how things were done, or it would make a difference only by leading to less productive technology. Yet in the Marxist view, the choice of technology – the way things are produced – is not a technical choice; it is a social choice, a product of social struggle between capitalists and workers. Capitalists choose technologies that maintain their control of the production process and therefore their profits, rather than technologies that are most productive. One can think of myriad examples: assembly lines where team production would yield higher output; computers used primarily to audit workers' activity instead of being used to enhance their production; work stations designed to separate workers from one another; and on and on. We do not need the labour theory of value to see that these technologies are poor ones, but the labour theory of value does give us a firmer foundation for our arguments against the ideologues of capitalism.[7]

Finally, the labour theory of value is politically useful because it treats ordinary people as actors in economic life, rather than simply as objects. It sees the production process as an arena of conflict, with workers, organized and individually, affecting the course of economic decisions. Technology, prices, the distribution of income, profits, and the overall level of output

– all these factors not only impinge on workers' lives, but they are also determined by workers' struggles. Socialists of all types have emphasized the way that workers are victims of capitalism, but Marxism stands out because it also emphasizes that workers are actors in creating their own history. This way of looking at things can provide an injection of power to workers' struggles.

The theory of accumulation is a second Marxist pillar in building an understanding of what's going on in the world. One of the distinguishing features of capitalism is its tremendous dynamism, its tremendous capacity for growth and change. The theory of accumulation explains this dynamism as a product of the force of competitive markets. As society increasingly becomes organized under competitive conditions, as pre-capitalist legal constraints and protections for certain groups are reduced, individual capitalists are caught in a continuing battle to cut costs in order to survive. To cut costs, they must find new technologies, and, more often than not, new technologies can be effective only if firms grow. Consequently, the competitive struggle to survive becomes a growth imperative; in order to take advantage of economies of scale and thus reduce costs, firms must become larger and larger.[8]

Although the growth imperative derives from very practical considerations, it becomes an ideological force that drives the expansion of both firms and the entire system. Marx expressed this in his famous: 'Accumulate, accumulate! That is Moses and the prophets!' Growth defines the 'soul' of capitalism, and, while individual firms may provide exceptions, neither capitalist firms in general nor the capitalist system can 'choose' not to grow.

In leading to the conclusion that continual expansion is an essential feature of capitalism, the theory of accumulation carries powerful political implications. For when we identify various phenomena as products of expansion, we are in effect identifying those phenomena as intrinsic to capitalism. Capitalism is not an immutable system and expressions of accumulation may be attenuated through political action, but those phenomena which are intrinsic to the system will continually re-emerge while the system remains intact. Consider some examples:

*One of the major routes for firms' expansion is international expansion, a constant search for new markets and new resources. International expansion carries with it an extension of economic and political control, both directly by the firms and by the nation states which they rely upon in pursuit of their interests. This extension of control and the conflicts that come with it are what we call imperialism. The theory of accumulation thus ties imperialism and its multiple acts of military aggression to the fundamental nature of capitalism. The lesson is that a thorough anti-imperialist politics is necessarily also an anti-capitalist politics.[9]

Understanding the international operations of capitalism as part of the accumulation process, we also have a basis on which to interpret the recurring disorder of the world economy. This disorder has current expression in the so-called debt crisis of the third world, the huge build-up of the US foreign debt, and the extremely large US trade deficits. Each of these phenomena has been precipitated by a particular set of events (e.g., oil price increases in the 1970s) and policies (e.g., the US government's tight money strategy of the 1979–82 period). But a political response that focused on these immediate factors and did not challenge the structures of capitalist accumulation would neither resolve the disorder nor remove the huge burdens it places upon millions of people.[10]

Similar to the politics of anti-imperialism, the politics of environmental protection, to be effective, is also anti-capitalist. The capitalist growth imperative leads firms to devour the world's resources without taking account of the non-market, social costs of their actions. Moreover, to expand their profits, firms will always seek to have society bear as large a share as possible of their production costs; in practice, this means dumping sludge into rivers, smoke into the air, and laying barren once fertile lands. These actions take place not because capitalists are especially malicious people, who choose waste and spoilage for the environment. They are, by and large, normal people who are compelled to behave this way in order to compete; in the context of accumulation, they have no choice.[11]

Accumulation has also driven the great changes that have taken place in the economic activities of women during the last century. As the successful expansion of capitalism has created a 'universal market,' in which products and services traditionally supplied through women's labour in the home are produced and sold for profit, women have simultaneously been pushed out of the home and pulled into wage employment. The multitude of changes in the family and in public social services that have come as the consequence are not simply the result of individual 'choices' by women or policy makers; they are the product of the larger social process of accumulation. The theory of accumulation, then, provides a useful basis for building a politics that deals with the changes in the family and government's provision of social services, a politics that identifies the limits and impacts of various reforms and their relation to the general operation of capitalism.

Most generally, the theory of accumulation provides a basis for politics because in defining the foundation of capitalist expansion it helps us see the limits of reform within the confines of the system. It leads to an anti-capitalist politics because it demonstrates that the particular social disorders that motivate popular protest are outgrowths of the way capitalism works; and in particular circumstances, it helps us see how our demands can be formulated in a way that challenges the way capitalism works.

The theory of crisis is also valuable because of its implications for our politics. It has its usefulness largely in the realm of ideology, strengthening oppositional politics by demonstrating the fundamentally irrational nature of capitalism.

The theory of crisis takes several forms, and different people give emphasis to different mechanisms in their explanations of why capitalism repeatedly disrupts itself. Some argue that, especially in the era of monopoly capitalism, there is a powerful tendency for the system's productive capacity to outstrip society's consumptive capacity, and thus the output cannot be profitably sold. Others stress that overproduction leads to a tightening of labour markets and a resulting wage squeeze on profits. Still others emphasize the classical argument that the changing composition of capital, the continual substitution of machinery for direct labour power in production, creates a tendency for the rate of profit to fail. Regardless of which tack one takes, however, the force of all of these arguments is to draw attention to capitalism's self-contradictory nature.

Defenders of the system do not deny that periodically capitalism suffers depressions and inflations, but they argue that these disruptions are not intrinsic to the system itself. Instead they are explained by 'outside events,' 'bad luck,' and 'poor policy.' The impact of these arguments is to generate a popular ideology favourable to the system, leading people to think that, no matter how severe their economic problems, capitalism itself is not at fault and should not be tampered with. Marxist crisis theory provides a direct challenge to this sort of apologia for capitalism, locating the source of disruptions within the system itself. Capitalism runs into trouble precisely because of its own success, its success in expanding production which, by one mechanism or another, disrupts the flow of profits. The troubles cannot be eliminated by making the system work better, but only by changing the system.

The weakness in many presentations of Marxist crisis theory is that we often go beyond developing this politically useful ideological argument and attempt to predict systemic demise, or at least severe disruption. Capitalism still stands, however, and the severe disruptions occur much less frequently than we predict – obvious facts, it would seem, but often ignored by many of us.

Yet the theory does have an additional usefulness. The contradictions and social conflicts which it identifies still operate, and, while they may not set the system on its ear, they do force change and adjustment. Figuring out the direction of this change and adjustment and pointing out the costs it imposes upon society is an important part of our political work. For example, the growing role of the state has been a central issue of political controversy in the United States over the last two decades. Marxists are well situated to affect this controversy because crisis theory provides us with the beginnings of a coherent explanation of the state's expansion. It has come as a response to the system's contradictions; the state has intervened in economic affairs to avert disruptions. In doing so, however, the state has created new problems which appear to be problems of the state itself, but, by the Marxist argument, have their origin in the way the capitalist economy operates. Moreover, these new problems can be extremely costly, as witness the savings and loan fiasco currently underway in the United States and the international debt and trade problems I alluded to above, to say nothing of four decades of large scale Keynesian stimulation provided by military spending.

Paying attention to our Marxism

In attempting to pull Marxism out of its current difficulties and move forward in the struggle for socialism, we should pay some attention to our Marxism. At the roots of every component of Marxist analysis is a historical approach to social issues, an understanding of current events as a product of long term changes and conflicts. Marxist theory is not a set of abstractions with its own life, but a way of generalizing about historical processes. To use Paul Sweezy's phrase, we should view 'the present as history.'[12]

Often we set ourselves outside of history. With regard to both the situation in post-revolutionary societies and developments in the capitalist world, we often look for things to happen quickly. Yet a Marxist historical view should show us that, the excitement and sharp breaks of revolutionary moments notwithstanding, major social changes, revolutionary changes, do not take place quickly. A revolution, after all, is not a military seizure of power – though it will generally involve a seizure of power at some point. Instead, it is a long historical process of change. Paying attention to our Marxism means, first of all, that we recognize that the struggle for socialism is a long haul.

At the same time, we should not allow our Marxism to transform us into cynics who would say: oh, well, things take a long time to happen so we should not expect anything good in our lifetimes; we'll just have to wait a few centuries for a decent society. Aside from the fact that this attitude is depressing, the problem with such cynicism is that, regardless of how long it takes, we are going to get to a 'decent society' only if we continually engage in struggles to change things. Furthermore, there is really no such thing as an ultimate 'decent society.' The point is to keep pushing, to change things and make life now as decent as possible. By fully recognizing the limits on what we can achieve, by accepting the necessity of a long haul, we will avoid disillusionment and be more successful.

Paying attention to our Marxism and understanding the present as history also means that we should give a good deal of attention to the connection between the way we shape the struggle for socialism and the socialism we expect to attain. In particular, what can we do in building a socialist movement to assure that our 'victory' will not be an authoritarian, repressive perversion of socialism?

To begin with, it will help to devote some effort to elaborating our goal, to figuring out what we mean by 'socialism.' It is rather difficult to get someplace if you do not know where you want to go! My own view of socialism, as I would hope is evident from much of what I have said above, begins with democracy. Democracy certainly includes formal procedures, contested elections, rights of opposition, civil liberties. Yet it must also include mechanisms for effective empowerment of people, mechanisms that encourage and assure their participation because they know that participation will make a difference. At the very least this means social ownership (which may include state ownership, but would not be only state ownership) of productive facilities. It also means placing a major stress on equality and people's control over their own work, for, while these are desirable goals in themselves, they are also a means to popular empowerment.

These generalizations may be useful, but they are of course little more than platitudes. They only begin the discussion of the really difficult issues, such as how the roles of market and planning would be balanced in a socialist future. The principle of democracy precludes the option of allowing our lives to be dominated by either markets or highly centralized, and thus necessarily bureaucratic, planning. Yet markets of some sort are almost surely necessary as mechanisms of coordination in a complex economy. And planning, in the sense of employing conscious human choice as the controlling principle in our economic lives, is essential. There is, in any case, a great deal of useful discussion that can take place on these issues. Marxists have often argued that it is impossible to construct a blue print for the future, but that is no excuse for ignoring the question of where we are going.

Even an incomplete statement of goals helps us recognize some of the ways we should organize ourselves right now. If we want to build a democratic social system, a meaningful socialism, we had better build a movement that leads in that direction. Much of the left has recognized this and has talked a lot about internal democracy, the legitimacy of multiple struggles, equality, participation, education through struggle, and so on. But I doubt I am wasting paper in reiterating the point.

There are, moveover, some ways that we can reinforce the point in our practice. I have said that 'a Marxist way of doing things' involves placing emphasis on accomplishing our immediate goals through the popular struggle of a mass movement. Beyond our immediate goals of attaining structural reforms ('revolutionary reforms' that challenge capitalist domination), 'a Marxist way of doing things' also forces us to build the right kind of movement. For the most effective way to build the popular struggle of a mass movement is through internal democracy and respect for the interests of many groups.

It will also help if we make some adjustments in our ideas; we need to straighten out our Marxism. Overcoming the productionism and uni-dimensional focus on class struggle at the point of production would be good places to start, and there are certainly other aspects of Marxism that are in need of amendment. Correcting our ideas is a good thing in itself, but its true importance lies in the way it affects our practice. It should help us build the kind of movement we need to build the kind of socialism we need.

NOTES

1. This essay is based on a talk I gave at the annual meeting of the Union for Radical Political Economics (URPE), August 27th, 1989, Sandwich, Massachusetts. My ideas benefited a great deal from exchanges on the Progressive Economists' Network, an electronic mail network, and, in particular, from reactions by Tom Weisskopf, Michael Lebowitz and Michael Perleman.
2. Hinton, author of the famous *Fanshen: A Documentary of Revolution in a Chinese Village* (New York: Monthly Review Press, 1966) and several other books on China, was in Peking at the time of the Tiananmen massacre. He made his comment about the fascist character of the regime in a speech at the URPE conference referred to in the previous note.
3. Ralph Miliband, 'Reflections on the Crisis of the Communist Regimes,' *New Left Review*, No. 177, Sept.–Oct. 1989, presents this line of argument. At the same time, he very usefully calls attention to the problem, which I shall take up shortly, regarding Marxism's heavy emphasis on struggle at the point of production.
4. From *Wage Labour and Capital*, as published in Karl Marx, *Selected Works*, In Two Volumes, Prepared by the Marx-Engels-Lenin Institute, Moscow, Under the Editorship of V. Adoratsky (New York: International Publishers, n.d., *circa* 1936), vol. I, p. 269.
5. The formulation here and in the following paragraph originated, for me, in André Gorz, *Strategy for Labor: A Radical Proposal* (Boston, Beacon Press, 1967); see especially the 'Introduction.' Gorz uses the terms 'reformist reform' and 'non-reformist reform' and writes: 'A reformist reform is one which subordinates its objectives to the criteria of rationality and practicability of a given system and policy. Reformism rejects those objectives and demands – however deep the need for them – which are incompatible with the preservation of the system. . .[A] struggle for non-reformist reforms – for anti-capitalist reforms – is one which does not base its validity and its right to exist on capitalist needs, criteria, and rationale. A non-reformist reform is determined not in terms of what can be, but what should be. And finally, it bases the possibility of attaining its objective on the implementation of fundamental political and economic changes.' (pp. 7–8)
6. The issues of control of work and of income distribution are often seen as goals by socialists. What I want to stress, however, is the importance of these factors in relation to the analytics of the labour theory of value and hence in relation to our understanding of fundamental conflicts in capitalist society. Harry Braverman's *Labour and Monopoly Capital* (New York: Monthly Review Press, 1974) and other modern analyses of the labour process integrate the control issue effectively into general analysis. The role of income distribution in Marxist analysis has, I think, received less attention. I find the discussion in Marx's *Wage Labor and Capital* on this point to be especially useful, and the point is of course a key in Marx's theory of immiseration. Once we do recognize the importance of these two factors – as opposed to the mainstream concept that people increase their economic welfare by obtaining a higher absolute level of goods and services – we not only obtain a better understanding of conflicts in capitalist society. Perhaps we also get a better idea of how to structure a socialist society
7. This argument derives from Braverman's book and also from Stephen Marglin, 'What Do Bosses Do? The Origins and Functions of Hierarchy in Capitalist

Production,' *Review of Radical Political Economy*, Summer 1974, and Richard Edwards, *Contested Terrain: The Transformation of the Workplace in the Twentieth Century* (New York: Basic Books, 1979). Of course, the most profitable technology might coincide with the most productive; the point is that the two are not necessarily the same.

8. Economies of scale in production – a situation where a larger amount of output distributes, for example, the fixed cost of machinery over a larger number of units – are easy to understand. Yet they are only the beginning of the story. Economies of scale are also important in research and development, marketing and distribution, finance, and political influence.

9. It should go without saying, but unfortunately does require saying, that when I argue that imperialism has roots in the nature of capitalism I am not denying that imperialism – in the sense of international domination by powerful nations over weaker nations – can have and has had other roots as well. Here, as with many other ills, the elimination of capitalism may be necessary to achieve a cure, but it is not sufficient.

10. See Arthur MacEwan, *Debt and Disorder: International Economic Instability and U.S. Imperial Decline* (New York: Monthly Review Press, 1990) and various essays in Arthur MacEwan and William K. Tabb, eds., *Instability and Change in the World Economy* (New York: Monthly Review Press, 1989).

11. As I have noted above, flying the banner of socialism, post-revolutionary societies have embraced 'productionism' and adopted the growth imperative with which capitalism has presented them. The consequences for the environment have been disastrous. For socialism, however, there is the possibility of choice about growth, and therefore at least a possibility of avoiding environmental disaster.

12. See Paul M. Sweezy, *The Present as History: Essays and Reviews on Capitalism and Socialism* (New York: Monthly Review Press, 1953). Concerning the title of his book, Sweezy writes in the preface: 'The title is not an attempt to define the subject matter but rather to suggest the angle of vision from which the various pieces were written. Everyone knows that the present will some day be history. I believe that the most important task of the social scientist is to try to comprehend it as history now, while it is still the present and while we still have the power to influence its shape and outcome.'

EULOGY BESIDE AN EMPTY GRAVE: REFLECTIONS ON THE FUTURE OF SOCIALISM

RICHARD LEVINS

The starting point for examinining the present situation is the acknowledgement that we – all who struggle for a humane, cooperative and supportive society – have suffered a defeat of immense proportions. I do not refer here to the toppling of discredited governments in eastern Europe. That merely ratifies a process that has been going on for decades. We see this defeat in:

*The failure to build an alternative world system that could confront imperialism and support the break away of third world countries. This leaves the world capitalist system with its uneven exchange, debt slavery, profit maximizing allocation of investment and dictation of economic policy within formally sovereign states as the only international economic system.

*The failure to demonstrate a clearly superior way of life, more democratic, rational, creative and fulfilling as well as more egalitarian than the society it replaced.

*The absence of an international movement with a strategy or perspective or even the goal of overthrowing capitalism. The defiant 'we'll bury you!' of the 1950's has become the whimper 'please, please take us in!' Half a century ago, my grandmother could assure me that my grandchildren would live in a socialist republic. It now seems unlikely.

*The replacement of bullshit Marxism by bullshit liberalism as the dominant discourse in the East, with the adoption of liberal vocabularies and hardline 18th century doctrines of private enterprise. This has been accompanied by the retreat from the bold goals of changing social relations, new ways of relating to work, the complete emancipation of women, the struggle against racism, the critique of science and religion.

*The squandering within a few years in power of the support of tens of millions of people, won by the heroism, sacrifice, dedication and ingenuity of millions of communist men and women. It is almost forgotten now that Communist–led resistance movements liberated Yugoslavia and Albania from the Nazi occupation without the help of Soviet troops, that the Communists won the 1946 elections in Czechoslovakia, that communist

Giorgi Dimitrov was the most popular political leader in Bulgaria after the Second World War and that the Chinese revolution was the victory of the overwhelming majority of the peasants and workers.

This leaves us, those of us who do not believe that exploitation is either inevitable or rational or that greed is the highest organizing principle for social relations, in the role of a rearguard, defending the gains of 150 years of struggle, acknowledging the reality of the defeat and evaluating the reasons for it, regrouping and preparing for the second wave of revolutionary upsurge. It is an agenda of years and decades.

In order to understand the present situation we have to be able to look at it at several different magnifications. The lowest magnification, like looking through the wrong end of a telescope, sees a world historic scale of centuries. We do not see a grand march through the classic modes of production from lower to higher but a curious zigzag. We would see incipient capitalisms emerge and subside time and again: Bohemia under the Taborites during the Reformation, Egypt under Mohammed Ali in the 19th century, pre-British Bengal. We would see the rebirth of feudalism in 16th century Poland and of capitalism in late 20th century Poland.

When detail is lost we see the rise and fall of social systems, the birth of capitalism and imperialism, the industrial revolution and modern science, the development of bourgeois law and consciousness until they rise to the rank of common sense, the imposition of slavery and the invention of racism, the attempts to resist capitalism from behind or to overthrow it from in front. On this scale, the four internationals and the labour movement are seen not distinctly but as one massive movement that has ebbed and flowed over the last two hundred years. The victories and defeats are shared by all of us. Then the often bitter conflicts among revolutionaries are barely visible as passing aspects of social evolution and Emma Goldman and Rosa Luxemburg are sisters.

One analogy for the present time is the Europe of 1814. The French revolution, long since lapsed into the Napoleonic empire, had nevertheless continued to overturn feudal aristocratic ways and even inspired rebellions such as the Haitian Revolution that it tried to suppress. The Henry Kissinger of the time, the Austrian Metternich, organized monarchical Europe to celebrate the end of the Revolution and restore stability. But it was not the Bourgeois Revolution that fell at Waterloo, only Napoleon. Fifteen years later the aristocracy was out of power again in France, and 34 years later the new wave of a more radical revolutionary upsurge was shaking the foundations of European privilege.

At an intermediate magnification we see changing class configurations and their political expressions in different countries, the defeat of direct colonialism and the rise of neocolonialism to offset that defeat on a world scale (with important exceptions such as Puerto Rico and the West Bank and Gaza where direct colonial rule continues), the victories and defeats of particular revolutionary movements, the broad extension of formal political rights and of the rulers' skills at manipulating their exercise, the growing disparity between rich and poor countries, the similarities and differences among revolutionary societies and the rise of new emancipatory movements as political actors.

At high magnification we have to evaluate programmes of movements, parties and individuals. The blurred stream of history now comes apart. Interests and beliefs are seen in their expression as policies, and allies in the historical project meet as adversaries in the struggle to build the movement in accord with very different perceptions.

Each of these perspectives is necessary. We have to shift back and forth among them, but always being clear about what level of magnification we are working on.

In acknowledging the pervasiveness of this defeat we should not lose sight of the victories which had been won both by the socialist movements and by the first revolutionary societies. The socialist movement and the labour movement it inspired and helped to build established at least the elementary rights for the working class and moved the masses of the world to become actors in political life. This is a crowning achievement.

The first attempt to build socialism has been successful in some ways: the equitable allocation of scarcity, the rapid emergence from extreme poverty, the development of social consumption in health, education, cultural life; the rupture of some traditional forms of sexism and the achievement of more equitable participation by women in most occupations and in political life. It has reallocated resources in such a way as to reduce rather than increase the economic disparities among geographic regions. It initially unleashed great cultural creativity and mass participation in public life; and pioneered in raising issues such as the protection of nature, although all of these were aspirations which it could not follow through on systematically.

However it failed to overtake and surpass world capitalism economically on its own terms, providing more abundant consumer goods and services. This would not be a disaster in itself if the terms of the competition had been effectively challenged with alternative patterns of consumption and standards for validating people's lives as satisfactory and fulfilling. The relative equality (even with the privileges usurped by managers and leaders, these societies are far more egalitarian than capitalism), the priorities of social consumption in education, health, and culture, the absence of unemployment and cyclic crises, a commitment to a rational planned development based on examining human need as a whole, could be the basis for a viable set of alternative aspirations even in the face of lower production.

But the reorganization of consciousness and work relations which seems to be a prerequisite for realizing the economic potential of socialism was only partially and sporadically attempted. Where the regimes said to the workers, 'you work and we'll deliver consumption', they were setting themselves up for defeat because they accepted the capitalist rules. While they delivered, they could win acquiescence despite their other failings but once they could not, they had lost all justification. And if they thought about the long term future at all, it was with the belief that the social changes which motivated the struggle in the first place would come about in due time when abundance will have permitted a shorter work day and non-specialized education. Thus the valid idea that the full development of socialist democracy and 'socialist man' requires a material base became the justification for a single-minded pursuit of economic growth and a callous disregard for the self-determination of the people in the present.

Of course, it is no trivial matter to replace the aspirations and ways of thinking and feeling of the past with a new way of acting in the world. It does not come about by exhortation or self praise, but only when changed patterns of daily experience at work and out of work make the new ways realistic, even obviously better ways of understanding and acting in the world. Then they can be effectively reinforced by conscious effort in confrontation with the cultural domination by capitalism on a world scale. We will return to the issue of consciousness below.

To the extent that capitalist criteria remained unchallenged, the failure to overtake capitalism in production becomes a major defeat. Capitalism's growing technical division of labour, the multiplication of different kinds of products, the tighter hegemony of capitalist aspirations and the failure to sustain the productive potential of socialism has led to a kind of giving up. That this has happened independently in a number of countries with very different political histories suggests that it is more than the ideological foibles of poor, corrupt or treacherous leadership and has systemic causes.

Incompetent, corrupt and treacherous leadership then becomes a symptom as much as a cause of the failure. These leaders were not the old capitalist class surviving the revolution and returning to their old ways. Some were bona fide revolutionary leaders who accepted great risk and sacrifice to organize the oppressed. But there is a way in which capitalism is still the 'natural' system of our time. Just as subsistence agriculture and barter is a 'natural' system where the capitalist system of exchange breaks down, so capitalist exploitation, ideology, beliefs and goals reassert themselves whenever the nascent socialist way of life is weak.

There are many who decided long ago that this first experiment had failed, would deny it the name of socialism, and therefore would deny the relevance of its present crises. But at low magnification and on a world historic scale, the first major point is that a world wide effort to overthrow a world system of plunder and oppression has not succeeded.

There are exceptions, countries such as Cuba where the case for socialism has never been the promise of imminent consumer prosperity but rather of a richer shared collective life for all and where the ties between the people and the leaders are stronger, where democratic participation of a socialist kind has been tried in innovative ways and where crises have been confronted mostly by revolutionary rather than bourgeois solutions. Further, by third world standards, the Cuban economy is highly efficient. It does not suffer the waste of capital flight, luxury consumption, unused labour and talent. It has allocated top priority in consumption to guaranteeing the basic necessities for all, to social consumption in health and education and cultural life. The macro level efficiency, despite inefficiency at the level of the enterprise, has allowed Cuba to survive the world economic downturn far better than the rest of Latin America. The Cuban experience remains as a hint of the potential of socialism and is therefore the prime target for capitalist attempts to erase the promise of another road.

No criticism of the socialist experience can reconcile us to capitalism. The horrors of capitalism and imperialism remain. The disparity between the rulers and the ruled continues to increase both within and between countries and to take its toll in hunger, premature deaths and thwarted lives. With the decline of revolutionary opposition, the prerogatives of management are being reasserted with increasing cynicism, union busting has become a professional career and long won rights such as health care are being withdrawn as too expensive in our increasingly prosperous economy. A major instrument in this process is competition between workers, both internationally and within each country, sometimes even between locals of the same union.

Modern technology permits the commodity relation to penetrate ever more deeply into every corner of our lives so that kidneys are for sale, wombs are for rent, education is contracted to the highest bidder, the environment is either plundered or conserved according to a cost/benefit analysis, pollution rights can be leased, living things patented, and the personal is the marketable.

Bourgeois democracy itself, one of the truly great achievements of the capitalist revolution, has also become a marketable commodity. As formal democratic procedures become more widespread and voting becomes almost identified with democracy, the means for trivializing elections and nullifying their significance become more sophisticated. Opinion is manufactured and a technical speciality of electoral tactics and political manipulation stands between people's interests and people's choices while a whole series of buffers are in place to correct the 'errors' that slip through when people do organize and put forth real alternatives.

In the age of monopoly capitalism the corporation rather than the town meeting becomes the model for society and the 'bottom line' of profit becomes the ultimate rationale for ethics. Capitalist democracy brings in the rule of law, but the doctrine of plausible deniability and the craft of damage control institutionalize government illegality. Science and culture become commodities and are evaluated by their sales. Capitalism created modern racism and adapted older patriarchal ways, making sexism a commodity as well as a pillar of social stability.

Whether we date capitalism from the growth of merchant capital in 14th century Europe or the conquest of the Americas in the 16th or the industrial revolution or the seizure of power by the bourgeoisie in the English and French revolutions and by the local bourgeoisie in the American revolution, there is much in the historic experience of capitalism that gives it little to boast about. This is clearly seen if we put the Russian and American Revolutions in comparative historical perspective.

Seventy years after the Bolshevik Revolution, we see nationalist rioting in the Soviet Union; 70 years after the American Revolution the massacre of Native Americans was still in full swing and opposition to slavery was still a fringe movement. A hundred years after the revolution, Jim Crow laws were being imposed throughout the South. Seventy years after the Bolshevik Revolution, the formal but hollow structures of socialist democracy are just being revitalized; 70 years after the American Revolution we were still only halfway toward women's suffrage and more than a century from Black enfranchisement. Seventy years after the Bolshevik Revolution, the labour movement struggles for more direct workers' control and strikes threaten to bring down Communist-led governments; seventy years after the American Revolution union organizing was still the criminal offence of 'conspiracy to increase wages'; and now, two centuries later, unions are in decline.

Dating events from the major revolutions toward each social system is not completely fair. There is a sense in which we are one world, and comparisons have to be made also to what has been achieved anywhere. The purpose of relative dating is only to show that nowhere do the proclaimed goals of new societies become realities immediately.

This telescopic view also provides some perspective on the criticisms and rejections of socialism. While some enemies of the revolution had good class reasons for their opposition, and should have been its enemies, most enemies of the revolution should have been its supporters. The bourgeois revolutions in Europe and the United States were accompanied by all sorts of injustices and barbarities. Many people who had initial sympathies with the revolutions were repelled and disillusioned and became enemies of the revolutionary process. Furthermore, a lot of their specific criticisms were valid and infused with a bitter humane passion. With the distance that a century or more can give us, we can now see their criticisms as often more honest, accurate and valid than the rebuttals of those who defended the new social order. But this validity held only in the small and immediate while their abandonment of the revolution in favour of the old regime was reactionary in the larger scheme of things. We need this dual vision to understand these critics, from Dickens to Solzhenitsyn.

Marxist theory has responded to the defeat of the first revolutionary wave in several ways. One approach is to decide that a conceptual framework which was caught by surprise by recent events must be so basically flawed as to be discarded. But without a careful examination of where theory holds up and where it has been wrong or irrelevant, the call for newness too often neglects what must be continued, and each insight, whether a rediscovery of bourgeois wisdom or an original departure, is proclaimed self consciously to be a new paradigm. Thus we are afflicted with a proliferation of banalities.

A second approach attempts to cut Marxism down to size, to make it a respectable social programme for giving capitalism a human face and discarding the world-historic aims. It could reject even the theoretical possibility of meaningful generalization in favour of petty empiricism or a post-modern, post-Marxist, post-enlightenment, post-scientific, post-materialist retreat into those dismal shadows where exploitation is a state of mind or imperialism an unpleasant discourse.

In some cases theory has been trimmed in scope and in militancy to become social democratic econometrics, dogmatic finger pointing or academic soul searching. Marxists have generally been reluctant to take up the challenges of the new social movements except by abandoning Marxism to jump on bandwagons labelled 'neo' or 'post', etc. or to reject them as 'un-Marxist'.

Therefore the islands of flexible principled Marxism both in capitalist and socialist countries take on a special importance for preventing the defeats from becoming a rout, disappointment becoming depression or panic. They must be appreciated and nurtured.

It is one of the ironies of our history that during the Carter and Reagan years, when political and intellectual life had been shifting to the right, the United States has been emerging as one of the centres of world Marxism.

The particular circumstances of our theoretical enterprise give it its special features. In the absence of a mass unitary movement, the struggles for human advancement have often been carried out separately in movements focusing on anti-racist, feminist, ecological, trade union, solidarity, gay rights, health and social service, educational or other specific concerns. Therefore theoretical work has examined each of these areas separately. At the same time, the relations among them, and especially the relations among class, race and gender analysis had to become a major theme. Meanwhile, our exclusion from power meant that we were free of the incredible demands to resolve immediate urgent issues of providing for the population, issues that dominate the thinking of our comrades in countries where capitalism has been overthrown. This has given us the freedom to explore many long-range issues which Cuban or Nicaraguan or Vietnamese Marxists would place at the bottom of their intellectual agendas. Although excluded from power, we do share a little of the affluence of the American empire and that wealth provides the resources for the meetings, publishing, research and specialized organizations that maintain our efforts.

One consequence of these circumstances is that we more readily see the struggle as one of challenging the capitalist system as a whole, in all the ways it distorts our lives and thwarts our fulfillment. This does not mean that all US Marxists really approach our reality this way. American anti-intellectual pragmatism is too powerful for that. But it is nevertheless true that our conditions of existence place us in an occasion for wisdom.

Our isolation from practical responsibility often gives our work an overly abstract character, naivete about the complexities of the processes of social transformation and the inclination to try to deduce programmes from general principles. Too often US Marxists look at revolutionary societies not from the perspective of comrades in a common venture but as judges grading the revolution according to some grade sheet of their own. Nevertheless, our isolation from power also gives us a scope that is often lacking elsewhere.

Finally, since we do not hold a monopoly in publishing or education or research, our Marxism has developed in intimate confrontation with opposing ideologies. This condition also has contradictory consequences. We are inevitably influenced by the beliefs of those around us, sometimes accepting parts of their agendas and adopting their vocabularies, or resisting this pressure by retreating into fortress dogmatism. But we also have a robust Marxism unlike the flaccid hothouse varieties that have been protected by state power from serious challenge.

Many Marxists are taking a different tack. Instead of pruning Marxism, they are building on its greatest strength, the dialectical materialist view of the world as a complex, multilevel, contradictory and evolving whole. The call to look at the whole acknowledges that the task is forever incomplete, the whole far too big and strange to be comprehended simply. But it is an appeal always to look further at context, at connections, at process. Marxist holism is a constant reminder of permanent incompleteness, the challenge of revolutionary insight to the gender, class and racially bounded constraints on prevailing ideas.

The Marxist insistence on the historical contingency of what seems self evident, the cry that the real may be irrational, the injunction to doubt and criticize, is always in conflict with the historically bounded real socialist movements. Therefore Marxism regularly produces courageous and brilliant feminists from its ranks, and just as often thwarts and isolates them in the real socialist movements that are still deeply sexist.

The intellectual task of Marxists is to expand the scope of our theory so as to confront capitalism in all its manifestations, laying the groundwork for a political challenge more pervasive than anything yet attempted.

At higher magnification, what had looked like objective tendencies are now seen to be made out of the political choices of movements and the struggles among conflicting ideas as to how to confront the urgent problems of building the new. Now the objective processes are those which arise from the low economic levels, the needs of the various social actors in the revolution, and the power of ways of thought that grew up in the experience of underdevelopment.

One way of looking at the political choices made in the revolutionary process was proposed by Rosa Luxemburg: we are trying to build a future with the instruments of the past, the instruments of the society we are trying to overcome.

There is both a conservative and a radical side to the revolution. On the one hand, it draws on the aspirations which the past sets before everybody but only allows some to reach. The landless peasants who want to own land and hire labour, the enslaved men who want the full freedom to abuse their own women, the latent entrepreneurs among oppressed minorities who want their own opportunities to become exploiters, the individualist intellectuals who want to be free of the marketplace but also of social responsibility, the overworked and alienated workers who want freedom from work, the servants of the czars who want palaces for themselves, parents who want their children to receive an education so that they can 'get ahead' out of the working class or peasantry, all bring their own desires to the revolution. Those who want to consolidate the family by giving it economic stability and those who challenge the nuclear family as a way to live, people who want for everyone all the goods that capitalism can offer and those who reject the alienated consciousness of consumerism, those who want to free production from neocolonial constraint and those who want to subordinate economic growth to ecological necessity, nationalists for whom internationalism is only a way to get support for their own liberation and internationalists committed to world revolution all storm the Winter Palaces or go to the mountains together. Conservative and radical dreams live side by side in the revolution and even in the same revolutionaries.

At each crisis point in social development, it is possible to draw on the dreams and methods and resources of the past: an appeal to nationalism, to bourgeois enterprise, to administrative commandism, consumerism, sexism. Or it is possible to leap ahead to improvize temporary solutions which prefigure future social relations.

Each has its justifications and dangers. To use the past reinforces that past and may undermine the chance to move ahead. It may gain support, it broadens the movement but also reshapes that movement. It alienates those for whom the revolutionary commitment means a transformed way of life, often regarding them as utopians in a pejorative sense, fearing their innovations as divisive and calling on them not to be so different. Their long range concerns are pushed to a back burner as 'not yet on the agenda of history'. The feminist upsurges that pop up regularly within revolutionary movements are then dismissed as divisive, premature, of lesser importance than production, etc. Much of the creative impulse of the revolution can be dissipated and its advocates alienated.

The point here is not that retreats are unacceptable but that they have to be recognized as retreats and not converted into virtues, changing consciousness in ways that preclude future advances. What may begin as tactical retreats, even necessary corrections of past errors, can easily become the abandonment of socialism.

But to base politics on the future aspirations while neglecting the weight of the past as already obsolete, to leap without a sufficient base of preparation can result in advanced but empty forms and loss of support. Then there is strong pressure to coerce that support, strident and dishonest apologetics, self-praise amid lamentations about the 'backwardness' of the people, distrust of democracy and imposition of a centralized commandism.

Even the most forward looking decisions take on a retrograde significance when they are imposed. The net flow of capital from richer to poorer regions of the USSR or among socialist countries is an expression of internationalism and socialist planning aimed at equalizing the levels among the nations. But from the point of view of the nationalisms of richer areas such as the Baltic Republics of the USSR, it feels like exploitation. The fair exchange between richer and poorer regions which was partly instituted by the eastern bloc could then be regarded as subsidies. When advanced forms are imposed without an adequate base of active support, planning becomes a cover for careerism and corruption, discipline protects abuses from criticism, the very awareness of that process leads to cynicism, passivity and alienation.

This is not a necessary result of a leftward turn but of an ineffective one, an attempt to rush the future with all the coercive means and excuses of the past that really reinforces that past.

Both kinds of errors have been important in revolutionary history and disastrous to people. But at present the first kind, the compromise with the past, is dominant in European and Asian socialism.

In the face of lax labour discipline, it is possible to tighten authority over workers. This usually carries with it more administration, more narrowly defined jobs so that performance can be measured better. But the measures that are devised to evaluate performance are never directly the goal itself but rather some indicator. This means that where supervisors control people's fate and satisfying the higher ups becomes a major goal, ways always can be found to produce good measures of performance without the reality of performance. If uniform school exam scores are used to measure teachers' effectiveness, then helping the students to cheat on exams becomes rational individualist behaviour. If a factory's achievement is measured by meeting production targets, this can be done in the easiest way posible. There is a whole literature of humour based on ways of fulfilling someone else's measure of your performance: one Soviet cartoon showed the workers of a nail factory posed out in front with one giant nail balanced on all their shoulders. They grinningly boast 'we have over fulfilled our plan for a thousand tons of nails'! Railways ship barrels of water back and forth between Moscow and Vladivostok to meet their quotas of ton/miles of freight. The forestry service plants millions of trees, but there are no forests because the survival of trees was not part of the measure. Then there is more abusive supervision, efforts to invent better indices so that measures and goals will correspond more closely, and increased alienation making tighter control more necessary in a vicious circle.

The other direction is an expanded autonomy, self organization at the shop level, and 'consagración', the Cuban term for dedication to work and to social goals. Then a collective can evaluate its own work, and report what is has done to improve the life of the country. But this path becames a sham if not built with care, if the restructuring of work is not accompanied by a restructuring of ideology. In that case, autonomy merely creates organizations for the collective ripping off of society. But a new ideology can only develop when it is reinforced by daily experience at work, at home, at school and at play. It is in the rebuilding of consciousness that sexism as a school for domination emerges as a major brake on socialist development and feminist demands become an urgent necessity for the whole social process.

The greatest failures of most contemporary revolutions have been in the area of building socialist democracy, a self governing society of the associated producers and reproducers. Here again, it is important to reject simple caricatures. Socialist revolutions did bring large masses of people into political life as actors in history. In some cases, advanced political forms were established to allow for grass roots democracy of a kind much deeper than that of capitalist politics. The judicial systems with the demystification of the legal process and the development of peoples' and neighbourhood courts is one such area. The system of participation by volunteers in the working committees of legislative bodies, extensive nationwide discussion of proposed legislation, the required report back of representatives, the principle of collective leadership are among the formal achievements of socialist states. But forms are not enough, and in many ways these forms eroded and lost real content. How this happened is something that has to be studied very carefully. It is not a simple matter of authorities suppressing discussion and bypassing the legal democratic structures. Democratic participation also requires the self confidence, the time and the information to participate, practice in determination in daily living, encouragement to think independently. It requires the overthrow of deeply rooted attitudes and beliefs, deference to authority, dependence on outstanding leaders, timidities that are built into the socialization of people in class societies. Without these deeper social changes, the democratic forms become empty and a little bit of intimidation goes a long way.

The experience of popular movements that focus on consciousness – the feminist consciousness raising groups, liberation theology's base communities, participatory action research, Freire's concientizaciaõ, Makarenko's work with war orphans in the Ukraine in the 1920's and the theoretical concerns of Gramsci and Ché Guevara have provided some valuable lessons that could serve as as a starting point:

*Consciousness is formed during the daily experience of living and the interpretation of that experience on the basis of previous consciousness. Therefore it cannot be fabricated by exhortation or transformed by offering better arguments.

*The feminist slogan 'the personal is political' opened up the areas usually regarded as private to social analysis and criticism, and broadened the notion of consciousness from explicitly held political or social beliefs to include also feelings about the self and others, about how to deal with the world, about what used to be called philosophy of life as against philosophy. It provides a link between the social creation of consciousness in the large, considered by Lukacs, Gramsci and Brecht, and the reproduction of consciousness in the context of growing up and within families.

*Everybody can learn to lead as well as to follow, but this capacity has to be developed, nurtured and encouraged. Without the consciousness raising, collectivity can become a cover for domination by a few and a field for the expression of primitive chauvinisms and eloquent opportunisms.

Consciousness raising and socialist democracy go together, and are jointly a powerful force of socialist development that cannot be put on a back burner for some indefinite communist future. Especially now, when the hollowness of some of the socialist forms has made capitalist liberalism seem attractive, revolutionaries have to avoid talking about democracy in the abstract, without adjectives, or advocating particular democratic forms as if they were equivalent to democracy. The difference between socialist and bourgeois ideas of democracy remain valid: while the one aims at the mobilization of the creative and critical intelligence and knowledge of the whole people on behalf of a common enterprise, the other is organized around the management of dissent within a safe domain and the competition for office. Bourgeois democracy has never yet led to the liberation of the oppressed classes, but has often corrected particular abuses, made the struggle for that liberation less painful and has sometimes ratified victories that occurred elsewhere.

The critique of bourgeois democracy should not be used to dismiss democratic issues from socialist development but to transcend it, incorporating its best features.

National chauvinism was certainly not a socialist invention, and to some extent its survival in socialist countries is not unexpected. But where internationalism is actively promoted and equality institutionalized, where collective decision making makes solidarity a daily experience, ethnic identity would gradually lose its potential for ethnic antagonism. On the other hand where corruption prevails, it very often organizes privilege along ethnic lines. Where 'necessity' becomes the justification for policy which sacrifices all to development and sees national sensibilities as obsolete obstacles to progress, then chauvinism becomes a justification for privilege. Where oppression is not confronted with materialist analysis chauvinism can come to dominate the resistance to privilege. Each in its own way, the Bulgarian expulsion of Bulgarian Turks, the Rumanian violation of ethnic rights of Hungarians, the anti-Vietnamese chauvinism of the Khmer Rouge and East European anti-semitism are all in part reactionary opportunisms in the face of the problems of socialist transition.

In recent decades the decisions made by most socialist regimes as they coped with problems that had long been denied have been in the backward looking direction, attempting to salvage the present with the resources and beliefs of the past. We cannot declare a general rule that this should never be done, but the over all pattern has been an abandonment of the revolutionary perspective: at best the tactic is swallowing up the strategy. A notable exception has been Cuba, where after a period of ineffective attempts to harness the past to progress, the critique of technocracy, economism and corruption is giving rise to a repoliticization, emphasis on consciousness and collectivity, and renewed interest in the ideas of Ché Guevara.

Thus one political conclusion from this analysis is not that revolutionary regimes have rushed too far away from capitalism but that they have not departed enough to realize the full potential of socialism. That is, issues which had been deferred to a distant communist future in fact belong on the agenda now. The most important of these issues involve the transformation of consciousness both to solve the problems of motivation for work and to mobilize the collective intelligence. But we know that consciousness does not change simply by urging it to change or even teaching systematically another world view. It requires altered practice so that daily experience supports the new outlook. This is the context in which socialist democracy and the fight against sexism acquire special importance for social development. And both of these require a restructuring of work, the division of labour, and the evaluation of what constitutes socially important work.

A similar argument applied to the revolutionary movement in capitalist countries leads to a similar conclusion: one weakness of the left has been its failure to challenge capitalism as a whole system, in every corner of our lives. This has allowed the struggles against separate evils to develop separately, often in antagonism to each other, and has not provided the options for us to switch emphases in our tactics as conditions shift.

I propose as a working hypothesis: when liberatory movements come into conflict, it is because they aspire to too little. When Afro-American and women's movements conflict over filling the few affirmative action slots in a university, they are failing to challenge the stinginess and turn off the rest into docility. When the ecology movement faces the ire of the trade unions because industry proves that environmental protection would reduce profits, a challenge is required of the sanctity of profit. Our hypothesis asserts that all struggles for human liberation and well being are complementary in the large. This does not mean abandoning class analysis or class politics but rather moving from economistic to historical materialist analysis.

Nor does it mean a utopian advocacy of a beautiful future divorced from immediate and short term practice. Rather, we have to struggle at different levels. At each level some conditions have to be taken as givens and others as potential variables. The failings of both opportunism and utopianism are in limiting the struggle to one level and therefore treating basic variables as givens or all givens as variables.

There are three major possible outcomes to the present situation. The least likely is that *perestroika* and its analogues results in a period of retreat, consolidation and a newly revitalized socialism with a more or less continuous leadership. It is unlikely not because there is a retreat in economic matters. These may or may not be necessary in order to rectify the failings of the past. If they were presented as such and if policy were debated in terms of socialist, revolutionary principles, a revived movement would be able to accept the detour, confront bourgeois alternatives and find a new revolutionary path. But this is unlikely because the economic reorganization is accompanied by massive ideological retreat from rhetorical Marxism to naive liberalism. *Glasnost* has yet to unleash a vigourous creative Marxist challenge to the liberalism and nationalisms which now seem to be its major beneficiaries.

A second possible outcome is that many of the present day socialist countries will rush, stagger or lapse into capitalism with or without the overthrow of their governments. This would open up whole new regions for capitalist expansion, possibly even postponing the next world crisis of capitalism. Having been burned once, their people will not be very receptive to socialist politics and may even play a reactionary role internationally. The recent hostility of part of the Hungarian press to Cuba, and the Polish student movements's enthusiastic reception of a former Batista policeman as a hero foreshadows this possibility. The focus of revolutionary movements would then shift to the present capitalist world.

There is also a third possibility. Although the slogans of the communist-led governments are often repudiated by their peoples as hollow exhortation or unjustified self praise, socialist ideas have penetrated to deeper levels of popular consciousness than has support for the governments. Demands for equal access to goods, against privilege, for workers' control of industry, job security, the right to housing and health care have become internalized even when thought of not as socialist but as elementary human rights. The future of socialism in eastern Europe may well be in the hands of people who are now subjectively anti-communist and whose nationalism or experience with bureaucratic abuses leaves them with considerable naivete about capitalism. This naivete about capitalism shows up in the trauma of emigrés from socialist countries upon meeting real live capitalism. Perhaps a third of them return home to eastern Europe, after they discover that America is after all in many basic ways much like the party propaganda said. One pair of Cuban emigrés actually approached the Cuban delegation to the UN demanding that it pay their rent for them because as Cuban citizens they had a right to housing, but who can pay for a New York apartment on New York wages?

The goals of at least part of the dissidents may eventually find expression in a workers' movement which even now has more power than workers' movements under capitalism and which can or has forged alliances with the peasants and intellectuals in textbook Bolshevik fashion. Just compare the political power of Soviet or Polish miners to their West Virginia and Kentucky counterparts.

These are very heterogeneous movements. Their own slogans do not provide a sufficient guide for what their future holds, and we really do not know yet what allies we will find there or what kind of societies will emerge when the dust settles.

The retreat of the European revolution creates special problems for the third world revolution. Internationalist support for their struggles will now have to come mainly from allies in capitalist countries; the dangers of direct military intervention or prolonged 'low intensity warfare' increase, the enormous tasks of reconstruction in a world of unequal exchange are not to be eased much by the more equitable trade patterns that previously had guided the relations of the Eastern bloc with the third world. This makes solidarity with third world revolutions and the reaffirmation of solidarity even more urgent than before. An irony of history is that American affluence and the stability of US capitalism provides both the resources and the relative freedom that makes us a centre of internationalism.

The task of the revolutionary is to change consciousness. At first impression, this is an awfully tame ambition compared to the much-cited 'the task of the revolutionary is to make revolution' of Ernesto Ché Guevara. But the first impression is misleading in two ways. It underestimates the complexities of Ché's thought on the importance of changing consciousness along with economic and social change, and it mistakenly assumes that changing consciousness is as tame as an academic lecture. The recognition that social changes do not drag consciousness along passively has made the analysis of consciousness formation both under capitalism and in revolutionary societies a major priority for all movements concerned with fundamental change.

On the theoretical level, we first have to expand the scope of Marxist analysis to deal with issues that have had only secondary importance, especially around ecology and feminism. In the past, Marxism has acknowledged its own sources in English political economy, French socialism and German philosophy. But organized Marxist movements have mostly stubbornly resisted accepting that it can learn anything important from any contemporary movements. One way of resisting their ideas is to claim that we had them all along. And indeed we can find the criticism of environmental destruction in Marx and the pioneering feminism of Engels or the militant struggles against the oppression of women in Soviet Asia. We can show that Marxists have indeed participated in feminist and ecological struggles and have important insights to contribute. But that is only part of the story. Revolutionary movements as they exist in reality mostly have been unsympathetic both to feminism and ecology and are the poorer for that. Rather than enter into polemics about who really said what first, the important thing is to take up issues which we have mostly neglected and which the other movements have emphasized, and to recognize that the struggle against capitalism has to become more rather than less pervasive.

A material reason for the Marxist reluctance to deal with feminist and ecological programmes has been that Marxist leaders have mostly been men, with real privileges to lose, and leaders of workers' movements for whom expanding employment was a necessary goal. The subjective side of the reluctance to deal both with feminism and ecology was that they feared that to consider those issues would dilute or even abandon a class analysis. However this is true only for the most economistic kind of class analysis. An historical materialist understanding of the present recognizes capitalism as a total system of exploitation which has invented or adapted many kinds of oppression and destructive practices and imposed the commodity relation and its spin-offs on all aspects of our lives. The maintenance of capitalism, the reproduction of its physical and human resources, political processes and social relations, beliefs and feelings is a full time task for its rulers, its licensed thinkers and institutions and for all its subjects. Communists have to recognize the pervasiveness of this system and challenge it wherever it produces misery, thwarts human creativity, threatens our existence and debases our world. We should gratefully accept the leadership of the feminists and ecologists who have placed these issues on the political agenda and mapped their intellectual landscape.

Marxists around the new journal *Capitalism, Nature and Socialism* and elsewhere have been developing a framework for this task. Some of the central notions are:

– Human history as a continuation of natural history.

– The interpenetration of organism and environment.

– The active nature of our ecology: 'We are what we do, but above all what we do to change what we are.' (Eduardo Galeano).

– Society/nature as a single entity, an eco-historical formation that combines the mode of production and the surrounding nature with which it interpenetrates. But the unity of this whole is not based on harmony or balance but on historical contingency, contradictions and change.

– The recognition of renewable and non-renewable resources as conditions of production that are also consequences of production.

– The unity of production and reproduction. This allows us to examine how the changing allocation of women's labour among these two activities helps to define their situation in society. This allocation has been the basis for the regulation of sexuality and power within the family. It also acts to determine, the structure of the labour force and the demographic changes which are part of the dynamics of each society, finally feeding back on the allocation of women's labour. This makes the situation of women not an epiphenomenon of social development but a part of the system's dynamics.

– The unity of production/reproduction with renewal, consumption and waste as they arise in our evolution first as activities within the body, then externalized and finally socialized. The labour of physical, intellectual, and emotional renewal has too often been dismissed as consumption and part of the private realm of women's work, while consumption has been abstracted from renewal and waste from ecological recycling.

Marxists are participating in the critique of science and technology. We are coping with the dual nature of both, as part of the growth of generic human knowledge of the world and as the socially determined product of a particular society interpreting and using nature according to its own priorities. Science is demystified to be recognized as an episode in the division of labour in which people are selected and institutuions established to organize experience for the direct purpose of finding out what the owners of science want to know.

There is a vigorous Marxist health movement which goes beyond the critique of inequitable health service to examine the social/biological nature of health and disease. Here some basic insights are:

– Health is capacity to carry out those activities deemed necessary according to each person's class, gender, race, and other specifications. The separation of the deemers from the deemed–about makes the definition of health an object of struggle.

– Human physiology is a socialized physiology. The unity of the physical, psychological and social in a holism that goes beyond the skin of the individual. All people share a common physiological network, but this is embedded in a larger socially created network that is unique to each individual according to her/his position in the world. It is in that larger network that the processes of health and disease unfold.

– Infectious disease is the relation between ourselves and parasitic organisms in a permanent co-evolution. Our medical technology and our changing society and environment set the terms for this co-evolution.

I refer to these fields because I have been involved with them and am familiar with the issues. There are other areas in which Marxists have been expanding our challenge of capitalist world views or in which such challenge is necessary.

One such area of priority for us is democracy. Here it is especially important never to discuss democracy without distinguishing socialist from bourgeois democracy or falling into the facile language of pluralism, identifying democracy with multiparty elections etc. The historical experience has been that nowhere has capitalist democracy given real power to the oppressed, but has often softened that oppression or made struggle against it less painful. While bourgeois democracy emphasizes the organization of dissent, in the socialist context the role of democracy is as the means to mobilize the creative intelligence of the whole people in solving problems and correcting errors. Therefore socialists must assimilate the achievements of bourgeois democracy while inventing its own forms of popular self government.

Another area of priority lies in establishing the theoretical underpinnings for rebuilding of the labour movement after half a century of retreat. This will place the struggle against racism and for local and international solidarity high on the agenda. Can North American and Japanese workers join together as effectively as GM and Nissan or Ford and Toyota?

We are living in a difficult time, a low point between periods of upsurge, when revolutionary optimism looks like a cruel joke. Neither the promise of quick victory nor a clear model of what that victory would be like is attracting millions to our cause. Our theories, so powerful in analyzing the large scale historical processes and the structures of capitalism, have been hard pressed to understand the particular, not only to anticipate particular futures but even to explain events satisfactorily after the fact, have been completely incapable of understanding post-revolutionary society, and have sometimes been used to justify barbarities.

Then why continue? First, because capitalism's half millenium has shown itself incapable of creating a humane and just world and is increasingly dangerous to us and all of life as technologies provide the power, and the commodity relation provides the motivation to turn all aspects of existence into investment for profit. The crises of power in the Eastern bloc cannot hide the deep structural crisis in the apparently triumphant system.

Second, because capitalism is an integrated system in which the correction of particular abuses can be achieved only at the expense of creating new ones.

Third, because it is also an exciting time in which the collapse of old approaches allows for new ways of posing the issues of human liberation in an expanded way.

And finally because understanding the world, breaking out of the Great Brainwash, is an exhilarating first step in reaching toward our own liberation. Immersing ourselves as a whole way of life in the struggle for *what might be* against *what is* provides the greatest degree of freedom possible for us in today's world.

Note: This essay is based on notes for a talk at the New York Marxist School in September 1989 and revised in December 1989 from a presentation at the Marxism Now conference at Amherst.

COUNTER-HEGEMONIC STRUGGLES*

RALPH MILIBAND

I

Hegemony, in Gramsci's meaning of the term, involves both coercion and consent. As consent, it means the capacity of dominant classes to persuade subordinate ones to accept, adopt and 'interiorise' the values and norms which dominant classes themselves have adopted and believe to be right and proper. This might be described as the strong meaning of hegemony-as-consent. A weaker version is the capacity of dominant classes to persuade subordinate classes that, whatever they might think of the prevailing social order, and however alienated they might be from it, any alternative would be catastrophically worse, and that in any case there was nothing much that they could do to bring about any such alternative. Weaker though this second version might be, it is not much less effective than the first one in consolidating the social order. In either version, however, hegemony is not something that can ever be taken to be finally and irreversibly won: on the contrary, it is something that needs to be constantly nurtured, defended and reformulated.

The dominant classes of capitalist-democratic regimes understand this very well, and do not take hegemony for granted. The whole history of these regimes, since the achievement of an extended suffrage, the creation of national working class movements, and serious political competition between bourgeois and labour or socialist parties, has been marked by a determined 'engineering of consent' on the part of conservative forces, and by their fierce striving to win the hearts and minds of their subordinate populations. The sources of these struggles have been extremely varied, and their forms have ranged from the most sophisticated and subtle to the most stridently demagogic. The purpose, however, is always the popular ratification of the prevailing social order, and the rejection by the working class (and everybody

---

*Many thanks to Marion Kozak, David Miliband and Leo Panitch for their comments and criticisms.

else) of any notion that there could be a radical and viable alternative to that order. This purpose, it should be added, is also served by real concessions to pressure from below, notably in the realm of welfare services: it would be a great mistake to take hegemony-as-consent to be purely a matter of mystification.

Be that as it may, the main reason why the struggle for hegemony-as-consent can never be taken to be finally won in capitalist-democratic regimes is that there exists a vast discrepancy between the message which hegemonic endeavours seek to disseminate, and the actual reality which daily confronts the vast majority of the population for whom the message is mainly intended. The message speaks of democracy, equality, opportunity, prosperity, security, community, common interests, justice, fairness, etc. The reality, on the other hand, as lived by the majority, is very different, and includes the experience of exploitation, domination, great inequalities in all spheres of life, material constraints of all kinds, and very often great spiritual want. Reality may not be conceived and articulated in these precise terms, but it is nevertheless adversely felt, and produces frustration, alienation, anger, dissent and pressure from below for the resolution of grievances. A crucial purpose of hegemonic endeavours is to prevent such sentiments from turning into a generalised availability to radical thoughts.

Were it not for the discrepancy between hegemonic message and lived reality, there would obviously be much less need, or no need at all, for the unremitting assault on popular consciousness. Nor would it be necessary to take much account of counter-hegemonic endeavours: such strivings would be the work of isolated individuals, who could be dismissed as eccentrics, and who would have no hope of achieving a serious hearing. As it is, the discrepancy between rhetoric, even when backed by real concessions, and reality as it is lived, does provide a very large terrain for counter-hegemonic endeavours. The terrain is sometimes more favourable, sometimes less, but it is never altogether barren, given the nature of capitalism.

These endeavours are as diverse in form as hegemonic ones; and one of the most notable features of the present epoch is how diverse also have been their sources. Much, for instance, has rightly been made in recent decades of the quite outstanding contribution which feminist, ecological, anti-racist and other 'new social movements' have made to the disturbance of the mental status quo of the countries in which they have flowered; and it must be assumed that they will continue to affect the political culture and the political agenda of these countries. There was a time, not very long ago, when it was taken for granted on the Left that the only source of 'real' dissent and challenge was the working class, and more specifically labour movements. The presence of 'new social movements' on the ideological and political scene has produced a general awareness on the Left that this was an aberration, and that these movements had a major and indispensable contribution to make. Indeed, the wheel has now come full circle, with many people on the

Left now persuaded that *only* 'new social movements' can be expected to provide an effective challenge to the status quo, and that labour and socialist movements are too steeped in ancient (and obsolete) modes of thought to be able to do so. This loss of confidence in 'traditional' socialist ideas, not to speak of labour and socialist agencies, has indeed been the dominant feature of the political culture of the Left in the eighties. 'New times', it has been insistently proclaimed, require new thinking; and new thinking requires the abandonment of many, perhaps most, of the long-cherished but by now quite irrelevant ideas which have been at the core of the socialist tradition. The message has been conveyed in many different versions; but it ultimately amounts to a retreat from the search and the striving for a socialist alternative to capitalism.

The present essay is written in the belief that this is a grievously mistaken perspective, and that socialists do have a distinctive contribution to make to counter-hegemonic struggles; and that the socialist alternative which they propose is now more than ever needed in the struggle against conservative hegemony. Of course, this socialist contribution does not in any way oppose the concerns of 'new social movements'. On the contrary, these concerns – anti-sexism, anti-racism, ecology, sexual liberation, peace, etc – are part of the socialist agenda; and there are many people in 'new social movements' who are themselves socialists and who conceive their concerns as bound up with socialism. But the question which I want to raise here is what are the fundamental positions which may nowadays be said to constitute the specific contribution which socialists can make to counter-hegemonic struggles. These positions need restating on at least two counts. The first, as already noted, is that they are now so often contested on the Left, or simply ignored. The second is that the crisis of Communist regimes, and the collapse of some of them, has given hegemonic forces a wonderful opportunity to proclaim not only that Communism was dead or dying, but that socialism in any version was in the same condition. Nothing, from a socialist perspective, could be more necessary than to counter this, and to provide a reasoned argument on behalf of the main propositions which define socialism.

II

The point of departure of such an argument has to be two closely related items: on the one hand, it involves a radical critique of the prevailing social order; on the other, an affirmation that an entirely different social order, based on radically different foundations, is not only desirable (which is easy enough), but possible.

Critiques of capitalism on the Left have increasingly tended in recent times to be piecemeal, and specifically related to immediate 'problems', shortcomings and failings over a multitude of issues. In other words, criticism on the Left tends to be directed at one aspect or another of the workings of a social order dominated by capitalism, without this criticism being related to the nature of the system as a whole. A socialist critique, on the other hand, is distinguished by the connections which it always seeks to make between specific ills and the nature of capitalism, as a system wholly geared to the pursuit of private profit, whose dynamic and ethos suffuse the whole social order, and which necessarily relegates all considerations other than the maximization of private profit to a subsidiary place, at best, in the scheme of things.

A socialist critique, unlike liberal or social democratic critiques, does not treat the economic, social, political and moral failings of the system as unfortunate deviations from normality, but on the contrary as intrinsic features of the system. It is the attenuation of ills by way of public intervention and regulation which must be taken as deviations from the essential dynamic of capitalism, and as contrary to its spirit and purpose. There is, from this point of view, a perverse logic in the 'libertarian' argument against all such intervention and regulation: 'libertarians' simply have the callous courage which politicians devoted to 'free enterprise' and the rule of the market cannot afford to have.

Socialists do of course support and demand piecemeal reforms. But they also offer a critique of the limited nature and palliative character of such reforms; they demand an enlargement of the scope of reform and struggle against the constraints imposed upon reforms by the capitalist context in which they occur; and they warn against the illusion that the deep ills generated by the system can be truly cured within its framework. Thus, a socialist critique of the 'welfare state' does not in the least denigrate the value of the reforms which are encompassed within this rubric; but it does point to the inadequacies which are bound to exist in a system unsympathetic to collective provision. Similarly, a socialist critique of public ownership points to the need to infuse it with an altogether different spirit from the spirit which moves capitalist enterprise, but also acknowledges that this, to be fully realised, requires the transcendance of capitalism itself.

I suggested earlier that a socialist critique of the prevailing social order is always coupled with the insistence that a radical alternative is not only desirable but possible. 'A radical alternative', as I understand it, simply means the creation of a cooperative, egalitarian, democratic, and ultimately classless society, to be replicated in due course throughout the world. Any such project was always utterly repellent to anti-socialists everywhere, and fiercely denounced by them as utopian nonsense and as a sure recipe, whatever the intentions of its proponents, for the creation of a murderously repressive and totalitarian social order. Some such view, however, is now also quite commonly held in many parts of the Left as well. Here too, there is now considerable suspicion of the radical transformations which socialism undoubtedly implies.

This, it should be noted, is not only a matter of saying that the project must be conceived as a long-term affair, as a *process* which is bound to extend over a very long period, and which may never come to be completed. All this is mere commonsense; and if commonsense was not sufficient, the experience of Communist regimes would show well enough that large-scale social change is a very difficult and complex business, even in the best of circumstances, which are not likely to exist anywhere, and which certainly did not exist in the countries where Communists assumed power. The view often found on the Left nowadays proceeds from a different position, namely that we don't really know where we are, that we certainly don't know where we should be going, that to try and impose a 'pattern' upon what is called reality is dangerously arrogant, and that the very notion of a radical alternative to the here and now is laden with dangerous consequences. Thus speaks 'post-modernism', and other currently fashionable modes of thought as well.

The experience of Communist regimes has many important lessons for socialists. But it cannot be taken to show that any attempt to create a society radically different from what capitalism has produced is bound to be disastrous. It is good conservative propaganda to argue that the only alternative to capitalism is the kind of regime which characterised Communist rule. But this is a very stunted view of what is possible by way of social arrangements; and one of the tasks of counter-hegemony is precisely to insist, with the help of programmes and policies and 'prefigurative' modes of behaviour and organisation, on the distance that separates socialism from Communist experience.

There is obviously no way of *proving* this, save in practice; and this makes it possible for conservatives to point with much glee to the fact – and it is a fact – that nowhere has the kind of society advocated by well-meaning socialists come into being; and the point is reinforced by the fact that societies claiming to be socialist *have* been created, but have not been, to say the least, good models of what a socialist society should be. The point cannot be brushed aside; but what it means is that the socialist case has to be presented with due regard for the many difficult questions it raises. In other words, the case has to be made without the naive and implausible claims which have often been advanced for socialism. Socialism is not a doctrine of instant salvation, with the promise of a perfectly harmonious, strife-free society, in which all ills which have always afflicted humankind will be miraculously dissipated. Its claims are rather more modest. What it offers is the promise of a social order in which remediable ills would at least be drastically attenuated, and in which altruism and fellowship would be made possible by a context altogether different from the context provided by capitalism.

There is, in this connection, a fundamental point which needs to be made: this is that the socialist project is based on the premise that 'ordinary people' are capable of ruling themselves and of ensuring the viablity of a cooperative, humane and rational social order. This too is a message that goes against the grain in an epoch soaked in blood. The twentieth century has been a century of war, massacre and horrors on an immense scale, in which masses of 'ordinary people' have been willing participants, and to which even larger masses of people have given their support, or to which they have at least acquiesced. Does it then really make sense, after the bloodbaths of World War I and World War II, and all the other wars which this century has witnessed, after Auschwitz and the Gulag and Hiroshima and Vietnam and a host of other infamous such names, to project a rosy picture of societies – indeed of a world – peopled by humans capable of sociality, cooperation, altruism, and guided by rational modes of thought and behaviour?

The answer, in socialist terms, is not to deny mass participation in, or support for, or acquiescence in, the horrors which have marked the twentieth century; but rather to note the crucial fact that these horrors were not *initiated* by 'the masses'. The ready attribution of guilt to everybody ('we are all guilty') masks the fact that the high policy decisions which led to the horrors were made by *rulers*, with very little if any 'input' by 'the masses'. It was not 'the masses' which decided to build gas chambers, or to build the Gulag, or to carry out saturation bombing in Korea or Vietnam. That 'the masses' supported their rulers and took part in the enterprises which the latter set in train shows well enough that 'ordinary people' are not innately good, which is hardly news, and that plenty of people easily develop an executioner's vocation. This is a sobering thought, but it cannot be taken to mean that people are innately bad and incapable of sociality and altruism. What any such ascription – positive or negative – misses is the importance of the context in which 'good' or 'bad' qualities flower. At the heart of the socialist perspective, there is the conviction that nothing in this realm is settled, predetermined, and that human nature is not implacably cursed by 'innate' cruelty and aggression.

Allied to this conviction, there is the further notion that societies based on domination and exploitation, and in the grip of crises which they cannot resolve, will inevitably produce deep pathological deformations, of which racism, sexism, antisemitism, xenophobia, ethnic hatreds, cruelty and aggression, are common manifestations; and that socialism (not to be confused with Stalinism) offers the only possible context in which these deformations can be effectively countered and thus turned into marginal and increasingly rare phenomena. 'Socialism or Barbarism' may be an over-dramatic slogan; but in so far as barbarism is compatible with great technological and cultural sophistication, the notion of Socialism or Civilized Barbarism embodies a truth which counter-hegemonic struggles need to stress.

III

Regrettably, any serious discussion of socialist alternatives has to tackle an exceedingly difficult question, namely the question of public ownership. I say 'regrettably', not because it is difficult, though it is, but because it is a subject which hardly quickens the blood or which provides much inspiration. Nor does it attract much support, even on the Left. Conservative propaganda, ever since the end of World War II, when measures of nationalisation were part of the agenda of social democratic parties, has succeeded in making the idea of public ownership all but synonymous with bureaucracy, inefficiency, sloth and neglect of the consumer; and this propaganda has been given further credence by the unattractive forms which nationalisation, under social democratic auspices, did acquire. Also, Communist experience, here too, has served to strengthen the view that state enterprise is inefficient, and that it also constitutes a sinister additional support for unbridled statism. The Left nowadays may not be wholly reconciled to capitalist enterprise, but it has become exceedingly uncertain about any alternative to it; and the uncertainty has been greatly enhanced by the new difficulties which measures of nationalisation in any single country, in the era of global capitalism, are deemed to entail.

Counter-hegemonic endeavours imperatively require a reasoned discussion of these questions, *and* a resolute defence of public ownership as an absolutely indispensable foundation for a social order radically different from capitalism. It needs to be said, for instance, that public ownership is not synonymous with state ownership, and that it can and must assume many different forms, from state ownership of the commanding heights of the economy to municipal and cooperative ownership. Nor need public or social ownership, even in its different forms, be all-encompassing. However disagreeable this may be to purists, it is desirable that a private sector, with a multitude of small-scale enterprises, catering to a variety of needs, should continue to exist alongside the public sector: the point about this 'mixed economy' is that the public sector should greatly outweigh the private one.

Furthermore, it is pure propaganda and prejudice which affirm that state enterprise is inherently bureaucratic, inefficient, slothful, and so forth. There are plenty of instances, drawn from many countries, including Communist countries, to show that it need not be so. As for the dangers of enhanced statism, everything here depends on the nature of the regime in which public enterprise is located. An authoritarian regime, in which the state is indeed dominant over society, will hardly turn state enterprises into models of democratic practice. A capitalist-democratic regime, for its part, which conceives such enterprises in capitalist rather democratic terms, will be as unsympathetic as private business to pressures for democratic control. A socialist regime, on the other hand, would be expected – in fact required – to include public enterprise in the general democratisation of life which it would seek to foster.

Nor can the growing internationalisation of economic life make impossible the transfer into public ownership of strategic sectors of the national economy. It no doubt complicates the process, but the notion that it spells disaster, ruin and chaos is, in this as in the case of other policies and measures which run counter to powerful interests and conventional modes of thought, born of ideological bias rather than cool assessment.

Still, there are problems here sufficiently acute to require a compelling answer to the question: why bother? What is the *point* of so demanding and fraught an enterprise?

The answer is made up of a combination of economic, political and also moral factors which cannot be neatly disentangled.

In so far as a fundamental purpose of socialism is the creation of a genuinely democratic society, it cannot admit the existence of a formidable concentration of power in the hands of a small group of people, who exercise that power with very little external control. But such precisely is the power exercised by corporate elites in capitalist societies; and economic concentration renders that power ever greater and more extensive with every day that goes by. Of course, corporate elites themselves are much given to scoff at this notion, and to point at the constraints to which they are subjected by the state, their shareholders, customers, public opinion, the market, and so forth; and it is indeed the case that their power is not absolute, and that they do not form a perfectly cohesive bloc. But it is also sheer obfuscation to claim that because corporate power is not absolute or perfectly cohesive, it is not very great. On the contrary, it is very great indeed, and affects very deeply all economic, political, and cultural aspects of their societies, not to speak of its impact upon what the state does or does not do. It is in this respect a good illustration of the meaning of hegemonic obfuscation that its ideologists should have been able to foster the notion that the 'special interests' which had real power in society and were able to 'hold it to ransom' were the trade unions rather than capitalist interests.

Corporate power turns 'capitalist democracy' into a contradiction in terms, into a formulation laden with tension and double speak. For democracy, in any but a formal and stilted sense, requires a rough equality between the members of society: capitalist power precludes it. It also requires that power should be directed to purposes democratically determined by society, and carried out by responsible and accountable agents. Corporate power evades that requirement.

This is not something for which the holders of corporate power can themselves be blamed. They too are the prisoners of a system whose rationality excludes so far as it can all considerations other than the maximization of profit for the firm. The notion that this is certain to produce the best possible results for everybody is belied by the whole history of the system. For throughout that history, it has been necessary for the state to step in and at least attenuate the socially detrimental effects of what capitalists, in the pursuit of private profit, were doing to their workers, consumers, and society at large. But this intervention, intended not least to save capitalism from itself, cannot – and is not intended to – cure the crucial and inherent fault of the system, namely the fact that it is not designed to assure the socially beneficial utilisation of the immense resources which it has itself brought into being. Its productive capacity has been and remains truly prodigious; and this provides the *basis* for humane societies. But having created that basis, capitalism is itself the greatest obstacle to the realisation of such societies.

There are many people on the Left who accept all this, and more, but who go on to argue that the failures, shortcomings and derelictions of capitalism require by way of remedy greater state intervention, regulation, direction and prohibition, rather than public ownership, which is declared to be irrelevant. It is obviously an attractive argument, since it appears to dispose so easily of all the great complications and problems which are certain to attend the implementation of measures of public ownership, even in conditions where it enjoys wide support; and the argument is all the more attractive since it has been possible to achieve a good deal of regulation of capitalist enterprise.

The trouble, however, is that this intervention has not normally impaired very materially the freedom of corporate power to make decisions of major local, regional, national and international importance without much or any reference to anybody. A more radical measure of interventionism is possible in crisis circumstances, but is difficult to maintain effectively, at least in capitalist-democratic conditions, against the opposition, ill-will, circumvention and sabotage which it is bound to encounter on the part of business. Nor obviously does interventionism change the essential character and dynamic of capitalism. In short, intervention and regulation, necessary though they are, are no substitute for public ownership, if the purpose is indeed the radical transformation of the system.

On this score, the rehabilitation of public ownership has to be a major task of counter-hegemonic struggles in the socialist mode. Given the present state of the issue, this is likely to be a lengthy and arduous business; but it is an essential contribution which socialists have to make. So too do they need, quite obviously, to produce realistic answers to the questions posed by the relation of plan to market. Planning forms part of the economics and the politics of socialism. But how to plan, and how much, remain questions high on the socialist agenda.

There is another, rather different reason why the transcendance of capitalism by way of the creation of a predominant public sector is necessary, namely that it is the only way in which may be initiated one of the crucial purposes of socialism: the abolition of wage labour.

Wage labour is here taken to mean work performed for a wage in the service of a private employer who is entitled, by virtue of his or her ownership or control of the means of work, to dispose of the surplus produced by workers as he or she thinks fit, and without any reference to the people who have produced that surplus. In other words, the abolition of wage labour means the end of a system in which people are employed for the sole purpose of enriching their employers. Wage labour thus understood is of course the essence of capitalism.

It will at once be said, quite rightly, that the exploitation which is inherent in wage labour is also possible, and may well be much worse, at the hands of controllers of state enterprise; and that public ownership does not therefore entail the end of wage labour. This, however, misses a crucial difference between private and public ownership. Public ownership does not *automatically* mean the end of wage labour; but exploitation under its auspices may be taken as a *deformation* of it, and capable of being avoided by means of democratic control. Exploitation, on the other hand, is the very purpose of capitalist enterprise: it may, under its auspices and by way of external intervention, be attenuated, but it cannot be eliminated. Public or social ownership under democratic control offers the possibility and promise of realising the abolition of wage labour; such a possibility and promise is rigorously excluded by the very nature of capitalism.

The point may be illustrated by reference to slave labour. The conditions under which slave labour occurred in history varied greatly, with the more humane treatment of slaves here, and their less humane treatment there. But slavery itself endured, was until not all that long ago generally taken to be quite 'natural', and required not attenuation but abolition. Wage labour is not slave labour. But while it too may be attenuated, and is taken to be quite 'natural', it needs to be abolished. This cannot be achieved very rapidly; but that is no reason for not beginning the process as soon as possible, and thus set in train a new and very different type of 'relations of production'. In due course, and with the generalised practice of these new relations, the notion of one person working for the personal enrichment of another will be seen to be as odious and 'unnatural' as the notion of one person owning another.

IV

Perhaps the greatest of all successes which conservative ideologists and politicians have scored in the struggle for hegemony has been in the appropriation of democracy as their particular cause and concern. This is all the more remarkable in that conservatism has historically fought tooth and nail against democratic advances; and when forced to retreat, has always striven to narrow as far as possible the meaning and scope of the concessions it has had to make. But hegemonic success in this respect is perhaps not so remarkable after all, given the nature of Communist regimes, and the opportunity which their repressive and undemocratic character offered to conservative ideologists to proclaim that, in opposing Communism, they were defending democracy against its enemies on the Left, whether those enemies called themselves Communists, socialists, or whatever.

It is clearly one of the main tasks of counter-hegemonic endeavours to expose the shallowness of these democratic proclamations, to point to the narrowness of the meaning which conservative, and liberal, and much social democratic discourse, attaches to democracy, and to point also to the crippling limitations which affect democratic forms and processes in class-dominated societies. So too is it necessary to stress that bourgeois democracy is never safe at the hands of the bourgeoisie, not only in periods of great social tension, when the authoritarian elements which form part of bourgeois democracy come to the fore, but also in 'normal' times, when hegemony-as-coercion permanently co-habits with hegemony-as-consent. Again, part of the socialist critique of bourgeois democracy has to be the latter's confinement of democracy to strictly 'political' forms, whereas democracy, in socialist terms, is conceived as a pervasive force in all areas of life.

To argue all this, and more, in detail, is very necessary. But it leaves open a very large question, which socialists have found it difficult to tackle. This is whether socialist democracy is essentially a radical extension of capitalist democracy, or whether it amounts to an entirely different system, which may be defined in terms of semi-direct democracy.

The social democratic Left has traditionally endorsed capitalist democracy, and only sought marginal improvements in its workings. This is quite logical: adaptation to capitalism is here parallelled by adaptation to capitalist democracy. For their part, Communist parties have gone through an evolution with two distinct phases. From their creation in the years immediately following World War I to the turn to the Popular Front in the mid-thirties, they coupled their wholesale denunciation of bourgeois democracy as a complete sham with a commitment to replace it by a local version of the Soviet model, which was defended as immeasurably more democratic than bourgeois democracy. In a second phase, they abandoned this posture and for all practical purposes accepted the framework of bourgeois democracy, with various proposals for its further democratisation, and this is their position today.

This 'reformist' position was adamantly rejected by other sections of the Marxist Left, which clung with unflagging dedication to the vision of a democratic order in which popular power would be barely mediated by representatives who would be delegates constantly accountable to and revocable by those who had chosen them. This was of course the vision evoked by Marx in his glowing defence of the Paris Commune in *The Civil War in France* in 1871; and it was also advanced in much greater detail by Lenin in *The State and Revolution* in 1917. This was indeed – or rather would have been if it had ever been realised – an entirely new form of regime, in which the power hitherto appropriated by the state would be re-appropriated by those in whom it should by right be vested, namely the people, who would not merely rule, but also govern, with the state in a process of rapid decomposition.

Attractive though this vision is, it does represent a jump into a far-distant future, and cannot be taken as a realistic view of the kind of regime that would be needed in the construction of a socialist society. Such a regime would undoubtedly welcome and foster a great extension of popular participation and power; and it would seek the radical democratisation of the state apparatus. But it would also need a state that was not, in any real meaning of the term, 'withering away'. The state would be representative, accountable, controlled and circumscribed; but it would nevertheless need a great deal of power to take care of all the functions which the state, at local, regional and national level, is alone able to fulfil. Not the least of these would be the settlement of conflicts that are certain to arise even in a democratic society freed from the shackles of capital. Also, it is to the state that would ultimately fall the duty to protect the rights of minorities and to ensure that popular power is not exercised arbitrarily. Popular power and state power, in this perspective, would complement each other, and would also, under agreed procedures, check each other.

Far from helping Marxists in counter-hegemonic struggles for democracy, the vision of an entirely new social order based on semi-direct democracy has tended to make them oblivious to the need to explore seriously the ways in which socialists ought to tackle the vast problems which the notion of a genuinely democratic system is bound to pose. Such an exploration, conducted soberly and without demagogic rhetoric, is an essential part of counter-hegemonic endeavours.

Meanwhile, there are democratic and civic rights to be defended against the conservative forces which constantly seek to curb them. Socialists are not alone in this struggle in the defence of what are misleadingly called bourgeois rights; but socialists should be their most resolute and principled partisans, and the most fervent advocates of their extension.

V

The discussion so far has concentrated on socialist concerns within capitalist societies. But socialism has always had a strong international, and internationalist, dimension. What does this mean nowadays? What, if anything, is there which distinguishes socialist internationalism from other versions of internationalism, and which may be said to constitute a specific socialist contribution to counter-hegemonic struggles?

In recent years, Mikhail Gorbachev has sought with great eloquence to define the kind of internationalism which the world requires today, and has done so in terms of universal values and aspirations, beyond boundaries of nations, classes and creeds – values and aspirations relating to peace, disarmament, the protection of the environment, and so on. These are indeed universal values, and socialists obviously subscribe to them. But such subscription cannot alone be taken to define socialist internationalism (nor for that matter does Gorbachev suggest that they can). For socialist internationalism has to proceed from the regrettable but crucial fact that, however much the decision-makers in capitalist countries may subscribe to univeral values, they are moved by very different considerations in regard to international affairs.

Uppermost among these considerations, ever since the Bolshevik Revolution and particularly since the end of World War II, has been the determination of major capitalist governments, to contain, curb or crush movements of radical reform and revolution throughout the world, and to contain, curb, crush or bring into line governments intent on pursuing policies of which these capitalist governments disapproved. Another way of making the same point is to say that, particularly since 1945, there has existed a state of global war, or an international civil war, between the major capitalist powers, led by the United States, on the one hand, and the movements and governments to which I have referred on the other. This conflict has assumed many different forms – economic, political, cultural, military. But it has defined much of the reality of international relations, not to speak of what it has meant for the countries concerned, for the best (or rather the worst) part of this century.

The Cold War made it appear that the conflict was above all a matter of confrontation between the United States and the Soviet Union, and their respective allies; and a massive hegemonic assault on the consciousness of the peoples of the 'Free World' turned into a not-to-be-questioned part of conventional wisdom the notion that the confrontation was based upon the aggressive and expansionist designs of the Soviet Union. In fact, that was never the issue at all. The real war, sometimes cold and often murderously hot, was always that between conservative forces, local and external, and the forces, notably but not exclusively in the 'third world', which sought a transformation of the status quo unacceptable to those conservative forces.

In this perspective, the collapse of Communist regimes in Eastern Europe (and its likely collapse elsewhere) clearly constitutes a great strengthening of the hope nurtured by conservative forces that the world might be shaped (or re-shaped) in an image acceptable to them. There is now a very good chance that some Communist countries at least will move towards the restoration of capitalism: some of them are already well advanced on that road. So too is it quite likely that countries in the 'third world' which had previously proclaimed a commitment to socialism and 'Marxism-Leninism' will follow the same path. No wonder that the defenders of capitalism should be celebrating a glorious victory, and proclaiming the end of socialism, which is also what is meant by the 'end of history'.

Such celebration and proclamation is, however, rather premature. Soviet-type Communism, with the centrally planned command economy and the monopolistic one-party political system, is out or on the way out, and will not be resurrected. But the notion that this is the end of socialist striving and eventual socialist advances leaves a vital fact out of account. This is that, despite the current apotheosis of capitalism, it has resolved none of the problems which give sustenance to socialist aspirations and struggles. Given the inherent and ineradicable failings of capitalism, there is no reason to doubt that the striving for radical alternatives will continue. Such striving is subject to phases of advance and phases of retreat; and the seventies and eighties have undoubtedly been a phase of retreat. But to believe that this is irreversible is naively unrealistic. No one can tell when advance will be resumed, or what forms it will take; but resume it will.

It is in the light of the permanent struggle on a global scale of conservative forces against forces of radical reform and revolution that socialist internationalism has to be understood. This does not exclude concern with large (or small) 'humanist' issues and causes. Nor of course does it preclude close collaboration with groups and movements primarily interested in such issues and causes. But socialists nevertheless have their own perspectives to advance in the realm of international relations and conflicts. Their most obvious task is eliciting support for movements and regimes which are subject to hostility and destabilisation by conservative forces at home and abroad. Another is the advancement of socialist explanations of the roots of the interventionism in which the United States and its allies have been and are engaged across the world; for in no area is hegemonic obfuscation, disinformation, and plain lying more common than in this realm.

This, it should be added, is by no means to say that socialist internationalism automatically resolves all the problems which frequently arise in relation to the support which it demands. There are movements which loudly proclaim their liberating and anti-imperialist commitments, but whose credentials, from a socialist point of view, may be exceedingly dubious. Similarly, governments issued from struggles against tyranny and imperialism may turn out to be themselves vicious tyrannies, notwithstanding their anti-imperialist rhetoric. The Iranian regime is an obvious example. What this means is that support based on socialist internationalism, even in the worthiest of cases, can never be wholly unconditional. Stalin once described an internationalist as 'one who is ready to defend the USSR without reservation, without wavering, unconditionally'; and this was long endorsed and followed by Communists everywhere. Socialist internationalism does not involve such a surrender of critical faculties in favour of any movement or regime.

There are obviously many other issues than those arising from the requirement of international solidarity which socialist internationalism does not automatically resolve, and which are susceptible to diverse and divergent positions. One of these issues has to do with institutional arrangements beyond the nation state. Socialists can have no concern with the preservation of national 'sovereignty' as such. At the same time, they cannot be indifferent to arrangements which, as in the case of the European Economic Community and the pressure for a federal structure for its members, are likely to confirm and solidify capitalist hegemony in the countries concerned. From a socialist point of view, it may well be that the most acceptable position is neither an insistence on national 'sovereignty', nor an acceptance of federalism under capitalist auspices, but regional confederal structures in which a degree of institutionalised cooperation between the members countries would be allied to a high degree of autonomy in the determination of major issues of policy.

Perhaps more immediately to the point, socialist internationalism requires the fostering of the closest possible ties between socialist movements (and trade union movements) across frontiers for the purpose of mutual reinforcement and the forging of common policies. The need for such cooperation has long been obvious, but in terms of real effectiveness has remained a largely unrealised aspiration. Given the ever-greater internationalisation of capital, it is now more urgent than ever; and the chances of it being advanced are now better than they have been since 1917, given the lessening of the divisions which have plagued Left movements thereafter.

VI

There was a time when many if not most socialists to the left of social democracy would have affirmed without hesitation that the indispensable basis of counter-hegemonic struggles was Marxism: on no other basis, it would be said, could such struggles be effectively waged, or even taken seriously by Marxists. Affirmations of this kind were based on some simple presumptions: one of them was that Marxism, or rather 'Marxism-Leninism', was a settled and mostly unproblematic body of thought, which held conclusive answers to all questions, from, in alphabetical order, astronomy to zoology. Another presumption was that failure to accept these answers showed a deplorable imprisonment in bourgeois thought.

Save in the few Communist regimes where such an approach to what passes for Marxism can still be imposed, most notably in China, Marxism has long been allotted a very different and much less exalted status on the left, and has in fact been subjected to sustained and fundamental criticism and attack from within the Left. There is by now a very long list of failings and lacunae which are said to afflict Marxism, drawn up by people who insist that they remain Marxists, or who continue to claim Marx as a major influence upon them. The list includes such items as economic and class reductionism, gender blindness, methodological deficiencies, untenable propositions, a propensity to authoritarianism, a dangerous utopianism, and so on. In any case, it is also said, the world of the 19th century, in which Marxism was forged, is long gone, so much so that the transformations which capitalism has undergone and has wrought upon the world, have turned much if not most of Marxism into something of an historical relic.

Other essays in this volume deal with these strictures; and I only wish to add in this connection that the criticisms levelled at Marxism in relation to many of its features do not seem to me to have undermined some of its key propositions. One such proposition, perhaps the most important of them all in social and political analysis, and the one which hegemonic endeavours are most at pains to befog or deny, is that capitalist societies are fundamentally divided between, on the one hand, dominant classes so defined by virtue of their ownership or control of the main means of domination – the means of production, the means of administration and coercion, i.e. the state, and the means of persuasion and consent; and, on the other hand subordinate classes, so defined by virtue of their relative (or absolute) lack of ownership or control of these means.* A related proposition is that the interests of these classes are fundamentally divergent and produce a permanent struggle between them, which assumes many different forms at different times but which is inherent in societies based on domination and exploitation. A third such proposition is that domination and subordination are not unalterable, but can be overcome by the collective endeavours of the subordinate classes themselves.

Critics rightly point to the fact that there are other divisions in society than those based on class, namely divisions based on gender, race, ethnicity, nationality, religion, or a combination of some of them. The critics tend to overlook the fact that these divisions are often related to class location, or are influenced by it; but the point is well taken that, whether so or not, Marxism has traditionally paid far too little attention to these other divisions.

Yet, it does not seem unreasonable to see these criticisms as qualifications, however important, of the Marxist emphasis on class, rather than its invalidation. There are many grounds for arguing that class and class division have been, *and remain*, 'primary'. Perhaps the most important such reason is that even if all the aims of feminist, anti-racist, ethnic, national and other movements could be realised, society would nevertheless remain fundamentally divided on class lines. No doubt, the composition of the dominant class, and much else about the social order, would be different, but domination and subordination, based on class lines, would endure. By contrast, the elimination of class divisions would at least make possible the elimination of division on the ground of gender, race, ethnicity, etc. This is the essential condition for the achievement of a social order from which these divisions would eventually be banished. 'New social movements' may well argue that it is not a *sufficient* condition for this to happen, and that it would be foolish to assume that the elimination of class *automatically* entails all other good things; but that (important) observation does not invalidate the Marxist emphasis on the 'primacy' of class divisions.

---

*What follows in the rest of this section is discussed at length in *Divided Societies. Class Struggle in Contemporary Capitalism* (Oxford University Press, 1989)

One of the most derided features of Marxism in recent years has been its focus on the working class as the principal agent for the liberation of society; and this has a clear bearing on counter-hegemonic struggles. For if the working class is not that agent, and never can be, counter-hegemonic endeavours directed towards that class are misguided, and ought to be directed to other, more receptive agents.

Criticisms of Marxism because of what is taken to be its 'labour metaphysic' also rest on different grounds. One of them is that the working class, which is taken to mean the male, industrial, manufacturing, working class, is steadily shrinking in advanced capitalist countries, and will continue to shrink in a 'post-Fordist' era. In any case, it is also said, the notion of the working class as a potentially revolutionary class was always a myth, as experience has richly demonstrated over the whole historical span in which the working class has been in existence; and even, it is added, if the working class *had* been a revolutionary class, there was no good reason to believe, and plenty of evidence to suggest, that the social order it would usher in would not mark the liberation of society at large.

One obvious flaw in the argument has to do with the meaning attached to the notion of 'working class'. For it is clearly an unwarranted limitation of that meaning to confine it to the industrial, manufacturing working class. On any reasonable view, it includes on the contrary the vast majority of the population of advanced capitalist countries, on the strength of the source of their income (mainly the sale of their labour power), the level of their income (which places them in the lower and lowest income groups), and, as noted earlier, their lack of ownership or control of the means of power and influence in their society. These combined characteristics define the working class, as the largest part of the subordinate population of the countries concerned.

A very different question is whether this 'sociological majority' is ever likely to turn into a 'political majority', that is, whether the working class and its allies in the rest of the subordinate class, are ever likely to want the kind of radical changes implied by the notion of socialism. In this respect, it is undoubtedly true that Marx, and Marxists after him, took much too sanguine of view of working class commitment to radical change, particularly to revolutionary change understood as proceeding from insurrectionary upheaval. But it seems all the same exceedingly premature to say that the working class, or at least a large part of it, can never be persuaded to support programmes of radical change pointing in socialist directions. Indeed, to say this flies in the face of much evidence: for majorities, of which members of the working class formed by far the largest part, have repeatedly been found in many countries to express support for parties which advanced precisely such programmes. The grounds for that support were no doubt varied, and cannot be taken to imply a generalised socialist consciousness and commitment. Nevertheless, support has been elicited for radical change from subordinate populations:

that the policies which were then pursued usually failed to match the promises made raises different questions about the *other* conditions of radical change.

As for the kind of society which radical change would bring about, I have already noted that socialism has to free itself of the salvationist and 'utopian' features which have commonly (and understandably) suffused it. But it is also quite mistaken, and debilitating, to argue that, because everything will not be immediately and radically transformed in a society moving towards socialism, the changes which will occur may therefore be discounted as trivial. So too is it perverse to invoke the example of Communist regimes to show the 'failure of socialism'. As already noted, there are important lessons to be learnt from the experience of these regimes; but they do not include the lesson, which advocates of the status quo are so eager to distil from that experience, that socialism cannot deal effectively with sexism, racism, ethnic discord, antisemitism and other manifestations of social morbidity. To argue this is to insist that here *was* socialism, and that no other version of it is plausible. It is not a good argument. Radical change, of the kind outlined here, would make possible the beginnings of a necessarily slow and arduous process of creating societies that would be genuine communities. This does not spell instant, or even distant, salvation; but it does offer a promise of real advance towards emancipation from remediable ills.

Class analysis in the Marxist mode claims to provide an organisational principle for the understanding of a vast range of seemingly disparate phenomena. It is a principle which is vulnerable to reductionist abuse, but this is not inevitable. Marxism's predictive capacity has proved again and again to be weak; but this latter point only shows that people who want to know the future should not consult Marx but Madame Olga. When all is said and done, Marxism as class analysis, handled with due care, remains an instrument of unsurpassed value in the interpretation of social and political life, and in the explanation of phenomena which, in other hands, remain unexplained or misunderstood. This is also to say that it is of unsurpassed value in counter-hegemonic struggles, since these struggles have as a primary object the 'laying bare' of a reality which hegemonic struggles seek to conceal.

The ultimate purpose of counter-hegemonic struggles, in socialist terms, is to make socialism 'the common sense of the epoch'. On any realistic view, this must be taken to be a very long-term project, spread over many generations and never likely to be wholly completed. But advances can at least be made, and clearly have to be made, for the socialist enterprise itself to make advances. Nothing much in this realm can move until a large number of men and women have 'interiorised' a socialist consciousness, and, in Cromwell's phrase about the New Model Army, know what they want and love what they know. There has, in this respect, clearly occurred a notable retreat, in so far as generations of men and women, nurtured in socialist ideas in earlier decades of the century, have gone, or lost heart, and have not been replaced by new generations in more recent decades. This is not at all to say that these new generations are less open, rebellious, iconoclastic, than preceding ones: it is rather that their rebelliousness and iconoclasm are not on the whole oriented in the direction of socialist ideas. Nor, all things considered, is this very surprising.

There are many people on the Left who now believe that this is an irremediable situation in the conditions of 'post-modernity'. This is a very short-term view, which ignores the degree to which the material and moral circumstances created by capitalism will in due course re-direct attention to the solutions which socialism proposes. On the other hand, it is quite certain that these solutions cannot amount to a simple reiteration of ancient nostrums, and will need to be in tune with the felt needs and aspirations of the epoch. Assuming, however, that this is an essential requirement for socialist renewal, it is also the case that while the formation of socialist consciousness will take many forms and draw from many different sources, it will also need to be fostered and advanced by socialist agencies.

Words like 'political education' and 'political training' are nowadays highly suspect on the Left, not surprisingly since they evoke the kind of frozen catechisms that long passed for socialist education in Communist and other Marxist organisations; and so too, from a different perspective, do the words attract suspicion and hostility because they are thought to have an 'elitist' ring, and are taken to convey the notion of experts passing on their wisdom and knowledge to the ignorant hewers of wood and drawers of water.

Yet, socialist education need not have these connotations, and can be a true process of cooperative learning, in which the questioning of everything is not only accepted but understood to be essential to that process. This also answers the accusation of 'elitism': for what is or should be involved in socialist education, properly understood, is not a one-way process of communication but on the contrary a dialogue in which teachers and taught enlighten and stimulate each other in a constant exchange of ideas.

At any rate, socialist education is a crucial component part of counter-hegemonic struggles, and requires organised and systematic, institutionalised forms as well as other, individual and independent forms. This requirement is something which earlier socialist generations took for granted, and did meet, well or ill is not here the point. Stalinist experience, in this realm as in all others, provides a salutary lesson in what ought not to be done. But the need remains for 'schools of socialism', open, flexible, critical and disputatious, and able to send out into the world activists better equipped to counter the propaganda which help dominant classes to maintain themselves in power, and to present a persuasive case for socialism.

It is of course true that these ideological struggles are only one part of a much wider class struggle; but they are an important part of it. For they help to inform and shape the language, the spirit and the aims of class struggle, and give it a greater resiliance than it would otherwise possess. The present may seem a bad time for counter-ideological strivings. But the collapse of Communist regimes, and the ever-greater adaptation of social democracy to capitalism, in fact offer a new space and new opportunities for such strivings, and make the coming years a period of hope rather than despair.